MW01079006

More than 2,000 years ago, Nehemiah undertook the rebuilding of his nation. As part of the process, he constructed a "House of Heroes" (Nehemiah 3:16) by which those in his generation could learn of the courage and sacrifices made by previous ones. Through *For You They Signed,* Marilyn has created a much-needed inspirational "House of Heroes" for this generation.

— David Barton, Wallbuilders

What a unique generation they were, those men of 1776. The intellectual culmination of eighteen centuries of Christian civilization, they possessed not only the most profound intellectual attainments, but each one was prepared to sacrifice his life, liberty, and sacred honor for the ideals of liberty. They were inheritors from the faithful guardians of English common law and constitutional tradition but were now developing a new application for the United States of America.

In a day when Americans confuse heroism with celebrity, and sacrifice with the lateness of a government welfare check, the new book, *For You They Signed,* by Marilyn Boyer comes as a refreshing reminder that our Founding Fathers were different; not only different, but exemplars of what we as Americans once were and ought to be again.

Not since B.J. Lossing's *Lives of the Signers* in 1848, has an historian so lovingly described the character and fortitude of the men who signed their names to the document that proclaimed independence from a tyrannical government. They risked their lives and those of their families and were forced to flee the invasion of a foreign army and attacks by their own neighbors. In the providence of God, most of them survived to celebrate the triumph of their cause. Most of the signers were men well known for their Christian lives; the legacy sealed by their autographs has blessed the whole world.

Mrs. Boyer has included a helpful study page and appropriate Scriptures, which make this book a handy teaching tool for learning the lives and lessons of the Founding Fathers. This is, in fact, one of those books that needs to be in every family's library, and parents would do well to insure that the next generation does not forget these men and the price they paid for our freedom.

— Bill Potter, Historian,
The Circa History Guild, Roswell, Georgia

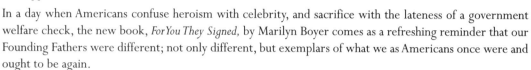

Many thanks for sending the copy of *For You They Signed.* This is a great book and a story that needs to be told! It is my hope that the Good Lord will bless all you do to glorify Him. Semper Fidelis,

— Oliver L. North,
Founder and Honorary Chairman of Freedom Alliance

Photo courtesy of Fox News

Thank you for your gift of *For You They Signed.* I have enjoyed reading of our founding fathers and the sacrifices they made to establish our beloved Country. Their dedication to principle and devotion to duty during the perils of the war for independence is an inspiration to our generation in the midst of present difficulties we face as a nation.

I want to thank you for the many hours and personal sacrifices you made to bring to us the story of the brave men who risked their lives for our freedom. May God bless your efforts to restore the integrity and Christian virtue of our founding fathers to our youth today. Your book will be kept as a valuable treasure to my library.

— Roy S. Moore,
Former Chief Justice, Alabama Supreme Court
President, Foundation for Moral Law

Thank you for your book. It is very informative. This information needs to be taught to our youth.

— Mathew D. Staver, Dean and Professor of Law,
Liberty University School of Law

Marilyn Boyer opens the pages of history to reveal the Christian character of many of our founders.

— Michael Farris, President, Patrick Henry College
Founder of Home School Legal Defense Association

Marilyn Boyer has given all of us who love our country a real treasure. *For You They Signed* captures an important but little-known history of 56 brave men who risked everything so we could be free. Marilyn's easy-to-read, succinct summaries of the lives and faith of these forefathers will inspire you and enable you to pass on this rich heritage to your children. The questions after each chapter help you to make this part of your American history curriculum or an effective weekly evening study. This interesting and challenging, well-researched collection of biographies is truly inspirational!

— Chris Klicka, father of seven
Senior Counsel, Home School Legal Defense Association

Thank you for your sacrificial work in creating this beautiful book. This is certainly a work for "such a time as this." The wonderful presentation and insightful content will assure this work will remain a well-used reference in our home. It is my prayer that this resource will find a way into every home so that this generation can know the sacrifice required to establish the God inspired design of our nation.

— Stanley John,
Senior Vice President, Focus on the Family

There are about a half-dozen resources that are "must-have" staples for the Christian homeschool family — *For You They Signed* is one of them. Easy to read and full of wonderful quotes, this is the book that will teach your children to thank God for the remarkable, God-blessed foundations of their country.

— Beall Phillips, homeschool mother of eight

There are three books that every home school family needs to bring to their table this year. For the foundations of our faith and worldview — bring your Bible. To help you define your words and build your vocabulary in terms of that Christian worldview — bring your *Webster's 1828 Dictionary*. But to teach your children to know, understand, and defend the remarkable providence of God in American history and to rejoice in the gift of liberty He has bestowed on them — you must bring Marilyn Boyer's *For You They Signed*.

Here is why: *For You They Signed* is an antidote to the rampant historical revisionism dominating the schools and media today. Our founders were not atheists. Nor did they believe in some deistic God who was disconnected from the affairs of men. In fact, they were one of the most theologically literate and God-fearing generations in the history of Western civilization.

Our Founders invoked the name of Jesus Christ in their public prayers, and appealed to the God of the Trinity in formal acts of Congress. They affirmed that Christian laws and Christian morals were the only safeguard for freedom. It was this foundation of Christianity that was used of the Lord to lay the foundations for liberty in America. To understand America, you must understand the character and faith of the men who built it. That is precisely what you get in *For You They Signed*.

— Douglas W. Phillips,
President, Vision Forum

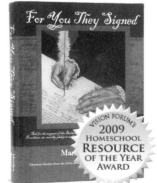

To understand America, you must understand the character and faith of the men who built it. That is precisely what you get in *For You They Signed* . . . We love it so much that we have given it Vision Forum's *2009 Homeschool Resource of the Year Award.* A beautiful, oversized, hardcover book, full of gorgeous illustrations, *For You They Signed* is a welcome resource of hope for the 2009 homeschool year.

For You They Signed

OTHER BOOKS BY MARILYN BOYER

Parenting from the Heart
Fun Projects for Hands-On Character Building
Home Educating with Confidence
Proverbs People Book One and Book Two
Crossroads of Character

For You They Signed

The Spiritual Heritage of Those Who Shaped Our Nation

By Marilyn Boyer

Illustrated by Linda Linder

First printing: January 2009
First Master Books printing: July 2010
Second printing: September 2011

Master Books® is a division of the New Leaf Publishing Group, Inc.

ISBN: 978-0-89051-598-3
LOC: 2010932465

Interior artwork by Linda Linder
Cover by Heidi Rohr Designs

Illustrations of Signers © 2009 by Linda Linder
Illustrations of the Signers' homes from
The Book of the Signers, edited by William Brotherhead, Philadelphia, PA, 1861

The font used for the headings and titles in this book is Caslon 76,
which was based on typefaces used in Colonial America at the time of the Revolutionary War.
It was designed by Professor Edward A. Edman of Liberty University and used by permission.

Proudly printed in the United States of America

Please visit our website for other great titles:
www.nlpg.net

For information regarding author interviews,
please contact the publicity department at (870) 438-5288.

Please consider requesting that a copy of this volume be purchased by your local library system.

Master Books®
A Division of New Leaf Publishing Group
www.masterbooks.net

Dedicated to those men
who put their
lives, fortunes, and sacred honor
in God's hands
to secure freedoms
for you
and me.

✒ Acknowledgments ✒

I would like to thank David Barton of Wallbuilders as the instrument God used to inspire me to write this book. As I watched him on several occasions refer to the painting of the signing of the Declaration of Independence, he would ask how many in the audience could identify more than three of the signers. I identified three. As he proceeded to tell some of their stories I was struck with my own ignorance of the incredible sacrifice these men made to secure my freedom today, and I couldn't shake the thought. I want my own kids to know who these men were and what they laid on the line for their posterity — for US! Thanks, Dave, for allowing God to use you to impart vision and inspiration to so many! The Boyers view you as a real American hero!

Without so many faithful helpers, I could never have accomplished this enormous undertaking. I would like to thank my family for allowing me the time for research and writing, and for listening to all the exciting bits of information as I discovered them. Specifically, a huge thanks to two of my daughters, Kate and Emily, who spent hours deciphering my handwriting and sitting at the keyboard to transcribe the entire manuscript!

Many thanks to Linda Linder, my awesome illustrator, whose expertise so accurately conveys the character of these men. She spent hundreds of hours masterfully drawing each signer and formatting the text. Linda, thanks for a job well done! This book would not have been a reality without your expertise and exceptional talent.

To my wonderful editors, Carol Arnold and Judy Saunders, who spent hours looking for misspelled words, missing periods and commas, indentations, etc., all the details I don't even see! I appreciate your time and devoted effort to make this book a work of excellence. Thank you!

Additional editing work was done by my dear friend Kati Grow, who has for many years helped in our ministry in too many ways to list here. Thanks, Kati!

Many thanks are due Ed and Mary Ann Edman. They made a huge contribution through many hours of hard work and an unusually high level of perceptiveness and creativity. Mary Ann was indispensable with her incredible eye for detail and passion for excellence in final preparation of the text for press.

ᴔ Table of Contents ᴔ

Contents, *continued*

❧ List of Illustrations ❧

Illustrations, *continued*

❧ Introduction ❧

It was a question David Barton posed that God used to challenge me to write this book. While showing a picture of the signers the Declaration of Independence, he asked who could identify more than three of the signers. Everyone knows Thomas Jefferson and Benjamin Franklin. I knew John Hancock, having grown up in Boston (his picture was often in bank logos), but those are all I could identify. The question continued to pierce my soul; I realized that a huge chunk of our history, that which is Christian in nature, has been carved from our public school classrooms (of which I was a product). God used that to challenge me to begin researching the lives of these men, and when I did I was astounded by what I found. The vast majority of these men were true Christians who were looking to their Savior for guidance and daily direction in the events which led to the signing.

What we now call the "American Revolution" was not, in fact, a revolution at all, nor did it occur as a protest of "taxation without representation" as I'd been led to believe. I felt like I was on a treasure hunt, constantly uncovering nuggets of our lost spiritual heritage. It has consumed hundreds of hours of work, but my hope is that what you learn from the study of these men's lives will inspire you to 1) value your freedom in a new and fresh way; 2) be inspired to actively protect that freedom so that future generations can benefit from it, and 3) catch a vision that God wants to use you and each member of your family to effect a permanent change in our society, a turning back to the godly principles upon which our country was founded, so that God will be able to continue extending His hand of blessing on this great land.

✌ Preface ✌

A nation which does not remember what it was yesterday does not know what it is today, nor what it is trying to do. We are trying to do a futile thing if we do not know where we have come from, or what we have been about.

— Woodrow Wilson

As President Woodrow Wilson so forcefully reminded us, we must understand where our country has come from in order to accurately attend to our duties as citizens today. Our country was, at the time of the American Revolution, a Christian nation. That means Christian principles governed the way people lived their lives. They had been trained to have a proper respect for God's principles and ways.

The Church was influential in shaping the beliefs of the founders. John Adams stated that Rev. Dr. Jonathan Mayhew and Rev. Dr. Samuel Cooper were two of the individuals "most conspicuous, the most ardent, and influential [in the] awakening and revival of American principles and feelings that led to our independence." [1]

The pulpits of America helped to shape what Americans thought about issues of the day. Current events were preached about, and the Bible was revered as having the answers to every dilemma in life. Even those who did not have a personal relationship with Jesus Christ (a true Christian) had a respect for Scripture and godly principles. John Adams declared, "The general principles on which the fathers achieved independence were . . . the general principles of Christianity . . . now I will avow that I then believed, and now believe, that those general principles of Christianity are as eternal and immutable as the existence and attributes of God." [2]

In a court case in 1854 the U.S. Congress stated:

> Had the people, during the Revolution, a suspicion of any attempt to war against Christianity, that Revolution would have been strangled in its cradle. At the time of the adoption of the Constitution and the amendments, the universal sentiment was that Christianity should be encouraged, but not any one [denomination]. In this age there can be no substitute for Christianity. That was the religion of the founders of the Republic, and they expected it to remain the religion of their descendants. [3]

When the fifty-six men signed their names to the Declaration of Independence, King George ordered his soldiers to find and execute them all, putting an end to the "foolish" rebellion. The British soldiers were just miles away from some of the homes of the New York signers on the day they placed their signatures on that document. They all knew, if captured, they would die the death of a traitor. John Adams, on the eve of the signing, wrote to his wife Abigail, "I am well aware of the toil, and blood, and treasure, that it will cost to maintain this declaration, and support and defend these states; yet, through all the gloom I can see the rays of light and glory. I can see that the end is worth more than all the means." [4]

They were laying their lives, fortune, and sacred honor on the line for you and me — their posterity.

> *Posterity* — "You will never know how much it has cost my generation to preserve your freedom. I hope you will make good use of it." [5] *–John Quincy Adams*

The statement pierced me deeply. We have forgotten. As a nation, we have forgotten; we never learned what sacrifices were made on our behalf. This was not a decision lightly made.

The first Congress, held in Philadelphia on September 5, 1774, opened with prayer which lasted for hours. They read Psalm 35 and felt God used it to speak direction into their lives.

Psalm 35

Plead my cause, O LORD, with them that strive with me: fight against them that fight against me.

Take hold of shield and buckler, and stand up for mine help.

Draw out also the spear, and stop the way against them that persecute me: say unto my soul, I am thy salvation.

Let them be confounded and put to shame that seek after my soul: let them be turned back and brought to confusion that devise my hurt.

Let them be as chaff before the wind: and let the angel of the LORD chase them.

Let their way be dark and slippery: and let the angel of the LORD persecute them.

For without cause have they hid for me their net in a pit, which without cause they have digged for my soul.

Let destruction come upon him at unawares; and let his net that he hath hid catch himself: into that very destruction let him fall.

And my soul shall be joyful in the LORD: it shall rejoice in his salvation.

All my bones shall say, LORD, who is like unto thee, which deliverest the poor from him that is too strong for him, yea, the poor and the needy from him that spoileth him?

False witnesses did rise up; they laid to my charge things that I knew not.

They rewarded me evil for good to the spoiling of my soul.

But as for me, when they were sick, my clothing was sackcloth; I humbled my soul with fasting; and my prayer returned into mine own bosom.

I behaved myself as though he had been my friend or brother; I bowed down heavily, as one that mourneth for his mother.

But in mine adversity they rejoiced, and gathered themselves together; yea, the abjects gathered themselves together against me, and I knew it not; they did tear me, and ceased not:

With hypocritical mockers in feasts, they gnashed upon me with their teeth.

Lord, how long wilt thou look on? Rescue my soul from their destructions, my darling from the lions.

I will give thee thanks in the great congregation; I will praise thee among much people.

Let not them that are mine enemies wrongfully rejoice over me; neither let them wink with the eye that hate me without a cause.

For they speak not peace; but they devise deceitful matters against them that are quiet in the land.

Yea, they opened their mouth wide against me, and said, Aha, aha, our eye hath seen it.

This thou hast seen, O LORD: keep not silence: O Lord, be not far from me.

Stir up thyself, and awake to my judgment, even unto my cause, my God and my Lord.

Judge me, O LORD my God, according to thy righteousness; and let them not rejoice over me.

Let them not say in their hearts, Ah, so would we have it: let them not say, We have swallowed him up.

Let them be ashamed and brought to confusion together that rejoice at mine hurt: let them be clothed with shame and dishonour that magnify themselves against me.

Let them shout for joy, and be glad, that favour my righteous cause: yea, let them say continually, Let the LORD be magnified, which hath pleasure in the prosperity of his servant.

And my tongue shall speak of thy righteousness and of thy praise all the day long.

The following was recorded of that day:

> Washington was kneeling there, and Henry, and Randolph and Rutledge, and Lee and Jay; and by their side there stood, bowed down in deference, the Puritan patriots of New England, who at that moment had reason to believe that an armed soldiery was wasting their humble households… They prayed fervently for America, for the Congress, for the province of Massachusetts Bay, and especially the town of Boston… "It was enough," said Mr. Adams, "to melt a heart of stone. I saw the tears gush into the eyes of the old pacific Quakers of Philadelphia." John Adams wrote to his wife Abigail, "We have appointed a continental fast. Millions will be upon their knees at once before their great Creator, imploring His forgiveness and blessing; His smiles on American councils and arms." [7]

Minutemen were often groups of laymen from local churches, led by their pastor or deacon. It wasn't unusual following militia drills for the men to then attend their church service for preaching of the Word and prayer. The spiritual nature of the American troops was reported by a Crown-appointed British governor, writing to Great Britain, "If you ask an American, who is his master, he'll tell you he has none, nor any governor but Jesus Christ." [8]

One of their early biographies made this declaration:

> It was fortunate for the cause of America, and for the cause of freedom, that there was a class of men at that day, who were adequate to the high and mighty enterprise of sundering the ties which bound the colonies. For this they were doubtless specially raised up by the God of heaven; for this they were prepared by the lofty energies of their minds, and by that boldness and intrepidity of character, which, perhaps, never so signally marked another generation of man. [9]

God clearly showed His providence in mighty ways during the Revolution. "It was truly a miracle that the American Navy would attempt a battle with the British warships. They fought with rowboats, furnished with a cannon at each end. They had taken out two British warships, one loaded with sixty-four guns and the other with twenty guns. As Adams later told his wife of the victory at Fort Mifflin, 'It appears to me the eternal Son of God is operating powerfully against the British Nation.' " [10]

Even George Washington wrote: "The Hand of Providence has been so conspicuous in all this, that he must be worse an infidel that lacks faith, and more than wicked, that has not gratitude enough to acknowledge His obligations." [11]

In his first inaugural address, he stated:

> No people can be bound to acknowledge and adore the invisible hand which conducts the affairs of men more than the people of the United States. Every step by which they have advanced to the character of an independent nation seems to have been distinguished by some token of Providential agency… We ought to be no less persuaded that the propitious smiles of heaven cannot be expected on a nation that disregards the eternal rules of order and right, which heaven itself has ordained. [12]

Even the standards to which Washington held his troops reflect the Christian nature of our country at the time.

Washington wrote, "every officer and man will endeavor so as to live and act as becomes a Christian soldier, defending the dearest rights and liberties of his country." [13]

He charged his troops, "To the distinguished character of Patriot, it should be our highest glory to add the more distinguished character of Christian." [14]

The Massachusetts Legislature gave the following orders to the Minutemen on December 10, 1774:

> You are placed by Providence in [the] post of honor because it is the post of danger. And while struggling for the noblest objects — the liberties of your country, the happiness of posterity, and the rights of human nature

— the eyes not only of North America and the whole British Empire, but of all Europe are upon you. Let us be therefore, altogether solicitous that no disorderly behavior, nothing unbecoming our characters as Americans, as citizens and Christians, be justly chargeable to us.[15]

Congress officially recognized the hand of God in the victory at Saratoga and issued a proclamation on November 1, 1777:

Forasmuch as it is the indispensable duty of all men to adore the superintending providence of Almighty God, to acknowledge with gratitude their obligation to Him for benefits received and to implore such further blessings as they stand in need of; and it having pleased Him . . . to crown our arms with most signal success: It [a day] is therefore recommended . . . for solemn thanksgiving and praise; that with one heart and one voice the good people may express the grateful feelings of their hearts, and consecrate themselves to the service of their Divine Benefactor; and that together with their sincere acknowledgments and offerings, they may join the penitent confession of their manifold sins . . . and their humble and earnest supplication that it may please God, through the merits of Jesus Christ, mercifully to forgive and blot out of remembrance [and] . . . to take schools and seminaries of education, so necessary for cultivating the principles of true liberty, virtue and piety, under His nurturing hand, and to prosper the means of religion for the promotion and enlargement of that kingdom which consisteth "in righteousness, peace, and joy in the Holy Ghost" [Romans 14:17].[16]

Alexis de Tocqueville, a French observer, came to America in the 1830s seeking to find what made Her great. This was his conclusion:

Upon my arrival in the United States, the religious aspect of the country was the first thing that struck my attention. And the longer I stayed there the more did I perceived the great political consequences resulting from this state of things to which I was unaccustomed. In France, I had almost always seen the spirit of religion and the spirit of freedom pursuing courses diametrically opposed to each other. But in America, I found that they were intimately united, that they reigned in common over the same country.[17]

As you study the lives and character of these men who birthed our great country, consider the words of President James Garfield, spoken over a century ago.

Now, more than ever before, the people are responsible for the character of their Congress. If that body be ignorant, reckless, and corrupt, it is because the people tolerate ignorance, recklessness, and corruption. If it be intelligent, brave, and pure, it is because the people demand these high qualities to represent them in the national legislature. . . [I]f the next centennial does not find us a great nation . . . it will be because those who represent the enterprise, the culture, and the morality of the nation do not aid in controlling the political forces.[18]

Let what you learn guide you as you and your family strive to be salt and light where you live today. Let us, with a clear conscience, be able to echo the words spoken by John Adams after his long years of service in Congress: "Whatever becomes of me, my friends shall never suffer by my negligence."[19]

❧ Suggestions for Using This Book ❧

THIS BOOK IS DESIGNED TO BE USED IN ANY OF THE FIVE FOLLOWING WAYS:

A YEAR'S WORTH OF FAMILY DEVOTIONAL CHARACTER STUDIES

Dads may use this book to lead their family in character studies through history. Contained in this book are studies of the fifty-six signers of the Declaration of Independence. Studying the life of one signer per week, there are more than a year's worth of lessons. As the dad leads his family in the character studies, the family learns character, history, and Scripture together. Traditionally, the study of the period of the American Revolution is covered in one chapter of a history textbook. This book is designed to challenge and inspire the entire family by learning history in a practical way that will change the way you live your life!

It's also a way for dads to relieve a bit of the pressure on the homeschooling mom, as the whole family will learn together, retaining and applying information learned to their own lives. Read a selection and ask thought-provoking questions (provided in each chapter) to encourage family discussion and challenge family members to set specific goals for applying character qualities to their own lives.

The family is trained to build character into their own lives. Learn what some signers said about their relationship with Jesus Christ — in their own words! Definitions of character qualities are taught, as it is hard to implement character goals in our lives if we don't understand what they mean. The family sees character exemplified in the life stories of our own founders. This motivates family members to live lives that make a difference. The family is inspired with vision as they study the impact these men made in their time.

A Family Activity Guide is available online as a companion book. Coloring pages are included so little ones can keep their hands busy in a profitable manner while Dad is reading and they are absorbing much of what is taught. Weekly character qualities with verses for memorization are available as calligraphy prints to hang on the refrigerator for the week or to place in a frame on the coffee table as the family learns together. Fun quizzes are provided for use during family fun night. There is one provided for every other week throughout the year. In our home, Rick and I ask the questions and have candy to share for correct answers. This way, the practical facts learned are reviewed and drilled in a fun way, effectively and easily implanting them in your memory. You may download this companion guide online at www.thelearningparent.com. Just sign in on the website and enter the code SIGNERS at the checkout and you may have this resource free of charge to help you use this book effectively.

A COMPLETE RESOURCE FOR A SINGLE MOM

This book can be a valuable tool in the hands of a single mom who struggles to balance work time, household time, and teaching. This book is a tool that can enable her to make a significant contribution to teaching her children Bible, character, and history in a way she and her kids will never forget! We have designed the book so she can pick it up and use it without preparatory work on her part.

A PRACTICAL, LIFE-CHANGING SELF-STUDY

Is your family looking for a practical character/history curriculum for your children to work through on their own? One signer per week affords a year's worth of study and review. This study documents the movements of God's hand in the founding of our country.

A Group Study Designed to Make a Difference

This book may also be used for group study and discussion. A unit study undertaken by members may include other material from the time of the American Revolution, if desired. Check out suggested readings in the Appendix!

Inspirational General Reading

The original intent of this book was as general reading for junior high age through adults. As an adult, I found this to be totally new information to me, which I felt would greatly benefit any reader's life. I was inspired by the sacrifices made on our behalf by men whose names I had never heard. My prayer is that you will be inspired to be a productive citizen whose focus is on our Lord and whose life exemplifies His principles for godly living. May others be drawn to our Savior by the life they see reflected in you!

Be sure to take advantage of our online companion guide to this book at
www.thelearningparent.com
Use code: SIGNERS

The Signatures

The actual signing of the document did not take place until August 2, 1776. An embossed copy (hand-copied with calligraphy) was prepared. The custom of the day was to sign beginning on the right side of the paper, under the text. They signed in groups of states geographically from north to south, starting with the State of New Hampshire.

		John Hancock			
			Rob Morris	Wm Floyd	Josiah Bartlett
Button Gwinnett	Wm Hooper	Samuel Chase	Benjamin Rush	Philip Livingston	Wm Whipple
Lyman Hall	Joseph Hewes	Wm Paca	Benj Franklin	Francis Lewis	Sam Adams
George Walton	John Penn	Thos Stone	John Morton	Lewis Morris	John Adams
		Charles Carroll	George Clymer		Rob Treat Paine
	Edward Rutledge	of Carollton	Ja Smith		Elbridge Gerry
			Geo Taylor	Rich Stockman	Step Hopkins
	Thos Heyward Jr.		James Wilson	Jon Witherspoon	William Ellery
	Thomas Lynch Jr.	George Wythe	George Ross	Fra Hopkinson	Roger Sherman
	Arthur Middleton	Richard Henry Lee		John Hart	Sam Huntington
		Th Jefferson	Caesar Rodney	Abra Clark	Wm Williams
		Benj Harrison	Geo Read		Oliver Wolcott
		Th Nelson Jr.	Tho McKean		Matthew Thornton
		Francis Lightfoot Lee			
		Carter Braxton			

		President of Continental Congress			
Georgia	N. Carolina	Maryland	Pennsylvania	New York	N. Hampshire
					Massachusetts
	S. Carolina			New Jersey	Rhode Island
		Virginia	Delaware		Connecticut
					N. Hampshire

IN CONGRESS, JULY 4, 1776

The unanimous Declaration of the thirteen united States of America

When in the Course of human events it becomes necessary for one people to dissolve the political bands which have connected them with another and to assume among the powers of the earth, the separate and equal station to which the Laws of Nature and of Nature's God entitle them, a decent respect to the opinions of mankind requires that they should declare the causes which impel them to the separation. —We hold these truths to be self-evident, that all men are created equal, that they are endowed by their Creator with certain unalienable Rights, that among these are Life, Liberty and the pursuit of Happiness. —That to secure these rights, Governments are instituted among Men, deriving their just powers from the consent of the governed, —That whenever any Form of Government becomes destructive of these ends, it is the Right of the People to alter or to abolish it, and to institute new Government, laying its foundation on such principles and organizing its powers in such form, as to them shall seem most likely to effect their Safety and Happiness. Prudence, indeed, will dictate that Governments long established should not be changed for light and transient causes; and accordingly all experience hath shewn that mankind are more disposed to suffer, while evils are sufferable than to right themselves by abolishing the forms to which they are accustomed. But when a long train of abuses and usurpations, pursuing invariably the same Object evinces a design to reduce them under absolute Despotism, it is their right, it is their duty, to throw off such Government, and to provide new Guards for their future security. — Such has been the patient sufferance of these Colonies; and such is now the necessity which constrains them to alter their former Systems of Government. The history of the present King of Great Britain is a history of repeated injuries and usurpations, all having in direct object the establishment of an absolute Tyranny over these States. To prove this, let Facts be submitted to a candid world. — He has refused his Assent to Laws, the most wholesome and necessary for the public good. — He has forbidden his Governors to pass Laws of immediate and pressing importance, unless suspended in their operation till his Assent should be obtained; and when so suspended, he has utterly neglected to attend to them. — He has refused to pass other Laws for the accommodation of large districts of people, unless those people would relinquish the right of Representation in the Legislature, a right inestimable to them and formidable to tyrants only. — He has called together legislative bodies at places unusual, uncomfortable, and distant from the depository of their Public Records, for the sole purpose of fatiguing them into compliance with his measures. — He has dissolved Representative Houses repeatedly, for opposing with manly firmness his invasions on the rights of the people. — He has refused for a long time, after such dissolutions, to cause others to be elected, whereby the Legislative Powers, incapable of Annihilation, have returned to the People at large for their exercise; the State remaining in the mean time exposed to all the dangers of invasion from without, and convulsions within. — He has endeavoured to prevent the population of these States; for that purpose obstructing the Laws for Naturalization of Foreigners; refusing to pass others to encourage their migrations hither, and raising the conditions of new Appropriations of Lands. — He has obstructed the Administration of Justice by refusing his Assent to Laws for establishing Judiciary Powers. — He has made Judges dependent on his Will alone for the tenure of their offices, and the amount and payment of their salaries. — He has erected a multitude of New Offices, and sent hither swarms of Officers to harass our people and eat out their substance. — He has kept among us, in times of peace, Standing Armies without the Consent of our legislatures. He has affected to render the Military independent of and superior to the Civil Power. — He has combined with others to subject us to a jurisdiction foreign to or constitution, and unacknowledged by our laws; giving his Assent to their Acts of pretended Legislation: — For quartering large bodies of armed troops among us: — For protecting them, by a mock Trial from punishment for any Murders which they should commit on the Inhabitants of these States: — For cutting off our Trade with all parts of the world: — For imposing Taxes on us without our Consent: — For depriving us in many cases, of the benefit of Trial by Jury: — For transporting us beyond Seas to be tried for pretended offences: For abolishing the free System of English Laws in a neighbouring Province, establishing therein an Arbitrary government, and enlarging its Boundaries so as to render it at once an example and fit instrument for introducing the same absolute rule into these Colonies: — For taking away our Charters, abolishing our most valuable Laws and altering fundamentally the Forms of our Governments: — For suspending our own Legislatures, and declaring themselves invested with power to legislate for us in all cases whatsoever. — He has abdicated Government here, by declaring us out of his Protection and waging War against us. He has plundered our seas, ravaged our coasts, burnt our towns, and destroyed the lives of our people. — He is at this time transporting large Armies of foreign Mercenaries to compleat the works of death, desolation, and tyranny, already begun with circumstances of Cruelty & Perfidy scarcely paralleled in the most barbarous ages, and totally unworthy the Head of a civilized nation. — He has constrained our fellow Citizens taken Captive on the high Seas to bear Arms against their Country, to become the executioners of their friends and Brethren, or to fall themselves by their Hands. — He has excited domestic insurrections amongst us, and has endeavoured to bring on the inhabitants of our frontiers, the merciless Indian Savages whose known rule of warfare, is an undistinguished destruction of all ages, sexes and conditions. In every stage of these Oppressions We have Petitioned for Redress in the most humble terms: Our repeated Petitions have been answered only by repeated injury. A Prince, whose character is thus marked by every act which may define a Tyrant, is unfit to be the ruler of a free people. Nor have We been wanting in attentions to our British brethren. We have warned them from time to time of attempts by their legislature to extend an unwarrantable jurisdiction over us. We have reminded them of the circumstances of our emigration and settlement here. We have appealed to their native justice and magnanimity, and we have conjured them by the ties of our common kindred to disavow these usurpations, which would inevitably interrupt our connections and correspondence. They too have been deaf to the voice of justice and of consanguinity. We must, therefore, acquiesce in the necessity, which denounces our Separation, and hold them, as we hold the rest of mankind, Enemies in War, in Peace Friends. —

We, therefore, the Representatives of the united States of America, in General Congress, Assembled, appealing to the Supreme Judge of the world for the rectitude of our intentions, do, in the Name, and by Authority of the good People of these Colonies, solemnly publish and declare, That these united Colonies are, and of Right ought to be Free and Independent States, that they are Absolved from all Allegiance to the British Crown, and that all political connection between them and the State of Great Britain, is and ought to be totally dissolved; and that as Free and Independent States, they have full Power to levy War, conclude Peace, contract Alliances, establish Commerce, and to do all other Acts and Things which Independent States may of right do. — And for the support of this Declaration, with a firm reliance on the protection of Divine Providence, we mutually pledge to each other our Lives, our Fortunes, and our sacred Honor.

New Hampshire

Josiah Bartlett
Matthew Thornton
William Whipple

Josiah Bartlett

Enthusiastic Patriot

Colossians 3:23

"He made the rafters echo with his approval."

❧

BORN
November 21, 1729

BIRTHPLACE
Amesbury, Massachusetts

EDUCATION
Common Schools

OCCUPATION
Physician

MARRIED
Mary Bartlett, 1754

CHILDREN
12

AGE AT SIGNING
46

DIED
May 19, 1795; age 65

As Josiah Bartlett took up the quill to put his name to the document, William Ellery saw a rugged-looking man in his forties. Bartlett was tall, his curly hair had a reddish tint, and he moved with determination and vigor. When the vote for independence had been tallied, he had "made the rafters echo with his approval," according to fellow delegates. Now he had the privilege of being the first of the regular delegates to sign the Declaration.[1]

The youngest of seven children, Josiah Bartlett was born November 21, 1729, in Amesbury, Massachusetts. His parents ran a farm by the name of Lin's Mouth and his father was a shoemaker. Even as a young boy, Josiah was determined to be a doctor. He received some schooling from the town teacher, but by the time he was 16 years old he had mastered Latin and Greek, and was apprenticed to an Amesbury physician (who was also a relative), Dr. Ordway. Josiah learned to mix medicines, deliver babies, and treat patients. By the time Josiah was 21, his master declared him ready to enter the ranks of physicians and he became known as Dr. Bartlett.

A physician was needed in Kingston, New Hampshire, ten miles from Amesbury. Bartlett set up practice and became known for his expertise in treating fevers and using quinine.

The story is told that Bartlett became seriously ill with a high fever. The physician who treated him insisted that the windows to his room be tightly closed and that he should receive no liquids. The fever continued to rise, and the doctor diagnosed Bartlett's condition as hopeless. Finally, rallying slightly, Bartlett prevailed upon friends to bring him a jug of cider which he drank in small quantities throughout the night. In the morning, the cider he had drunk enabled him to perspire heavily; the fever broke, and his life was saved. Later, one of his most important discoveries as a physician was the use of Peruvian bark, or cinchona, to relieve cases of severe sore throat. This was long before the drug quinine had been extracted from cinchona.[5]

In 1754 he married his cousin, Mary Bartlett. The couple had twelve children, eight of whom lived to adulthood. Three of their sons became physicians, as did seven of their grandsons.

Bartlett's devotion to his profession, his friendliness, and his intelligence, soon won him a wide medical practice and many friends. Although he had no formal training in the law, he was elected as a local justice of the peace because the community knew it could rely on his impartiality. His rising community leadership also led to his appointment by the royal governor as a commander of militia troops.[6]

In 1774, New Hampshire's House of Representatives created the Committee of Correspondence as part of the patriotic network. The royal governor, recognizing Bartlett's role in this patriotic activity, ordered him to be removed from his office as justice of the peace and dismissed him from his command in the militia. He was elected delegate from his colony to the First Continental Congress in 1774, but declined, due to the loss of his house by fire, presumably set by the British.

The royal governor repeatedly ordered the dissolution of the legislature. Bartlett and other members would disband and meet elsewhere, and soon formed the Committee of Safety, which became the governing body of New Hampshire when the governor fled to the protection of the British troops in 1775. In August, Bartlett was appointed colonel of a militia regiment.

On August 27, 1775, Bartlett was chosen for the Second Continental Congress to represent New Hampshire along with John Langdon.

With permission of Congress, on January 5, 1776, the Assembly of New Hampshire established a government which was, however, only "to Continue During the Present Unhappy and Unnatural Contest with Great Britain. Protesting and Declaring that we Never Sought to throw off our Dependance upon Great Britain…And that we Shall Rejoice if Such a reconciliation…can be Effected."[7]

Colonel Bartlett, attending Congress at Philadelphia, wrote to John Langdon about the instructions disavowing independence which had been given the Portsmouth representatives in the New Hampshire Assembly: "…by the instructions I find the town (Portsmouth) is very much afraid of the idea Conveyed by the frightful word *Independence!* This week a pamphlet on the subject *(Common Sense)* was printed here, and greedily bought up and read by all ranks of people — I shall send you one of them which you will please to lend round to the people: perhaps on Consideration there may not appear anything so terrible in that thought as they may at first apprehend if Britain should force us to break off connections with her."[8]

New Hampshire was torn between the patriot faction and that group which felt need of Great Britain's protection. Colonel Bartlett requested explicit instructions.

Colonel Bartlett wrote on June 6 to Nathaniel Folsom: "The affair of declaring these Colonies Independent States…must soon be Decided whatever may be the opinion of the Delegates of New Hampshire on that matter they think it their duty to act agreeable to the minds of their Constituents and…Desire the Explicit Directions of the Legislature…" On the day of the postponement, June 10, Bartlett wrote to John Langdon, requesting instructions and urging that favorable ones "would Carry great weight with it (independence)."

Folsom, who was present in the Council, replied to Colonel Bartlett on the 15th: "…I doubt not that you will be pleased to hear that a pretty General harmony in the Grand American Cause Prevails here — the vote for independency you will see is unanim' in both Houses…I wish you the divine blessing at the Congress — I doubt not if we remain firm and united we shall under God disappoint the Sanguenary designs of our Enemies — "

The instructions were "to join with the other Colonies in declaring The Thirteen United Colonies, A FREE & INDEPENDENT STATE…" [9]

Over a week later, John Langdon, now being considered for Congress' agent of prizes in New Hampshire, wrote from Portsmouth to his colleague Bartlett that he then knew of none who opposed independence.

New Hampshire's instructions reached Philadelphia just in time:

…Colonel Bartlett tells that the independence resolve of their colony "came to hand on Saturday, very seasonably, as that Question was agreeable to order this Day taken up in a Committee of the whole House and every Colony fully represented…" [10]

Josiah Bartlett is thought to have been the second to sign the Declaration on August 2, following John Hancock. Bartlett's signature, just under the pledge of "our Lives" in the text, is at the head of the extreme right-hand column of names on the priceless parchment — a signature which might have hanged him! [11]

During the year 1777, Bartlett remained in New Hampshire. He occupied himself mainly in recruiting soldiers to serve in the state's regiments in the Continental Army. He also aided in the administration of the government of the state. Bartlett returned to Congress in May, 1778, while it was meeting at York, Pennsylvania. When the British evacuated Philadelphia, Congress adjourned to that city in July. In a letter written shortly after his arrival in Philadelphia, Bartlett described changes made in the city by the British occupation:

ᔰ Public Service ᔰ

1750	**Began practicing medicine in Kingston, New Hampshire**
1765–1775	**Delegate of New Hampshire legislature**
1775–1776	**Delegate of New Hampshire to the Continental Congress; first delegate to vote approval of the Declaration of Independence**
1778	**Delegate of New Hampshire to the Continental Congress; first delegate to sign the Articles of Confederation**
1779–1782	**Chief justice of New Hampshire Supreme Court**
1782–1788	**Associate justice of New Hampshire Supreme Court**
1788	**Member of State Ratification Convention of U.S. Constitution**
1788–1790	**Chief justice of New Hampshire Supreme Court**
1790–1793	**President of State of New Hampshire**
1791	**First president of the New Hampshire Medical Society**
1793–1794	**First governor of the State of New Hampshire**

The Congress meets in the college hall, as the state house was left by the enemy in a most filthy and sordid situation, as were many of the public and private buildings in the city; some of the genteel houses were used for stables, and holes cut in the parlour floors, and their dung shoveled into the cellars. The country northward of the city for several miles is one common waste; the houses burnt, the fruit trees and others cut down and carried off, fences carried away, gardens and orchards destroyed; Mr. (John) Dickinson's and Mr. (Robert) Morris's fine seats all demolished; in short, I could hardly find the great roads that used to pass that way: the enemy built a strong abbatis with the fruit and other trees, from the Delaware to the Schuylkill, and at about forty or fifty rods distance along the abbatis, a quadrangular fort for cannon, and a number of redoubts for small arms; the same on the several eminences along the Schuylkill, against the city.[12]

During the war, Bartlett worked in Congress to build the American navy, and also treated wounded soldiers.

In October of 1778, Dr. Bartlett obtained leave of absence from Congress and returned home to attend to his personal affairs, which had suffered greatly in his absence. In 1779, he was appointed chief justice of the common pleas, and in 1780, muster-master of the troops. In January 1782, when Judge Thornton retired, he was appointed a justice of the superior court and in 1788 was made chief justice.

Dr. Bartlett attended the Constitutional Convention in Philadelphia to help draft the constitution, and strenuously supported its adoption. He was chosen senator in the same year, but because of infirmities that came from being 60 years old, he declined. In June 1790, he was elected president of New Hampshire, in which office he continued until he was elected the first governor of the state in 1793.

He discharged the duties of this high station with his usual promptitude and fidelity: he was a ruler in whom the wise placed confidence, and of whom even the captious could find nothing to complain.[13]

On the 29th of January, 1794, he addressed the following letter to the legislature:

Gentlemen of the Legislature,

After having served the public for a number of years, to the best of my abilities, in the various offices to which I have had the honour to be appointed, I think it proper, before your adjournment, to signify to you, and through you to my fellow-citizens at large, that I now find myself so far advanced in age, that it will be expedient for me at the close of the session, to retire from the cares and fatigues of public business, to the repose of a private life, with a grateful sense of the repeated marks of trust and confidence that my fellow-citizens have reposed in me, and with my best wishes for the future peace and prosperity of the state.

I am, Gentlemen, your most obedient, And very humble servant, JOSIAH BARTLETT.

To the President of the Senate and Speaker of the House of Representatives, to be communicated.[14]

His well-deserved rest was short-lived. On May 19, 1795, this distinguished patriot was "gathered to his fathers," at the age of 65. The following is an excerpt from Rev. Dr. Thayer's funeral sermon for Dr. Josiah Bartlett:

The New Hampshire stern patriotism and inflexible republicanism which adorned the character of Doctor Bartlett, have already been developed. His mind was quick and penetrating, his memory tenacious, his judgment sound and perspective. His natural temper was open, humane, and compassionate. In all his dealings he was scrupulously just, and faithful in the performance of all his engagements.[15]

The town of Bartlett, New Hampshire was named in his honor.

John Greenleaf Whittier composed a poem in honor of Josiah Bartlett entitled, "One of the Signers." One verse says: "Amidst those picked and chosen men, Than his, who here first drew his breath, No firmer fingers held the pen That wrote for liberty or death."[4]

❧ Questions for Discussion ❧

1. What qualities did William Ellery observe in Josiah Bartlett?

2. How was Bartlett called to suffer for signing the Declaration?

3. What qualities caused Bartlett to be ready to practice medicine on his own at the early age of 21?

4. How did Bartlett prove to be innovative when he was seriously ill?

5. What qualities in Bartlett's life helped to build a successful medical practice? What quality caused folks to elect him as justice of the peace?

6. What caused the Royal Governor to remove Bartlett from his position as justice of the peace?

7. What character quality did Bartlett demonstrate to help form the Committee of Safety?

8. Were the patriots at first actually desiring a break from Great Britain, or reconciliation?

9. What did Josiah Bartlett do when the vote for independence was tallied? What does this tell us about him?

10. Describe Bartlett's description of British destruction in and around Philadelphia.

11. Tell of Bartlett's duties during the war. After the Revolution?

12. List the character qualities of Josiah Bartlett, as described in Dr. Thayer's funeral sermon.

13. Look up the definition of "enthusiasm." How did this characterize Bartlett's life?

14. About what aspect of your life could you ask God to help you be more enthusiastic?

Matthew Thornton

Matthew Thornton

Temperate Patriot

1 Corinthians 9:25

"We recommend a serious and steady regard to the rules of temperance, sobriety, and righteousness."

❧❧

BORN
1714

BIRTHPLACE
Ireland

EDUCATION
Common Schools

OCCUPATION
Physician

MARRIED
Hannah Jack, 1760

CHILDREN
5

AGE AT SIGNING
62

DIED
June 24, 1803; age 89

And such the confidence reposed in him by the people, that he was invested, at the same time, with the highest offices, legislative, judicial, and executive, in which he was continued by annual elections during the whole war. He was not a person of an original and inventive genius, but he possessed an extensive knowledge, an accurate judgment, a calm temper, a modest deportment, an upright and benevolent heart, and a habit of prudence and diligence in discharging the various duties of public and private life.[2]

Matthew Thornton was born in 1714 in Ireland. He sailed to America with his family at the age of four. The first winter there, the family had no place to live, so they spent the cold, long winter months on their ship which was anchored along the coast of Maine. They settled in Worcester, Massachusetts, where Matthew grew up attending common schools, and became a doctor by studying with an established physician, Dr. Grout, of Leicester, Massachusetts.

Young Dr. Thornton moved to Londonderry, New Hampshire, and built up a successful medical practice there. Matthew remained a bachelor until he was 46 years old, when he married Hannah Jack, who was only about 18. They had five children.

In 1745, the British launched an attack on the French in Nova Scotia, and Thornton was the surgeon for the unit of five hundred New Hampshire men.

Louisburg was a fortress upon the island of Cape Breton, Nova Scotia, then in possession of the French, and was considered one of the strongest fortifications in America… Louisburg was the "Dunkirk" of America; yet it surrendered to the valour of our troops. It is recorded to the praise of Dr. Thornton, and as an evidence of his professional abilities, that of the corps of five hundred men, of whom he had charge as a physician, only six died of sickness, previous to the surrender of the city, although they were among those who assisted in dragging the cannon over the abovementioned morass.[7]

Thornton returned to his practice after the Battle of Louisburg, and prior to the Revolutionary War became a member of New Hampshire's colonial legislature, representing Londonderry. In 1771, the royal governor was forced to flee from New Hampshire and a provincial convention was created. Colonel Thornton was elected president, and made the following speech:

(In Provincial Congress, Exeter June 2, 1775; To the Inhabitants of The Colony of New Hampshire)

Friends and brethren, you must all be sensible that the affairs of America, have, at length, come to a very affecting and alarming crisis. The horrors and distresses of a civil war, which, till of late, we only had in contemplation, we now find ourselves obliged to realize. Painful beyond expression, have been those scenes of blood and devastation, which the barbarous cruelty of British troops have placed before our eyes. Duty to God, to ourselves, to posterity, enforced by the cries of slaughtered innocents, have urged us to take up arms in our own defence. Such a day as this was never before known, either to us or to our fathers. You will give us leave, therefore, in whom you have reposed special confidence, as your representative body, to suggest a few things, which call for the serious attention of everyone, who has the true interest of America

Dr. Thornton was greatly beloved by all who knew him, and to the end of his long life he was a consistent and zealous Christian. He always enjoyed remarkably good health, and by the practice of those hygiene virtues, temperance and cheerfulness, he attained a patriarchal age.[4]

at heart. We would, therefore, recommend to the colony at large, to cultivate that Christian union, harmony, and tender affection, which is the only foundation upon which our invaluable privileges can rest with any security, or our public measures be pursued with the least prospect of success.

The most industrious attention be paid to the cultivation of lands and American manufactures, in their various branches, especially the linen and woolen, and that the husbandry might be managed with a particular view thereto; accordingly, that the farmer raise flax, and increase his flock of sheep to the extent of his ability.

We further recommend a serious and steady regard to the rules of temperance, sobriety, and righteousness; and that those laws which have, heretofore, been our security and defence from the hand of violence, may still answer all their former valuable purposes, though persons of vicious and corrupt minds would willingly take advantage from our present situation.

He was noted as a wit who particularly enjoyed puns, satires, and humorous fables. An early biographer said of him: "He exhibited the very essence of hilarity and humour, in the infinite variety of his stories, and his mode of narrative, which was particularly inviting. In this rational pastime, he never descended to vulgarity, but afforded general amusement, while he instructed the minds, and improved the morals, of his hearers: like the great Franklin, whom he, in many traits of his character, resembled, he illustrated his sentiments by fable…His inventive powers in exercises of this nature were quick and judiciously directed…His posture, and manner of narrating, were as peculiar as the faculty itself; when he placed his elbows upon his knees, with his hands supporting his head, it was the signal for the arrectis auribus of the assembly. Their attention became instantly arrested and irresistibly fixed upon the narrative; the curious incidents of which were evolved in the most masterly manner. Commencing with a slow articulation and a solemn countenance, he gradually proceeded in his tale, casting, at intervals, his black and piercing eyes upon the countenance of his hearers, to detect the emotions excited in their breasts, and pausing to observe its full effects."[3]

RES. OF MATTHEW THORNTON.

Residence of Matthew Thornton
Derry, New Hampshire

> *H*is house was, at all times, open to those who were houseless, and his table as frequently surrounded by individuals, from whom gratitude alone could be anticipated in return for his kindness and hospitality.[5]

In a word, we seriously and earnestly recommend the practice of that pure and undefiled religion, which embalmed the memory of our pious ancestors, as that alone upon which we can build a solid hope and confidence in the Divine protection and favour, without whose blessing all the measures of safety we have, or can propose, will end in our shame and disappointment. Matthew Thornton, President.[8]

He worked so intently on New Hampshire business that he didn't get to change his clothes for ten days in a row. New Hampshire became the first of the original thirteen colonies to create a government totally independent of Great Britain.

On the great question which was decided in favour of our national independence, he was invariably steadfast, and at all times evinced his readiness to support with his property and life, the declaration to which he had publicly subscribed. His political character may be best estimated by the fact, that he enjoyed the confidence, and was the unshaken disciple of Washington.[6]

In September of the following year, he was chosen as a delegate to the Continental Congress. Although he couldn't be present to vote for the Declaration of Independence, he did sign it on November 4, 1776, the day he took his seat in Congress.

He was one of the last of the fifty-six men to sign the document. The space directly below the signatures of New Hampshire's other two signers was already taken by Samuel Adams of Massachusetts, so Thornton signed his name at the bottom of the right-hand column, apart from Josiah Bartlett and William Whipple.[9]

During the same year he was appointed Chief Justice of the Court of Common Pleas and soon afterward was raised to the office of Judge of the Superior Court of New Hampshire. He retained this office until 1782.

In 1780, he purchased a farm near Exeter on the banks of the Merrimack, and involved himself in agriculture. Even though he was growing aged, he cheerfully granted folks his professional medical services when required. He took an active interest in affairs of the town. He was a member of the General Court for a year or two as well as a senator in the state legislature. He also served as a member of the council in 1785. He held the office of Justice of the Peace from January 1784, until his death.

Matthew Thornton continued to write political articles for newspapers until he was in his eighties, and about this time he prepared a work of 73 manuscript pages for the press, entitled, *Paradise Lost, or, the Origin of the Evil called Sin, examined,* or *how it ever did, or ever can come to pass, that a creature should or could do anything unfit or improper for that creature to do.* Dr. Thornton contracted whooping cough after his eightieth year, but survived it and even went on practicing medicine, though feeble with age.

Dr. Thornton died while visiting his daughter at Newburyport, Massachusetts, on June 24, 1803, at age 89. Dr. Burnap, at his funeral, said of him,

> He was venerable for his age, and skilled in his profession, and for the several very important and honourable offices he had sustained; noted for the knowledge he had acquired, and his quick penetration into matters of abstruse speculation; exemplary for his regard for the public institutions of religion, and for his constancy in attending the public worship, where he trod the courts of the house of God, with steps tottering with age and infirmity. Such is a brief outline of one who was honoured in his day and generation; whose virtues were a model for imitation, and while memory does her office, will be had in grateful recollection.[10]

His grave is in Thornton's Ferry Cemetery near the site of his Munich home. On the marble slab over his grave is the inscription, "An Honest Man."

> That no man was more deeply impressed with a belief in the existence and bounties of an over-ruling

[Dr. Thornton's] character as a Christian, a father, a husband, and a friend, was bright and unblemished.[12]

Providence, which he strongly manifested by a practical application of the best. In relation to the religious sentiments and opinions of Doctor Thornton, it is not ascertained that he ranked himself among any of the established sects of Christians. It is, however, certain and wisest injunctions of the Christian religion: a believer in the divine mission of our Saviour, he implicitly followed the great principles of his doctrine, so far as human frailty would permit. Exemplary for his regard to the public institutions of religion, and for his constancy in attending public worship, he trod the courts of the house of God with steps tottering with age and infirmity." [11]

As a neighbour he was universally loved, as a citizen respected, and as a physician, he gained the confidence of people, by his skill and punctuality. He cherished with fondness the remembrance of those individuals of merit, with whom he had formed

❧ Public Service ❧

1740	Began practicing medicine in Londonderry, New Hampshire
1745	Took part in the first Battle of Louisburg in Nova Scotia as a surgeon with the New Hampshire militia
1775	President of the first Patriotic Provincial Congress of New Hampshire
1776	Speaker of the General Assembly of the New Hampshire legislature
1776–1778	Delegate to the Continental Congress; signed the Declaration of Independence
1776–1782	Associate justice of the Superior Court of New Hampshire

an acquaintance during the chequered scenes of his life…His own children, who were absent from home, participated largely in his warmest affections: he visited them annually, and expended some time in their society. Their love and veneration for him, and unceasing solicitude for his welfare, amply repaid his paternal anxiety, and were a soothing consolation to his declining years. He was greatly recreated by these excursions, and never returned from them without apparent satisfaction.[13]

Questions for Discussion

1. What character qualities in Thornton's life prompted the people to place their confidence in his leadership?

2. What quality particularly endeared him to his listeners?

3. What do others attest about the qualities of his Christian testimony?

4. What kind of individuals did Thornton open his home to? What qualities did he bestow upon them?

5. How might his political character best be described?

6. What quality is seen in Matthew's studying to be a doctor?

7. How was his skill as a doctor demonstrated while surgeon for his unit of 500 New Hampshire men at the Battle of Louisburg?

8. List the practical suggestions Thornton makes to the people of New Hampshire in his speech at the Provincial Congress.

9. What does he cite to be the primary response for taking up arms?

10. What character qualities does Thornton appeal to the people to demonstrate in their behavior?

11. Describe his call to Christianity and faith in Almighty God. What does he see to be the deciding factor in victory?

12. In what way did New Hampshire set an example for the other colonies?

Questions for Discussion

13. Tell what quality Thornton demonstrated when he went ten days without changing clothes.

14. What office did Thornton hold in useful service to his country?

15. Even in old age, what quality did he show when providing medical care to those in need?

16. Tell of his desire to spread the gospel, even in his old age.

17. What do we know of his Christian testimony and dedication?

18. From what earthly pastime did he derive pleasure in his later years?

19. Look up "temperance" in the appendix and give instances to show this to be one quality which governed Thornton's life.

20. Choose an area in which you could use more temperance and set a goal to achieve this week.

William Whipple

Patriot of Great Faith

Hebrews 11:1

"May God Unite Our Hearts"

BORN
January 14, 1730
BIRTHPLACE
Kittery, Maine
EDUCATION
Common Schools
OCCUPATION
Merchant
MARRIED
Catherine Moffat
CHILDREN
one–died in infancy
AGE AT SIGNING
46
DIED
November, 1785; age 55

His letters showed that he was a forthright, practical-minded man with strong views and an optimistic disposition. Even when the outlook seemed darkest, he never doubted that the colonies would be victorious.[1]

William Whipple, the eldest of five children, was born in 1730 in Kittery, Maine. After attending public school, where he was taught reading, writing, arithmetic, and navigation, he went to sea as a boy and rapidly rose to become a ship's captain while still in his twenties. In voyages chiefly confined to the West Indies, he obtained a considerable fortune; by the time he was 29, he retired from the sea.

In 1759, he went into business with his brother Joseph at Portsmouth, New Hampshire. The business prospered and he became a leading citizen in town. He married his cousin, Catherine Moffat. They had only one child who died in infancy.

Whipple, known for his honesty and responsibility, represented Portsmouth to the Provincial Congress. He was appointed to the Committee of Safety and was also a delegate to the general Congress in 1776. He was the third person to sign the Declaration of Independence.

The memorable day which gave birth to the Declaration of Independence afforded, in the case of William Whipple, as a writer observes, a striking example of the uncertainty of human affairs, and the triumphs of perseverance. The cabin boy, who thirty years before had looked forward to a command of a vessel as the consummation of all his hopes and wishes, now stood amidst the Congress of 1776, and looked around upon a conclave of patriots, such as the world had never witnessed. He whose ambition once centered in inscribing his name as commander upon a crew-list, now affixed his signature to a document, which has embalmed it for posterity." [5]

In 1777 he was appointed brigadier general by the assembly of New Hampshire. Great alarm prevailed at this time in New Hampshire because of the evacuation of Fort Ticonderoga by the Americans, the fort now being under possession of the British. General Burgoyne, with a larger force, was headed for the state. The militia of New Hampshire was divided into two brigades under command of General John Stark and General Whipple.

General Stark was immediately ordered to march "to stop the progress of the enemy on our western frontiers," with one-fourth of his brigade, and one-fourth of three regiments belonging to the brigade of General Whipple. His army was principally composed of veteran corps of the best troops of Britain and Germany, and American loyalists, furnished it with spies, scouts, and rangers: a numerous body of savages, in their own dress and with their own weapons, and the characteristic ferocity, increased the terrors of its approach...of the number of friendly loyalists, the British general dispatched lieutenant colonel Baum from fort Edward, with about fifteen hundred of his German troops, and a body of Indians, to pervade the Grants as far as the Connecticut river, for the purpose of collecting horses to mount the dragoons and cattle, both for labour and provisions. He was encountered at Bennington by the intrepid Stark, who carried the works which he had constructed, by assault, and killed or captured the greater part of his detachment; a few, only, escaped into the woods, and saved themselves by flight.

This victory gave a severe check to the hopes of the enemy, and revived the spirits of the people after a long depressions. The courage of the militia increased with their reputation, and they found that neither British nor German regulars were invincible. Burgoyne was weakened and disheartened by the event, and beginning to perceive the danger of his situation, he now considered the men of New Hampshire and the Green Mountains, whom he had viewed with contempt, as dangerous enemies: in a letter, written about this time, he remarks to lord Germaine, that "the New Hampshire Grants, till of late but little known, hang like a cloud on my left."

The northern army was now reinforced by the militia of all the neighbouring states. Brigadier general Whipple marched with a great part of his brigade; and volunteers from all parts of New

Once independence was declared, William Whipple wanted to fight — even though he was starting to suffer from a heart condition that caused him to faint at times. Whipple was one of sixteen signers who served as soldiers during the war. [2]

His life and character present one of those bright examples of self-reliance which cannot be too often pressed upon the attention of the young; and, although surrounding circumstances had much to do in the development of his talents, yet, after all, the great secret of his success was doubtless a hopeful reliance upon a conscious ability to perform any duty required of him. [3]

Hampshire, hastened in great numbers to join the standard of general Gates. In the desperate battles of Stillwater and of Saratoga, the troops of New Hampshire gained in a large share of the honour due to the American army. The consequence of these engagements was the surrender of general Burgoyne. When the British army capitulated, he was appointed, with colonel Wilkinson, as the representative of general Gates, to meet two officers from general Burgoyne, for the purpose of propounding, discussing, and settling several subordinate articles and regulations springing from the preliminary proposals of the British general.

…[t]hey signed the articles of capitulation. After the attainment of this grand object, general Whipple was selected as one of the officers, under whose command the British troops were conducted to their destined encampment on Winter-hill, near Boston. General Whipple was attended on this expedition by a valuable negro servant, named Prince, whom he had imported from Africa, many years before. On his way to the army, he told his servant that if they should be called into action, he expected that he would behave like a man of courage, and fight bravely for his country. Prince replied, "Sir, I have no inducement to fight; but if I had my liberty, I would endeavour to defend it to the last drop of my blood." The general manumitted him on the spot.[6]

In the summer of 1778, the American army under General Whipple and General Sullivan neared Providence for the purpose of the "reductions" of Rhode Island.

From July to September 1778, Whipple and his militia troops served under Major General John Sullivan in an unsuccessful effort to recapture Rhode Island from the British. During this period of military duty, Whipple is said to have narrowly missed death when a British cannonball smashed through his headquarters.[7]

After entering the house, the cannonball passed under the table where the officers were sitting and shattered the leg of the brigade-major of General Whipple's brigade. His leg was injured so badly that amputation was necessary. According to the payroll records it appears that

⚜ Public Service ⚜

1775	**Member of the Provincial Congress of New Hampshire; member of New Hampshire's Committee of Safety.**
1776	**Member of the first executive council of the State of New Hampshire**
1776–1779	**Delegate to the Continental Congress; signed the Declaration of Independence**
1777–1778	**Fought in the Revolutionary War as a brigadier general of the New Hampshire militia**
1780–1784	**Member of the New Hampshire Legislature**
1782–1784	**Receiver of finances for Congress in New Hampshire**
1782	**President of a court of commissioners to settle a land dispute between Connecticut and Pennsylvania**
1782–1785	**Associate justice of the Superior Court of New Hampshire**

Whipple took command on July 26, and retired on September 5, 1778.

The following year he was elected a member of the legislature to which he was repeatedly chosen, showing that his fellow citizens had confidence in him.

In 1780, Whipple was appointed by Congress as a commissioner of the board of admiralty, but he declined the appointment, writing: 'I am confident that your wishes, that I would accept the office you mentioned, are founded on the best principles, viz., the public good; though I am not altogether so clear that you would not be mistaken. No doubt some other person may be found that will fill the place much better; at least this is my sincere wish, for I have nothing more at heart than our navy. The official account of my appointment did not reach me till sometime in January, although the letter was dated the 27th November; this may account for my answer's being so long delayed: indeed, I took a fortnight to consider the matter before I gave my answer, and I assure you considered it very maturely; and, in casting up the account, I found the balance so greatly against it, that I was obliged, on the principle of self-preservation, to decline.[8]

In May 1782, Robert Morris, superintendent of finance, appointed Whipple receiver for the State of New Hampshire.

Confiding in his inclination and abilities to promote the interest of the U.S., Mr. Morris was known to appoint to this position men of "tried integrity and invincible patriotism." His duty was to "receive money from the state and send them to Congress for use in paying the costs of the war." This was an extremely thankless job, for money was scarce in New Hampshire, and the state legislators were reluctant to send any money to Philadelphia. Whipple attempted to resign, but was persuaded to remain in the position when Robert Morris...wrote to him in August, 1783:

Res. of Gen'l WM WHIPPLE
Portsmouth, NH~ Now Res. of CH Cobb, Esq.

Residence of General William Whipple
Portsmouth, NH ~ Now Residence of C.H. Cobb, Esq.

"If a number of competitors would appear, I am well persuaded that you would not have accepted. Your original motives must continue to exist, until the situation of our affairs shall mend. Persist then, I pray you, in those efforts which you promised me, and be persuaded that the consciousness of having made them will be the best reward. If this is not the case, I have mistaken your character." Finally, in 1784, Whipple succeeded in collecting three thousand dollars from New Hampshire and sent it to Morris, then in July of that year he resigned.

From 1782 until his death, Whipple served as an associate justice of the superior court of New Hampshire. During this period...he also served briefly as president of a court of commissioners appointed by Congress that settled a dispute between Connecticut and Pennsylvania over lands lying in the Wyoming Valley region.[9]

Presenting the situation in the Continental Congress through the eyes of a New Hampshire delegate, Colonel Whipple wrote on June 17: "…there is a great change here since my arrival (February 28) as there was in New Hampshire between the time that the powder was taken from the fort and the battle of Bunker Hill… Affairs go bravely as you'll see by the papers." A week later he wrote: "The middle colonies are getting in a good way. Next Monday being the first of July, the grand question is to be debated and I believe determined unanimously. May God unite our hearts in all things that tend to the well being of the rising Empire."4

About this time, Whipple began to experience a heart ailment which at times was quite painful. Exercise would irritate it and riding horseback often brought it on, frequently causing him to faint and fall from his horse. He therefore declined any further military command. On December 25, 1784, he was appointed a justice of the peace and quorum throughout the state under the new constitution.

In the fall of the next year, his medical condition forced him to resign before his circuit was completed. He was immediately confined to his bed chamber, but the nature of his heart problem necessitated him to sleep in a chair. The medical profession at the time did not know how to deal with blocked arteries, and as a result, he died on November 28, 1785, at 55 years old. He was buried in Portsmouth.

General Whipple was possessed of a strong mind, and quick discernment: he was easy in his manners, courteous in his deportment, correct in his habits, and constant in his friendships. He enjoyed through life a great share of the public confidence, and although his early education was limited, his natural good sense, and accurate observations, enabled him to discharge the duties of the several offices with which he was entrusted, with credit to himself and benefit to the public…he constantly manifested an honest and persevering spirit of emulation, which conducted him with rapid strides to distinction. As a sailor, he speedily attained the highest rank in the profession; as a merchant, he was circumspect and industrious; as a congressman, he was firm and fearless; as a legislator, he was honest and able; as a commander, he was cool and courageous; as a member of many subordinate public offices, he was alert and persevering. Such was William Whipple, whose memory will be long cherished in New Hampshire, and whose name, united with the great charter of our freedom, will perish only with the records of the Republic.10

❧ Questions for Discussion ❧

1. What character qualities do Whipple's letters reveal?

2. What character trait could have motivated Whipple to serve as a soldier despite his heart condition?

3. What was the great secret of his success?

4. How did his words prove his reliance on God in the matter of independence?

5. What qualities would have caused him to be financially successful by age 29?

6. For what two qualities was Whipple distinguished which led to his representing Portsmouth to the Provincial Congress?

7. On what committee did Whipple serve in the general Congress?

8. Tell how God had much greater plans for Whipple's life than Whipple first thought. What quality drove him to achievement?

9. What was Burgoyne's comment about the New Hampshire regiments?

10. Tell of the incident which led Whipple to free his trusty servant, Prince. What quality does this reveal?

11. Tell of Whipple's narrow escape from a British cannonball.

12. Tell of an incident which shows Whipple had a sane estimate of his own capabilities.

13. Tell how Whipple served his country in various appointments.

14. What caused him to finally decline military appointments? List qualities related at his funeral.

15. Look up the definition of "faith" and show how it was an integral part of Whipple's life. How can you implement this in a specific way in your life?

Massachusetts

John Adams
Samuel Adams
Elbridge Gerry
John Hancock
Robert Treat Paine

John Adams

Diligent Patriot

Proverbs 12:24

"Independence Forever"

❧❧

BORN
October 30, 1735

BIRTHPLACE
Braintree, Massachusetts

EDUCATION
Harvard College

OCCUPATION
Lawyer

MARRIED
Abigail Smith, 1764

CHILDREN
5

AGE AT SIGNING
40

DIED
July 4, 1826, age 90

John served in the Continental Congress from 1774 to 1777. One of the hardest-working congressmen, he awoke at four each morning and kept going until ten at night. By 1775 he believed that America must become independent. "The die is now cast," he wrote in a letter. "Sink or swim, live or die, survive or perish with my country is my unalterable determination."[1]

John Adams

John Adams was born on October 30, 1735, in a nondescript frame house in Quincy (formerly Braintree), Massachusetts. He was a descendant of John Alden, one of our Pilgrim fathers. Young Adams showed an early love of reading, and his father provided for his early education by a tutor. When John was sixteen he was enrolled at Harvard College.

Upon graduation, he accepted a position as schoolmaster in Worcester, Massachusetts. He was given a horse as his means of transportation, and made the 60-mile ride to Worcester in a day's time. He was well liked by his students, as we see in his diary:

> I find by repeated observation and experiment in my school, that human nature is more easily wrought upon and governed by promises and encouragement and praise, than by punishment and threatening and blame.[3]

After teaching about a year, he decided to become a lawyer and moved into the house of John Putnam, a Worcester attorney. Free time was given to reading in Putnam's fine library. Two years later, in 1758, he was admitted to the bar and began practicing law in Braintree.

In October 1764, he married Abigail Smith, a nineteen-year-old daughter of a clergyman. They had an extremely happy marriage that lasted 54 years until Abigail's death, and they had five children, one of whom later became the sixth president of the United States, John Quincy Adams.

When the Stamp Act was passed in 1765, Adams published (in the Boston Gazette) several articles entitled, "A Dissertation on the Canon and the Federal Law."

He appealed to the people to oppose the Stamp Act because lack of action by the people has "always prompted the princes and nobles of the earth, by every species of fraud and violence, to shake off all the limitations of their power.

In conclusion, he exclaims, "let the pulpit resound with the doctrines and sentiments of religious liberty. Let us hear the danger of thraldom to our consciences, from ignorance, extreme poverty and dependence, in short, from civil and political slavery. Let us see delineated before us, the true map of man — let us hear the dignity of his nature, and the noble rank he holds among the works of God! That consenting to slavery is a sacrilegious breach of trust, as offensive in the sight of God, as it is derogatory from our own honour, or interest, or happiness; and that God Almighty has promulgated from heaven, liberty, peace, and good will to man." [4]

The next year Adams moved his law office to Boston. At the time of the Boston Massacre, Adams volunteered to defend the soldiers as he felt the higher British authorities who had ordered their stationing in Boston to be at fault. Robert Treat Paine, a future signer, was the prosecutor in their case.

It is testimony to the eloquence and legal abilities of Adams and Quincy that they won the acquittal of Captain Preston and all but two of his soldiers — these two being convicted of the lesser charge of manslaughter and released with little more than a reprimand. The case did not hurt Adams' popularity, for shortly after he was elected to the Massachusetts General Court (legislature). Recognizing that his election was but the first step in what was to be a long career of public service devoted to his country, Adams said of it, "I consider the step as a devotion of my family to ruin and myself to death." [5]

That same year he was elected as one of the representatives in the general assembly, and then appointed a member of the Continental Congress from Massachusetts. Adams was placed on many important committees.

A few years before his death, Adams wrote a letter to a friend expressing his thoughts at the close of that convention.

When congress had finished their business, as they thought, in the autumn of 1774, I had finished with Mr. Henry, before we took leave

A discussion between Thomas Jefferson and John Adams about who should write the Declaration:

TJ: "You should do it!"

JA: "Why will you not? You ought to do it."

JA: "I will not."

TJ: "Why?"

JA: "Reasons enough."

TJ: "What can be your reasons?"

JA: "Reason first — you are a Virginian, and a Virginian ought to appear at the head of this business. Reason second — I am obnoxious, suspected, and unpopular. You are very much otherwise. Reason third — you can write ten times better than I can."

TJ: "Well, if you are decided, I will do as well as I can."[27]

The piety of [Adams] had been always fervent and sincere, and the regular attention to the duties of public worship in the church of which he was a member, for sixty years, and to which he afterwards bequeathed property worth ten thousand dollars, was one of the habits of his life that endured to the last. [2]

of each other, some familiar conversation, in which I expressed a full conviction that our resolves, declaration of rights, enumerations, and addresses, associations, and non-importation agreements, however they might be viewed in America, and however necessary to cement the union of the colonies, would be but waste water in England. Mr. Henry said they might make some impression among the people of England, but agreed with me, that they would be totally lost upon the government. I had but just received a short and hasty letter, written to me by Major Joseph Hawley, of Northampton, containing a few broken hints, as he called them, of what he thought was proper to be done, and concluding with these words, "after all, we must fight!" This letter I read to Mr. Henry, who listened with great attention, and as soon as I had pronounced the words, "after all, we must fight," he raised his head, and, with an energy and vehemence that I can never forget, broke out with, "I am of that man's mind." The other delegates from Virginia returned to their state in full confidence that all our grievances would be redressed. The last words that Mr. Richard Henry Lee said to me, when we parted, were, "we shall infallibly carry all our points. You will be completely relieved; all the offensive acts will be repealed; the army and fleet will be recalled, and Britain will give up her foolish project." [6]

The Second Continental Congress gathered in a state of alarm in Philadelphia on May 10, 1778; on June 15, Washington was appointed commander-in-chief of the American armies. It was John Adams who recommended him for this position.

When first suggested by Mr. Adams, to a few of his confidential friends in Congress, the proposition was received with a marked disapprobation. Washington, at this time, was almost a stranger to them; and, besides, to elevate a man who had never held a higher military rank than that of colonel, over officers of the highest grade in the militia, and those, too, already in the field, appeared not only irregular, but likely to produce much dissatisfaction among them, and the people at large. To Mr. Adams, however, the greatest advantage appeared likely to result from the choice of Washington, whose character and peculiar fitness for the station he well understood. [7]

John Adams wrote of this time, "I was incessantly employed through the whole fall, winter, and spring of

> *John told Abigail, "We have appointed a continental fast. Millions will be upon their knees at once before their great Creator, imploring His forgiveness and blessing; He smiles on American councils and arms." [29]*

1775 and 1776: in Congress during their sittings, on committees in the mornings and evenings, and unquestionably did more business than any other member of the house." [28] By this time it became unlikely that reconciliation with Great Britain would be possible. On May 6, 1776, Adams offered a resolution:

that the colonies should form governments independent of the crown. On the 10th of May, this resolution was adopted, in the following shape: "That it be recommended to all the colonies, which had not already established governments suited to the exigencies of their case, to adopt such governments as would, in the opinion of the representatives of the people, best conduce to the happiness and safety of their constituents in particular, and Americans in general." This significant vote was soon followed by the direct proposition, which Richard Henry Lee had the honour to submit to Congress, by resolution, on the 7th day of June. [8]

> *It appears to me the eternal Son of God is operating powerfully against the British nation. [26]*

The vote was postponed until July 1, but a committee was chosen to draft the Declaration of Independence. While Adams was on the committee, he deferred to Jefferson in the actual writing of the document. Adams' most important role was in influencing some of the more reluctant delegates to vote in favor of the declaration.

When Lee's resolution for independence was discussed on July 1, Adams took a leading role in the arguments. Thomas Jefferson declared:

Mr. Adams was its great supporter on the floor of Congress. This was the unequivocal testimony of Mr.

Jefferson. "John Adams," said he, on one occasion, "was our Colossus on the floor; not graceful, not elegant, not always fluent in his public addresses, he yet came out with a power, both of thought and of expression, that moved us from our seats;" and at another time, he said, "John Adams was the pillar of its support on the floor of Congress; its ablest advocate and defender against the multifarious assaults, which were made against it."[9]

The resolution was adopted on July 4th unanimously agreed to. Adams, in a letter written to his wife the following day, best describes his elation:

"Yesterday," says he, "The greatest question was decided that was ever debated in America; and greater, perhaps, never was or will be decided among men. A resolution was passed, without one dissenting colony, 'That these United States are, and of right, ought to be, free and independent states.' The day is passed. The 4th of July, 1776, will be a memorable epoch in the history of America. I am apt to believe it will be celebrated by succeeding governments as the great anniversary festival. It ought to be commemorated as the day of deliverance, by solemn acts of devotion to Almighty God. It ought to be solemnized with pomp, shows, games, sports, guns, bells, bonfires, and illuminations, from one end of the continent to the other, from this time forward, forever. You will think me transported with enthusiasm, but I am not. I am well aware of the toil, and blood, and treasure, that it will cost to maintain this declaration, and support and defend these states; yet through all the gloom, I can see the rays of light and glory. I can see that the end is worth more than all the means; and that posterity will triumph, although you and I may rue, which I hope we shall not."[10]

Britain's Lord Howe, at this time, sent word to Congress that he would like to meet with them. Adams, Franklin, and Rutledge were chosen to visit Howe at British headquarters on Staten Island, New York.

Upon their arrival, they were conducted through an army of twenty thousand men, drawn up for the purpose of show and impression. But the display was lost on the commissioners, who studiously avoided all signs of wonder or anxiety. As had been predicted by

❧ Public Service ❧

1758	**Began practicing law**
1774–1777	**Delegate from Massachusetts to the Continental Congress; he signed and also helped write the Declaration of Independence**
1777–1779	**Served as U.S. Diplomat in France**
1779	**Wrote new constitution for the Commonwealth of Massachusetts**
1780–1785	**Served in Europe as diplomatic representative for the Continental Congress and as a member of the commission that negotiated peace with Great Britain**
1785–1788	**U.S. minister to Great Britain**
1789–1797	**First vice-president of the United States**
1797–1801	**Second president of the United States**
1820	**Helped write a new constitution for the Commonwealth of Massachusetts; served as a presidential elector, voting for President Monroe**

Mr. Adams, the interview terminated without any beneficial result. On being introduced, Lord Howe informed them that he could not treat with them as a committee of congress, but only as private gentlemen of influence in the colonies; to which Mr. Adams replied, "You may view me in any light you please, sir, except that of a British subject."[11]

For the remainder of 1776 and 1777, Adams worked tirelessly as a member of ninety different committees, and chaired twenty-five of them. His most important assignment was chairman of the Board of War and Ordnance, similar to Secretary of War in present day.

On June 14, 1777, he introduced the following resolution which passed unanimously:

> Resolved, that the flag of the thirteen United States shall be thirteen stripes, alternate red and white; that the union be thirteen stars, white on a blue field, representing a new constellation.[12]

Late in 1777, Adams was appointed by Congress to join Benjamin Franklin and Arthur Lee in Paris to negotiate aid from France. He took his son, John Quincy Adams, then a boy of ten. When they returned, the citizens of Braintree elected Adams to the Massachusetts State Constitutional Convention.

He was on the committee to prepare a draft of the Massachusetts Constitution, a work which was interrupted by a mission to help negotiate peace with Great Britain.

> …Congress appointed Adams as "minister plenipotentiary for negotiating a treaty of peace and a treaty of commerce with Great Britain." He set sail for France in October, taking with him his oldest two sons, John Quincy and Charles. Their ship sprang a leak and was forced to put into port in Spain. From there the Adamses had to travel across

Birthplaces of John and John Quincy Adams at Quincy Massachusetts

Birthplace of John and John Quincy Adams at Quincy, Massachusetts

Europe by land, finally reaching Paris in February, 1780. Meanwhile, the British had lost interest in discussing peace, having become more confident they would finally beat Washington's army.[13]

Adams carried on negotiations with the Netherlands. He wrote articles which were published in Dutch newspapers. In the summer of 1781, he became extremely ill with typhoid fever. He did recover, and by October, 1782, the Netherlands had signed treaties of friendship and trade and they even agreed to loan the U.S. eight million gilders to carry on the war with Britain.

His success with the Dutch influenced Great Britain, and they redeveloped an interest in peace negotiations. On November 30, 1782, with John Adams, Ben Franklin, John Jay, and Henry Laurens serving as peace commissioners, a provisional peace treaty was signed. A few days after the signing, Adams again fell ill to a fever.

> In an effort to regain his health, he visited England. There, while attending a meeting of parliament, he had the satisfaction of hearing King George III announce Britain's recognition of American independence.[14]

For the rest of 1784 Adams lived in Paris, where he was joined by Abigail. He worked on negotiating another loan with the Netherlands and concluding trade treaties with European nations. In 1785, Congress appointed Adams as America's first minister to Great Britain, which kept him in England for three years.

The general principles on which the fathers achieved independence were...the general principles of Christianity. I will avow that I then believed, and now believe, that those general principles of Christianity are as eternal and immutable as the existence and attributes of God.[24]

His report on his first reception by the British king illuminates his character and his abilities as a diplomat: The king then asked me, whether I came last from France? And upon my answering in the affirmative, he put on an air of familiarity, and smiling, or rather laughing, said, "There is an opinion among some people that you are not the most attached of all your countrymen to the manners of the French." I was surprised at this, because I thought it an indiscretion, and a descent from his dignity. I was a little embarrassed, but determined not to deny the truth on one hand, nor leave him to infer from it any attachment to England on the other, I threw off as much gravity as I could, and assumed an air of gaiety, and a tone of decision, as far as it was decent, and said, "that opinion sir is not mistaken; I must avow to your majesty I have no attachment but to my own country." The king replied, as quick as lightning, "an honest man will never have any other."[15]

He found England, although friendly, to be disinterested in seriously discussing an American trade treaty. While there he wrote *The Defence of the Constitutions of Government of the United States of America.*

In it he upheld the American use of constitutional authority to establish a balance of power between the executive, legislative, and judicial branches of government.[16]

Tired of his long stay overseas, Adams asked Congress to relieve him of those duties. They returned home in June, 1788, just as the new United States Constitution was ratified.

In February of 1789, when votes were counted for the President of the United States, George Washington won unanimously, with Adams as Vice President.

Upon his election, Adams observed wryly, "My country has in its wisdom contrived for me the most insignificant office that ever the invention of man contrived or his imagination conceived."[17]

When Washington declined to run for a third term the Federalists chose John Adams as their candidate and the Anti-Federalists chose Jefferson. The vote in the election was close, with Adams receiving 71, only three more than Jefferson's 68. Adams became President, Jefferson his Vice President.

Adams described his own inauguration in a letter to Mrs. Adams, who was unable to attend.

"A solemn scene it was indeed," Adams wrote, "and it was made affecting to me by the presence of the General [Washington], whose countenance was as serene and unclouded as the day. He seemed to me to enjoy a triumph over me. Methought I heard him say, 'Ay! I am fairly out and you fairly in! See which of us will be the happiest!' "[18]

Adams' administration had trouble at the start. England was at war with France, and both nations wanted the U.S. on their side. Adams was caught in the middle, wanting to avoid war, and pleasing neither the Federalists nor the Anti-Federalists.

James Madison wrote to Jefferson in 1799, this comparison of Adams and Washington:

There never was perhaps a greater contrast between two characters than those between those of the present President and his predecessor...The one cool, considerate and cautious, the other headlong and kindled into flame by every spark that lights on his passions; the one ever scrutinizing into the public opinion, and ready to follow where he could not lead

We have no government armed with power capable of contending with human passions unbridled by morality and religion... Our Constitution was made only for a moral and religious people. It is wholly inadequate to the government of any other.[25]

it; the other insulting it by the most adverse sentiments and pursuits. Washington a hero in the field, yet overweighing every danger in the Cabinet — Adams with not a single pretension to the character of a soldier, a perfect Quixote as a statesman; the former Chief Magistrate pursuing peace everywhere with sincerity, though mistaking the means; the latter taking as much pains to get into wars, as the former took to keep out of it…[19]

Adams was strong in military preparedness. Under his urging the Department of the Navy was established and construction of warships begun.

"From the day when he took his seat as President of the Senate," John Quincy Adams later wrote of his father, "until that when his administration expired, he was assailed with unappeasable virulence; nor did it even cease with his retirement to private life."[20]

In the election of 1800, the Federalists were divided. Hamilton urged Adams to go to war against France, and when he refused, Hamilton withdrew his support for Adams. Adams lost by eight electoral votes. Jefferson and Burr tied, and the House of Representatives declared Jefferson the winner.

Adams, disappointed, returned home to Quincy, where he spent 25 years in quiet retirement. It should be noted, that after Jefferson's administration was replaced, the mutual friendship which had been broken by political disagreements was restored, and in their last years, Adams and Jefferson carried on a friendly correspondence.

Abigail died in 1818. Two years later, at the age of 85, Adams was honored as a presidential elector for the Commonwealth of Massachusetts, casting his vote for James Monroe.

He was also elected president of a Massachusetts Constitutional Convention to revise the state constitution he'd written 40 years earlier. He declined due to his age, but attended and took part in some of the debates. In 1825, he had the joy of seeing his oldest son, John Quincy Adams, elected President.

The last words uttered by the ninety-year-old John Adams were, "Thomas Jefferson still survives"; but unknown to Adams, the author of the Declaration of Independence had died a few hours earlier.[23]

He saw around him that prosperity and general happiness, which had been the object of his public career and labours. No man ever beheld more clearly, and for a longer time, the great and beneficial effects of the services rendered by himself to his country. That liberty, which he so early defended, that independence, of which he was so able an advocate and supporter, he saw, we trust, firmly and securely established. The population of the country thickened around him faster, and extended wider, than his own sanguine predictions had anticipated; and the wealth, respectability, and power of the nation, sprang up to a magnitude, which it is quite impossible he could have expected to witness, in his day. He lived, also, to behold those principles of civil freedom, which had been developed, established, and practically applied in America, attract attention, command respect, and awaken imitation, in other regions of the globe; and well might, and well did he exclaim, "Where will the consequences of the American revolution end!"[21]

He remained in good health until late June, 1826.

The morning of the fourth of July, 1826, he was unable to rise from his bed. Neither to himself, or his friends, however, was his dissolution supposed to be so near. He was asked to suggest a toast, appropriate to the celebration of the day. His mind seemed to glance back to the hour in which, fifty years before, he had voted for the Declaration of Independence, and with the spirit with which he then raised his hand, he now exclaimed, "Independence forever." At four o'clock in the afternoon he expired.[22]

Questions for Discussion

1. What was John Adams' most outstanding character quality, according to Thomas Jefferson?

2. About what character deficiency did Adams poke fun at himself?

3. John Adams was described as one of the hardest working congressmen. What kind of hours did he often keep?

4. What statement did John Adams make which revealed the degree of his commitment to the patriots' cause?

5. What reason did John Adams give for wanting Thomas Jefferson to pen the Declaration of Independence?

6. What do we know of John Adams' Christian character? What was his practice concerning public worship?

7. From which Pilgrim father was John Adams descended?

8. What type of training would John Adams have received at Harvard? (See appendix.)

9. How did Adams prepare to become a lawyer?

10. What was Adams' comment on how to treat students in order to enable the best learning atmosphere?

11. For what reasons did Adams commit himself to fight for independence?

12. Why did Adams feel justified by God to fight for liberty?

13. Tell an incident in which Adams, committed to justice, defended some British soldiers.

14. Who recommended George Washington for commander-in-chief?

15. What resolution did Adams propose to Congress in May of 1776?

16. What was Adams' most influential role in Congress? What quality did it demonstrate in his life?

17. How did Adams demonstrate persuasiveness in his public addresses in support of independence?

18. What did Adams suggest to his wife about how July 4th should be commemorated?

Questions for Discussion

19. Show how vision and commitment to his posterity was foremost in his mind. How do you know he knew the reality of what it might cost?

20. During 1776-77, how many committees did Adams serve on? On how many did he serve as chairman? What character quality is reflected by this?

21. Adams helped to draft the Massachusetts State Constitution. Read about it in the appendix and comment on its Christian nature.

22. Tell what quality Adams had that led Congress to appoint him to negotiate a treaty with Great Britain.

23. Tell of the result of Adams' negotiations with the Netherlands.

24. Why was John Adams in England right after the signing of the Declaration of Independence? What did he have the pleasure of hearing?

25. Tell of an incident with the British king that illuminates Adams' character and abilities as a diplomat.

26. What comment did Adams make when he was elected Vice-President?

27. Tell of James Madison's comparison of George Washington and John Adams.

28. What department was established under John Adam's urging?

29. Describe the liberty John Adams witnessed in his lifetime, the liberty for which he had so diligently worked.

30. According to John Adams, upon what principles was independence achieved? Give his actual quote about the type of people for whom our Constitution was written.

31. Give evidence that our nation looked to God for guidance, for victory, and for acknowledged blessings on their efforts.

32. Discuss John Adams' powerful declaration in his letter to Abigail on December 15, 1777.

33. How did Adams demonstrate diligence in his fervent convictions?

34. What special task has God given you right now to accomplish? How can you apply diligence to bring it to completion?

Samuel Adams
Passionate Patriot

Proverbs 29:19

"Father of the Revolution"
"For Millions Unborn"

✿✿

BORN
September 27, 1722
BIRTHPLACE
Boston, Massachusetts
EDUCATION
Tutors; Harvard College
OCCUPATION
Merchant, Politician
MARRIED
Elizabeth Checkley, 1749
Elizabeth Wells, 1769
CHILDREN
6
AGE AT SIGNING
53
DIED
October 2, 1803, age 81

A man of medium height, Sam Adams had the upbringing and deep religious convictions of a Puritan. He had steel-gray eyes, and in his portraits his face appears severe; but his friends regarded him as a genial companion. The evidence is indisputable that he knew how to get along with other people, and he perhaps can best be described as the popular "political boss" of Boston at his time. His forte was in moulding opinion in a backroom meeting or in haranguing a street mob.[1]

Samuel Adams was born in Quincy (formerly Braintree), Massachusetts, on September 27, 1722. "He was of pilgrim ancestors, and had been taught the principles of Freedom, from his infancy."[14]

His father, a man of wealth and a member of the Massachusetts Assembly under the Colonial government, endeavored to give Sam a good education. He taught him at home, enrolled him in the Boston Latin School, and at the age of fourteen, Samuel entered Harvard, desiring to be a minister of the gospel.

He gave evidence of already leaning toward becoming a revolutionary by choosing as the topic for his master's thesis: "Whether it be lawful to resist the supreme magistrate, if the commonwealth cannot be otherwise preserved?" While he was a student, he also saved enough money from his allowance to pay for the publishing of a pamphlet he wrote called "Englishmen's Rights." [15]

Although Sam desired to become a minister, His parents disagreed. His father wanted him to be a lawyer, and he began this study, but his mother wished for him to be a merchant. At her request he became a clerk apprenticed to a prominent businessman, Thomas Cushing. He was never able to fully concentrate on business pursuits, and formed a club of young men who wrote political essays for the *Boston Independent Advertiser.*

> His father furnished him with ample capital to commence business as a merchant, but his distaste for the profession and the diversion of his mind from its demands by politics, soon caused him serious embarrassment, and he became almost a bankrupt.[16]

> The genius of Adams was naturally bent on politics. It was with him an all engrossing subject. From his earliest youth, he had felt its inspiration. It occupied his thoughts, enlivened his conversation, and employed his pen.[17]

When he was twenty-five his father died, and the cares of the family and estate were left to Samuel. Through lack of interest and poor management, his inheritance was used up within a few years. About this time he married Elizabeth Checkley, with whom he had six children and was happily married. Several years after his dear wife's death, he remarried, to Elizabeth Wells in 1764.

> In 1763 it was announced, that the British ministry had it in view to "tax the colonies, for the purpose of raising a revenue, which was to be placed at the revenue of the crown."[18]

The citizens of Boston held a meeting to discuss this act of Parliament. They recorded the first public document which denied Parliament the right of taxation. They also suggested corresponding with the other American colonies. At the meeting,

> Adams observes: "If our trade may be taxed, why not our lands? Why not the produce of our lands, and every thing we possess, or use? This we conceive annihilates our charter rights to govern and tax ourselves. It strikes at our British privileges, which, as we have never forfeited, we hold in common with our fellow subjects, who are natives of Britain. If taxes are laid upon us in any shape, without our having a legal representation, where they are laid, we are reduced from the character of free subjects, to the state of tributary slaves. We, therefore, earnestly recommend it to you, to use your utmost endeavours to obtain from the general court, all necessary advice and instruction to our agent, at this most critical juncture. We also desire you to use your endeavours, that the other colonies, having the same interests and rights with us, may add their weight to that of this province; that by united application of all who are agreed, all may obtain redress."[19]

Sam Adams became well known as an advocate for independence of the people. In 1765, he was elected a representative to the general

John Adams, his kinsman, said of Samuel that he was "born and tempered with a wedge of steel to split the knot which tied North America to Great Britain."[2]

Most of his adult life was devoted to serving the cause of freedom, for which he received little financial reward. In fact, when he was elected a delegate to the Continental Congress, his friends had to furnish the money to buy him suitable clothing and a horse.[3]

John Adams penned this eulogy: "Without the character of Samuel Adams, the true history of the American Revolution can never be written. For fifty years his pen, his tongue, his activity, were constantly exerted for his country without fee or reward."[4]

Samuel Adams was so poor that his family would have starved had not the rich merchant John Hancock helped support them.[5]

William Ellery observed as Samuel Adams signed the Declaration, "His effectiveness was due to the depth of his conviction rather than to personality or eloquence."[6]

> *For his country he laboured both by night and by day, with a zeal which was scarcely interrupted, and with an energy that knew no fatigue.*[7]

court of Massachusetts for the town of Boston, given the office of clerk. (Note: in Massachusetts, the general court is the name of the legislature).

> He was appointed upon almost every committee, assisted in drawing nearly every report, and exercised a large share of influence, in almost every meeting, which had for its object the counteraction of the unjust plans of the administration.[20]

He originated the *Massachusetts Circular,* a periodical which proposed a Continental Congress to be held in New York in 1766.

> It was known to the British that Adams was now a poor man. It was suggested to Governor Hutchinson to offer him a bribe in the form of a lucrative offer for the British government. He replied in a manner highly complimentary to the integrity of Mr. Adams, "Such is the obstinacy and inflexible dispositions of the man, that he never can be conciliated by any office or gift whatever." The offer, however, it is reported, was actually made to Mr. Adams, but neither the allurements of fortune or power could for a moment tempt him to abandon the cause of truth, or to hazard the liberties of the people. He was indeed poor; but he could be tempted neither by British gold, nor by the honours or profits of any office within the gift of the royal governor. Such patriotism has not been common in the world; but in America it was to be found in many a bosom, during the revolutionary struggle. The knowledge of facts like this, greatly diminishes the wonder, which has sometimes been expressed, that America should have

> *He was a strict Calvinist; and probably, no individual of his day had so much of the feelings of the ancient puritans, as he possessed.*[8]

successfully contended with Great Britain. Her physical strength was comparatively weak; but the moral courage of her statesmen, and her soldiers, was to her instead of numbers, of wealth, and fortifications.[21]

A story is told that illustrates Adams' means of inspiring a crowd. At a Boston meeting, Adams listened to speaker after speaker discuss the problems that were faced, with each speaker carefully avoiding any remark that might be considered treasonous. Finally, Adams in disgust rose and told this fable:

> A Grecian philosopher who was lying asleep on the grass was suddenly roused by the bite of some animal on the palm of his hand. He closed his hand as he awoke, and found that he had caught in it a small field-mouse. As he was examining the little animal which had dared to attack him, it bit him unexpectedly, a second time; he dropped it, and it made its escape. Now, fellow citizens, what think you was the reflection which this trifling circumstance gave birth to in the mind of the philosopher? It was this: that there is no animal, however weak and contemptible, which cannot defend its own liberty, if it will only fight for it.[22]

After the Boston Massacre, a public meeting was called where Sam Adams addressed the crowd. A committee was chosen to go to Governor Hutchinson requesting that British troops be withdrawn immediately from Boston.

> Mr. Adams, who was one of this committee, strongly represented to the governor the danger of retaining the troops no longer in the capital. His indignation was aroused, and in a tone of lofty independence, he declared, that the removal of the troops would alone satisfy his insulted peril, that they were continued in the town, and that he alone must be answerable for the fatal consequences, which it required no gift of prophecy to predict must ensue.[23]

The governor at last gave his consent to remove one of the two regiments, stating he had no authority over the other.

> Adams replied angrily that if Hutchinson had the power to remove one regiment, then he obviously had the power to remove both, and that unless this were done

immediately, he alone must be answerable for the fatal consequences that would ensue.[24]

The Governor, fearing the consequences, called for the removal of all troops from Boston. Thus, through the decisive and spirited conduct of Samuel Adams, and a few other kindred spirits, the obstinacy of a royal governor was subdued, and further hostilities were for a still longer time suspended.[25]

More offers were to be made attempting to bribe Sam Adams. In 1773, Governor Gage tried again:

At that time Colonel Fenton was requested to wait upon Mr. Adams, with the assurance of Governor Gage, that any benefits would be conferred upon him which he should demand, on the condition of his ceasing to oppose the measures of the royal government. At the same time, it was not obscurely hinted, that such a measure was necessary, on personal considerations. He had incurred the royal displeasure, and already, such had been his conduct, that it was in the power of the governor to send him to England for trial, on a charge of treason. It was suggested that a change in his political conduct, might save him from this disgrace, and even from a severer fate; and might elevate him, moreover, from his circumstances of indigence, to the enjoyment of affluence.

To this proposal, Mr. Adams listened with attention; but as Colonel Fenton concluded his communication, with all the spirit of a man of honour, with all the integrity of the most incorrupted and incorruptible patriotism, he replied: "Go tell Governor Gage, that my peace has long since been made with the King of kings, and that it is the advice of Samuel Adams to him, no longer to insult the feelings of an already exasperated people."[26]

Governor Gage, irritated that his plan had failed, issued a proclamation in response to Adams' reply:

"I do hereby," he said, "in his majesty's name, offer and promise his most gracious pardon to all persons, who shall forthwith lay down their arms, and return to the duties of peaceable subjects: excepting only from the benefits of such pardon, Samuel Adams, and John Hancock, whose offences are of too flagitious a nature to admit of any other consideration but that of condign punishment."[27]

His aspect was mild, dignified, and gentlemanly. In his own state, or in the congress of the union, he was always the advocate of the strongest measures; and in the darkest hour, he never wavered or desponded. He engaged in the cause with all the zeal of a reformer, the confidence of an enthusiast, and the cheerfulness of a volunteer martyr. It was not by brilliancy of talents, or profoundness of learning, that he rendered such essential service to the cause of the revolution; but by his resolute decision, his unceasing watchfulness, and his heroic perseverance. In addition to these qualities, his efforts were consecrated by his entire superiority to pecuniary considerations; he, like most of his colleagues, proved the nobleness of their cause, by the virtue of their conduct: and Samuel Adams, after being so many years in the public service, and having filled so many eminent stations, must have been buried at the public expense, if the afflicting death of an only son had not remedied this honourable poverty.[9]

So it was that this action merited the respect of their countrymen. In Sam Adams' view,

The die was cast, and a further friendly connexion [sic] with the parent country was impossible. "I am perfectly satisfied," said he, in a letter written from Philadelphia to a friend in Massachusetts, in April, 1776, "of the necessity of a public and explicit declaration of independence. I cannot conceive what good reason can be assigned against it. Will it widen

As a warning to future generations, Sam Adams once said, "Neither the wisest constitution nor the wisest laws will secure the liberty and happiness of a people whose manners are universally corrupt."[10]

> *Let ministers and philosophers, statesmen, and patriots, unite their endeavors to renovate the age by impressing the minds of men with the importance of educating their little boys and girls — of inculcating in the minds of youth — the love of their country; of instructing them in the art of self-government…and in short, of leading them in the study and practice of the exalted virtues of the Christian system.[11]*

the breach? This would be a strange question, after we have raised armies, and fought battles with the British troops; set up an American navy; permitted the inhabitants of these colonies to fit out armed vessels, to capture the ships belonging to any of the inhabitants of Great Britain; declaring them the enemies of the United Colonies; and torn into shivers their acts of trade, by allowing commerce, subject to regulations to be made by ourselves, with the people of all countries, except such as are subject to the British king. It cannot, surely, after all this, be imagined that we consider ourselves, or mean to be considered by others, in any other state, than that of independence."[28]

When the British granted a monopoly to the British East India Company and placed the tax on tea, the Sons of Liberty were enraged. On the evening of December 6, 1773, Adams gathered a crowd on the Boston waterfront to protest the arrival of the British ships. Following Adams' lead, a group of patriots, dressed as Indians, boarded the ships and dumped several hundred chests of tea into Boston Harbor.

The British Parliament reacted angrily. They passed the Coercive Acts ordering Boston Harbor closed to all trade until the tea destroyed had been paid for.

The Massachusetts Legislature met, at the urging of Sam Adams, on June 17, 1774, to discuss sending delegates to a meeting in Philadelphia with the representatives of the colonies. As a precaution, Adams locked the door and kept the key in his pocket. Governor Gage heard of the meeting and sent his secretary with an order dissolving the assembly, but finding the door locked, the secretary was forced to read the order from outside the locked door. The representatives elected their delegates to the Constitutional Congress — one of whom was Sam Adams — and then dissolved the meeting.

ᔆᔆ Public Service ᔆᔆ

1756	Elected as a tax collector in Boston
1765–1777	Member and clerk of the Massachusetts legislature
1770	His patriotic agitation brought about the Boston Massacre
1772	On his motion, the Boston town meeting established a Committee of Correspondence
1773	Instigated the Boston Tea Party
1774–1781	Member of the Constitutional Congress
1779	Helped write the Massachusetts state constitution
1781–1788	President of the Massachusetts senate
1789–1793	Lieutenant Governor of Massachusetts
1794–1797	Governor of Massachusetts

The Continental Congress met on September 5, 1774. They began in a deadlock over who should pray to open the meeting. Although a Puritan, Sam Adams suggested,

> that he was no bigot, and could hear a prayer from a gentleman of piety and virtue who was, at the same time, a friend to his country. He was a stranger in Philadelphia, but he had heard that Mr. Duché (Reverend Jacob Duché) deserved that character, and therefore he moved that Mr. Duché, an Episcopal clergyman, might be desired to read prayers to the Congress tomorrow morning. Adams' motion was accepted, and the next day the clergyman was present, reading the militant thirty-fifth Psalm.[29]

From the reading of this Psalm, the members of Congress felt, as John Adams wrote later to his wife, Abigail, "that it seemed as if Heaven had ordained that Psalm to be read on that morning." He begged his wife and her father, also, to read this psalm. It would be wise for us to read it, also, to understand how God used this portion of Scripture in the life of His people in their time of need. His prayer was no shallow one. Some writings indicate that it lasted several hours. Congress understood that America could not succeed without God's help, and they even appointed a continental fast to implore God's blessing. Adams left the Convention at the conclusion of the meetings, satisfied that progress had been made and the patriots' cause strengthened.

On the evening of April 18, 1775, Adams and Hancock were at Lexington preparing to leave for the Second Continental Congress. They were awakened about midnight by Paul Revere, who had ridden from Boston to spread the word that British soldiers were on the way to arrest them both. Revere rode on, was captured by the British, escaped, and returned to join Adams and Hancock, meeting them in a coach that carried them away from Lexington about dawn. Adams, realizing that the British were about to be met with American minutemen, remarked:

> "This is a fine day!" "Very pleasant, indeed," answered one of his companions, supposing he alluded to the beauty of the sky and atmosphere — "I mean," he replied, "this day is a glorious day for America!" His situation at that moment was full of peril and

If we would most truly enjoy the gift of Heaven, let us become a virtuous people; then shall we both deserve and enjoy it. While, on the other hand, if we are universally vicious and debouched in our manners, though the form of our Constitution carried the face of the most exalted freedom, we shall in reality be the most abject slaves.[12]

uncertainty, but throughout the contest, no damage to himself or his country ever discouraged or depressed him.[30]

Adams worked tirelessly at the Second Constitutional Convention. When John Adams nominated George Washington as commander-in-chief, Sam Adams seconded the motion. It was the high point of Sam Adams' life when he penned his own name and witnessed the signing of the Declaration of Independence.

In the autumn of 1777, the fortunes of war were running at a low ebb; attendance at Congress was reduced to less than 30 members, and spirits were low. However, Adams' resolute courage helped hold the national government together. Hearing some delegates bemoaning the desperate nature of events, he is quoted to have said:

> If this be our language, it is so, indeed. If we wear long faces, they will become fashionable. The people take their tone from ours, and if we despair, can it be expected that they will continue their efforts in what we conceive to be a hopeless cause? Let us banish

*C*ommenting on the rights of the Colonists as Christians, Sam Adams, said, "These may best be understood by reading and carefully studying the institutes of the great Law-Giver and Head of the Christian Church, which are to be found clearly written and promulgated in the New Testament."[13]

America triumphed, and a grateful nation called Samuel Adams "the Father of American Independence" and "the Father of the Revolution." Thomas Jefferson called him "truly the Man of the Revolution." [35]

such feelings, and show a spirit that will keep alive the confidence of the people, rather than damp their courage. Better tidings will soon arrive. Our cause is just and righteous, and we shall never be abandoned by Heaven while we show ourselves worthy of its aid and protection. [31]

His unshaken courage, and his calm reliance upon the aid and protection of heaven, contributed in an eminent degree to inspire his countrymen with a confidence of their final success. [32]

It was said of Sam Adams, the man responsible for managing the expresses (mails) which were continually moving between Philadelphia and Boston:

He eats little…drinks little, sleeps little, thinks much, and is most indefatigable in the pursuit of his object. It was this man, who by his superior application, managed at once the factions in congress at Philadelphia, and the factions of New England. [33]

Adams retired from Congress in 1781, to become a member of the Massachusetts state senate. Sam Adams, along with his cousin John Adams, wrote the Massachusetts Constitution. It states: "All persons elected must make and subscribe the following declaration, viz. " 'I do declare that I believe the Christian religion and have firm persuasion of its truth.' " [34]

In 1789, he was elected lieutenant governor, and upon the death of Hancock in 1794, became governor of Massachusetts. He remained in that office until his death in October of 1803 in his eighty-second year.

Samuel Adams often said that he worked, not for personal glory, but so that "millions unborn" could enjoy independence. That means you!

Mr. Adams was a Christian. His mind was early imbued with piety, as well as cultivated by science. He early approached the table of the Lord Jesus, and the purity of his life witnessed the sincerity of his profession. On the Christian Sabbath, he constantly went to the temple, and the morning and evening devotions in his family proved, that his religion attended him in his seasons of retirement from the world. The last production of his pen was in favour of the Christian truth. He died in the faith of the gospel. [36]

I…rely upon the merits of Jesus Christ for a pardon of all my sins. [37]

🐾 Questions for Discussion 🐾

1.   We are told that Sam Adams was taught the principles of freedom and religious truth from INFANCY. What can we learn of this regarding a parent's job? Look up several passages in Scripture concerning the teaching of one's children.

2.   Look up the definition of disinterestedness in the dictionary. What evidences show that Sam Adams possessed this quality regarding his patriotism?

3.   What can we learn from William Ellery's observation of Sam Adams? Look up I Samuel 16:7. What can we learn of this concerning how God uses people? Do we have to possess exceptional talents to be used by God?

4.   What did Sam Adams understand about how our attitude affects those around us? Does God really use individual people to effect the course of nations? Consider if there is an attitude in your life that needs changing. God wants to use YOU to help bring America back to her godly foundations. Set a personal goal to bring this attitude under God's control and ask God to use you. (Read Isaiah 55:8.)

5.   What was Sam Adams' passion and vision? How did God use that to impassion and encourage others? How did God use his passion and faith to secure your freedom? Ask God to give you passion and vision and empowerment to accomplish mighty things for Him.

6.   Give evidence that Sam Adams invested in others more than in personal gain.

7.   Tell instances of Sam Adams displaying the quality of boldness. How did God bless it?

8.   Give examples of persuasiveness in Sam Adams' life.

9.   Keeping in mind the poverty of his family, what can we tell about Sam Adams' life from the fact that he turned down two bribes from the British?

10.   Give instances in which Adams put his words into action.

11.   Tell of an instance when Sam Adams had the foresight to predict future trouble and took precautions against it (Proverbs 22:3).

☙Questions for Discussion❧

12. Give proof of Sam Adams' relationship with Jesus Christ.

13. Give examples of Sam Adams displaying courage and resoluteness.

14. To what did Sam Adams attribute the boldness to oppose the British? Why did he expect victory even when circumstances looked bleak (Proverbs: 28:1)?

15. List all the character qualities you see in Sam Adams' life. Choose one to ask God to build into your life. Learn corresponding Bible verses and plan some specific steps of action to implement it in your life.

16. Sam Adams labored tirelessly for your freedom. He had the vision that the freedom to be won would affect "millions yet unborn." So it is with your life. Ask God to build vision into your life for "millions yet unborn."

17. Describe passion in Adam's life. Show how he lived and breathed for freedom.

18. Passion is a wonderful quality when applied with godly motives. Ask God for passion to participate in moving forward His plans in this time of history.

19. Comment on the willingness of Robert Morris to finance someone with a vision such as Sam Adams possessed.

Elbridge Gerry

Dutiful Patriot

Matthew 7:12

"The Soldier's Friend"

✦✦

BORN
July 17, 1744

BIRTHPLACE
Marblehead, Massachusetts

EDUCATION
Harvard College

OCCUPATION
Merchant, Politician

MARRIED
Ann Thompson, 1786

CHILDREN
10

AGE AT SIGNING
32

DIED
November 23, 1814; age 70

John Adams once wrote that if his fellow congressmen were all like Elbridge Gerry, "the Liberties of America would be safe."[1]

E lbridge Gerry, the third of twelve children, was born on July 17, 1744, in Marblehead, Massachusetts, the son of a merchant whose main export was codfish. When his preparatory studies were concluded, he entered Harvard College.

To receive his master's degree from Harvard in 1765, Gerry had to present an argument on a subject. Twenty-year-old Elbridge Gerry argued that Americans should resist the British Stamp Act, a tax on paper goods that had been passed that year.[9]

Upon graduating in 1762, Gerry entered his father's business and soon became a leading merchant in Marblehead, amassing a considerable fortune.

Gerry was elected to the General Court of Massachusetts in 1773. He was active in all the leading political movements in Massachusetts until the war broke out, and was elected a delegate to the provincial Congress.

Mr. Gerry was an active contributing member on many useful committees. He served on the Committee of Safety and adopted measures necessary to obtain a badly needed supply of arms and ammunition. They reorganized the militia and appointed general officers. They appealed to the people to be ready to take up the arm of defense if necessary.

In the spring of 1775, it appeared that the British planned to seize arms the colonists had stockpiled, especially at Concord and Worcester. The Committee of Safety stood watch to give an alarm should such an attempt be made. It wasn't long until their apprehensions were realized and the munitions at Concord were threatened.

> "Among the objects of this expedition," observes Mr. Austin, in his life of Mr. Gerry, "one was to seize the persons of some of the influential members of Congress, and to hold them as hostages for the moderation of their colleagues, or send them to England for trial as traitors, and thus strike dismay and terror into the minds of their associates and friends." [10]

A committee of Congress had been in session that day near Cambridge. John Hancock had departed for Lexington, and Mr. Gerry and Mr. Orne remained at Menotomy near Cambridge. The other members had dispersed.

> Some officers of the royal army had been sent out in advance, who passed through the villages just before dusk; in the afternoon of the 18th of April, and although the appearance of similar detachments was not uncommon, these so far attracted the attention of Mr. Gerry, that he dispatched an express to Colonel Hancock, who, with Samuel Adams, was at Lexington. The messenger passed the officers, by taking a by-path, and delivered his letter. The idea of personal danger does not seem to have made any strong impression on either of these gentlemen. Mr. Hancock's answer to Mr. Gerry bears marks of the haste with which it was written, while it discovers the habitual politeness on the part of the writer, which neither haste nor danger could impair. *Lexington, April 18th, 1775* Dear Sir, I am much obliged for your notice. It is said the officers are gone to Concord, and I will send word thither. I am full with you, that we ought to be serious, and I hope your decision will be effectual. I intend doing myself the pleasure of being with you to-morrow. My respects to the committee. I am your real friend, John Hancock. [11]

Mr. Gerry and Colonel Orne retired to bed until the sound of the advancing British awoke them. It was a fine moonlit night. The British advanced and some passed on, until the center was opposite the house occupied by the committee. An officer and file of men given a signal, marched towards it. It was not until this moment that Gerry and Orne felt any apprehension of danger. While the officer posted his files, Gerry and Orne, in their nightclothes, fled

In New England, from the earliest times, they had been the political as well as spiritual leaders of the people; and in the mother country, the duties of the magistrate were almost generally united with the pious care and instruction of their flocks. The other resolution perhaps arose from feelings somewhat similar to those which dictated this, at least from feelings which would seek to separate, as much as possible, the offices and profession of religion from all that might be deemed peculiarly worldly, either in the performance of duties or the enjoyments of amusement. In the journal of the succeeding October is found the following entry.

A motion was made that congress pass the following resolutions: Whereas true religion and good morals are the only solid foundations of public liberty and happiness: Resolved, that it be, and it is hereby earnestly recommended to the several states, to take the most effectual measures for the encouragement thereof, and for the suppressing theatrical entertainments, horse-racing, gaming, and such other diversions as are productive of idleness, dissipation, and a general depravity of principles and manners. Resolved, that all officers in the army of the United States be, and hereby are strictly enjoined, to see that the good and wholesome rules provided for the discountenancing of profaneness and vice, and the preservation of morals among the soldiers, are duly and punctually observed. [2]

The fiery little Marbleheader who stuttered when speaking became one of his colony's leading revolutionaries, among other things helping to gather military supplies and distribute them to Massachusetts minutemen. [3]

to a nearby cornfield and remained there concealed for more than an hour until the troops withdrew. Every nook and cranny of the house was searched for members of the rebel Congress. The beds they had lain in were searched, although personal property was not stolen. Mr. Gerry's watch remained under his pillow where he'd left it. Gerry and Orne then helped spread the alarm that resulted in the Minutemen's resistance the next day.

A few days after the Battles of Lexington and Concord the provincial Congress met again. It was now apparent that a force of arms was necessary. What was needed most was gunpowder and Mr. Gerry was commissioned to procure it. He wrote to many gentlemen in different parts of the country to ask for munitions. Mr. Gerry advanced his own funds where immediate payment was required. During the war evidence of these payments was lost, and the final settlement was accounted for with heavy financial loss to Mr. Gerry.

Gerry was absent when most of the delegates signed the Declaration of Independence, but added his signature on November 19, 1776. On the evening before June 17, the provincial Congress was in session at Watertown. Mr. Gerry shared a bed that night with Dr. Joseph Warren, then president of the Congress, who was planning to take an active role at Bunker Hill the next day. In the morning, Dr. Warren, in leaving, said, "It is sweet and glorious to lay down one's life for one's country." At that, Gerry left for his seat in Congress, and General Warren to the place where duty called, to be slain on the battlefield of Bunker Hill fighting for the liberty of his country.

Early in 1775, Gerry introduced a bill to encourage the fitting out of armed vessels. In another bill he introduced, John Adams:

> pronounced one of the most important measures of the Revolution. Under the sanction of it, the Massachusetts cruisers captured many of the enemy's vessels, the cargoes of which furnished various articles of necessity to the colonies.[12]

He was again elected delegate to the Continental Congress of 1776. Among his achievements were arranging the plan of a general hospital, introducing better discipline into the army, and regulating commissary departments. He often visited the army to examine the state of the country's finances.

"Mr. Gerry," observes the late President Adams, "was a financier, and had been employed for years on the committee of the treasury in the old congress, and a most indefatigable member too. That committee had laid the foundation for the present system, and had organized it almost as well, though they had not the assistance of clerks and other conveniences, as at present. Any man who will look into the journals of the old congress, may see the organization, and the daily labours and reports of that committee, and may form some judgment of the talents and services of Mr. Gerry in that department.

I knew the officers of the treasury in Hamilton's time, dreaded to see him rise in the house on any question of finance, because, they said he was a man of so much influence, that they always feared he would discover some error, or carry some point against them."

Such is the testimony of a man who was himself amongst the most active of our revolutionary leaders, and who, in a long life, had the opportunities as well as the sound abilities which enabled him to form strong and correct opinions of the leading statesmen of his age.[4]

Gerry "took a particular interest in those dealing with military affairs, winning the nickname of the 'soldier's friend' because of his support for better pay and equipment for the troops."[20]

Gerry signed the Declaration in November, and forever after considered it the crowning achievement of his life.[5]

Gerry was such a slight, thin man that one of his fellow signers of the Declaration of Independence is said to have told him that if all the signers were hanged by the British he would be the unluckiest because he was so light that he would kick the longest.[6]

A resolution was brought [to the Congress] and warmly supported by Mr. Gerry, recommending the subject to the different states; urging them to procure, in addition to the allowances of clothing heretofore made by congress, supplies of blankets, shoes, stockings, shirts, and other clothing for the comfortable subsistence of the officers and soldiers of their respective battalions. During the year 1778, Mr. Gerry renewed his exertions to improve the state and conduct of the commissary and hospital departments of the army; two branches of the military art, of paramount importance to the common soldiers, but greatly liable to neglect and abuse. He also exerted all his efforts to obtain an allowance for the soldiers, after their term of service had expired, not only those who were citizens of the United States, but the foreigners who had united their fortunes with them. No officer, however high, escaped his vigilant inquiries into the performance of his duties; every act of oppression or misconduct which came to his knowledge was brought promptly before congress, and fairly and fully investigated. The military committees of congress found him an active member, or a ready coadjutor, and the soldiers knew him as their steady advocate and friend.[13]

At the age of 41, he retired from Congress and returned to Cambridge, Massachusetts. He married Ann Thompson of New York; they had seven children who survived childhood. In 1787, he was appointed to be a delegate from Massachusetts to the Constitutional Convention. He was one of the most vocal; he did not sign the Constitution. He explained:

> My principal objections to the plan are, that there is no adequate provision for a representation of the people; that they have no security for the right of election; that some of the powers of the legislature are ambiguous, and others indefinite and dangerous; that the executive is blended with, and will have an undue influence over the legislature; that the judicial department will be oppressive; that treaties of the highest importance may be formed by the president, with the

⚘ Public Service ⚘

1772–1773	Representative in the Massachusetts colonial legislature
1774–1775	Member of the Massachusetts provincial congress
1776–1780, 1783, 1785	Delegate from Massachusetts to the national Congress; signed the Declaration of Independence and the Articles of Confederation
1786	Member of the Massachusetts House of Representatives
1787	Delegate from Massachusetts to the Constitutional Convention; declined to sign the United States Constitution
1789–1793	Represented Massachusetts in the U.S. House of Representatives
1797–1798	U.S. diplomatic representative in France during the XYZ Affair
1810–1812	Governor of Massachusetts
1813–1814	Vice president of the United States

advice of two-thirds a quorum in the senate; and that the system is without the security of a bill of rights.[14]

Although he had formerly opposed the adoption of the constitution, he now cheerfully united in carrying it into effect, since it had received the sanction of his country. Indeed, he took occasion, on the floor of congress, not long after taking his seat in that body, to declare, "that the federal constitution having become the supreme law of the land, he conceived the salvation of the country depended on its being carried into effect."[15]

Gerry was elected to the U.S. House of Representatives in 1789 and served two terms in Congress. He was sent to France in 1797 by President John Adams to negotiate peaceful relations.

Adams wrote of Gerry: "He was nominated and approved, and finally saved the peace of the nation, for he alone discovered and furnished the evidence that X. Y. and Z. were employed by Talleyrand; and he alone brought home the direct, formal, and official assurances, upon which the subsequent commission proceeded, and peace was made."[16]

In 1812 he won the office of governor of Massachusetts.

"Elmwood" formerly the Res of Elbridge Gerry Cambridge, Mass Now Res of Jas Russell Lowell the Poet

"Elmwood" formerly the residence of Elbridge Gerry Cambridge, Massachusetts

*O*f this committee, [General Court of Massachusetts] Mr. Gerry was chosen a member, a proof of the high standing and character, he had attained even before he entered the legislature.[7]

The term "gerrymander" dates from this time and grew out of a redistricting bill Gerry supported which obviously benefited his own party. One district was so oddly shaped that it resembled a salamander, and angry Federalists coined the word gerrymander to describe it.[17]

*T*he conduct of the American army to the unfortunate British troops had been marked with generosity and kindness: a resolution Gerry proposed to Congress:

"Whereas, the army of the United States of America have by their patriotism, valour and perseverance in the defence of the rights and liberties of their country, become entitled to the gratitude as well as the approbation of their fellow citizens: Resolved, that it be, and it is hereby recommended to the several states that have not already adopted measures for that purpose, to make such further provision for the officers and for the soldiers enlisted for the war, to them respectively belonging, who shall continue in the service till the establishment of peace, as shall be an adequate compensation for the many dangers, losses and hardships they have suffered and been exposed to in the course of the present contest; either by granting to their officers half pay for life, and proper rewards to their soldiers; or in such other manner as may appear most expedient to the legislatures of the several states. Resolved, that it be, and hereby is recommended to the several states, to make such provision for the widows of such of their officers and such of their soldiers enlisted for the war, as have died or may die in the service, as shall secure to them the sweets of that liberty, for the attainment of which their husbands had nobly laid down their lives."[8]

In March 1813, he was inaugurated as Vice President to James Madison, and much of his work entailed presiding over the Senate. The citizens from his state honored him and ended their congratulations with the words, "We trust in Heaven, that the enemies of our country will not prevail, while the arm of Gerry is uplifted to oppose them."[18]

A year and a half after taking office, Gerry was in a carriage on his way to the Capitol to preside over the Senate when he became suddenly ill and died. He was seventy years old.

Thus fulfilling his own memorable injunction — "It is the duty of every citizen, though he may have but one day to live, to devote that day to the service of his country." [19]

Questions for Discussion

1. What did Elbridge Gerry believe to be the duty of every citizen? What can we tell about his character from this?

2. What was John Adams' comment about Gerry? What does this tell us about his character?

3. We are told that Elbridge Gerry stuttered. Did this hinder God's ability to use him?

4. List some ways God used Gerry during the American Revolution.

5. What did Elbridge Gerry consider to be the crowning achievement of his life?

6. What qualities did Gerry demonstrate which aided him in being a financier?

7. Give a couple of instances which show Mr. Gerry to have been a courageous man.

8. How did prudence on the part of Mr. Gerry help to save the lives of others?

9. Why was Mr. Gerry called "the soldier's friend"? What did he do to earn this title?

10. What were Mr. Gerry's objections to signing the Constitution? Have any of his concerns been proved valid? What quality did he show to support it after it had been ratified?

11. How did the citizens of his state show him honor?

12. Read the qualifications and entrance requirements to Harvard located in the appendix.

John Hancock

Benevolent Patriot

II Corinthians 9:6–8

"Charity was the business of his life."

❧

BORN
January 23, 1737

BIRTHPLACE
Quincy (then Braintree)
Massachusetts

EDUCATION
Harvard College

OCCUPATION
Merchant

MARRIED
Dolly Quincy, 1775

CHILDREN
2

AGE AT SIGNING
39

DIED
1793; age 56

Charity was the common business of his life. Hundreds of families, from his private benevolence, received their daily bread; and there is, perhaps, no individual mentioned in history, who has expended a more ample fortune in promoting the liberties of his country.[3]

John Hancock was born in Braintree, Massachusetts in 1737, the son of a dedicated minister of the gospel. When John was seven years old his father died, and John was sent to live with his grandparents. His uncle, Thomas Hancock, who had no children of his own, took John under his wing and sent him first to Boston Grammar School and then Harvard College. Upon graduation at age 17, John became clerk in his uncle's mercantile business.

> Four large ships were constantly plying between Boston and London, and other businesses in proportion. He became an example to all the young men of the town. Wholly devoted to business, he was as regular and punctual at his store as the sun in his course."[7]

His uncle sent John on a business mission to England in 1760. In 1764, Thomas Hancock died, leaving most of his fortune to John, his shipping business and estate worth 80,000 pounds. At 27 years of age, John was one of the richest people in Massachusetts.

John enjoyed his wealth. He owned enough suits to open a clothing store, drove about in a fancy carriage, and gave parties that were the talk of Boston. He also used his money for the public good, which made him very popular. For example, he helped rebuild damaged structures after a fire, and every winter he donated food to poor Bostonians.[8]

The people of Boston elected John to the office of selectman. "John Adams quotes his cousin Sam Adams as remarking that Boston's citizens had done a wise thing because 'they had made that young man's fortune their own.' "[9]

In 1776, Hancock was elected to the colonial legislature of Massachusetts. Sam Adams recruited Hancock for the Liberty Party, as patriots were called. Hancock, at a meeting of fellow patriots, was heard to say: "Burn Boston, and make John Hancock a beggar, if the public good requires it."[10]

They made an interesting contrast — Sam Adams in his threadbare suit and Hancock a dashing young merchant. "Hancock poured his heart, soul — and money — into the patriot cause. He gave so much money to the rebels that Bostonians joked, "Samuel Adams writes the letters [to the newspapers], and John Hancock pays the postage.' "[11]

In 1768, one of Hancock's ships, the *Liberty,* arrived with a cargo of Madeira wine on which Hancock refused to pay British taxes. The customs officer was held prisoner on the ship while it was unloaded. To retaliate, the customs officers seized the *Liberty,* and it was never returned to Hancock. An angry mob of citizens attacked the customs officers and burned a customs boat. Although Hancock didn't take part in the riot, he as owner was held responsible.

Citizens of Boston elected Hancock as chairman of a committee to try to persuade the British governor to withdraw troops from Boston after the Boston Massacre. They were successful and gained much respect from the people of Boston.

While the Boston port was closed under the Coercive Act, in punishment for the Boston Tea Party, the fourth anniversary of the Boston Massacre passed. In an oration on March 5, 1774, Hancock said:

> The town of Boston, ever faithful to the British crown, has been invested by a British fleet; the troops of George the third have crossed the Atlantic, not to engage an enemy, but to assist a band of traitors in trampling on the rights and liberties of his most loyal subjects; those rights and liberties, which, as a father, he ought ever to regard, and as a king, he is bound in honour to defend from violation, even at the risk of his own life.

Previous to the demise of his paternal uncle, whom we have already mentioned as his patron and benefactor, the hall of the university had been destroyed by fire. The deceased, it was said, had expressed the intention of leaving five hundred pounds for the reparation of its library. No such appropriation was, however, made by his will; yet the sum was paid, without hesitation, by Mr. Hancock, his heir.[1]

The salary allowed by the constitution to the chief magistrate of the commonwealth of Massachusetts, had occupied, for several years, the debates of the legislature. By many it was declared to be exorbitant, and was enumerated amongst the grievances that had occasioned riot and insurrection in the state. An act for its reduction from eleven to eight hundred pounds, had passed both houses of the legislature, but was negated by the governor; and the subject being resumed, under the administration of Mr. Hancock, he intercepted all farther discussion of it, by a voluntary remission of the sum.[2]

An enterprise was undertaken in 1778, in cooperation with the fleet of the French admiral D'Estaing against Newport, in Rhode Island, by a detachment from the regular army under Washington, and seven thousand of the militia of New England, which excited in the whole continent the most extravagant expectations. On the arrival of these troops in the island, the fleet of lord Howe appeared upon the coast. D'Estaing, regardless of his obligations with the American troops, instead of supporting, assisting and defending them, and solicitous only for his own glory, hastened to the pursuit of the enemy, and exposed the army of his allies to all the calamities of a fatal defeat. In consequence of this manoeuvre, the Americans were left in the midst of innumerable difficulties and danger, to make good their retreat; which they achieved, however, without the loss of artillery or baggage; and the fleet arrived at the same time in the harbour, shattered by a furious storm.

Under these circumstances the French were received in Boston with sullen displeasure and in many instances with feelings of irritation, which had, no doubt, produced violent consequences, had not the evil been counteracted by the address and liberal hospitality of Mr. Hancock. His house, which was elegant and spacious, was thrown open, with every species of splendid entertainment, to the French admiral and all his officers; from thirty to forty of whom dined every day at his table. In addition to which, he gave, at his own expense, a grand public ball at Concert Hall, attended by the count and his officers, with the principal ladies and gentlemen of the town. Thus harmony was restored, a friendly intercourse with the inhabitants was re-established, and the dispute terminated in a reciprocation of esteem and respect.[5]

Residence of John Hancock, Boston, Massachusetts

In 1775, it was proposed by the American officers, who carried on the siege of Boston, in order to procure the expulsion of the enemy, to bombard or destroy the town. The entire wealth of Mr. Hancock was exposed, by the execution of this enterprise, to ruin; but whilst he felt for the sufferings of others with a very generous compassion, he required that no regard to his personal advantages should obstruct the operations of the army. His private fortune, he observed, should, on no occasion, oppose an obstacle to the interests of his country.[4]

These troops, upon their first arrival, took possession of our senate house, pointed their cannon against the judgment hall, and even continued them there, whilst the supreme court of the province was actually sitting to decide upon the lives and fortunes of the king's subjects. Our streets nightly resounded with the noise of their riot and debauchery; our peaceful citizens were hourly exposed to shameful insults, and often felt the effects of their violence and outrage. But this was not all; as though they thought it not enough to violate our civil rights, they endeavoured to deprive us of the enjoyment of our religious privileges; to vitiate our morals, and thereby render us deserving of destruction. Hence the rude din of arms, which broke in upon your solemn devotions in your temples, on that day hallowed by heaven, and set apart by God himself for his peculiar worship. Hence, impious oaths and blasphemies, so often tortured your unaccustomed ear. Hence, all the arts which idleness and luxury could invent, were used to betray our youth of one sex into extravagance and effeminacy, and of the other to infamy and ruin; and have they not succeeded but too well? Has not a reverence for religion sensibly decayed? Have not our infants almost learned to lisp curses, before they knew their horrid import? Have not our youth forgotten they were Americans, and

regardless of the admonitions of the wise and aged, copied, with a servile imitation, the frivolity and vices of their tyrants? And must I be compelled to acknowledge, that even the noblest, fairest part of all creation, have not entirely escaped their cruel snares? — or why have I seen an honest father clothed with shame; why a virtuous mother drowned in tears?

But I forbear, and come reluctantly to the transactions of that dismal night, when in such quick succession we felt the extremes of grief, astonishment, and rage; when heaven in anger, for a dreadful moment suffered hell to take the reins; when Satan, with his chosen band, opened the sluices of New England's blood, and sacrilegiously polluted our land with the dead bodies of her guiltless sons.

Let this sad tale of death never be told, without a tear; let not the heaving bosom cease to burn with a manly indignation at the relation of it, through the long tracks of future time; let every parent tell the shameful story to his listening children, till tears of pity glisten in their eyes, or boiling passion shakes their tender frames.

Dark and designing knaves, murderers, parricides! How dare you tread upon the earth, which has drunk

ॐ Public Service ॐ

1766–1772	Member of the Massachusetts colonial legislature
1774–1775	President of the Massachusetts provincial congress
1775–1777	President of the second Continental Congress; signed the Articles of Confederation
1778	Major general in charge of Massachusetts militia in effort to recapture Rhode Island from the British
1780–1785	First governor of the Commonwealth of Massachusetts
1785–1786	Member of the Congress of the Confederation
1787–1793	Governor of Massachusetts
1788	President of the Massachusetts state convention that ratified the United States Constitution

Of the character of Mr. Hancock, the limits which we have prescribed to ourselves, will permit us to say but little more. It was an honourable trait in that character, that while he possessed a superfluity of wealth, to the unrestrained enjoyment of which he came at an unguarded period of life, he avoided excessive indulgence and dissipation. His habits, through life, were uniformly on the side of virtue. In his disposition and manners, he was kind and courteous. He claimed no superiority from his advantages, and manifested no arrogance on account of his wealth.[6]

the blood of slaughtered innocence shed by your hands? How dare you breathe that air, which wafted to the ear of heaven the groans of those who fell a sacrifice to your accursed ambition? — But if the labouring earth doth not expand her jaws; if the air you breathe is not commissioned to be the minister of death; yet, hear it, and tremble! The eye of heaven penetrates the darkest chambers of the soul; and you, though screened from human observation, must be arraigned, must lift your hands, red with the blood of those whose death you have procured, at the tremendous bar of God.

But I gladly quit this theme of death — I would not dwell too long upon the horrid effects, which have already followed, from quartering regular troops in this town; let our misfortunes instruct posterity to guard against these evils. Standing armies are sometimes, (I would by no means say generally, much less universally,) composed of persons who have rendered themselves unfit to live in civil society; who are equally indifferent to the glory of George, or a Louis; who for the addition of one penny a day to their wages, would desert from the Christian cross, and fight under the crescent of the Turkish sultan; from such men as these what has not a state to fear? With such as these, usurping Caesar passed the Rubicon; with such as these he humbled mighty Rome, and forced the mistress of the world to own a master in a traitor. These are the men whom sceptered robbers now employ to frustrate the designs of God, and render vain the bounties which his gracious hand pours indiscriminately upon his creatures.[12]

In October 1774, Hancock was elected president of Massachusetts' provincial Congress of patriots that met in Concord. Governor Gage began to regard Hancock as a traitor and outlaw.

Under Hancock, Massachusetts raised bands of "minutemen." These soldiers, who claimed they could get ready to fight in sixty seconds, were soon needed.[13]

In April 1775, British troops were sent from Boston to capture Hancock and Samuel Adams at Lexington, as well as stored munitions at Concord. Paul Revere spread the warning during his famous midnight ride. Hancock was at this time engaged to Dorothy "Dolly" Quincy, who later became his wife, and this night, the two were at a dinner in the parsonage of Rev. Jones Clarke at Lexington. About midnight the silence of the night was broken by a messenger galloping up on horseback. The rider, out of breath, yelled,

"Where's Mr. Hancock?"

"Don't make so much noise!" the sentry ordered.

"Noise!" hollered Paul Revere. "You'll have noise enough before long. The Regulars are coming out!"[14]

Hancock flung open his bedroom window and invited Revere into the house. When told the news, his first reaction was to join the Minutemen on the village green. The others persuaded him to run to avoid risk of capture. He and Samuel Adams, also residing there for the night, fled toward the village of Woburn. They heard the sound of the Minutemen's drum and fife as they barely escaped the village. They then journeyed on to the meeting of the second Continental Congress.

Shortly afterward, Governor Gage issued a proclamation offering a pardon to any patriot who would lay down his arms, "excepting only from the benefit of such a pardon, Samuel Adams and John Hancock, whose offences are of too flagitious a nature to admit of any other consideration than that of condign punishment." [15]

At the Second Continental Congress, Hancock was elected president after Peyton Randolph resigned.

In May of 1775, John Hancock married Dolly Quincy, with whom he would have two children. Their daughter, Lydia, lived less than a year. Their son, John George Washington Hancock, hit his head while ice skating and died at the age of eight.

John Hancock was president of the Continental Congress and the first man to sign his name to the document.

 Reportedly, while signing in large, bold letters on July 4, 1776, Hancock said, "There! John Bull [a nickname for England] can read my name without spectacles and may double his reward on my head!" [16]

The printed version of the Declaration that was sent to all the colonies to be read on July 5, carried only the signature of John Hancock, as the official document wasn't drawn up and ready for all to sign until August 2. As a result, John Hancock's name swiftly became second only to that of George Washington as a symbol of freedom in the colonies.

Hancock resigned his presidency of the Continental Congress in October, 1777, due to a severe case of gout. He did, however, continue on as a member of the Massachusetts delegation and in 1778, signed the Articles of Confederation.

The legislature of Massachusetts commissioned him as Major General of the Militia in 1778. He was in command of approximately 6,000 New England troops on a mission to free Rhode Island from British occupancy. When the French fleet failed to carry out their part, the campaign ended in retreat. Hancock took part in the Massachusetts legislature and helped write the state constitution. He was elected first governor of Massachusetts in 1780.

Hancock was reelected President of Congress in 1785, but did not serve due to recurring illness. Again, he was elected governor in 1787 and held this office for the remainder of his life. Sometimes the gout was so painful he couldn't walk and had to be carried around Boston. He died on October 8, 1783, at fifty-five years of age. The funeral procession was extremely impressive. It included public officials, the militia, and thousands of citizens. Lieutenant Governor Samuel Adams (his lifelong friend) walked in front of the coffin and Vice President of the United States, John Adams, walked behind.

John Adams summed up Hancock's career and characteristics in the following words:

> Mr. Hancock had a delicate constitution. He was very infirm; a great part of his life was passed in acute pain. He inherited from his father, though one of the most amiable and beloved of men, a certain sensibility, a keenness of feeling, or, in more familiar language, a peevishness of temper, that sometimes disgusted and afflicted his friends. Yet it was astonishing with what patience, perseverance, and punctuality, he attended to business to the last. Nor were his talents or attainments inconsiderable. They were far superior to many who have been much more celebrated. He had a great deal of political sagacity and penetration into men. He was by no means a contemptible scholar or orator. Compared with Washington, Lincoln, or Knox, he was learned. [18]

Questions for Discussion

1. What commitment of his paternal uncle did John Hancock fulfill? What quality does this reflect?

2. Why did Hancock forego receiving a salary? What character trait is seen in this willing act?

3. What evidence do we have that charity was a common business of Hancock's life?

4. What selfless patriotic declaration did John Hancock make concerning his own property and belongings?

5. How did Hancock use generosity and hospitality to ward off disaster with the French?

6. What was his father's profession? What does this tell us of John's early training?

7. What is proof of John's punctuality in business?

8. What evidences do we have that Hancock put the public good above his own?

9. How did Hancock's influence with the British influence the people of Boston?

10. Tell why Hancock was in favor of independence, from his own words in his oration on March 5, 1774.

11. Who helped to raise groups of Minutemen? What were Minutemen called to do?

12. In April 1775, what two people were British troops sent to capture? What else did they try to seize?

13. Tell of Paul Revere's ride and circumstances surrounding his warning to Hancock. Where was Hancock? What was Hancock's response?

14. What was Governor Gage's proclamation regarding pardons?

15. What was Hancock reported to say when signing his name to the Declaration of Independence?

16. What other important document did Hancock sign?

17. What military campaign did Hancock lead?

18. Hancock helped write the Massachusetts state constitution. What are its religious implications?

19. What can be said of Hancock who gave his life and freedom to the American cause, even though he suffered physically much of the time?

20. Hancock was the epitome of benevolence. Plan to take action this week to show benevolence to a family less fortunate than yours.

Robert Treat Paine

Moral and Just Judge

II Samuel 23:3

"His forgiving mercy is revealed to the world through Jesus Christ."

ᏵᎡᎡ

BORN
March 11, 1731
BIRTHPLACE
Boston, Massachusetts
EDUCATION
Harvard College
Seminary Degree
OCCUPATION
Lawyer
MARRIED
Sally Cobb, 1770
CHILDREN
8
AGE AT SIGNING
45
DIED
May 11, 1814; age 83

Previously to his commencing the study of law, he devoted some time to the subject of theology, which tended to enlarge his views of Christianity, and to confirm his belief of its truth.[1]

Robert Treat Paine was born on March 11, 1731, in Boston, Massachusetts. His father had been pastor of a church in Weymouth for many years when his health began to fail him, and he moved to Boston and began mercantile pursuits. His mother was the daughter of a pastor. Robert received his early education at Boston Latin School. At age 14, he entered Harvard College and pursued theology, graduating at age 18. He then served as chaplain with New England troops in the French and Indian War in 1755. He also preached in pulpits in and around Boston. "He devoted some time to the subject of theology, which tended to enlarge his views of Christianity, and to confirm his belief of its truth."[2]

His father's fortune had been much reduced, and Robert sought to help support his family. He took up the practice of law, studying under Benjamin Pratt in New York, and he taught school in order to support himself. In a letter to his sister Abigail, he wrote: "I began my school. O how [the students] did hum & haw & whine & sings & everything else disagreeable."[3]

Once qualified to practice law in 1759, he established himself at Taunton, Massachusetts, where he resided for many years. About this time he and Sally Cobb married, and they had eight children. Paine took an early role as a patriot. He was a delegate from Taunton in a convention called by the people in 1768 protesting the royal governor's closing of the colonial legislature. He also prosecuted British soldiers who had killed five people in the Boston Massacre. In 1774 he was elected delegate to the Continental Congress.

> In concluding their session, in October of the same year, they presented a solemn appeal to the world, stating that innovation was not their object, but only the preservation and maintenance of the rights which, as subjects of Great Britain, had been granted to them by their ancient charters. "Had we been permitted," they say, "to enjoy in quiet the inheritance left us by our fathers, we should, at this time, have been peaceably, cheerfully, and usefully employed in recommending ourselves, by every testimony of devotion to his majesty, and of veneration to the state from which we derive our origin. Though now exposed to unexpected and unnatural scenes of distress, by a contention with that nation, in whose general guidance, on all important occasions, we have hitherto with filial reverence constantly trusted, and therefore can derive no instruction, in our present unhappy and perplexing circumstances, from any former experience; yet we doubt not, the purity of our intentions, and the integrity of our conduct, will justify us at that great tribunal, before which all mankind must submit to judgment. We ask but for peace, liberty, and safety. We wish not a diminution of the royal prerogatives; nor do we solicit the grant of any new right in our favour." [4]

In 1775, he was again a delegate to the Continental Congress, which met at Philadelphia in May. He also did considerable work to encourage the production of gunpowder.

> At that time, the colonies were greatly in want of gunpowder. The manufacture of salt petre, one of its constituents, was but imperfectly understood. Congress appointed a committee, of which Mr. Paine was chairman, to introduce the manufacture of it. In this particular, he rendered essential service to his country, by making extensive inquiries into the subject, and by inducing persons in various parts of the province to engage in the manufacture of the article. [5]

Mr. Paine affixed his signature to the Declaration of Independence in August, 1776.

In the December following, the situation of congress became justly alarming. The British army was, at this time, making rapid advances through New Jersey, towards Philadelphia. The troops of Washington, amounting to scarcely one third of the British force, it was thought would not be able to resist their progress, or prevent their taking possession of Philadelphia. During the alarm excited by an approaching foe, congress adjourned to Baltimore. Of the state of congress, at this time, the following letter of Mr. Paine gives an interesting account. "Our public affairs have been exceedingly agitated since I wrote you last. The loss of fort Washington made way for that of fort Lee; and the dissolution of our army happening at the same time, threw us into a most disagreeable situation. The interception of an express gave the enemy full assurance of what they must have had some knowledge of before, the state of our army; and they took the advantage of it. In two days after the possession of fort Lee, on the 20th of November, where we lost much baggage, and the chief of our battering cannon, they marched to the Hackensack, and thence to Newark, driving General Washington before them, with his 3,000 men; thence to Elizabethtown. General Washington supposed, from the best information he could get, that they were 10,000 strong; marching with a large body of horse in front, and a very large train of artillery. We began to be apprehensive that they were intended for Philadelphia; and congress sat all Sunday in determining proper measures on the occasion. I cannot describe to you the situation of this city. The prospect was really alarming. Monday, 9th; yesterday, General Washington crossed the Delaware, and the enemy arrived at Trenton on this side, thirty miles from this place; close quarters for Congress! It obliges us to move; we have resolved to go to Baltimore." [6]

From 1777 to 1778, Mr. Paine served on multiple committees of the Congress and held several important positions in the Commonwealth of Massachusetts. In 1777 and for the next 13 years, he was appointed attorney general of Massachusetts; in 1779, he became a member of the Massachusetts legislature and also served as delegate to the convention to draw up a new constitution for the Commonwealth of Massachusetts. He was then appointed Judge of the Supreme Court of Massachusetts. He was tough on the incorrigible offenders and made sure all the penalties of law were passed upon them. Where crime was followed by repentance, though, he was moved to tenderness, although always careful to uphold the law.

> The important duties of a judge, he discharged with honour and great impartiality for the space of fourteen years. During the latter part of this time, he was affected with a deafness, which, in measure, impaired his usefulness on the bench. Few men have rendered more important services to the literary and religious institutions of a country, than did Judge Paine. He gave them all the support and influence of his office, by urging upon grand jurors the faithful execution of the laws, the support of schools, and the preservation of a strict morality.[7]

He helped form the American Academy of the Arts and Sciences, and he supported both Washington and Adams in their administrations.

In 1803, increasing deafness caused him to resign from the Supreme Court. He died on May 11, 1814, at 83 years of age.

> His memory was of the most retentive character, and he was highly distinguished for a sprightly and

> *I* am constrained to express my adoration of the Supreme Being — the Author of my existence — in full belief of…His forgiving mercy revealed to the world through Jesus Christ, through Whom I hope for never ending happiness in a future state.[9]

agreeable turn in conversation. A witty severity sometimes excited the temporary disquietude of a friend; but if he was sometimes inclined to indulge in pleasant raillery, he was willing to be the subject of it in his turn. As a scholar, he ranked high among literary men, and was distinguished for his patronage of all the useful institutions of the country. He was a founder of the American Academy established in Massachusetts in 1780, and active in its service until his death. The honorary degree of doctor of laws was conferred upon him by Harvard University. Judge Paine was a firm believer in the divine origin of the Christian religion. He gave full credence to the scriptures, as a revelation from God, designed to instruct mankind in a knowledge of their duty, and to guide them in the way to eternal happiness.[8]

❧ Public Service ❧

1773–1775	**Representative in the Massachusetts legislature**
1774–1778	**Massachusetts delegate to the Continental Congress**
1777–1778	**Member of the Massachusetts House of Representatives**
1777–1790	**Attorney general of Massachusetts**
1779	**Member of the Massachusetts Constitutional Convention**
1790–1804	**Justice of the Supreme Court of Massachusetts**
1894	**Elected a counselor of the Commonwealth of Massachusetts**

⚘ Questions for Discussion ⚘

1. Robert received his seminary degree from Harvard. Look up information in the appendix as to the Christian nature of the school.

2. What positions did he hold as pastor?

3. What event occurred which caused Robert to enter the study of law? What character quality does he show to be willing to do this?

4. As a delegate to the Continental Congress in 1774, what reasons did he list for wanting independence?

5. What major role did Robert Treat Paine perform in gathering munitions?

6. What do we learn from Mr. Paine's letters about the state of affairs at that time?

7. What character quality did he display as Judge of the Supreme Court of Massachusetts?

8. Tell of any evidences we have that Robert Treat Paine was indeed a Christian.

9. In the final quote about Robert Treat Paine, what insight can we glean about the founder's attention to duty? Where might he have learned this?

10. Robert Treat Paine helped to draw up the Massachusetts state constitution. What can we learn from it in the appendix concerning Paine's worldview?

11. Look up the definition for "moral" in the character qualities appendix. Tell how Paine was indeed a moral and just judge.

12. In today's world, many have loose morals. Purpose to be true to God's holy standards for behavior.

Rhode Island

William Ellery
Stephen Hopkins

William Ellery

Dutiful Patriot

Romans 15:27

"High Son of Liberty"

❧❧

Born
December 22, 1727

Birthplace
Newport, Rhode Island

Education
Harvard College

Occupation
Merchant, Lawyer

Married
Ann Remington (6 children)
Abigail Carey (10 children)

Children
16

Age at Signing
48

Died
February 15, 1820; age 92

The British invaded Rhode Island and occupied Newport from December 1776 to October 1779. During the occupation, they occupied Ellery's home for three years, burning it to the ground when they left. They destroyed most of the town.[5]

William Ellery

William Ellery was born on December 22, 1727, in Newport, Rhode Island, the second son in a family of four children. His father gave much attention to his education and sent him to Harvard College where he excelled in Greek and Latin.

Upon graduating, he married Ann Remington, with whom he had six children. He wanted to become an attorney, but worked as a merchant for 20 years. Finally, at age 40, he had enough money to pursue his dream and began studying law. In 1769, he went to work as an attorney. His first wife had died two years before, and he had since married Abigail Carey, with whom he had 10 more children. William loved to garden, growing both vegetables and flowers. When the British began taxing the Americans, Ellery became known as one of Newport's "High Sons of Liberty" — a term describing the most fervent patriots.

In 1776, Samuel Ward, a Rhode Island delegate to the Continental Congress, died of smallpox, and Ellery was sent to take his place. He set out in May and probably made most of the 250-mile trip to Philadelphia on horseback. He earned the name "the Congressman on Horseback" as he disliked riding in carriages, unlike most of the other delegates.

He arrived in Congress in time to sign the Declaration of Independence.

 William Ellery of Rhode Island — a witty, literary chap who wrote epigrams about his fellow delegates while they spoke in Congress — sought a spot where he could witness the signature of each man. "I was determined," he said, "to see how they all looked as they signed what might be their death warrants. I placed myself beside the secretary, Charles Thompson, and eyed each closely as he affixed his name to the document. Undaunted resolution was displayed on every countenance."[1]

During the next three years, Ellery worked diligently on many committees of Congress. The British invaded Rhode Island and occupied Newport from December, 1776, to October, 1779. During the occupation they overtook Ellery's home for three years, burning it and most of the town to the ground when they left. Ellery later had to borrow money from his friends to pay his expenses.

In November, 1781, Ellery returned to Congress and continued to serve as a delegate until 1785. He often spoke out against slavery while in Congress. In 1790, President George Washington appointed him U.S. Collector of Customs for Newport: a position he held for the next 30 years. He never lost his sense of industry or sharpness of mind, though he lived to be 92 years old. The day on which he died, he got up, dressed himself, and sat upon his flag-bottomed chair, just as he'd done for half a century, and read Tully's Offices in Latin without his glasses, though the print was tiny. The doctor stopped in on his way to the hospital, as was his usual custom, and taking Ellery's hand, found his blood pressure gone. After the doctor gave him a little water and wine, Ellery's pulse became stronger. Ellery remarked,

> O! Yes, Doctor, I have a charming pulse, But it is idle to talk to me in this way. I am going off the stage of life, and it is a great blessing I go free from sickness, pain, and sorrow.[2]

Later his daughter found him extremely weak, and moved him to his bed so he could continue to read. Shortly after, they found him dead, with his book, Cicero, propped up under his chin, as a man who just got drowsy and fell asleep.

During his life, he gave much diligence to studying the Bible.

> He studied the scriptures with reverence, diligence and a liberal spirit; feeling their value, seeking for the truth, and aiming at the obedience they require. …Those who knew him only during the last twenty or thirty years of his life, speak of the religious serenity with which he looked upon the world… "The Lord reigneth," were the words with which he usually ended whatever he had to say, of public sufferings and dangers here and abroad. To the young he was dear, for good, cheering counsel, and almost youthful sympathy. His mind and affections never seemed to grow old, but only to ripen with age. His conversation never lost its humour, richness and variety — its freedom and temperate earnestness, and the originality of a thoroughly sincere and natural mind; nor his advice its authority…[3]

As a patriot and a Christian, his name will ever be revered.[4]

❧ Public Service ❧

1776–1779, **Represented Rhode Island in Congress; signed the**
1781–1785 **Declaration of Independence and the Articles of Confederation**
1790–1820 **U.S. Collector of Customs at Newport**

Questions for Discussion

1. What quality did William demonstrate while working toward a law career?

2. To what type of individual did the term "High Sons of Liberty" refer?

3. Why did he get the nickname "the congressman on horseback"?

4. For what reason did William Ellery carefully choose his seat at the signing of the Declaration?

5. What was Ellery's home used for during the British occupation of Newport?

6. What was the quality he observed in every signer?

7. What did the British do to Ellery's home when they left Newport?

8. How did this effect Ellery's finances?

9. What was an issue that Ellery devotedly represented in Congress?

10. Tell of the day Ellery died. What does this tell us about his character?

11. Tell of Ellery's habit of studying the Scriptures.

12. What was one of his common sayings when hearing of sufferings?

13. Look up the definition of "fervent" in the appendix. How can you become fervent in the mission God has for you?

Step. Hopkins

Stephen Hopkins

Consistent Christian

Colossians 2:5

**"My Hand Trembles,
but My Heart Does Not."**

❧❧

BORN
March 7, 1707
BIRTHPLACE
Cranston, Rhode Island
EDUCATION
self-taught
OCCUPATION
Merchant
MARRIED
Sarah Scott, 1726
Anne Smith, 1775
CHILDREN
7
AGE AT SIGNING
69
DIED
July 13, 1785; age 78

One of the other delegates to the [Continental Congress] described him as a venerable man "of an original understanding, extensive reading, and great integrity," who thoroughly believed in liberty, while fully recognizing its inevitable costliness.[1]

Stephen Hopkins was born the son of a farmer on March 7, 1707, in Cranston, Rhode Island. He educated himself by extensive and varied reading. He grew up as a Quaker and adopted their plain dress and many of their beliefs. He earned his living as a farmer and surveyor, and married at the age of 19. He and Sarah Scott had seven children. Following her death, he married Anne Smith.

At the age of 25, he was chosen as Scituate's town clerk. He later became governor of Rhode Island, and Supreme Court Chief Justice. He also founded a patriot newspaper, *The Providence Gazette*, in which he published an article, "The Rights of the Colonies Examined," criticizing British taxation and supporting colonial rule. It was made into a pamphlet and circulated widely throughout the colonies and Great Britain; it confirmed Hopkins as a firm patriot leader. He served on the Rhode Island committee of correspondence, as well as continuing to serve in the legislature and Superior Court while a member of the Continental Congress. He helped prepare the Articles of Confederation and helped form the Continental Navy.

While serving as chief justice in 1772, Hopkins became involved in one of the events that sparked the Revolutionary War. A group of Americans burned the British ship *Gaspee* off the Rhode Island shore and shot a British officer. Everyone knew who the culprits were, but instead of punishing them, Hopkins did all he could to make sure they weren't caught. The British hated him for this, but to the American patriots he was a hero. [9]

In June 1774, Rhode Island became the first of the thirteen colonies to elect delegates to the First Continental Congress. Stephen Hopkins and Samuel Ward were chosen. While many other delegates hoped to make peace, Hopkins warned that Americans would have to fight for their liberty: "Powder and ball [meaning gunpowder and bullets] will decide this question.

Often it was venerable Stephen Hopkins of Rhode Island who, as John Adams put it, "kept us all alive." This witty Quaker entertained until midnight with his anecdotes, dissertations on history, and gems from Milton and Pope... Adams recalled his memories of them as the most delightful of all his years in Congress. [2]

Even before 1760 Hopkins favored some plan of union for the colonies, and he and Benjamin Franklin became firm friends because of their similar views. [3]

⚘ Public Service ⚘

1732–1741	**Town clerk of Scituate, Rhode Island**
1732–1738	**Member of the Rhode Island colonial legislature**
1735–1741	**President of the town council of Scituate**
1736–1739	**Justice of the peace and judge of the court of common pleas**
1739–1740	**Chief justice of the court of common pleas**
1741–1742, 1744–1754	**Speaker of the House of Representatives in the state legislature**
1750	**Helped found the public library in Providence**
1754	**Delegate from Rhode Island to the Albany Convention**
1755–1768	**Governor of Rhode Island, except for four years during this period**
1765	**Chairman of committee opposing the Stamp Act; wrote *The Rights of the Colonies Examined***
1772–1775	**Member of the Rhode Island legislature; led in forbidding the importation of slaves**
1774-1776	**Delegate from Rhode Island to the Continental Congress; signed the Declaration of Independence**
1775–1776	**Chief justice of the superior court of Rhode Island**
1777–1779	**Member of the state legislature of Rhode Island**
1776	**Delegate to the Continental Congress from Rhode Island**

Just before the Revolutionary War, Hopkins became a leading advocate of the abolition of slavery. In 1773, he freed the slaves that he owned, and the next year he prepared a legislative act forbidding the further importation of slaves into Rhode Island. He persuaded the legislature to adopt the act in 1774, the first such anti-slavery legislation adopted in America.[4]

All his life Hopkins had been interested in learning…When Rhode Island College (now Brown University) was founded in 1764, Hopkins became its first chancellor, a position that he held for many years.[5]

The life of Mr. Hopkins exhibits a fine example of the rewards of honest, persevering industry. Although his early education was limited, yet he became a distinguished mathematician, and filled almost every public station in the gift of the people, with singular ability. He was a sincere and consistent Christian, and the impress of his profession was upon all his deeds.[6]

Stephen Hopkins was a firm believer in the Christian Religion.[7]

A decided advocate, and zealous supporter, both of civil and religious liberty, he was the friend of his country, and the patron of all good works.[8]

The gun and bayonet alone will finish the contest in which we are engaged, and any of you who cannot bring your minds to this mode of adjusting the question had better retire." [10]

Hopkins was the second oldest signer, being 69 at the time. He had a stroke which left the right side of his body affected. With his left hand, he picked up his right hand and guided it in recording his signature. So all would know he was not shaking from fear, he said, "My hand trembles, but my heart does not." [11]

His house was the resort of the ministers, elders, and other members engaged in religious visits; and the usual place of meeting in Providence being contracted, the general religious meetings of the society were, in the winter season, frequently held at his dwelling.[12]

In July, 1785, he acquired a lingering fever. He retained full possession of his faculties, and remained tranquil in spirit until his death on July 13. Inscribed on his tombstone are the following words: "Blessed are the dead which die in the Lord; they rest from their labours, and their works do follow them." [13]

Questions for Discussion

1. What was one of Hopkins' outstanding character qualities?

2. What made others glad to have Hopkins around?

3. Was Hopkins a Christian?

4. By what writings did Hopkins persuade others?

5. On what committees did Hopkins serve?

6. What role did he play in an event that helped spark the Revolutionary War?

7. What warning did Hopkins give the Americans?

8. Why did Hopkins' hand tremble?

9. How did Hopkins show hospitality?

10. What words are inscribed on his tombstone?

11. Look up the definition of "consistent." How did Hopkins demonstrate this?

12. Discern an area in your life that needs work to be more consistent. Learn an associated Scripture verse and meditate on it.

Connecticut

Samuel Huntington
Roger Sherman
William Williams
Oliver Wolcott

Samuel Huntington

Lover of Justice

Proverbs 21:3

"I shall always love my Country"

❧❧

BORN
July 3, 1731

BIRTHPLACE
Windham, Connecticut

EDUCATION
Common Schools

OCCUPATION
Lawyer

MARRIED
Martha Devotion

CHILDREN
2 adopted

AGE AT SIGNING
45

DIED
January 3, 1796; age 64

A shy, quiet man who wasn't much of a speaker or writer, Samuel Huntington won the respect of Connecticut people for his fairness and hard work.[2]

Benjamin Rush described him as a "sensible, candid and worthy man and wholly free from state prejudices."[4]

Sam Huntington

Samuel Huntington was born on a farm near Windham, Connecticut on July 3, 1731. As a boy, he learned to read and write in common schools, but he had an insatiable desire to learn, and so borrowed books whenever he was able. Every spare moment he had, he would be found reading and studying. He spent much time doing chores on his father's farm and at the age of 16, he was apprenticed to a cooper to learn how to make barrels. When at the age of 22, he had completed his apprenticeship, he began studying law on his own; by the time he was 27 years old, he was admitted to the bar and began to practice law in Windham.

In 1760 he moved to Norwich and began to win law cases. Word of his legal prowess spread among all the farmers in that area. The fact that he was one of them, from humble beginnings, helped him to gain their confidence.

He married Martha Devotion, daughter of the Reverend Ebenezer Devotion, a godly, well thought of woman. They had no children, yet later adopted two of Joseph Huntington's children, one of whom was later to become governor of Ohio.

At the age of 33, he embarked upon his career of public service, when elected to the colonial legislature. He served there over the next

Residence of Samuel Huntington
Norwich, Connecticut

22 years. He also took on other duties, such as King's attorney, which he held until the Revolutionary War ended colonial government.

He was a member of the second Continental Congress in 1775, a strong advocate for freedom, and voted for and signed the Declaration of Independence. He also signed the Articles of Confederation in 1778.

When John Jay resigned as President of Congress in 1779, the delegates elected Huntington to replace him. His duties during the war were strenuous and began to affect his health, forcing him to resign in July, 1781.

Returning to Connecticut, he resumed his duties as an associate justice of the superior court and a member of the upper house of the legislature. He was reelected to Congress and took his seat in 1783.

He continued to serve throughout his life in important offices in Connecticut, such as chief justice, lieutenant governor, and finally governor; and was re-elected to this position for ten years. He was well-loved by the citizens of Connecticut.

He supported ratification of the U.S. Constitution in 1787. Connecticut's government flourished under his wisdom and fidelity, until he was afflicted with a "dropsy of the chest." His faith in God remained firm and unwavering, and January 5, 1796, at 64 years of age, his useful life ended at his Norwich, Connecticut home.

Although he had held the post of King's attorney right up to the outbreak of revolution, he never faltered in his work for the patriot cause once the colonies had set their course toward independence.[3]

Governor Huntington lived the life of the irreproachable and sincere Christian, and those who knew him most intimately, loved him the most affectionately. He was a thoughtful man, and talked but little — the expression of his mind and heart was put forth in his actions. He seemed to have a natural timidity, or modesty, which some mistook for the reserve of haughtiness, yet with those with whom he was familiar, he was free and winning in his manners. Investigation was a prominent characteristic of his mind, and when this faculty led him to a conclusion, it was difficult to turn him from the path of his determination. Hence as a devoted Christian and a true patriot, he never swerved from duty, or looked back after he had placed his hand to the work.[5]

It may truly be said that no man ever possessed greater mildness or equanimity than Mr. Huntington; a living witness can attest, that during a long residence of twenty-four years in his family, he never, in a single instance, exhibited the slightest symptoms of anger, nor spoke one word calculated to wound the feelings of another,

In a letter to George Washington, Huntington once wrote, "I shall always love my Country." On the day before his forty-fifth birthday he voted for independence, and later he signed the Declaration for his state.[1]

Being truly an upright man, one of the leading traits of his character was the love of justice; this principle was so deeply and indelibly impressed upon his heart, that in whatever circle of society he moved, and whatever situation of life he was placed, he was steadfastly and strenuously its advocate and promoter.[6]

or to injure an absent person. He was the friend of order and of religion, a member of the Christian church, and punctual in the devotions of the family… For many years a professor of religion, Mr. Huntington appeared to enjoy to great satisfaction both in the doctrines and ordinances of the gospel; a constant attendant upon public worship, 'he was occasionally the people's mouth to God, when destitute of preaching.' As a professor of Christianity, and supporter of its institutions, he was exemplary and devout: he manifested an unshaken faith in its doctrines, amid the distresses of declining life, until debility of mind and body, produced by his last illness, rendered him incapable of social intercourse.[11]

❧❧

His conversation, studiously avoiding frivolous topics, was eminently instructive, and he delivered his sentiments in few, but weighty words.[7]

His deportment in domestic life was excellent; his temper serene; and his disposition benevolent. The whole tenor of his conversation was ingratiating and exemplary; and although he sometimes absorbed deep in meditation, he was generally friendly, cheerful, and social.[8]

Thus the private beneficence of Mr. Huntington could have been amply attested, particularly by those relatives whose situation required his assistance.[9]

Ever interested in education, despite his own lack of a college degree, in the 1780's Huntington received honorary degrees from Princeton, Yale, and Dartmouth; and was appointed one of the original trustees of Plainfield (Conn.) Academy. Before that time, he had acted as adviser to the president of Yale.[10]

❧ Public Service ❧

1758	Admitted to the bar to practice law
1764–1775	Member of the lower house of the Connecticut legislature
1765–1774	King's attorney for Connecticut
1774–1783	Associate justice of Connecticut's superior court
1776–1783	Member of Connecticut's delegation to the Continental Congress; signed the Declaration of Independence and the Articles of Confederation
1779–1781	President of the Congress
1784	Chief justice of the superior court of Connecticut
1785	Lieutenant governor of Connecticut
1786–1796	Governor of Connecticut

ເ◈Questions for Discussion◈ວ

1. With what character qualities did Huntington win the respect of the people of Connecticut?

2. What evidence do we have of Samuel Huntington being a Christian?

3. Samuel Huntington was said to be a man of few but weighty words. Look up Bible verses in a concordance about these qualities.

4. Tell how he demonstrated determination in his life.

5. Show how, as a patriot, he demonstrated a sense of duty.

6. Did Samuel Huntington demonstrate generosity in his life? How?

7. Samuel Huntington was given honorary degrees from Harvard, Yale, and Dartmouth. Look up doctrinal statements of these schools.

8. How was Samuel Huntington a "redeemer of time" as a young boy?

9. How did having humble beginnings benefit Huntington in his career?

10. What evidences do we have that Samuel Huntington felt a strong sense of duty and usefulness to his country?

11. Look up the definition of "just." How is this reflected in Huntington's life?

12. How can you work to develop this quality in your life?

Roger Sherman

Steadfast Christian

Hebrews 10:23

"Strong Pillar of the Revolution"

❧❧

BORN
April 19, 1721

BIRTHPLACE
Newton, Massachusetts

EDUCATION
Self-taught

OCCUPATION
Lawyer

MARRIED
Elizabeth Hartwell,
Rebecca Prescott

CHILDREN
15

AGE AT SIGNING
55

DIED
July 23, 1793; age 72

Possessed of a strong, discriminating mind, and guided by the most rigid rules of prudence, his stern integrity and general good sense, together with his cautious perseverance, elevated him to a prominent station among the most successful politicians of his time, and gave him a great and merited ascendancy in the several deliberative bodies of which he was a member.[1]

Roger Sherman

Roger Sherman was born on April 19, 1721, in Newton, Massachusetts. His father was a hard-working farmer and shoemaker. As a young boy he acquired a great desire to study and read about many subjects, especially theology, politics, and law. His father taught him how to make shoes, and when his father died, Roger, 19, was responsible to care for his younger brothers and sisters. He worked as a cobbler for two years and then moved the family to New Milford, Connecticut, where his older brother was working. The story is told that Roger walked the entire distance of more than 100 miles with his shoemaker's tools on his back.

He would work at the cobbler's bench, with a book propped up in front of him. He became instructed in mathematics, and that led to his being appointed as a surveyor in 1745. This position supplemented his regular income and enabled him to pay for the education of his younger brothers, who later became clergymen. He pursued his mathematical interests and later had astronomical observations he made published in an almanac in New York.

His mind was early impressed with the truth of the Christian religion, and, faithful to its precepts, he passed through the turbulent and conflicting scenes of the revolution without a blemish on his character. Before he had attained the age of twenty-one years, he made a public profession of his religion, and continued more than half a century a zealous defender of its doctrines. Exemplary in his attention to the forms and discipline of the church to which he was attached, he evinced, by his conduct, the importance of the application of the moral doctrines of Christianity to the duties of social life.[2]

During the revolutionary war, he was placed on a committee of congress to examine certain army accounts, among which was a contract for the supply of shoes. He informed the committee that the public had been defrauded, and that the charges were exorbitant, which he proved by specifying the cost of the leather and other materials, and of the workmanship. The minuteness with which this was done exciting some surprise, he informed the committee that he was by trade a shoemaker, and was perfectly acquainted with the cost of the article.[3]

In the controversy which arose between Great Britain and her colonies, Mr. Sherman was one of those who from the commencement of hostilities, foresaw the necessity of our entire union and complete independence, and urged, with energy, the boldest and most decisive measures. He engaged in the defence of our liberties, not with the rash ardour of political enthusiasm, nor the ambitious zeal of a lover of popularity, but with the deliberate firmness of the undertaking, able to forsee dangers, resolute to meet them, and sagacious in devising the means of successful opposition. The revolutionary war was a contest of principles.[4]

When he was 28 years old he married Elizabeth Hartwell of Stoughton, Massachusetts, his sweetheart from his hometown in Massachusetts. They had seven children before she died at the age of 34. Roger later married Rebecca Prescott, with whom he had eight more children.

Through handling disputes of landholders while surveying, he became interested in law. He studied on his own, and at the age of 33 was admitted to the bar and began practicing law.

In 1755, his political career began when he was appointed local justice of the peace, and also to the lower house of the Connecticut legislature, and later judge of the court of common pleas. After the death of his first wife, at the age of 40, he moved his family to New Haven. Soon he was elected to the colonial legislature representing New Haven. In 1765, he was appointed judge of the court of common pleas for New Haven county.

In 1766, he was elected to three offices simultaneously — member of the governor's council of the upper house of Connecticut legislature, which he held for 19 years; judge of the superior court of Connecticut, a position he held for 23 years; and treasurer of Yale College, which he held until the Revolutionary War.

In 1774, Sherman was sent to the Continental Congress. Some of the delegates laughed, looking at him. Instead of a wig, he wore his own brown hair cut short. He had a strong New England accent, and gestured often with his hands. He soon won the Congressmen's respect when he opened his mouth with wisdom.

Sherman took a firm stand in support of colonial rights. He served in Congress for the rest of his life, on many committees including the committee of war which directed the war effort; the maritime committee that built a navy; and the board of treasury, whose job it was to raise funds for the war.

Sherman was appointed to the committee to draft the Declaration of Independence.

> Jefferson [once] recalled this of his association with Sherman: "I served with him in the old congress in the years 1775 and 1776: he was a very able and logical debater in that body, steady in the principles of the revolution, always at the post of duty, much employed in the business of committees, and particularly, was of the committee of Dr. Franklin, Mr. J. Adams, Mr.

Livingston, and myself, for preparing the Declaration of Independence. Being much my senior in years, our intercourse was chiefly in the line of our duties. I had great respect for him." [9]

Throughout the war, Sherman divided his time between serving in Congress, sitting on the superior court bench of Connecticut, and serving as a member of the governor's committee of safety. He helped codify the laws of the state of Connecticut.

> One of Sherman's greatest service[s] to the nation came in 1787 when he helped forge the U.S. Constitution, which replaced the early national laws called the Articles of Confederation. Sherman helped solve a giant problem. The states with large populations wanted to have more lawmakers than those with fewer people. The small states were afraid that if that happened, they wouldn't have much power. Sherman introduced the Connecticut Compromise: Heavily populated states would have more members in the House of Representatives, but each state would have an equal number of U.S. senators. This system was adopted and has worked well for more than two centuries. Sherman's compromise may have inspired Connecticut's nickname, the Constitution State. [10]

In 1789, Sherman was elected to the U.S. House of Representatives at age 68, the oldest man in the new Congress. He took a leading role in preparing the Bill of Rights. His views were published in an essay signed, *A Citizen of New Haven,* in which he said:

> The immediate security of the civil and domestic rights of the people will be in the government of the particular states. And as the different states have different local interests and customs, which can be best regulated by their own laws, it would not be expedient to admit the

Residence of Roger Sherman
Norwich, Connecticut

federal government to interfere with them, any further than is necessary for the good of the whole… [11]

When Samuel Johnson resigned as U.S. senator in 1791, the Connecticut legislature appointed Sherman to fill the seat. He served as Senator until his death on July 23, 1793, in New Haven, Connecticut at age 72.

> Mr. Sherman expressed his opinion of the constitution which had been agreed upon, in a letter to general Floyd: "Perhaps," he remarks, "a better could not be made upon mere speculation: it was consented to by all the states present in convention, which is a circumstance in its favour, so far as any respect is due to them. If, upon experience, it should be found deficient, it provides an easy and peaceable mode of making amendments. If it should not be adopted, I think we shall be in deplorable circumstances. Our credit as a nation is sinking; the resources of the country

> *J*ohn Adams wrote of him: "The honourable Roger Sherman was one of the most cordial friends which I ever had in my life. Destitute of all literary and scientific education but such as he acquired by his own exertions, he was one of the most sensible men in the world. The clearest head and the steadiest heart. It is praise enough to say, that the late Chief Justice (Oliver) Ellsworth told me that he had made Mr. Sherman his model in his youth. Mr. Sherman…was one of the soundest and strongest pillars of the revolution." [5]

*J*ohn Adams called him, "an old Puritan, as honest as an Angel and as firm in the course of American Independence as Mount Atlas."

*P*atrick Henry considered him one of the greatest statesmen he knew.[6]

*H*aving helped to draft the Declaration, he signed it with a stiff, clear hand as plain and uncomplicated as his Yankee upbringing.[7]

*M*r. Sherman had no instructor or guide in the study of the law, neither had he any books but such as he borrowed, yet he became one of the most profound jurists of his day.[8]

could not be drawn out to defend against a foreign invasion, nor the forces of the union to prevent a civil war. But if the constitution should be adopted, and the several states choose some of their wisest and best men, from time to time, to administer the government, I believe it will not want any amendment. I hope that kind Providence, which guarded these states through a dangerous and distressing war to peace and liberty, will still watch over them, and guide them in the way of safety." [12]

The following inscription is recorded upon the tablet which covers his tomb:

In memory of THE HON. ROGER SHERMAN, ESQ. Mayor of the City of New Haven, and Senator of the United States. He was born at Newton, in Massachusetts, April 19th, 1721, And died in New Haven, July 23d, A.D. 1793, aged LXXII. Possessed of a strong, clear, penetrating mind, and singular perseverance, He became the self-taught scholar, eminent for jurisprudence and policy. He was nineteen years an assistant, and twenty-three

years a judge, of the superior court, in high reputation. He was a delegate in the first congress, Signed the glorious act of Independence, and many years displayed superior talents and ability in the national legislature. He was a member of the general convention, approved the federal constitution, And served his country with fidelity and honour, in the House of Representatives, and in the Senate of the United States. He was a man of approved integrity; a cool, discerning Judge; a prudent, sagacious politician; a trued, faithful, and firm patriot. He ever adorned the profession of Christianity which he made in youth; and, distinguished through life for public usefulness, died in the prospect of a blessed immortality.[13]

"In short," to use the language of the Rev. Dr. Edwards, "whether we consider him in public or private life; whether we consider him as a politician, or a Christian; he was a great and a good man. The words of David concerning Abner, may, with great truth, be applied on this occasion; *know ye not that there is a great man fallen this day in Israel.*[14]

Mr. Jefferson…pointed in a certain direction, and exclaimed, "That is Mr. Sherman, of Connecticut, a man who never said a foolish thing in his life." Mr. Macon, now a distinguished member of the senate of the United States, once remarked to Mr. Reed, of Marblehead, formerly a member of congress, that, "Roger Sherman had more common sense than any man he ever knew." Washington uniformly treated Mr. Sherman with great respect and attention, and gave undoubted proof that he regarded his public services as eminently valuable. The late Dr. Edwards, one of the most eminent divines which this country has produced, was accustomed to speak of him under the appellation of "my great and good friend, senator Sherman." [15]

Jonathan Edwards said of Sherman:

As an avowed professor of religion, he did not hesitate to appear openly in its defence, and maintain the peculiar doctrines of grace. He was exemplary in attending all the institutions of the gospel, in the practice of virtue in general, and in showing himself friendly to all good men.[16]

When he resided at home, he was accustomed, as a peculiar gratification, to retire to his closet, and commit his thoughts to writing, or extract from books the wisdom of other times. His mind was always employed; and those hours which were not interrupted by business, or public engagements, were generally devoted to reading and contemplation. The volume which he consulted most especially, was the Bible: it was his custom to purchase a Bible at the commencement of every session of congress, to peruse it daily, and to present it to one of his children on his return. To his familiar acquaintance with the pages of inspiration may be attributed much of that extraordinary sagacity which he uniformly exhibited.[17]

I believe that there is one only living and true God, existing in three persons, the Father, the Son and the Holy Ghost...[and] that at the end of this world there will be a resurrection of the dead and a final judgment of all mankind when the righteous shall be publically acquitted by Christ the Judge and admitted to everlasting life and glory, and the wicked be sentenced to everlasting punishment.[18]

❧ Public Service ❧

1745	Appointed county surveyor
1754	Admitted to the bar to practice law
1755–1761	Member of the Connecticut legislature
1759–1761	Judge of the court of common pleas of Litchfield County
1765	Judge of the court of common pleas of New Haven County
1766–1785	Member of the governor's council of Connecticut
1766–1789	Judge of the superior court of Connecticut
1766–1776	Treasurer of Yale College
1774–1781	Delegate from Connecticut to the Continental Congress; signed the Declaration of Independence and the Articles of Confederation
1781–1789	Delegate from Connecticut to the Congress of the Confederation
1784–1793	Mayor of New Haven, Connecticut
1787	Member of the Constitutional Convention; signed the United States Constitution
1789–1791	Representative from Connecticut in the United States Congress
1791–1793	U.S. senator from Connecticut

Questions for Discussion

1. What qualities in Roger Sherman's life led to his prominent position in civil government?

2. Quote Roger Sherman's proclamation of the Gospel.

3. How did his life prove his faithfulness to the Lord?

4. What seemingly unimportant skill that Sherman had learned in an earlier season of life proved of benefit to the American cause?

5. What qualities did Sherman exemplify in the defense of our liberties?

6. What qualities did John Adams see in Roger Sherman?

7. How did Roger Sherman learn the profession of law?

8. What can be learned from the character of Sherman as a young man? How did he learn to "redeem the time"?

9. How did Sherman sacrifice for his brothers? Did it prove to be a good investment?

10. What three offices did Sherman hold simultaneously?

11. How did Roger Sherman impress the other Congressmen? What had their first impression of him been from just his appearance? Read I Samuel 16:7. How does God see you?

12. What offices did Roger Sherman hold in usefulness to his country?

13. What character traits did Thomas Jefferson observe in Roger Sherman?

14. What may have led to Connecticut being named the Constitution State?

15. What news did Roger Sherman promote in his essay entitled, *A Citizen of New Haven*?

16. What did Sherman think of the Constitution?

17. What did Jonathan Edwards say of Roger Sherman?

18. What was Sherman's custom at home regarding reading?

19. Do you think Roger Sherman could be said to be a wise user of time? Why or why not?

20. What book did Sherman read the most?

21. What was Sherman's custom at the beginning of each session of Congress?

22. What was Sherman's personal declaration of his belief in Jesus Christ?

23. Give proof that Sherman was "a Steadfast Patriot."

24. Read the definition of "steadfast." Purpose to be a person of steadfast commitment to the Lord Jesus and ask Him for an avenue of personal ministry or service.

William Williams

Honest Politician

Proverbs 22:21

"The Cause of Liberty is the Cause of God"

✤✤

BORN
April 8, 1731
BIRTHPLACE
Lebanon, Connecticut
EDUCATION
Harvard College
OCCUPATION
Merchant
MARRIED
Mary Trumbull, 1771
CHILDREN
3
AGE AT SIGNING
45
DIED
August 2, 1811; age 80

During the revolutionary era, Williams wrote letters to newspapers complaining of British injustice, signing them with such pen names as "America," and "A Friend to His Country." As war came, he wrote that independence was "a Cause unspeakably important," and added that "the Cause of Liberty is the Cause of God."[1]

William Williams was born in Lebanon, Connecticut, in 1731. Both his grandfather and father were pastors for over 50 years. After graduating from Harvard, William studied for the ministry under his father. William had a strong faith, and served as church deacon for 43 years. During the French and Indian War, William served with his uncle, Colonel Ephraim Williams, the founder of Williams College. His uncle was shot through the head by an Indian and died. At the close of the campaign, William returned to Lebanon.

He returned dissatisfied and disgusted with the British commanders: their haughtiness and arbitrary conduct, and their inattention to the interests of America, made a powerful and lasting impression upon his mind. Even at that early period, he formed the opinion that the prosperity of his native country would never be secured under the administration of officers who had no common interests nor feelings with the people; and that to enable them to profit by the means within their reach, a government dependent on themselves was necessary.[4]

He was a merchant for a short time, until the age of 25, when he began his political career as town clerk, in which he continued for 45 years.

He also served as selectman for 20 years, a member of the Upper House for 23 years, and a judge for 35 years. It has been said that to hold all these offices one at a time he would have had to live to 170 years of age.

That his life was useful cannot be doubted. In June, 1776, Oliver Wolcott had to leave the Continental Congress due to sickness and Williams was sent to substitute for him. He was too late arriving in Philadelphia to vote for independence, but he signed the Declaration on August 2. He served in Congress for about a year.

During the war he was a member of the Committee of Safety which met daily. He held numerous offices in service to his country throughout his lifetime, as well as being a colonel of the twelfth militia, over 1,700 men.

He married Mary Trumbull, daughter of Connecticut's first state governor, Jonathan Trumbull. They married on Valentine's Day of 1771 and had three children. During the war, the couple opened their home to American soldiers and their French allies. William truly sacrificed his fortune for the cause of liberty: He purchased supplies repeatedly for the American forces with his own money, and went door-to-door throughout his district, raising funds and collecting blankets and lead for the American soldiers. He collected more than 3,000 blankets, and recovered a large quantity of lead by removing the lead weights from clocks.

> Soon after the battle of Germantown, Mr. Williams was instrumental in preventing the capture of one of his colleagues, (colonel Dyer, of Windham,) and narrowly escaped himself from falling into the hands of the enemy. On the approach of the British towards Philadelphia, he retired with the congress to Yorktown, where he remained during the winter. The acknowledged aim of Mr. Williams, in his political career, was to merit the title of an *honest* politician, and no one was more successful in obtaining it: he never desired any office in which he could not promote the public good. He was scrupulously honest in all the transactions of private life.[5]

At a time when continental currency was not trustworthy, he knowingly exchanged $2,000 of his personal money for continental currency and lost the entire amount. It was a loss he never regretted, and demonstrates his true practical patriotism.

> His mind was so fully bent upon the one great object, that he scarcely took the trouble of collecting the notes which he had received: he was accustomed to remark, that many of his debtors had been impoverished by the war, some had died, and others had been killed in the public service, and that he would never enforce payment from the widow and the fatherless — more especially from those whose husbands and fathers had perished in the cause of their country. He was

His voice was strong and powerful, and his eloquence gathered fresh force as he became animated by the increasing interest of his subject. His political career was untainted by selfishness, unless, indeed, it was selfish to seek elevation in the public opinion, by pure and disinterested patriotism. He was never wealthy, but he abandoned a lucrative business, and sacrificed the greater part of his estate in the public service: the property, which a life of plodding industry, divested of every care or feeling in the contest, excepting such as might relate to the great goal of gain, might have swelled into an ample fortune, was, at the death of the patriot, dwindled down to less than five thousand dollars.[2]

When, in 1781, Arnold, the traitor, made an attack upon New London, Williams, who held the office of colonel of militia, hearing of the event, mounted his horse and rode twenty-three miles in three hours, but arrived only in time to see the town wrapped in flames.[3]

a prudent and economical, but liberal, man. After our present form of government was fully established, he often observed, that no person could possibly conceive the troubles that were encountered in obtaining our independence, but those who achieved it.[6]

In 1781, he and his family gave up their home to house officers stationed in Lebanon for the winter. When his health permitted, during the course of the war he rarely went to bed before 2 AM, working tirelessly on behalf of freedom.

Toward the end of 1776, Williams was housing two members of the Committee of Safety in his home overnight. In the course of discussion the conversation led to the dangers of the time, should they fall into the hands of the British. Mr. Williams remarked that he would in all probability be hung, as he had signed the Declaration, and had written many public papers, which would all be considered an act of rebellion the British government would never pardon. One of the gentlemen observed that as he, himself, had neither signed the Declaration nor written anything in opposition to the British government, he was, in all events, secure from the gallows. To this, Mr. Williams instantly replied: "Then, sir, you ought to be hanged for not doing your duty."[7]

A few years after the war Williams was sent to the convention to decide whether or not to approve the U.S. Constitution. He voted for it, convinced it was best for the country. Connecticut became our fifth state when Williams and his fellow delegates approved the Constitution on January 9, 1788.

His oldest son, a man well loved and respected, died at age 38. Williams, now an elderly man, was shocked by this death, and thereafter his own health began to decline. He died on August 2, 1811, at 81 years of age, 35 years to the day after he had signed the Declaration of Independence.

In the domestic circle, Mr. Williams was tender and affectionate, anxious for the welfare of his children, and particularly solicitous in procuring them the benefits of education: his sons were both educated at Yale college. His public engagements, and frequent absence from home, deprived him of many of the enjoyments of domestic life; but

❧ Public Service ❧

1755	Served in the French and Indian War
1756–1801	Town clerk of Lebanon, Connecticut
1756–1804	Member of the Connecticut legislature
1764–1804	Probate judge and county judge for Windham County, Connecticut
1773–1778	Delegate to the Continental Congress; signed the Declaration of Independence
1783–1784	Delegate to the Congress of the Confederation
1788	Member of Connecticut state ratification convention for United States Constitution

it served to impart fresh warmth to the pleasure with which he joined the family circle, and merged for a season the cares of the patriot, in the blessings and comforts of home. His domestic government was regular and uniform; his domestics participated in his paternal kindness; and this constant and endearing system resulted in the strictest bonds of union and love.[8]

Mr. Williams was a man of piety: he entertained the religious opinions of the Congregationalists, of which communion he became a member in his youth, and through the course of a long life he never varied from his professions…he preserved, unblemished, his Christian character, conduct, and conversation. The high opinion which his brethren of the church entertained relative to his piety and virtue, may be inferred from his election, when a young man, to the office of deacon, which he retained until his death. He honoured the sacred ordinances, and was a strict attendant at church; his liberality towards clergymen, and all religious, charitable, and missionary societies, was very conspicuous. Although rigid in his religious opinions, he was free from bigotry, and loving, as he did, all real Christians, conscientiously maintained that every man ought to worship the Creator after his

RES. OF Wᴹ WILLIAMS
Lebanon, Conn.

*Residence of William Williams
Lebanon, Connecticut*

own heart. At the close of his life, being deprived in a great measure of the enjoyments and benefits of social intercourse by his deafness, he spent a great portion of his time in reading, meditation, and prayer.[9]

ॐॐ

ॐQuestions for Discussionॐ

1. **William Williams graduated from Harvard. What was required of one in order to obtain entrance to this school?**

2. **What personal possessions did Williams devote to the cause of liberty?**

3. **In what manner of influence did God use Williams to persuade his countrymen?**

4. **Tell the account of Williams' famous horseback ride, what prompted it and the outcome. What character qualities did he demonstrate in taking immediate action?**

5. **Tell about Williams' training as a minister of the gospel.**

6. Show how God used tough circumstances in William's life during the French and Indian War to prepare him for future usefulness.

7. What evidence do we have that Williams lived a useful, productive life of service to his country?

8. What offices did Williams hold during the Revolution?

9. How did the Williams family demonstrate hospitality?

10. Tell how Williams sacrificed his own fortune for the cause of liberty.

11. Tell of his resourcefulness in supplying lead for the American soldiers.

12. How many blankets did he personally collect?

13. Tell how Williams was instrumental in preventing the capture of one of his colleagues and how he narrowly escaped capture himself.

14. What character trait did Williams strive to be known for in his political dealings?

15. What decision regarding his personal finances shows a true spirit of patriotism and selflessness?

16. What proves him to be a compassionate, merciful, and generous man regarding debts owed him?

17. What sacrifice did his family make for officers of the militia?

18. How does a report concerning his usual bedtime show him to be a man of great diligence and focus?

19. Tell of the instance where Williams rebuked a man for cowardice and not having a sense of duty.

20. What is one interesting fact regarding the day Williams died?

21. What evidence do we have that Williams was a Christian? What spiritual disciplines did he engage in as an elderly man?

Oliver Wolcott

Resourceful Hero

James 1:5

"I shall most cheerfully render my country every service in my power."

❦❦

BORN
November 20, 1726

BIRTHPLACE
Windsor, Connecticut

EDUCATION
Yale College

OCCUPATION
Lawyer, Politician

MARRIED
Laura Collins, 1755

CHILDREN
5

AGE AT SIGNING
49

DIED
December 1, 1797; age 71

Wolcott was a tall man with a dignified, military bearing. Although he was modest, he was firm and tenacious in his opinions and freely expressed them. He loved books and read widely in medicine, law, science, history, and literature.[1]

Oliver Wolcott was the youngest son in a family of 15 children. He was born on November 20, 1726, in Windsor, Connecticut. His father had been a colonial governor in Connecticut. Oliver received a good education, graduating from Yale at the head of his class in 1747. At the time of his graduation, the British were fighting the French in Canada. After Wolcott received a commission as captain in the army from the governor of New York, he rounded up a company of men and defended the northern frontier with Canada. He returned in 1748 to Connecticut when the war ended.

Next, Oliver took up the study of medicine under his brother, Dr. Alexander Wolcott, but before he established a practice, he was appointed as sheriff of Litchfield, Connecticut in 1751 and began to study law.

In 1755, in his late twenties, he married Laura Collins of Guilford, Connecticut. Together they had five children. Laura was quite remarkable, managing their small farm and rearing their children while Oliver was absent, fulfilling his patriotic duties.

Wolcott served as a member of the state council for 12 years. At the same time, he held the office of chief judge of the court of common pleas of Litchfield, and judge of probate as well. Wolcott was appointed by the Continental Congress of 1775 as one of the commissioners of Indian Affairs trying to get the Indians to remain neutral during the Revolutionary War. He also worked settling boundary disputes between the northern states. He was a powerful voice to frontier settlers, winning their support for independence.

In 1775, Wolcott was appointed a member of the Connecticut delegation to the Continental Congress. He took his seat in January 1776, but became ill in June, so was not present for most of the discussions concerning the Declaration of Independence. He continued to serve in the Connecticut militia, rising from Captain to Major General. He led 14 regiments in 1776 to aid in the defense of New York City.

> While returning to Connecticut, Wolcott passed through New York City, where George Washington ordered the Declaration of Independence read to his troops on July 9. That night New York patriots, excited by the separation from England, pulled down a statue of Great Britain's king George III. Oliver Wolcott placed pieces of the headless statue into wagons and took them home to Litchfield with him. There the statue was melted. According to a count someone kept, the two Wolcott daughters and their friends shaped the metal into more than 42,000 bullets. American soldiers later fired the bullets at English troops. [4]

Mary Ann Wolcott, 11, (daughter of General Wolcott) made 10,140 of them, and her eight-year-old brother Frederick turned out 936 bullets.

Wolcott then returned to Congress, where on September 4, 1776, he added his signature to the Declaration of Independence. He relocated with Congress when it moved to Baltimore during the winter of 1777.

> He was made a general and placed in command of Connecticut troops. He helped defeat the British at the Battle of Saratoga in New York in the fall of 1777. Reportedly some of the bullets made from the statue of the king were used in this battle. [5]

The person of Mr. Wolcott was tall and erect, indicating great personal strength and dignity. His countenance manifested a sedate and resolute mind. His manners were urbane, and through life he was distinguished for modesty. Though firm and tenacious of his own opinions, which he distinctly expressed on all suitable occasions, he ever manifested great deference for the opinions of others. [2]

General Wolcott kept busy recruiting units of militia in Connecticut during the summer of 1777. In the fall, he commanded several thousand militiamen aiding General Horatio Gertis in his victory over British General John Burgoyne at Saratoga, New York.

When Wolcott resumed his seat in Congress in 1778, it was meeting in York, Pennsylvania. During the summer of 1779, he commanded a troop of militia defending the Connecticut sea coast from a British invasion. He remained in service with the militia during 1780.

After the war, Wolcott was highly respected in his state. He held the seat of lieutenant governor from 1786-1796. He took part in enthusiastic deliberations over the U.S. Constitution. In 1796, Connecticut elected him governor of the state. It was while serving in this office that he died on December 1, 1797 in East Windsor, Connecticut, at the age of 71.

> As a patriot and statesman, a Christian and a man, Governor Wolcott presented a bright example; for inflexibility, virtue, piety and integrity, were his prominent characteristics. [6]

> His integrity was inflexible, his morals were strictly pure, and his faith that of an humble Christian,

I shall most cheerfully render my country every service in my power."

— *Oliver Wolcott* [3]

Residence of Oliver Wolcott
South Street, Litchfield, Connecticut

untainted by bigotry or intolerance. Mr. Wolcott was personally acquainted with, and esteemed by, most of the great actors of the American revolution, and his name is recorded in connexion with many of its most important events. It is the glory of our country, that the fabric of American greatness was reared by the united toils and exertions of patriots in every state, supported by a virtuous and intelligent people. It is peculiar to our revolution, and distinguishes it from every other, that it was recommended, commenced, conducted, and terminated under the auspices of men, who, with few exceptions, enjoyed the public confidence during every vicissitude of fortune. It is therefore sufficient for any individual to say of him, that he was distinguished for his virtues, his talents, and his services.[7]

✦ Public Service ✦

1747–1748	**Captain in the army during King George's War with the French in Canada**
1751	**Appointed sheriff of Litchfield County, Connecticut**
1774–1786	**Member of the upper house of the Connecticut general assembly**
1776–1778	**Represented Connecticut in the Continental Congress**
1776–1780	**Major general in command of militia troops during the Revolutionary War**
1780–1784	**Represented Connecticut in the Continental Congress**
1786–1796	**Lieutenant governor of Connecticut**
1796–1797	**Governor of Connecticut**

❧Questions for Discussion❧

1. Oliver Wolcott has been described by others as tenacious. Look up the definition in the dictionary and give an example of it in his life.

2. What type of education would Oliver have received from Yale where he graduated at the top of his class? (See appendix.)

3. What are some of the duties Wolcott performed in service to his country?

4. What character qualities were reflected in the way Wolcott dealt with the Indians? How did this benefit his country?

5. How did Wolcott serve in the militia? How many regiments did he lead in defense of New York City?

6. Tell of his resourcefulness with the statue of King George.

7. Tell how his family helped with the statue and how many bullets were made.

8. Reportedly, in what battle was Wolcott involved where some of his bullets were used?

9. How did Wolcott make himself useful during the summer of 1777?

10. What offices of service did Wolcott hold after the revolution?

11. What evidence do we have that Oliver Wolcott was a Christian?

12. Wolcott was said to have great "deference" toward the opinions of others. Look up this quality and see what it means. Did this prevent him from being tenacious in his own opinions?

13. Think of a specific way to implement resourcefulness in your life this week.

New York

William Floyd
Francis Lewis
Philip Livingston
Lewis Morris

William Floyd

Sincere Patriot

I Peter 1:22

"Life, Liberty, and the Pursuit of Happiness"

❧❧

BORN
December 17, 1734

BIRTHPLACE
Brookhaven, Long Island

EDUCATION
At home, by his father

OCCUPATION
Landowner

MARRIED
Hannah Jones
Joanna Strong

CHILDREN
8

AGE AT SIGNING
41

DIED
August 4, 1821; age 86

William Floyd, in [Benjamin] Rush's estimate, was "A mild and decided Republican. He seldom spoke in Congress, but always voted with the zealous friends to liberty and independence."[1]

William Floyd's family had been in America since 1654 when his great-grandfather emigrated from Wales. He became a very successful farmer and served as a judge in Suffolk County and a colonel in the militia.

William was born in Brookhaven, Long Island, in 1734 to a very wealthy and respected family. William was taught at home by his father, Nicoll Floyd. When he was but a teenager his father died, leaving William in charge of a huge estate and the upbringing of his brothers and sisters. He had a passion for hunting and enjoyed entertaining at his large white house at Mastic.

Six years after his father died he married Hannah Jones, with whom he had three children. One of his daughters, Mary Floyd, later became the wife of Colonel Benjamin Talmadge, chief of General Washington's Secret Service, who played an important part in uncovering the treason of Benedict Arnold.

His political course was uniform and independent, and marked with a candour and sincerity which attracted the approbation of those who differed from him in opinion. The most flattering commentary upon his public life will be found in the frequent and constant proofs of popular favour, which he received for more than fifty years.[2]

In 1769, William became an official of Brookhaven, the Long Island town in which his estate was located. From early in his career, he spoke out strongly against British taxes.

> There was in his conduct, both in public and private life, a characteristic sincerity which never failed to inspire confidence; and which combined with the warmth and spirit with which he opposed the usurpations of the British government, had acquired for him an extensive popularity.[5]

He was elected as a delegate to the First Continental Congress in 1774, and was given command over the militia in his county of Suffolk. Upon returning from the Continental Congress, he found that the British naval force had invaded Long Island with the purpose of gathering supplies. As soon as Floyd heard of the impending danger he assembled his force and marched to the point of attack.

> It was perhaps fortunate for his little army, composed of raw and undisciplined militia, that the terror of their approach left nothing for their arms to accomplish.

In his political character, there was much to admire. He was uniform and independent. He manifested great candour and sincerity towards those from whom he happened to differ; and such was his well known integrity, that his motives were rarely, if ever, impeached.[3]

The activity displayed, however, had an important effect in inducing the enemy to abandon their design.[6]

In April 1775, he was chosen as delegate to the Second Continental Convention.

News that Long Island had been surrendered without a battle soon reached Philadelphia, and Floyd was angered. A short time before, he had written from Philadelphia: '[I]s New York to be evacuated as well as Long Island without fighting, or will our army like the Ravens of Old consider the invaluable prize for which they are contending and with their fortitude attack the enemy wherever they can find them?[7]

William Floyd's wife and children were luckier [than some]. Friends rode to warn them of the approach of armed Tories, out in force now that the British army was on Long Island. Mrs. Floyd gathered her family and fled across the countryside to the shore of Long Island Sound. Here, she found some loyal fishermen, who took the Floyds across to Connecticut, where, fortunately, they had friends.

On the island, William Floyd's estate was looted. The house was stripped of everything. The farm implements and livestock in his pastures were stolen; the extensive timberlands he had preserved were razed. After the house and grounds were looted, a party of British cavalry was quartered on the estate. Men and horses alike turned the house into a shambles.[8]

His fine estate was exposed to the rude uses of the British soldiery, and his family were obliged to seek shelter and protection in Connecticut. His mansion was the rendezvous for a party of cavalry, his cattle and sheep were used as provision for the British army, and for seven years he derived not a dollar of income from his property.[9]

Floyd, all of whose estates were on Long Island, suffered deprivation of income for seven years. His wife and children were forced to live off the hospitality of friends. Hannah Jones Floyd never saw her home again; she died in exile in 1781. The loss of income, property, and homes by the patriots of the day worked a greater hardship than it might at first seem for men in public service. Not only did the men who expended their personal fortunes in the Revolutionary cause

have no real knowledge they would be reimbursed, but most claims were not paid until Washington's Administration. The majority of all the Signers expended their personal funds to a remarkable degree in many ways.[10]

On May 8, 1777, General Floyd was appointed to the senate of the state of New York. He became a leading and influential member of this body who helped organize the government and adopt a code of laws. In October of 1779, he was unanimously re-elected as a delegate to the second Continental Congress, and there chosen as a member of the treasury board and numerous other committees. In April, 1783 he was finally able to return home after having faithfully seen his country through a long and perilous war.

When the fighting virtually ended after Yorktown in 1781, and some said the war was over, it was recorded that people of Suffolk County stubbornly insisted, *the war was not over until General Floyd returns*. He was not able to return until after the British departed.

His return was triumphant, with hundreds of people turning out to cheer him or shake his hand. He found his estate despoiled of almost everything but the naked soil.

However, Floyd remained prominent in state government, and he was able to recoup. He purchased lands in Oneida County, in western New York, and eventually moved there. Floyd's losses, though great, were only temporary.[11]

In 1784 he purchased a tract of land upon the Mohawk River and developed it, though he was of advanced age. His first wife having died, he remarried, to a lady named Johanna Strong, with whom he would have five more children.

In 1800, he was chosen as an elector of the president and vice president of the United States. He remained incredibly strong and healthy, and lived to the age of 87, "meeting death with the characteristic firmness which distinguished him through life."[12]

The public career of William Floyd can be summarized by a quotation from his old adversary John Jay concerning Floyd's service in the Continental Congress. "Colonel Floyd's conduct while here gained him much respect," Jay wrote. "He moved on steady uniform principles, and appeared always to judge for himself which, in my opinion, is one very essential qualification in a delegate, and absolutely necessary to prevent his being a mere tool of factions."[13]

A decent tomb has been erected over his ashes; but his name is inscribed upon the more imperishable monument of his country's independence. ...To the benighted victims of oppression — a pillar of fire to light them in the path to liberty; and to the tyrants of the earth — a scroll more appalling than that emblazoned upon the wall before Belshazzar, which caused the joints of his loins to be loosed, and his knees to smite together; it will long be held in veneration as the charter of their national existence, by a grateful people, and will never be forgotten so long as liberty has a friend, and man yields homage to the empire of reason.[14]

⚜ Public Service ⚜

1774–1783	Member of New York delegation to the Continental Congress; signed Declaration of Independence
1777–1788	State senator in New York assembly
1789–1791	U.S. representative from New York in first United States Congress
1808	State senator in New York assembly

Most revolutions begin in favor of some program, or with the burning desire to make change. Floyd had no desire for power, either for himself or his friends; he did not even want to throw the people he considered rascals out. What he wanted above all else was for the American colonies to be let alone — no taxes, no ministerial encroachments, no interference with the personal pursuit of life, liberty, and happiness. This was a view that pervaded the American gentry interested in abstract philosophy. His reasoning processes tended to be logical, practical, and based on his own experience — the mark of an intelligent man with little theoretical education. Floyd took time to make up his mind on an issue, but once he had, he rarely changed his view because of other men's arguments. Very early, he decided the taxes and other measures of the British ministry were an encroachment upon, even a usurpation of, American liberties. He entered the Assembly controversies on the Whig, or patriot, side. He had many rich and fashionable friends who tried to persuade him otherwise, but the squire from Long Island refused to change his mind.[4]

❧ Questions for Discussion ❧

1. How did sincerity enable Floyd to win public favor? Look up the definition for "sincerity" in the appendix.

2. What qualities are exemplified in Floyd's life which caused him to refuse to be influenced by his rich and fashionable friends?

3. How did Floyd react when he heard of the surrender of Long Island? What is one character trait shown by his reaction?

4. Tell of the Floyd family's escape from the Tories.

5. What happened to the Floyds' property, livestock, and timberlands? Specifically, what happened to his house?

6. How did this affect Floyd's income? For what period of time?

7. In what capacities did Floyd render service to his country?

8. When was General Floyd able to return home? What evidence do we have of the loyalty and respect of the residents of Suffolk County to General Floyd?

9. What does the statement of John Jay tell us of Floyd's character?

10. What could you do to make this quality a part of your life?

Francis Lewis

Steadfast Patriot

Joshua 10:25

"He sacrificed on the altar of patriotism"

❧❧

BORN
March 21, 1713

BIRTHPLACE
Llandoff, Wales

EDUCATION
Westminster, London

OCCUPATION
Merchant

MARRIED
Elizabeth Annesley, 1745

CHILDREN
7

AGE AT SIGNING
63

DIED
December 31, 1802; age 89

He early espoused the patriotic cause, against the encroachments of the British government, and was among the first to unite with an association, which existed in several parts of the country, called the "sons of liberty."[1]

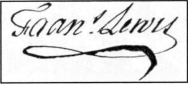

Francis Lewis was the only native-born Welshman among the signers of the Declaration. He was born March 21, 1713, in Llandoff, Wales, the only son of an Episcopal minister. Between the ages of four and five years he was orphaned and came into the care of a maiden aunt before being sent to Scotland to live with relatives. His uncle was responsible for sending him to Westminster School where he became a classic scholar.

After graduating, Francis entered the counting room of a merchant in London, where he acquired an extensive knowledge of commerce. Upon receiving a modest inheritance, he purchased a cargo of goods for trading and sailed to America in the spring of 1735.

He entered into a friendship and partnership with Mr. Edward Annesley and later married this friend's sister, Elizabeth. They had seven children, although four died as infants.

Mr. Lewis was an enterprising and active merchant who traveled widely and had many adventures, including visiting Russia, most of Europe, and several islands; he was shipwrecked off the Irish Coast twice.

During the French and Indian War Lewis was an agent to supply British troops with clothing. He was present when Fort Oswego was captured in 1756, under command of British Colonel Mersey, who was killed at Lewis' side. The garrison of 1,004 men, including Francis Lewis, surrendered as prisoners of war. Lewis was one of only 30 prisoners turned over to the chief warrior of the Indians to do with them whatever he pleased. Tradition reports that because Lewis spoke Welsh, which was similar to the Indians' dialect and understandable to them, he was kept alive and sent to France. Some time later, he was exchanged for other prisoners and sent back to America. For his services during the French and Indian conflict, the King of England rewarded him with a grant of 5,000 acres on Long Island, New York.

In the 1760s Lewis gave firm support to the patriotic cause, joining the Sons of Liberty.

He early espoused the patriotic cause, against the encroachments of the British government, and was among the first to unite with an association, which existed in several parts of the country, called the "sons of liberty," the object of which was to concert measures against the exercise of an undue power on the part of the mother country.[1]

The independent and patriotic character which Mr. Lewis was known to possess, the uniform integrity of his life, the distinguished intellectual powers with which he was endued, all pointed him out as a proper person to assist in taking charge of the interest of the colony in the continental congress. Accordingly, in April, 1775, he was unanimously elected a delegate to that body. In this honourable station he was continued by the provincial congress of New York, through the following year, 1776; and was among the number who declared the colonies forever absolved from their allegiance to the British crown, and from that time entitled to the rank and privileges of free and independent states.[2]

He served on many committees and rendered valuable service to his country over the next few years, including the establishment of a navy for the colonies, working in secret services, purchasing provisions and clothing for the army, and importing of military stores, especially arms and ammunitions.

On the twenty-first of December, 1775, he was continued, by the provincial congress of New York, a delegate from that state for the year 1776, and affixed his signature to the Declaration of Independence with a pride and exultation, only equaled by the ardour with which he supported its adoption. In a convention of the representatives of the state of New York, held at White Plains, on the ninth of July, 1776, the conduct of her congressional delegates was, as has been mentioned, fully approved, and it was unanimously resolved that the reasons assigned by the continental congress for declaring the united colonies free and independent states, were cogent and conclusive; and that, while they lamented the cruel necessity which had rendered that measure unavoidable, they would, at the risk of their lives and fortunes, unite with the other colonies in supporting it.[3]

In 1775, when he was elected to Congress, Mr. Lewis moved his family and personal belongings to his county seat on Long Island, which proved to be an unfortunate event.

In the fall of 1776, the British cavalry, under command of Colonel Birteh, galloped toward Lewis' fine country estate. Not finding Lewis at home "so he could get the hanging he deserved,"[5] Birteh was extremely angry and instead took vengeance upon his wife, wantonly destroying all his property. The cavalry confiscated silver, clocks, clothing, china, food, and drink. Everything that could be carried away was stuffed into British saddlebags. Lewis' extensive library and valuable papers were piled up and burned. With undue brutality, Mrs. Lewis was made to watch her property destroyed, then taken prisoner and treated with unusual cruelty. She was carried off by horseback and, during captivity, was closely confined, given no bed to lie on, or even a change of clothes for several months. The aging woman slept on the floor of an unheated prison with only a slop bucket at her side.

Finally, General Washington arranged a prisoner exchange for her, but her health was irreparably damaged by the effects of imprisonment and she died soon afterward.

From the report of a committee of congress, in April of 1777, it appears that the whole track of the British army through New Jersey was marked with the most wanton ravages and desolation, and that places of worship, ministers, and religious persons of certain protestant denominations, were particularly treated with the most rancorous hatred, and at the same time with the greatest contempt. Prisoners, instead of that humane treatment which those taken by the United States experienced, were in general treated with the greatest barbarity. Many of them were kept nearly four days absolutely without food; and when they received a supply, it was both insufficient in point of quantity, and of the worst quality. They suffered the utmost distress from cold, nakedness, and close confinement. Freemen, and men of substance, suffered all that a generous mind could suffer from the contempt and mockery of British and foreign mercenaries. Multitudes died in prison; nor was any charitable assistance afforded to the sick and dying, a neglect which was probably never known to happen, in a similar case, among Christians. The prisoners captured by sir William Howe, in 1776, amounted to many hundreds, who were shut up, in the coldest season of the year, in churches, sugar-houses, and other large buildings. Many hundreds of these unhappy men expired from the severity of the weather and the rigour of their treatment. The filth of their places of confinement was both offensive and dangerous; and seven dead bodies have been seen in one building, at a time, all lying in a situation shocking to humanity. When those who survived were ordered to be sent out for exchange, some of them fell dead in the streets, while attempting to walk to the ves-

sels, and others were so emaciated that their appearance was horrible. It has been asserted, on as good evidence as the case will admit, that, during the last six years of the war, more than eleven thousand persons died on board the Jersey prison-ship, which was stationed in East river, near New York; and for some time after the war the bones of many of these victims lay whitening in the sun on the shores of Long Island. Conyngham, the provost-marshal at New York, was a fellow who would not, says Graydon, have disgraced the imperial throne of the Caesars, in the darkest days of Roman tyranny; nor the republic of France at the most refulgent era of Jacobinism. It is recorded, as a trait of his villainy, that in the evening he would traverse his domain with a whip in his hand, sending his prisoners to bed with a ruffian-like exclamation of "kennel, ye sons of b—s! kennel G—d d—n ye!" Colonel Ethan Allen, than whom few have ever felt more severely the hand of arbitrary power, declares that Joshua Loring, the commissary of prisoners, was even a greater villain than Conyngham. His language on this occasion, so violent, yet characteristic of that singular man, demonstrates the irresistible excitement occasioned by a series of the most inhuman oppressions, and which once caused him to twist off with his teeth the nail which fastened the bar of his hand-cuffs: "Loring," he remarks, "is the most mean-spirited, cowardly, deceitful, and destructive animal in God's creation below; and legions of infernal devils, with all their tremendous horrors, are impatiently waiting to receive Howe and him, with all

Public Service

1756	Captured by the French at Fort Oswega, NY during the French & Indian War
1765	New York delegate to Stamp Act Congress
1775–79	New York delegate to Continental Congress; signed Declaration of Independence

their detestable accomplices, into the most exquisite agonies of the hottest regions of hell-fire."

With regard to the butchery of unresisting prisoners, many facts might be produced. It was the general opinion that the enemy, the day before the battle of Princeton, had determined to give no quarter; and the treatment of several particular persons, at different times, was of the most shocking description, and gave too much countenance to the supposition. Wounded and disabled officers, some of whom were of the first rank, were barbarously mangled, or put to death. A minister of the gospel in Trenton, who neither was nor had been in arms, was massacred in cold blood, though humbly supplicating for mercy. A young American was killed by the British cavalry, and his body so cruelly hacked and mangled by their sabers, that general Washington thought proper to send it in for inspection: it was carried to the post of sir George Osborne, who with much admired sang-froid, simply returned for answer, that *he was no coroner*. This circumstance became a theme of considerable merriment ,and the bon mot of sir George was not a little applauded. Such was the treatment of prisoners, and the inhumanity of the enemy, when Mrs. Lewis was subjected to the unmanly exercise of their power.

The property of Mr. Lewis was almost all sacrificed on the altar of patriotism; and the peace which established the independence of his country, found him reduced from affluence to nearly a state of poverty; his real estate being little more than sufficient for the discharge of his British debts.[4]

Despite his personal grief, Lewis remained in public service. He had served four years in Congress in 1779. In addition to congressional service, Lewis was a commissioner of the Admiralty Board until July

*O*n the thirtieth day of December, 1802, this venerable man, and excellent citizen, was gathered to his fathers, in the ninetieth year of his age, bequeathing to his posterity a name which shall long flourish in the annals of liberty, and affording an example of virtue, constancy, and personal sacrifice, which, if properly appreciated, will serve as a model upon which the rising patriot may found his fame, and to which the veteran statesman may look with mingled emotions of rivalry and emotion.[8]

1781. When he finally saw Whitestone again after the British evacuation of New York City in 1783, nothing but rubble remained. The Revolution deprived Francis Lewis of his home and much of his wealth. He did not rebuild Whitestone, living his remaining years with the families of his sons. In remembering Lewis, Dr. Benjamin Rush, a fellow Declaration signer from Pennsylvania, called him "A moderate Whig, but a very honest man, and very useful in executive business." [6]

In his declining years, Lewis took pride in the achievements of his son Morgan Lewis (1754-1844), who had served as an officer during the Revolutionary War, rising to become chief justice of New York from 1801 to 1807. His daughter, however, married a British General and settled in England, and therefore was estranged from her family.[7]

❧ Questions for Discussion ❧

1. What quality is shown by Lewis' immigration to America in 1735?

2. When he was a prisoner of the Indians, what character quality did he possess that helped obtain his release?

3. How did he acquire his Long Island estate?

4. What qualities resulted in him being chosen to represent the colonies in their struggle against England?

5. How did he prove useful to his country? What services did he render?

6. How did moving his family and personal belongings to his county seat on Long Island prove to be unfortunate?

7. What destruction was Mrs. Lewis forced to witness?

8. How was Mrs. Lewis treated by the British? What effect did it have on her?

9. What are we told of the British treatment of prisoners?

10. In what financial condition was Francis Lewis left by the British?

11. What quality could be evident which induced Lewis to remain active in the service of his country after facing such devastation at the hand of the enemy?

12. What evidence do we see of the vision of patriotism Lewis passed on to his son?

13. Look up the meaning of "steadfast" in the appendix and tell how this quality characterized Lewis' life. How could you implement this in your life?

Phillip Livingston

Available Patriot

Isaiah 6:8

"Impressed by his country's great need"

✦

BORN
January 15, 1716
BIRTHPLACE
Albany, New York
EDUCATION
Tutored at home; Yale College
OCCUPATION
Merchant
MARRIED
Christina Ten Broeck
CHILDREN
9
AGE AT SIGNING
60
DIED
June 12, 1778; age 62

He has been called the reluctant rebel. As a conservative patriot, he tried to avoid open rebellion with Great Britain; but when war came, he supported it in every way he could.[2]

Phillip Livingston's grandfather was a Scottish minister of the Gospel whose son Robert, Phillip's father, emigrated to America and obtained a grant to a large tract of land on the Hudson River which became known as Livingston's Manor. Phillip was born in Albany, New York in 1716 on his family's estate which covered 160,000 acres. He was the fourth of six brothers. The land made Phillip and his family one of the richest in all the colonies. Phillip was taught at home as a boy by tutors before completing his education at Yale College in 1737. Phillip followed his older brother Peter into business as a successful and respected merchant, and was known for his personal integrity and upright dealings. He and Christina Ten Broeck were married in 1740 and raised nine children, five boys and four girls, in a lovely home on Duke Street in Manhattan. Later, as his business prospered, they acquired a 40-acre estate in Brooklyn Heights, overlooking New York Harbor.

While extremely wealthy, Phillip had the character quality of generosity. In 1735, Royal Governor and Admiral Sir Charles Hardy said of him, "No one is more esteemed for energy, promptness, and public spirit." [1] He devoted his energies and growing fortune to philanthropic

None possessed a more patriotic spirit, or was more ready to rise in opposition to British aggression, than Phillip Livingston.[3]

and civic efforts and financially supported Kings College (later Columbia University), the New York Society Library, the New York Chamber of Commerce and the New York Hospital.

Livingston appeared stern to many, but was affectionate and tender toward family and friends. He much preferred reading to conversation, and was knowledgeable in many areas as a result. He had a natural intuitive grasp of the motives of men which not only showed his intelligence, but was almost a necessity for a public figure of immense wealth and prestige.

As Britain began to impose unfair taxes on the colonists, he grew to be a leader of New York's conservation patriots and was elected to New York's colonial legislature in 1758. He resented the riotous behavior of the Sons of Liberty and dreaded the prospect of war. Livingston was in a very enviable position and stood nothing to gain materially from joining the Patriot cause, but very much to lose. It was said that he was one of the richest men in the New York colony at the time.

In September of 1754, he was elected alderman of the east ward of the city of New York and served in public service from this time forward.

At a meeting of the general assembly on the eleventh of September, 1764, Mr. Livingston reported an answer to lieutenant governor Colden's speech, which contained the following passage, deserving of the highest praise for its spirit of genuine patriotism, its recognition of the orthodox principles of the revolution, and its laying the foundation of that opposition and resistance which produced the glorious work of American independence: 'But nothing can add to the pleasure we receive from the information your honour gives us, that his majesty, our most gracious sovereign, distinguishes and approves our conduct. When his service requires it, we shall ever be ready to exert ourselves with loyalty, fidelity, and zeal; and, as we have always complied in the most dutiful manner with every requisition made by his directions, we, with all humility, hope that his majesty, who, and whose ancestors, have long been the guardians of British liberty, will so protect us in our rights, as to prevent our falling into the abject state of being forever hereafter incapable of doing what can merit either his distinction or approbation. Such must be the deplorable state of that wretched people, who (being taxed by a power subordinate to none, and in a great degree unacquainted with their circumstances,) can call nothing their own. This we speak with the greatest deference

❧ Public Service ❧

1754	Elected alderman of east ward of New York City
1758	Elected to New York's colonial legislature
1774	Chosen as member of New York delegation to First Continental Congress
1775	Appointed as president of a provincial congress
1776	Appointed as member of colonial general assembly; signed the Declaration of Independence
1777	Chosen as state senator and served on treasury board and on marine committee

to the wisdom and justice of the British parliament, in which we confide. Depressed with this prospect of inevitable ruin, by the alarming information we have from home, neither we nor our constituents can attend to improvements conducive either to the interests of our mother country or of this colony. We shall, however, renew the act for granting a bounty on hemp, still hoping that a stop may be put to those measures, which, if carried into execution, will oblige us to think that nothing but extreme poverty can preserve us from the most insupportable bondage. We hope your honour will join with us in an endeavour to secure that great badge of English liberty, of being taxed only with our consent, to which we conceive all his majesty's subjects at home and abroad [are] equally entitled to.[4]

In 1774, Livingston was chosen as a member of the New York delegation to the First Continental Congress. Eventually, after repeated appeals to the British king were denied, he accepted the fact that fighting was inevitable.

While serving in Congress, he continued to be active in politics in New York and was appointed president of a provincial congress in 1775. In February 1776, he was unanimously appointed as member of the colonial general assembly. In April of 1777, after a constitution for the state of New York was adopted, he was chosen as state senator and served on the board of treasury and as a member of the marine committee.

He was also a member of the Secret Committee which imported weapons and gunpowder for the army. He spent a huge amount of his own personal resources in purchasing military supplies for the army.

Phillip Livingston, the austere aristocrat who feared the Sons of Liberty, did not escape the wrath of the British. Before the British landed, his lucrative mercantile business was already bankrupt. In 1774, Livingston had strongly supported the voluntary boycott of British imports, which was so effective that imports to the value of 437,937 pounds at New York in 1774 dropped to only 1,228 pounds in 1775.

When Phillip Livingston signed the Declaration, he believed he was putting his vast fortune in jeopardy, and indeed it was so. All his business interests fell to the enemy. His mansion on Duke Street was seized by the British and turned into a barracks for enemy troops. His county estate on Brooklyn Heights was turned into a British naval hospital. Homeless, his family fled up the Hudson River to Kingston, New York. They were again endangered when the British burned Kingston. Phillip Livingston was never able to return home, and his health was devastated because of the strain from the war. Remaining faithful to the cause, he and his family sold some of their remaining property to help maintain the country's credit.

For Phillip Livingston, the revolution meant personal ruin and yet his spirit remained strong. Although in poor health by 1778, his country's great need impressed upon him so much that despite his doctor's report of dropsy in the chest with no rational prospect of recovery, he bid his final goodbye to his loved ones and pressed himself to take his seat in Congress. The British had taken possession of Philadelphia, forcing Congress to leave the city and meet in New York.

> Yet in this dubious and anxious state, his love to his country continued strong and unwavering. For her good he had made many sacrifices; and now that her interests seemed to require his presence in Congress, he hesitated not to relinquish the comforts of home, and those attentions which, in his feeble and declining state, he peculiarly needed from a beloved family.[5]

His son Henry, who was now a member of George Washington's family by marriage, attended his father in the last few days of his life. On June 12, 1778, he breathed his last and was deeply mourned by family, friends and all of Congress.

> His last moments were correspondent with the tenor of his well-spent life. He met, with characteristic firmness and Christian fortitude, the trying hour which separated him from this world.[6]

He never lived to see Cornwallis' surrender and freedom procured.

> May we give honor to him, by remembering what was said of him by those who knew and loved him. "He was a firm believer in the great truths of the Christian system, and a sincere and humble follower of the divine Redeemer."[7]

Questions for Discussion

1. Where did Phillip Livingston receive his early education? Tell what preparation he must have received since he later entered Yale. (See appendix.)

2. Tell how supporting the voluntary boycott of British goods affected Livingston's lucrative business.

3. What became of Livingston's properties on Duke Street and Brooklyn Heights? What peril did his family encounter from the British?

4. What outstanding character quality was shown in Livingston's dealings as a successful businessman?

5   Describe instances of Livingston's generosity and philanthropic efforts.

6. What qualities exemplified Livingston's attitude toward his family?

7. What form of communication did Livingston prefer over speaking?

8. Tell how the text describes Livingston as a discerning man.

9. Tell in what way Livingston sacrificed personally as a member of the Secret Committee.

10. How did Livingston and his family again sacrifice with what remained of their property, demonstrating their faithfulness to the patriot cause?

11. In 1778, when Livingston's health was declining, how did he show selfless devotion to his country?

12. What testimony do we have that Phillip Livingston was a Christian?

13. Look up "availability." How does Livingston's life exemplify this quality? Consider his final duty to attend Congress while dying.

14. Purpose to be available to God. Ask Him to use you in a specific way this week.

Lewis Morris [signature]

Lewis Morris

Disinterested Patriot

I Peter 2:21

"Every attainment of his heart yielded to the love of his country."

BORN
April 8, 1726
BIRTHPLACE
Morrisania, New York
EDUCATION
At home by father;
Yale College
OCCUPATION
Landowner
MARRIED
Mary Walton, 1749
CHILDREN
10
AGE AT SIGNING
50
DIED
January 22, 1798; age 71

A cheerful, amiable man and a most disinterested [selfless] patriot... He suffered the loss of many thousand pounds by the degradations of the British army upon his property near New York without repining. Every attainment of his heart yielded to his love of his country.[1]

Lewis Morris descended from a distinguished ancestry, of whom one was a leader in Cromwell's army. His great-great-grandfather came to America and settled in New York where he purchased a large estate near Haarlem, in West Chester County, within a few miles of the city. He there established his domain of more than 3,000 acres as a manor with a grant from Governor Fletcher. He named the estate Morrisania. He died in 1673 leaving an only child called Lewis, who afterward became chief justice of the province of New York and governor of New Jersey. In the next generation, the sons of Lewis held prestigious positions, and Lewis Morris the judge was father to signer Lewis.

Lewis was born on April 8, 1726, at Morrisania, the eldest of three sons. His father personally managed his early education, teaching him at home until he entered Yale College at the age of sixteen, "where under the care of the learned and pious Dr. Clap, he was taught the learned languages and mathematics; and his youthful mind was infused with the lessons of morality and religion."[4]

Upon graduation in 1746, he returned to Morrisania and devoted himself to managing the family estate and experimenting with new

agricultural ideas he'd heard about from the agricultural revolution in full swing in England. He had considerable success and acquired much profit from the farm; and for a few years enjoyed considerable peace and prosperity.

On September 24, 1749, he married Mary Walton, daughter of Jacob and Maria Walton, also a wealthy family. Morris and Mary would have six sons and four daughters.

> Lewis Morris possessed a lofty stature, a singularly handsome face, and the most graceful demeanor, with a temperament so enthusiastic and ardent, and a disposition so benevolent and generous, as to render him in his native province the universal favourite of his coevals.[5]

It was the Stamp Act that broke the peace of Morris' life. In New York, it was

> lamented as a calamity and upbraided as an oppression in every form of public and private expression. The newspapers were decorated with black borders, and awful emblems of death…all the indications of a universal and sincere sense of wrong and injury abounded,[6]

upon which the British governor closed down the New York newspapers.

Morris opposed the Stamp Act as an affront to freedom, even though it had no direct effect on him, and in 1764 he was elected to serve in the Assembly.

Tall, distinguished, and immaculately dressed, the fifty-year-old Morris stepped forward, took the quill and put his huge fortune on the line with a few strokes of the pen and a bold calligraphic flourish.[2]

To better understand the sacrifice of the New York signers it is necessary to understand the cause of the conflict in the colonies. In 1767, New York was put through a severe trial by the act requiring residents to provide for the needs of the British troops. It was called the Quartering Act. The people of New York bore the heaviest burden, as the majority of British forces were stationed there. Despite their protest, the Crown simply requisitioned the salt, beer, vinegar and cider for the troops, which Mr. Morris pronounced "unconstitutional, tyrannical, and not to be submissively borne."[7] It is said that act produced "a sullen silence" on inhabitants of New York, but not acquiescence among men like Morris. The governor dissolved the Assembly.

In 1774, the first Congress was assembled. Morris was not chosen to represent New York, as he was considered too decided and zealous an assertor of the rights of the colonies, and too bold a declaimer against the arbitrary acts of the ministry. The Congress was:

> not to prepare for war, but by pacific consultation and explanations, to produce a restoration of tranquility and good understanding. The fervent loyalty which breathes in their eloquent addresses to the king, the British people, and their fellow subjects in the colonies, and the entire absence of all hints of resistance, show the purposes for which they considered themselves brought together.

> There could not have been a fairer experiment made of the efficacy of humble petitions to the royal government, and of affectionate appeals to the people of England. And no experiment, begun with such rational prospect of at least partial success, could have terminated in a more total failure.[8]

The appeals of the colonies were met with "entire indifference" and the "manifestations of a determined perseverance" on the part of England. It was determined that the colonies must resort to "something more vigorous than the issuing of humble memorials."[9]

The following year the Second Continental Congress was formed. "The choice of delegates included men of 'less timid' disposition, and more enthusiastic spirit."[10] Lewis Morris was chosen to represent New York in this Congress which assembled shortly after the bloody skirmish of Lexington.

The tone of the Second Continental Congress was different. It mixed affection and fidelity towards the king with bitter complaints about the injustices forced on the colonists, and a stern resolution to defend the rights of its citizens with a recognition that preparations

for war must be made. Following are the resolutions of this Congress:

That his majesty's most faithful subjects in these colonies are reduced to a dangerous and critical situation, by the attempts of the British ministry to carry into execution, by force of arms, several unconstitutional and oppressive acts of the British parliament for laying taxes in America; to enforce the collection of those taxes, and for altering and changing the constitution and internal police of some of these colonies, in violation of the natural and civil rights of the colonists. Hostilities being actually commenced in the Massachusetts Bay, by the British troops under the command of General Gage, and the lives of a number of the inhabitants of the colony destroyed, the town of Boston having not only been long occupied as a garrisoned town in an enemy's country, but the inhabitants thereof treated with a severity and cruelty not to be justified even towards declared enemies; large reinforcements too being ordered and soon expected, for the declared purpose of compelling these colonies to submit to the operation of the said acts; that therefore, for the express purpose of securing and defending these colonies, and preserving them in safety against all attempts to carry the said acts into execution by force of arms, these colonies be immediately put into a state of defense.

But, as we most ardently wish for a restoration of the harmony formerly subsisting between our mother country and these colonies, the interruption of which must, at all events, be exceedingly injurious to both countries, that with a sincere design of contributing by all the means in our power, not incompatible with a just regard for the undoubted rights and true interests of these colonies, to the promotion of this most desirable reconciliation, an humble and dutiful petition be presented to his majesty.

That measures be entered into for opening a negotiation, in order to accommodate the unhappy disputes subsisting between Great Britain and these colonies, and that this be made a part of the petition to the king.

That the militia of New York be armed and trained, and in constant readiness to act at a moment's warning; and that a number of men be immediately embodied and kept in that city, and so disposed of as to give protection to the inhabitants, in case any insult should be offered by the troops that may land there, and to prevent any attempts that may be made to gain possession of the city, and interrupt its intercourse with the country.[11]

A committee was established, with George Washington as chairman, to consider best how to supply the colonies with munitions. They appealed to the patriotism of citizens as there were no supplies at all. The Battle of Bunker Hill was a determining factor in the minds of the Congress as to the course they were being forced to adopt.

✎ Public Service ✎

1775–1777	Served as Delegate from NY in the Constitutional Convention; signed the Declaration of Independence
1776–1783	Served as General in the New York Militia
1777–1790	Member of the senate in the New York Legislature
1788	Member of the State Convention that ratified the U. S. Constitution

During this time Mr. Morris served on several committees, and was also given the job of trying to persuade the Indians to join forces with the colonists. He served his country by purchasing bayonets and muskets, and encouraging the manufacture of saltpeter and gunpowder.

Lewis Morris was, very early, an advocate of independence, though many citizens were slow in following, especially in New York where they had developed relationships with the British living among them. The Committee of Safety began to discourage colonists from personal contact with the British warships. However, it wasn't rigidly obeyed; so much so, that when Washington came to establish headquarters at New York, "he found that Governor Tryon was a more formidable adversary,

by the use of letters, proclamations, and conciliatory addresses, than General Gage had been, with all his well appointed army." [12]

Washington then issued a proclamation punishing offending colonists with the threat of treason should they violate the regulation, thereby jeopardizing the colonial army. Meanwhile, as Congress deliberated its declaration of independence, the British fleet arrived at Sandy Hook and threatened New York with destruction such as Boston had incurred. There was a plot against General Washington's life that stemmed from Governor Tryon, who was now safe on a British warship in the bay. The fact that his estate lay in imminent danger did not affect the decisions made by Lewis Morris. As put by Sanderson in *Biography of the Lives of the Signers,*

> But, if he had an estate to be devastated and destroyed by the British troops, he had also a character for consistency to preserve, which he valued much more highly; and he had also a sincere, high minded love of liberty and justice, which would not permit him to hesitate, if pride of reputation had been out of the question, between the safety of his individual property and the honour of his country.
>
> In voting for the declaration of independence, and putting his name to the instrument, at the very time when a large British army had landed within a few miles of his estate, and their armed ships were lying within cannon shot of the dwelling of his family, he felt and knew that he was devoting his fine farm and mansion, and valuable timber, to the special vengeance of the British commanders, and therefore to the unrestrained devastations of the soldiery; but he had higher aims than the preservation of his own property; motives of action in which self-interest formed no part. [13]

Although the colony of New York was slow to agree upon independence from England, they did on July 9 assemble at White Plains and resolved unanimously:

> …the reasons assigned by the continental congress for declaring the united colonies independent states, were cogent and conclusive, and that while they lamented the cruel necessity which rendered that measure unavoidable, they approved of the same, and would at

*M*orris, who signed after August 2, was concerned but resolute in supporting the Declaration. His own family and estate, at Bronk's Land, was within cannon shot of the British anchorage. But he said that although he felt and knew he was devoting his fine farm and mansion and valuable timber to the special vengeance of the British commanders, he had motives of action in which self-interest played no part.

The Morris's, like the Floyd's, were able to evacuate Morrisania before the British redcoats arrived. The enemy decided to make an example of the manor as an object lesson to the rebellious gentry of New York. The manor house was looted and vandalized. The furnishings were destroyed. All the stock was taken for food by the army; the fences, put up at great labor and expense, were deliberately burned. All of Morris's servants and tenants were turned out and driven from their homes. Some of these poor people suffered greatly.

Lewis Morris had owned about 1,000 acres of fine woodlands in West Chester. These trees were cut down, and the land was left littered with stumps. [3]

> *"[The American troops appear to be] retreating to King's Bridge; if so, Morrisania will fall of course."*[15]
> — *Lewis Morris to his father, September 6, 1776*

the risk of their lives and fortunes join with the other colonies.[14]

General Washington, who had come in April to fortify New York City, gave an order on July 9 regarding the celebration of independence: "The several brigades are to be drawn up this evening on their respective Parades, at six o'clock, when the Declaration of Congress…is to be read with an audible voice. The General hopes this important Event will serve as a free incentive to every officer, and soldier, to act with Fidelity and Courage, as knowing that now the peace and safety of his Country depends (under God) solely on the success of our arms…"

The brigades were formed in hollow squares and in the middle of one the Commander in Chief, on horseback, listened while an aide read the matchless proclamation in a clear voice, under the guns of the enemy ships and in view of the British troops occupying Staten Island. It was during this evening that the King's statue was brought down. Later the royal governor wrote from his safe vantage point on board the warship *Duchess of Gordon*, "…every vestige of Royalty, as far as has been in the power of the Rebels, done away…"

"Molten Majesty" was a great help in the desperate scarcity of lead. Collections of lead weights from windows were made in New York, and Philip Livingston was among those contributing.

At the Signing in Philadelphia on August 2, Livingston, Lewis and Floyd were present to inscribe their names. The British forces at New York had built up great strength, so they were literally risking everything they had, as was Morris, too, a post-signer.[16]

It was less than one month later that Morrisania, as could have been expected, was under British control. Knowing it belonged to one of the signers, the British wasted no time in plundering and destroying everything.

> …His fine woodland of more than a thousand acres, all upon navigable water, and within a few miles of the capital — of a value not easily measured, but evidently worth an immense price — was totally laid bare and given up to plunder and conflagration. His house, from which his family were obliged to retreat, was spoiled and injured; his fences burnt or prostrated; his stock driven off; his domestics and tenants dispersed; and his whole estate laid waste and ruined, as much as was within the power and opportunity of the British forces.[17]

Thus began a period that lasted until the fall of 1783, when the British finally evacuated New York, that plunged Mr. Morris and his family into great suffering.

> His house was greatly injured, his fences ruined, his stock driven away, and his family obliged to live in a state of exile. Few men during the revolution were called to make greater sacrifices than Mr. Morris; none made them more cheerfully.[18]

> The spirit with which he had met the difficulties of the contest, and which sustained him under the pressure of these misfortunes, was shared equally by his family, who did not regret the loss of their comforts or the enjoyments to be purchased by wealth, knowing for what cause their father subjected them to such privations.

> His three eldest sons had taken up arms, and exerted themselves as faithfully for their country, in the field, as their father did in council. Of these the eldest, Lewis, commenced his military career as aide-de-camp to general Sullivan, with the rank of major. He served in that arduous campaign which terminated in the defeat of the Indians, and their expulsion from the northern and western parts of the state of New York. He afterwards accepted general Green's invitation to enter his family, and distinguished himself in all the brilliant campaigns of that most active and enterprizing [sic] commander, in the Carolinas. When the persevering valour of the forces under general Greene's

command had finally delivered that portion of the union from the horrors of a protracted war, major Morris received the thanks of congress and the commission of colonel, as a testimonial of their exalted sense of his services.

The second son, Jacob, had been educated for a merchant at Philadelphia, but impelled by the same patriotic ardour, he offered his services to congress, and was appointed aid-de-camp to general Charles Lee, with whom he went to the south, and had an opportunity to prove his bravery at the gallant defence of Fort Moultrie, and in many subsequent actions.

The third, whose name was William, was very young, but being tall enough for a soldier, he entered the corps of artillery as a lieutenant, and served with reputation to the close of the war. [19]

Once his family was relocated to Philadelphia, he remained in New York serving as a member of the legislature and officer in the militia. In the legislature his "high character, undaunted spirit, and untiring zeal, [which] were of most important value to the cause of independence." [20]

He rose to the rank of major general and contributed to the efficiency of the militia in New York. Lewis Morris lived to see peace restored to his country and a wise constitution ever established for her protection.

He lived his final days at Morrisania and resumed farming his land. He died on January 22, 1798, at the age of 72 and was buried with military honors in the family vault at Morrisania.

Questions for Discussion

1. Lewis Morris is described as the "disinterested patriot." Look up "disinterested" in the dictionary. How did he demonstrate this quality in his life? How is it illustrated in his letter to his father on September 6, 1776?

2. Tell what the British did to his fine estate, furnishings, livestock and fences, and servants.

3. What qualities did Morris possess that made him a favorite of his friends?

4. What quality is demonstrated in Morris' opposition to the Stamp Act?

5. What duties did Lewis Morris undertake to help prepare the militia?

6. How did the British occupancy of New York affect military plans? What steps were taken to overcome this?

7. What qualities are demonstrated by Lewis Morris' being willing to sign the Declaration of Independence? What special dangers did this place him under?

8. How was Lewis Morris' income affected by his signature on the Declaration?

9. What hardships did Morris and his family have to endure?

10. How did this suffering affect his three sons?

11. How did Morris rise to the call of duty by serving in the militia? In the legislature?

12. How could you manifest this trait in your family?

New Jersey

Abraham Clark
John Hart
Francis Hopkinson
Richard Stockton
John Witherspoon

Abraham Clark

Enduring Patriot

Hebrews 12:1–3

"It has gone so far that we must now be a free, independent state or a conquered country."

BORN
February 15, 1726

BIRTHPLACE
Elizabethtown, New Jersey

EDUCATION
Self-taught

OCCUPATION
Lawyer, farmer

MARRIED
Sarah Hatfield, 1749

CHILDREN
10

AGE AT SIGNING
50

DIED
September 15, 1794; age 68

...his patriotism and integrity attracted the respect and admiration of his colleagues.[1]

Abraham Clark was born in Elizabethtown, New Jersey, on February 15, 1726. He was a frail child who was not able to help with farm chores. He devoted much time to reading and was especially fond of mathematics; he became a surgeon. Abraham married Sarah Hatfield of Elizabethtown at the age of 22, and together they had 10 children. He became known as the "poor man's counselor" because he freely gave advice to neighbors on legal matters. His popularity with farmers won him election to the office of sheriff of Essex County, New Jersey.

> He had arrived at an age when the actions of men are more frequently guided by principle than passion, and the calm circumspection of experience has succeeded the hot and hasty ebullitions of youth. It was, therefore, under a well settled and solemn conviction of the justice of the cause, that he appeared in the first ranks of the revolutionary phalanx, and devoted his remaining years to the service of his country. The oppressive claims of the British parliament, the inveterateness

*P*atriotism was the most distin-guishing trait in the character of this plain and pious man. In private life, he was reserved and contempla-tive: preferring retirement to compa-ny, and reflection to amusement, he appeared to be continually absorbed in the affairs of the public...His habits were extremely temperate, and his manner thoughtful and sedate.[2]

*M*r. Clark was a warm partisan, and his feelings of attachment or repulsion were very strong. He had witnessed so much of the cruelty and oppressions of Great Britain, in her war upon the declared freedom of the colonies, that his feelings of hatred could not be soothed by the treaty of peace, although he patriotically acquiesced in whatever tended to his country's good. He therefore took sides with France when questions concerning her came up in Congress; and, early in 1794, he laid before Congress a resolution for suspending all intercourse with Great Britain, until every item of the treaty of peace should be complied with. It was not sanctioned by Congress.[3]

with which they were pursued, and the hostile spirit which charac-terizes all measures touching the government of the colonies, were incitements which aroused all the energies of his mind, and led him to become a principal actor in the eventful scenes which marked the course of the liberating contest.[4]

In June 1776, Clark was appointed as a delegate to the provincial congress for the purpose of uniting with the other colonies:

in the most vigorous measures for supporting the just rights and liberties of America; and if it should be deemed necessary or expedient for this purpose, to join with them in declaring the United colonies independent of Great Britain.[5]

Clark and the other new delegates from New Jersey arrived in Phil-adelphia and took their seats on July 1, in time to hear the debate be-tween John Dickinson of Pennsylvania and John Adams of Massachusetts on whether or not the colonies should declare themselves independent. On the following day, Clark cast his vote for independence. He voted for the adoption of the Declaration of Independence on July 4, and signed his name to the document with the other members of Congress on Au-gust 2.

His patriotism was of the purest character. Personal considerations did not influence his decision. He knew full well that fortune and indi-vidual safety were at stake. But what were these in comparison with the honour and liberty of his country. He voted, therefore, for the declara-tion of independence, and affixed his name to that sacred instrument with a firm determination to meet the consequences of the noble, but dangerous action, with a fortitude and resolution becoming a free born citizen of America.[6]

Abraham Clark wrote from Philadelphia on July 4:

Our Congress is an August Assembly — and can they support the Declaration now on the Anvil, they will be the Greatest Assembly on Earth...We can die but once...We are now embarked on a most tem-pestuous sea...It is gone so far that we must now be a free independent State or a Conquered Country.[7]

Knowing law as he did, Clark was well aware of the penalties for trea-son which, under British law, all the Founding Fathers incurred when they put their signatures to the Declaration. To have been a Signer is a proud title now, but Abraham Clark wrote to a friend: 'As to my title, I know not yet whether it will be honourable or dishonourable; the is-sue of the war must settle it. Perhaps our Congress will be exalted on a high gallows.[8]

Clark was often in bad health, but that did not deter him from fulfilling his duty to Congress. The Library of Congress still contains many reports in his handwriting on various subjects of concern to the patriots of 1776.

Abraham labored greatly to gather the supplies General Washington's army so badly needed. Three times he was re-elected to Congress while giving interim service in the New Jersey legislature. He was chosen a representative of his state to the Philadelphia Convention that formed the Federal Constitution in 1787, although he was unable to attend due to bad health.

When the British forces landed on Staten Island they were a few miles across the water from Clark's New Jersey home. Accounts vary as to whether his estate escaped destruction at the hands of the British. It is known that Clark so neglected his private affairs while serving his country that he did suffer great loss during the Revolution.

Two of Clark's sons served as officers in the American army; both were captured by the enemy. Because their father was a Signer, they were subjected to especial brutality and confined on a prison ship, the *Jersey*.

> Britain's prisons were loathsome enough; its prison ships were worse, They provided the cheapest means of disposing of prisoners because they died off so fast. On the *Jersey*, where Clark's boys were held, 11,000 American prisoners perished. New York harbor smelled of death.[9]

His son Thomas, a captain of artillery, was put in solitary confinement in a dark hole of the ship and was not fed. He managed to stay alive only because other prisoners pushed him small bits of bread through a keyhole in the door. Abraham Clark was informed by the British that his sons were held captive and would be released only if he deserted the American cause.

> But patriotism was strong in this plain and pious Signer, and he rejected the enemy's offer to free his sons if he would renounce his cause in favor of King and Parliament…[10]

Because of the treatment inflicted by the British, more men were lost on the prison ship *Jersey* than in battle during the Revolution.

Abraham Clark refrained from exerting his influence in Congress in favor of his sons, although, when he heard of Thomas's plight, Congress was informed. Congress threatened to treat one of Britain's prisoners in like manner, and only then was the suffering of Captain Clark's sons mitigated.

> The British had not passed gently through New Jersey. In addition to the despoliation of the Signers, there were dozens of incidents in the wake of the armies. Homes were looted or burned, women raped. American clergymen, other than Anglican or Presbyterian, were treated with contempt. One such pastor was bayoneted in Trenton. British cavalry hacked a dead

☙ Public Service ❧

1776–1783	Represented New Jersey in the Continental Congress; signed the Declaration of Independence
1784–1787	Member of the New Jersey state legislature
1786	Delegate to the Annapolis Convention
1789–1790	Representative from New Jersey in the U.S. House of Representatives

Res of Abraham Clark
Elizabeth County, New Jersey

American soldier to pieces. This mutilation was protested by General Washington, who sent the bloody remains to Sir George Osborne, a British officer. Osborne's reply that *he was no coroner*, and his refusal to condemn the act, caused merriment on the British staff, but cold rage among Americans. The foreign Hessians were especially feared and hated, but there do not appear to have been more atrocities on their part than from the British Grenadiers. Under the common assumption that the Americans were rebels and *vile traitors*, as one officer wrote, no real effort was made to control the troops or observe the amenities of civilized warfare.[11]

General Washington, on the other hand, would not permit similar treatment of British prisoners. Usually, if the prisoner promised not to fight again, he was returned to Britain by ship.

The British commander in New Jersey, Charles Earl Cornwallis, made the mistake of despising his ragged enemy too much. He put the invading army into winter quarters at Trenton, Bordentown, and other sites, and took personal leave…On Christmas night, 1776, Washington crossed the Delaware and defeated and captured almost a thousand Hessians under Colonel Johann Rall at Trenton; a few days later he outwitted and outflanked Cornwallis and inflicted another defeat on the British at Princeton…Across the countryside, the British Army's repressive policies had not conquered the state, and above all, they had failed to seal the peace…the troops were pulled back to New York.[12]

Upon adjournment of Congress in June 1794, Mr. Clark retired from public life, being exhausted by political toils and infirmities of his feeble condition. In the autumn of 1794 he experienced a heat stroke while watching a bridge being built across one of his fields. Realizing his danger, he stepped into his chaise and drove himself home. Two hours later he died, at age 69. He was buried in the church yard at Rahway, the same church to which he had given so generously. This inscription is on his grave:

Firm and decided as a patriot,
Zealous and faithful as a friend to the public,
He loved his country,
And adhered to her cause
In the darkest hours of her struggles
Against oppression.[13]

Questions for Discussion

1. Why did Abraham Clark win election as sheriff of Essex County, New Jersey? What character quality did this demonstrate?

2. What two character qualities in Clark's life are we told attracted the respect and admiration of his colleagues?

3. What character traits were evidenced by Clark's willingness to sign the Declaration?

4. What was Clark's own declaration on July 4th concerning the fight for liberty? What was his remark in Congress?

5. What quality was demonstrated when Clark worked for freedom, despite frequent illness?

6. How did Clark render service to the army?

7. How did revolution affect Clark's personal finances?

8. Tell of the plight of Clark's two sons who were officers in the American army. Tell of Thomas' harsh treatment.

9. What character quality kept Clark from relinquishing his signature on the Declaration in order to obtain the release of his sons?

10. Tell of the British treatment of prisoners on the ship *Jersey*.

11. What was George Washington's policy on the treatment of prisoners?

12. Tell of the devastation the British caused on their path through New Jersey.

13. One of Cornwallis' mistakes was despising the American patriot soldiers. Look up the word "despise" in the dictionary. How did God use this "mistake" to aid the patriots?

14. To what institution did Clark extend generosity?

15. What was Abraham Clark's distinguishing trait?

16. Look up the definition for "endurance" in the appendix. How did Clark live it out?

17. What do you know God wants you to do right now? Ask God for inner strength to endure and be victorious for His sake.

John Hart

Honest Patriot

I Thessalonians 4:11–12

"Honest John Hart"

ക്ക

BORN
1711
BIRTHPLACE
Stonington, Connecticut
EDUCATION
Self-taught
OCCUPATION
Farmer
MARRIED
Deborah Scudder, 1740
CHILDREN
13
AGE AT SIGNING
65
DIED
May 11, 1779; age 68

"Honest John Hart" had been a tall, dark-haired youth whose good looks and good manners had endeared him to his neighbors. Although he had received a meager education, his honesty, hard work and common sense had marked him as a leader in his community.[2]

Honest John Hart, as his neighbors called him, was born in Stonington, Connecticut. His parents moved to Hopewell, New Jersey before John's second year. His actual birth date is uncertain except that it was in the year 1711.

John's father Edward Hart had commanded a volunteer corps called the New Jersey Blues in the French-Canadian War, and later settled down to farm in Hopewell. Young John was raised to work the farm with his father. He was self-taught in his spare time and grew rich enough to acquire a 380-acre farm in 1739. Over the years, by diligence and good character, he won the reputation as "the most considerable man in his community." At the age of 29 he married Deborah Scudder of Ewing, New Jersey. The couple had 13 children, and with hard work became rather well-to-do.

> His farm grew yearly better in value and improvement, his stock increased, and his family was augmented by a biennial addition of a son or a daughter, until he was surrounded by thirteen children. In their education, together with the care of his farm, the exercise of friendly acts of assistance to his neighbours, and in serving brief tours of duty

as a member of the colonial legislature, he found occupation of that enviable kind which, at once useful and tranquil, brings old age with no wrinkles but those which time has traced, and preserves for advanced years the cheerfulness of youth.[4]

His public life began when he was chosen justice of the peace, where he won the reputation for fairness. In 1761, he was elected to the New Jersey legislature, and was reelected until it was dissolved in 1771. Hart opposed the Stamp Act in 1765.

Three years later he favored sending a message to the king bluntly saying that the right to tax the colonies lay with the colonies only — and not with Great Britain.[5]

He also backed the refusal to pay British troops stationed in the colony.

A farmer! What had he to do with stamped paper? He had no occasion to sign bills of exchange or promissory notes. Far advanced in years! What improvement in his condition could he look for in civil strife and commotion? Possessed only of a farm and farmer's stock! What inducement of pecuniary saving could persuade him to join in measures that would invite a hostile army, with devastation in its train, to make his fields the theatre of war? Far different motives from the love of self could induce such men to assume an attitude of resistance against arbitrary power…

It was not the amount, but the principle of the poll-tax, and the ship-money, that made those exactions so intolerably odious to the people of England…their freshness to Plymouth-rock by the first pilgrims — to say that a free people might be taxed without their consent seemed to the colonists equivalent to the pretension that they might be chained, scourged and branded as the vilest slaves. It is certain that at this early period independence was not thought of, or if suggested at all, was not in the least desired by the respectable and loyal subjects who assembled at New York in the autumn of 1765.[6]

The consequences of this assertion of a maxim so important in the relations between the colonies and the mother country, were of great moment to the interests of both. It roused the pride of the British aristocracy,

While the most tempting offers of pardon were held forth to all rebels that would give in their adhesion to the royal cause, and while Washington's army was dwindling down to a mere handful, this old man was carrying his gray hairs and his infirmities about from cottage to cottage, and from cave to cave, while his farm was pillaged, his property plundered, his family afflicted and dispersed; he was, through sorrow, humiliation and suffering, wearing out his bodily strength and hastening the approach of decrepitude and death. Yet he never despaired, never repented the course he had taken, but was always hoping for the best, and upheld by an approving conscience, and by a firm trust that the favour of Heaven would not be withheld from a righteous cause.[1]

while it excited also the attention of the colonists, and gave them a principle to contend for, which being approved by their understandings and impressed upon their hearts, became of dearer value than their money or their trade, their farms or their houses; all of which, as well as their peace and safety, were willingly sacrificed in their determination to maintain it.[7]

John Hart, in the midst of his quiet comforts, appreciated the extent of the evil that impended. Valuing all the blessings which were his own, he felt that they might all be rendered valueless if he were to possess them but as the slave of a despotic master. The amount of tax that he would pay was not worth a thought; he had little occasion for English paper, pasteboard, glass, or paint; and tea was a luxury that hardly found its way to the tables of such plain country families as his. "But the sense of personal security and unalienable rights, the sturdy pride of freedom, which every Englishman of that day, and every inhabitant of the British colonies was accustomed to cherish as his birth-right — these were indispensable to him. Without these, all the advantages he possessed were of no avail — his riches might increase, his friends might multiply, his honours thicken upon him, his children might be all that his parental wishes could suggest — still if he might be taxed, to the value of

a straw, by a parliament in which he had no share of actual or virtual representation, he could be no more than a slave. It was a noble sentiment which actuated such men to join the plans of resistance — a sentiment alloyed by no hope of personal aggrandizement, excited by no restlessness of temper, fomented by no artful demagogues — but pure and disinterested, founded on a sincere belief…[8]

When the British closed the port of Boston, the congress of 1774 was called and assembled. Hart was elected in July.

> Of that august and venerable body nothing can be said in commendation, that would be beyond the truth. To that body will future statesmen look, and learn what it is to be a patriot. There was no selfish intrigue for power, no aim at personal distinction, no factious striving for individual honours…with them the republic was all in all; for that alone they consulted; the only faction they formed was against the common enemy; their minds, their bodies were exerted sincerely and greatly and nobly, not for personal power, but for the liberties, the rights, and the honour of their country.[9]

He contributed his zeal to the meeting which drafted an appeal to King George and the citizens of Great Britain.

> He returned, after the adjournment of congress, to the unvaried occupations of his farm; and waited, with anxious hope, the effect of the appeal that had been

made to the generosity of the king and the British people.[10]

In January of 1775, the general assembly of New Jersey reappointed him a representative to Congress. Mr. Hart was one of the oldest members, at 60 years of age, and his cool and refined judgment served to temper the impetuous zeal of some of the youthful delegates from the southern colonies. During the recess he turned his attentions again to his farm and family, and when congress resumed in September:

> he requested the colonial assembly to excuse him from serving any longer as their delegate, setting forth at the same time the peculiar situation of his family and private affairs, as an excuse for thus seeking to withdraw from their public service. The assembly considered his apology satisfactory, and in November of the same year accepted his resignation.[11]

John Hart's talents were considered far too important to the public to remain inactive, and he was again elected delegate to the Provincial Congress of New Jersey, and then to the general congress in 1776.

> He was too deeply impressed with the paramount importance of his county's claims, to permit him to refuse the office.[12]

> The hope of a happy reconciliation with the royal government was not yet extinct. The intelligence received from England of the total failure of every

❧ Public Service ❧

1761–1772	Member of New Jersey's colonial legislature
1774–1776	Member of provincial congress of New Jersey
1775–1776	Member of the New Jersey Committee of Safety
1776	Delegate to the Continental Congress; signed the Declaration of Independence
1776–1777	First speaker of the House of Representatives in the New Jersey state legislature

proposal offered in the House of Commons, tending towards a pacific policy; the treaty with the duke of Brunswick and the elector of Hesse Cassel, stipulating for the employment of foreign mercenaries in the reduction of the colonies; and the indifference shown by the British people, who it had been hoped, would have felt the wrongs attempted to be done to the Americans as outrages on their own liberties, all conspired to show a gloomy and a warlike prospect.

At home, too, the feelings of the people had become exasperated, and New Jersey, which had been second to no one of the colonies in loyalty of love and peace, became thoroughly and rapidly changed. The machinations said to be detected early in the year of 1776, which had been directed against the fidelity and spirit of the army and the safety of the commander in chief, excited the indignant patriotism of the people of this province, perhaps more than even the proofs of determined and violent hostility on the part of the British government.[13]

Accordingly, on the twenty-first of June, a new appointment was made in which John Hart was retained as being of accord with the people in their determination to risk all and suffer all that might be necessarily risked or suffered in the effort to gain independence; but some of his colleagues were not continued, because their zeal or their firmness could not so safely be trusted.

This new appointment was accompanied with instructions "to join with the delegates of the other colonies in continental congress, in the most vigorous measures for supporting the just rights and liberties of America, and if you shall judge it necessary or expedient for this purpose, to join with them in declaring the United Colonies independent of Great Britain, entering into a confederation for union and common defence, making treaties with foreign nations for commerce and assistance, and to take such other measures as may appear to them and you necessary for those great ends, promising to support them with the whole force of this province, always observing that whatsoever plan of confederacy you enter into, the regulating the internal police of this province is to be reserved to the colonial legislature."[14]

A few days after this decisive step of the New Jersey provincial congress, British General Howe arrived at New York and was soon followed by his army.

We have Dr. Benjamin Rush's report that John Hart was a plain, honest, well-meaning Jersey farmer, with little education, but with good sense and virtue eno' to discover and pursue the true interests of his country.[3]

…having put his hand to the plough, he [Hart] would not turn back. He voted for the declaration of independence, without hesitation or reluctance; although well knowing the peril that he was bringing upon his property, his family, and himself. . . When the declaration of independence was first promulgated, the British army had just landed on Staten Island; and no one could tell which of the members of the congress had voted for a manifesto so offensive to the royal government. The president and secretary alone could be identified as individually responsible. Soon afterwards the battle on Long Island was fought; the American army was defeated with considerable loss; and it was known that the royal army was numerous, well disciplined and brave: under these circumstances a new publication of the declaration was made, with the names of all the members, both those who were actually present, and those who subsequently came into congress.

Far from shrinking at this alarming crisis, from the share of responsibility and contingent punishment attaching to each individual, by a concealment of the part that each had taken, every one seemed desirous to affix his name to an instrument which would have brought down on all the signers the direst vengeance of the British government, if the contest, apparently so unequal, had ended in the overthrow of the colonists.

It is impossible to contemplate without admiration the moral courage, the generous disinterestedness, and the conscientious resolution that could impel such a man as John Hart to sign his name to a paper which he could not but know would be a signal for the devastation of his farm, the dispersion of his family, and the total impoverishment of himself and his children. Not impelled by personal ambition, nor sustained by the ardour of youth; already trembling with the feebleness of age, and having neither hope of a protracted life to enjoy in his own person the restoration of peace and the establishment of political rights; nor suited by temperament, habit or education, for the attainment of political distinction; what could have supplied him with the motive for such heroic self-devotion? His motive is to be sought only in a sober conviction of rights invaded, in the dictates of a pure and enlightened patriotism, and a pious reliance on the protection of Heaven upon those who conscientiously performed their duty.

Accustomed during all his life to guide his conduct by the rules of right, and not by considerations of expediency, the same principle of rectitude which had made him the chosen arbiter of all disputes among his neighbours, and acquired for him the title of "honest" — a distinction which immortalized Aristides; this honesty impelled him to execute all his duties faithfully in whatever situation he might be placed, and guided him in the most elevated public act which was to be known and judged by the whole world, as well as in the most trivial concerns of his domestic circle.[15]

New Jersey was soon to become the theatre of war. The British army advanced to the bank of the Delaware, marked by the unrestrained destruction of property in its path. Congress was shocked by the odious details of their ravages. The signers of the Declaration were marked for vengeance, and Mr. Hart's estate was their target as they descended upon New Jersey.

The British were determined to make John Hart their prisoner. Neighbors warned John that the British were marching down the road to his house, but John was unwilling to leave his family. His wife was suffering from a debilitating disease which prevented her being removed from her bed. His neighbors begged him to flee, promising to care for his wife while his 13 children fled. At the last moment, John fled to the woods and was hunted with a fierce perseverance. Scarcely able to elude his enemies, he was often in desperate need of food and necessities. He lived in the woods and the hills, sleeping in caves or out in the open in the frigid December weather, never sleeping in the same place two nights in a row. One night he concealed himself in the presence of a large dog who was his companion for a time and afforded him some warmth.

Hart's farm was pillaged and destroyed by the Hessians. The British officials offered to pardon him if he would surrender and give up the patriot cause, but he refused. He wasn't able to return home until George Washington's troops won the Battle of Princeton on January 3, 1777. When the British evacuated New Jersey John Hart returned to find his home in ruins, his wife dead, and his children scattered by the British. His health suffered immensely, and he never fully recovered, though he set about repairing the damages done to his plantation.

Hart did not return to his seat in Congress, as he was required to devote all his attention to the restoration of his farm. He did, however, share his energies with friends and neighbors who sought him out. He lived long enough to see brighter prospects of freedom with the surrender of Burgoyne and the French alliance.

Happy in the strengthening of this hope into a confident anticipation, and in the consciousness of having well performed his duty during the whole of his life, he sunk into the arms of death, in the year 1780; leaving a character as free from any stain of sordid, or selfish motive, as it has ever fallen to the lot of man to sustain.[16]

He never repented the course he had taken. He enlisted himself in a good cause; and in the darkest periods, still believed that a righteous Providence would ultimately enable that cause to prevail, and finally to triumph.

He was greatly beloved by his family and friends, and highly respected by a large circle of acquaintance, who often appealed to his wisdom and judgment in the settlement of their local affairs. In addition to this, he enjoyed the reputation of being a sincere and humble Christian. He was exceedingly liberal to the Baptist church of Hopewell, to which community he belonged; and greatly assisted them in the erection of a public house of worship; the ground for which he presented to the church, and also as the ground for a burial place. Such was the life, and such the last end, of "honest John Hart."[17]

Questions for Discussion

1. What character traits marked John Hart as a leader in his community?

2. What did young John do in his spare time?

3. What character traits won John a reputation as "the most considerable man in his community"?

4. By what quality did Hart reach the point of being "well-to-do"?

5. For what quality was he known while serving as justice of the peace?

6. What motivated Hart's patriotism?

7. How was John Hart involved in an appeal to the British government?

8. Comment on how loyalty to the Crown changed in the minds of the colonists.

9. Tell how John Hart made the determination to do right and leave the consequences to God.

10. List character qualities seen in the life of John Hart, who was willing to sign his name to the Declaration knowing the location of the British army at the time.

11. Tell the account of the British who were determined to take John Hart prisoner. What became of his children? His wife?

12. Tell of the hardships John Hart personally endured until the British finally evacuated New Jersey in 1777.

13. What did John Hart find when finally able to return home?

14. In whom did Hart trust to bring about the righteous cause of freedom?

15. What do we know of Hart's generosity to his neighbors?

16. What evidence do we have that John Hart was a Christian?

17. Look up "honest" in the appendix. Give examples of it in Hart's life. Purpose to act upon it in your life.

Fra.ˢ Hopkinson

Francis Hopkinson

Kind Patriot

Romans 12:10

"America's First Hymnwriter"

Born
October 2, 1737
Birthplace
Philadelphia, Pennsylvania
Education
College of Philadelphia
Occupation
Lawyer, composer
Married
Ann Borden
Children
5
Age at Signing
38
Died
May 9, 1791; age 53

His person was a little below the common size. His features were small, but extremely animated. His speech was quick, and all his motions seemed to partake of the unceasing activity and versatility of the powers of his mind.[1]

F rancis Hopkinson was born on October 2,1737, one of the eight children of Thomas and Mary Johnson Hopkinson. Francis' father, a lawyer, had emigrated to Pennsylvania from England in 1731 and held many influential offices once in America. It is to him that Ben Franklin attributed his introduction to the study of electricity.

When Francis was only 14, his father died and his mother took upon herself the responsibility for her children's religious and intellectual education.

> How she acquitted herself of that awful responsibility, may be inferred from the character afterwards sustained by her offspring, and from the exemplary moral and religious sense which has been observed essentially to pervade the writing and intellectual effusions of her descendants, and particularly of the subject now before us, who was only fourteen years of age at the time of his father's death.[5]

> [His mother] brought every assistance that could be derived from her admirable precepts, enforced by her own excellent example; and relinquishing for this most sacred purpose, every enjoyment and every pursuit which was not recommended to her judgment by its direct tendency to the accomplishment of this, her most delightful duty,

Mr. Hopkinson possessed uncommon talents for pleasing in company. His wit was not of that coarse kind which was calculated to "set the table in a roar." It was mild and elegant, and infused cheerfulness, and a species of delicate joy, rather than mirth, into the hearts of all who heard it. His empire over the attention and passions of his company was not purchased at the expense of innocent. They who have passed many delightful hours in his society, declare that he was never once heard to use a profane expression, nor utter a word that would have made a lady blush, or have clouded her countenance for a moment with a look of disapprobation. It is this species of wit alone what indicates a rich and powerful imagination.[1]

His disposition and demeanour were marked by benignity and kindness, and the following anecdote will be deemed rather apposite and affecting than trivial, since it displays them in so amiable a light. He was accustomed to cherish an acquaintance with a little mouse, which would come from its hiding place and sit by him at his meals, in order to receive the crumbs with which its boldness was plentifully rewarded. His pigeons also became so much attached to him, from his constant attention to them, that, when he walked in the yard, they would light on his person, and contend for a place, crowding upon his head, shoulders, arms, and indeed wherever they could rest.[2]

she never suffered her attention to relax till, with his manners softened by the purest moral habits, and his virtues fenced in from every attack by strict religious instruction, she transferred his literary education to the college of Philadelphia, afterwards the University of Pennsylvania.[6]

Francis graduated in 1757 with a degree in law.

At the age of seventeen, he began to study the harpsichord and showed his musical talent by being able to play in public three years later. He loved music, composed tunes, and his song, *My Days Have Been So Wondrous Free,* and his publication, in 1763, of a collection of Psalm Tunes mark him as our first American composer.[17]

After graduating from college, young Hopkinson studied law under Benjamin Chew, attorney-general of the province; and in 1761, at the age of twenty-four, he was admitted to practice before the Supreme Court of Pennsylvania. He was hardly more than a boy when he began to display literary, as well as musical, leanings. Many of his poems appeared in the American Magazine.[18]

Dr. Benjamin Rush, one of the most sagacious and discriminating of his contemporaries, who for the greater part of his life was personally acquainted with him, [said of him] that, "he excelled in music and poetry, and had some knowledge in painting. These arts, however," he continues, "did not monopolize all the powers of his mind; he was well skilled in many practical and useful sciences, particularly mathematics and natural philosophy, and he had a general acquaintance with the principles of anatomy, chemistry, and natural history. But his forte was humour and satire, in both of which he was not surpassed by Lucian, Swift, or Rabelais. These extraordinary powers were consecrated to the advancement of the interests of patriotism, virtue and science."[19]

The year after the Stamp Act was repealed, Francis left to visit his relatives in England, where he stayed for two years, visiting also with various dignitaries of the day including Dr. Benjamin Franklin, a personal family friend who was involved in diplomatic relations in England.

Upon returning to America, he married Ann Borden of Bordentown, New Jersey where the couple settled and raised a family of five children. Francis practiced law again and received appointments to various offices, including collector of customs and executive counselor under the royal governor. These appointments he soon had to sacrifice for the cause of his country.

Had his feelings permitted it, he would not have been allowed to remain a quiet spectator of the contest; for his character for abilities and patriotism pointed him out to his countrymen, in a peculiar degree, as one in whom their confidence ought to be reposed in the most trying exigencies of their affairs. He was conspicuous in all the public measures which preceded the revolutionary contest, and in the year 1776 was chosen by the state of New Jersey as one of her representatives in congress; in this capacity he voted for and subscribed the ever memorable Declaration of Independence.[20]

 Hopkinson voted for independence and signed the Declaration on August second. On the twenty-first, John Adams, writing to his wife Abigail, described him: "Yesterday morning I took a walk into Arch Street to see Mr. Peale's painter's room…At this shop I met Mr. Francis Hopkinson, late a Mandamus Counsellor of New Jersey…who, it seems, is a native of Philadelphia, a son of a prothonotary of this country, who was a person much respected. The son was liberally educated, and is a painter and a poet. Have a curiosity to penetrate a little deeper into the bosom of this curious gentleman, and may possibly give you some more particulars concerning him. He is one of your pretty, little, curious, ingenious men. His head is not bigger than a large apple…I have not met with anything in natural history more amusing and entertaining than his personal appearance; yet he is genteel and well bred, and is very social."[21]

Hopkinson, despite his Tory relatives in England, was an open Whig. He used his talents as a writer to pamphleteer and satirize the British party as the controversy deepened. In 1775, he prophesied that the colonies would declare independence. Hopkinson's talent was delicate and elegant, rather than hard-hitting, but his wit had a deep bite. His pen was credited for irresistible influence through its clever ridicule of the Tory and British side. These political writings were widely read, and resulted in his being chosen by the newly-dominant Whigs for the Congress in 1776. He voted unhesitatingly for independence.

Hopkinson's greatest service to the cause was through his pen. His best known work, *The Ballad of the Kegs*, was written and published early in 1778, when the American inventor David Bushnell prepared

The Jerseyman

Gallants, attend, and hear a friend, trill forth harmonious ditty:
Strange things I'll tell, which late befell in Philadelphia city.…

These kegs, I'm told, the rebels hold, packed up like pickled herring,
And they're come down t'attack the town in this new way of ferrying.'

The soldier flew, the sailor too, and scared almost to death, sir,
Wore out their shoes to spread the news, and ran till out of breath, sir.…

Sir William, he, snug as a flea, lay all this time a snoring;
Nor dreamed of harm, as he lay warm in bed with Mrs. L.[oring].

Now in a fright, he starts upright, awaked by such clatter;
He rubs his eyes and boldly cries, "For God's sake, what's the matter?"

Therefore prepare for bloody war; these kegs must all be routed,
Or surely we despised shall be, and British courage doubted'

The cannons roar from shore to shore, the small-arms loud did rattle;
Since wars began, I'm sure no man e'er saw so strange a battle.…

An hundred men with each a pen, or more upon my word, sir.
It is most true would be too few, their valour to record, sir.

Such feats did they perform that day, against these wick'd kegs, sir,
That years to come, if they get home, they'll make their boasts and brags, sir.

The kegs, 'tis said, though strongly made of rebel staves and hoops, sir,
Could not oppose their powerful foes, the conquering British troops, sir.…

Such feats did they perform that day against those wicked kegs, sir,
That years to come, if they get home, they'll make their boasts and brags, sir. [23]

a number of floating combustibles, or infernals, and set them floating down the Delaware against shipping in the British-held harbor of Philadelphia. These devices, the first known floating mines, were constructed of kegs and filled with explosives, set to go off on contact with British hulls. Their appearance alarmed the British, who fired a great amount of ordnance and small arms into the river, at every floating object for some hours. The attack failed, but Hopkinson's satire on the British reaction was credited with being as valuable, at that gloomy time, as an American victory.[22]

Among Hopkinson's other pieces were *Essay on White-washing, A Specimen of Modern Lawsuit,* in which Lawrence Landlord and Timothy Tenant "are sketched to nature;" *The Typographical Mode of Conducting a Quarrel,* and *The High Court of Honor.* A year after writing the latter, he composed an imaginary case which caused a scene in a real courtroom. The manuscript was stolen from the house of James Wilson, for whom it was intended. The thief thought that he had discovered a terrible plot and tried to have this "literary sport" read as evidence before Chief Justice Wilson! [24]

Hopkinson's musical talents were directed not only to satire but to psalms. In 1764 the vestry of Christ Church in Philadelphia thanked him for teaching the choir the art of psalmody. He later served as rector's warden. To Hopkinson has come the honor of being America's first native composer. His *My Days Have Been So Wondrous Free* is considered to be the earliest piece of music by an American. As for his appearance, "His person was a little below the common size. His features were small, but extremely animated. His speech was quick, and all his motions seemed to partake of the unceasing activity and versatility of the powers of his mind." Francis Hopkinson was church music director and choir leader, and the editor of a 1767 hymnal — one of the first purely American hymnals. His work took the one-hundred-and-fifty Psalms and set them all to music.[25]

The British marked Hopkinson as a prominent rebel. During the occupation of Philadelphia, the Hessians plundered his Bordentown house, and his family barely escaped.

He possessed a library, which contained the most distinguished literary productions of the times...After the evacuation of Philadelphia, by the British, a volume, which had been taken from the library of Mr. Hopkinson, , fell into his [a British officer's] hands. On a blank leaf, the officer, who took the book, had written in German an acknowledgement of the book, declaring that although he believed Mr. Hopkinson to be an obstinate rebel, the books and philosophical apparatus of his library were sufficient evidence, that he was a learned man.[26]

He continued in service to his country even after the revolution. Soon after the adoption of the Constitution, President George Washington appointed Mr. Hopkinson to the office of Judge of the U.S. for the

❦ Public Service ❦

1776	**Delegate from New Jersey to second Continental Congress, signed Declaration of Independence**
1779–89	**Judge of admiralty court of Pennsylvania**
1789–91	**Secretary of organizational conference of Protestant Episcopal Church**
1789–91	**Federal circuit court judge in Pennsylvania**

district of Pennsylvania. In this capacity, he was well-suited to give stability and direction to the national government.

Sir, I have the pleasure to enclose to you a commission as judge of the United States for the district of Pennsylvania, to which office I have nominated, and with the advice and consent of the senate have appointed you. In my nomination of persons to fill offices in the judicial department, I have been guided by the importance of the object. Considering it as of the first magnitude, and as the pillar upon which our political fabric must rest, I have endeavoured to bring into the high offices of its administration such characters as will give stability and dignity to our national government; and I persuade myself they will discover a due desire to promote the happiness of our country, by a ready acceptance of their several appointments. The laws which have passed relative to your office accompany the commission. [27]

RES. OF FRANCIS HOPKINSON.
Bordentown, N.J.

Residence of Francis Hopkinson
Bridgetown, New Jersey

Hopkinson continued to influence his country with his copious writings. One of his last was:

The New Roof, a pleasing little allegory, containing, in substance, the principal arguments used in the convention of Pennsylvania assembled in 1778, to consider the frame of government for the United States, and by them recommended to the people at large. It is upon this piece Dr. Rush observed that it "must last as long as the citizens of the United States continue to admire, and to be happy under the present national government." [28]

At the age of 53, Francis Hopkinson, while at breakfast in his Philadelphia home on May 9, 1791, suffered a stroke and died within two hours.

One of Hopkinson's endearing traits was his affection for his friends. In a letter to Thomas Jefferson written in 1790, Francis closed by saying, "I have but few words to spare. If I had but six left, three of them would be spent in saying I love you."[4]

His children followed in their father's distinguished steps to become active in service to their country. He had a son who was distinguished as a jurist and composed the song "Hail, Columbia." His daughter Maria Hopkinson Smith had a son who was distinguished as an author, engineer, and artist. He supervised in the construction of the foundation for the Statue of Liberty, the symbol of the freedom for which his grandfather and others sacrificed.

Francis Hopkinson "was the happy kind of creature who found it delightful just to be alive, with so many fascinating interests around him." This attractive and winning quality is probably what led to John Adams's amusing remarks:

There seemed to be no end to things that caught his interest. He is said to have designed the seals for the American Philosophical Society and for the University of the State of Pennsylvania. He designed the Great Seal of New Jersey. Hopkinson amused himself, too, by inventing such little articles as a shaded candlestick and an improved quill or "pick" for the harpsichord. He took an active interest in his church, too, and was known for his kindly disposition. [29]

"A Pretty Story"

Despite his position as an official of the royal government, Hopkinson became sympathetic to the patriotic cause, and in 1774 he published a biting satire on the conflict between the colonists and the British government which he entitled A Pretty Story. *This satire was written in the form of an allegory that represented the British King as a nobleman with a large farm. The citizens of the British empire were represented as the nobleman's children, and the British parliament was represented by the nobleman's wife. When the children moved to a distant farm, the "harsh and unconstitutional proceedings" of the nobleman and his wife "irritated" the "inhabitants of the new farm." Hopkinson followed this with another satire in 1776 called* The Prophecy, *in which he used Biblical language to forecast the Declaration of Independence.[3]*

Hopkinson is thought to have possibly helped design the American flag.

Of Francis Hopkinson there remains only this to say, in the words of Dr. Rush — that "the various causes which contributed to the history of the establishment of the Independence and the federal Gov't is ascribed to the irresistible influence of the Ridicule which he occasionally poured forth upon the enemies of those great political events." [30]

❧ Questions for Discussion ❧

1. How did Hopkinson's humor reflect his character?

2. What can be deduced about Hopkinson's character by his relationship with common criminals?

3. What can be learned about Hopkinson from his devotion to friends?

4. How did Hopkinson use persuasiveness through writing? Give two examples which show his biblical frame of reference.

5. What was Francis' mother's focus on the training of her children? What proved her successful?

6. What wonderful musical achievement did Francis Hopkinson give to America?

7. To what did Hopkinson consecrate his literary talents?

8. Why did Hopkinson have to sacrifice his professional appointments for the patriot cause?

9. What led his countrymen to trust in him?

10. What talent gave Hopkinson tremendous influence?

11. Tell of the *Ballad of the Kegs*.

12. Tell of his family's narrow escape from the British and the plight of his home.

13. Tell the story of his library and the observation of the British officer who kept one of his books.

Richard Stockton

Devoted Patriot

I Peter 4:19

"I ascribe to the entire belief of the great and leading doctrines of the Christian religion."

BORN
October 1, 1730

BIRTHPLACE
Stockton Manor, New Jersey

EDUCATION
College of New Jersey

OCCUPATION
Lawyer

MARRIED
Annis Boudinot

AGE AT SIGNING
45

NUMBER OF CHILDREN
6

DIED
February 28, 1781; age 50

Of his father-in-law, Benjamin Rush wrote: "An enlightened politician and a correct and graceful speaker. He was timid where bold measures were required, but was at all times sincerely devoted to the liberties of his country."[2]

He was a Christian who was an honour to the church.[1]

Richard Stockton was born on his family's estate near Princeton, New Jersey, on October 1, 1730. His father John Stockton was a wealthy landowner. Richard received an education in classical science at a private school in West Nottingham, Maryland, until at age 17 he entered the College of New Jersey at Newark. He was a member of the first graduating class in 1748. He then began studying law under David Ogden of Newark, New Jersey, who was considered the leading lawyer of that state. He was admitted to the bar in August, 1754.

When he was 22 years old, Richard married Annis Boudinot, the sister of his good friend and fellow student Elias Boudinot. Interestingly, Elias later married one of Stockton's sisters. Stockton and his wife had six children. One of their daughters, Julie, married Benjamin Rush, a signer of the Declaration of Independence.

Stockton was admitted to the bar to practice law in New Jersey at the age of 23. He soon built a flourishing law practice that made him quite wealthy. He enjoyed sports, was an excellent horseman and swordsman, and enjoyed entertaining his wife in a lavish style in their large mansion.

Stockton was absorbed in his legal work, and as late as 1764 wrote the following to his friend and pupil, Joseph Reed:

> The publick is generally unthankful and I never will become a Servant of it, till I am convinced that by neglecting my own affairs I am doing more acceptable service to God and Man.[5]

It wasn't long though, before he became convinced. As a trustee of his beloved alma mater, he was asked by the board to make a trip abroad to try to persuade the Reverend John Witherspoon of Paisley, Scotland, to accept the offer of president of the College of New Jersey. Reverend Witherspoon's wife had previously opposed the idea, but Richard Stockton helped to remove her objections.

During his tour through England, Scotland, and Ireland, he was received with the highest honors: The Marquis of Rockingham and Earl of Chatham consulted him on American affairs. On visiting Edinburgh, he was complimented with a public dinner given by the city authorities — a testimony of respect for his distinguished character. While in Edinburgh, he narrowly escaped death twice. He was waylaid by a furious robber, whom he managed to fight off and wound with his sword. The second instance occurred during his passage across the Irish Channel. He had purchased passage, but his luggage was detained and the voyage that had been scheduled was shipwrecked during a storm; all the passengers and crew died. The Lord twice spared him for future service.

The next year he was appointed one of the royal judges of the province. He was at this time highly elevated in royal favor. He possessed a huge fortune, a wonderful family, and honorable position under King George.

In 1773, he sent Lord Dartmouth a paper entitled, *An Expedient for the of the American Disputes Settlement,* warning him that immediate measures would have to be taken or there would be an "obstinate, awful and tremendous war."[6]

But the time at length arrived, when the question arose, whether he should renounce his allegiance to his sovereign, and encounter the sacrifices which such a step must bring upon him, or continue that allegiance, and forfeit his character as a friend to his country....

The sacrifices which he was called upon to make, were cheerfully endured. He separated himself from the royal council, of which he was a member in New Jersey, and joyfully concurred in all those measures of the day, which had for their object the establishment of American rights, in opposition to the arbitrary and oppressive acts of the British ministry.[7]

On June 21, 1776, he was elected by the provincial Congress of New Jersey as a delegate to the general Congress, which met in Philadelphia. Any doubts he had about independence were dispelled by John Adams.

> Richard Stockton's opinion of it was given by his son years later in a letter to Adams which read: "I have just alluded to my Father and shall take leave to mention an anecdote...I well remember that on his first return home from Congress in the summer of 1776 after the 4th of July he was immediately surrounded by his anxious political Friends who were eager for minute information in respect of the great event which had just taken place — Being then a Boy of some observation and of very retentive memory I remember these words addressed to his Friends — 'The Man to whom the Country is most indebted for the great measure of Independence is Mr. John Adams of Boston — I call him the Atlas of American independence — He it was who sustained the debate.' "[8]

All five New Jersey Delegates voted for independence on July 2. In September he was appointed by Congress to a committee whose task was to inspect the northern army.

> At the end of the month, he was appointed, with George Clymer of Pennsylvania, on a committee to visit the northern army. From Saratoga he wrote, toward the end of October, that the New Jersey soldiers were "marching with cheerfulness, but great part of the men barefooted and barelegged...There is not a single shoe or stocking to be had in this part of the world, or I would ride a hundred miles through the woods and purchase them with my own money." While absent on this errand, Stockton was appointed in late November as one of a committee to consider ways to reinforce General Washington and to hinder the progress of the British army.[9]

On the thirtieth of November he was unfortunately taken prisoner by a party of refugee royalists. He was dragged from his bed by night, and carried to New-York. During his removal to the latter place he was treated with great indignity, and in New York he was placed in the common prison, where he was in want of even the necessaries of life. The news of his capture and sufferings being made known to the congress, that body unanimously passed the following resolution:

Whereas congress hath received information that the honourable Richard Stockton, of New Jersey, and a member of this congress, hath been made a prisoner by the enemy, and that he hath been ignominiously thrown into a common gaol, and there detained – *Resolved*, that General Washington be directed to make inquiry into the truth of this report, and if he finds reason to believe it well founded, that he send a flag to General Howe, remonstrating against this departure from that humane procedure which has marked the conduct of these states to prisoners who have fallen...[10]

His constitution having been materially impaired, Stockton was only able to give occasional counsel and advice to his country after his release. His large fortune was greatly diminished by the depreciation of Continental currency and by the destruction visited on his property by the enemy army. Morven had been used as military headquarters in late 1776. His library, one of the best in the country, was destroyed. Benjamin Rush, his son-in-law, wrote to Lee after the Battle of Princeton: "The whole of Mr. Stockton's furniture, apparel, and even valuable writings have been burnt." Years later, Stockton's widow was still trying to locate those priceless papers which would have revealed so much of this Patriot's services to our country. His lands laid waste, Stockton was forced to ask temporary aid from friends.[11]

On top of all these discouragements, Stockton was stricken with cancer. He died in pain at his home near Princeton at the age of fifty, on February 28, 1781. In his will, he set forth his faith that had sustained his life: "As my children...will have frequent occasion of pursuing this instrument, and may probably be particularly impressed with the last words of their father, I think it proper here, not only to subscribe to the entire belief of the great and leading doctrines of the Christian religion, such as the being of a God, the universal defection and depravity of human nature, the

❧ Public Service ❧

1754	Admitted to the bar to practice law in New Jersey
1766–1776	Visited England, Scotland and Ireland; convinced John Witherspoon he should come to America to become president of the College of New Jersey
1768–1774	Member of the executive council of New Jersey
1774–1776	Associate justice of the supreme court of New Jersey
1776	Delegate to the Continental Congress; signed the Declaration of Independence
1776–1778	Captured and imprisoned by the British in New York City

divinity of the *Person,* and the completeness of the redemption purchased by the Blessed Saviour; the necessity of the operations of the divine Spirit, of divine faith accompanied with an habitual virtuous life, and the universality of the divine providence; but also, in the bowels of a father's affection, to charge and exhort them to remember that 'the fear of God is the beginning of wisdom.' "

After recommending an early attention to religion, he thus continues: "As Almighty God has not been pleased in the Holy Scriptures to prescribe any precise mode in which he is to be publicly worshipped, all contention about it generally arises from want of knowledge or want of virtue. I have no particular advice to leave to my children upon this subject, save only, that they deliberately and conscientiously, in the beginning of life, determine for themselves with which denomination of Christians they can most devoutly worship God, and that after such determination they steadily adhere to that denomination, without being given to change, and without contending against, or judging, others who may think or act differently in a matter so immaterial to substantial virtue and piety."[12]

The following is an excerpt from Dr. Samuel S. Smith's speech at Richard Stockton's funeral:

Behold, my brethren, before your eyes, a most sensible and affecting picture of the transitory nature of mortal things, in the remains of a man who hath been long among the foremost of his country for power, for wisdom, and for fortune; whose eloquence only wanted a theatre like Athens, to have rivaled the Greek and the Roman fame; and who, if what honours this young country can bestow, if many and great personal talents, could save man from the grave, would not thus have been lamented here by you. Behold there "the end of all perfection."

Young gentlemen, [the students of the college,] another of the fathers of learning and eloquence is gone. He went before in the same path in which you are now treading, and hath since long presided over, and helped to confirm the footsteps of those who were here labouring up the hill of science and virtue. While you feel and deplore his loss as a guardian of your studies, and as a model upon which you might form

*M*rs. Stockton was known for her literary talents. Her Pastoral on the subject of Lord Cornwallis' capture, addressed to General Washington after the surrender at Yorktown, was acknowledged by him in a letter. Her composition, "Welcome, Mighty Chief, Once More!" was sung by young ladies of Trenton while strewing flowers in front of General Washington as he passed through that city on his way to New York, just before his first inauguration as President.[3]

In the letter of thanks to Mrs. Stockton, General Washington said: "Your favor of the 17th conveying to me your Pastoral on the subject of Lord Cornwallis' capture has given me great satisfaction…I have only to lament that the Hero of your Pastoral is more deserving of your Pen; but the circumstance shall be placed among the happiest events of my life."[4]

yourselves for public life, let the memory of what he *was* excite you to emulate his fame; let the sight of what he *is* teach you that every thing human is marked with imperfection…Strictly upright in his profession, he scorned to defend a cause that he knew to be unjust. A friend to peace and to the happiness of mankind, he has often with great pains and attention reconciled contending parties…

Compassionate to the injured and distressed, he hath often protected the poor and helpless widow unrighteously robbed of her dower, hath heard her with patience, when many wealthier clients were waiting, and hath zealously promoted her interest, without the prospect of reward, unless he could prevail to have right done to her, and to provide her an easy competence for the rest of her days.

Early in his life, his merits recommended him to his prince and to his country, under the late constitution, who called him to the first honours and trusts of

Many of Richard and Annis Boudinot Stockton's descendants were prominent in the service of the Republic which he did not live to see established. Their son Richard was a lawyer and United States Senator. A grandson, Robert Field Stockton, a naval officer, helped secure California for the United States and the city of Stockton in that state is named for him. A great-grandson, John Potter Stockton, served as minister to Rome and United States Senator.

the government. In council he was wise and firm, but always prudent and moderate. Of this he gave a public and conspicuous instance, almost under your own observation, when a dangerous insurrection in a neighbouring county had driven the attorneys from the bar, and seemed to set the laws at defiance. Whilst all men were divided betwixt rash and timid counsels, he only, with wisdom and firmness, seized the prudent means, appeased the rioters, punished the ringleaders, and restored the laws to their regular course.

The office of a judge of the province, was never filled with more integrity and learning than it was by him, for several years before the revolution. Since that period, he hath represented New-Jersey in the congress of the United States. But a declining health, and a constitution worn out with application and with service, obliged him, shortly after, to retire from the line of public duty, and hath at length dismissed him from the world.

In his private life, he was easy and graceful in his manners; in his conversation, affable and entertaining, and master of a smooth and elegant style even in his ordinary discourse. As a man of letters, he possessed a superior genius, highly cultivated by long and assiduous application. His researches into the principles of morals and religion were deep and accurate, and his knowledge of the laws of his country extensive and profound. He was well acquainted with all the branches of polite learning; but he was particularly admired for a flowing and persuasive eloquence, by which he long governed in the courts of justice.

As a Christian, you know that, many years a member of this church, he was not ashamed of the gospel of Christ. Nor could the ridicule of licentious wits, nor the example of vice in power, tempt him to disguise the profession of it, or to decline from the practice of its virtues. He was, however, liberal in his religious principles. Sensible, as became a philosopher, of the rights of private judgment, and of the difference in opinion that must necessarily arise from the variety of human intellects; he was candid, as became a Christian, to those who differed from him, where he observed their practice marked with virtue and piety. But if we follow him to the last scene of his life, and consider him under that severe and tedious disorder which put a period to it, there the sincerity of his piety, and the force of religion to support the mind in the most terrible conflicts, was chiefly visible. For nearly two years he bore with the utmost constancy and patience, a disorder that makes us tremble only to think of it. With most exquisite pain it preyed upon him, until it reached the passages by which life is sustained: yet, in the midst of as much as human nature could endure, he always discovered a submission to the will of heaven, and a resignation to his fate, that could only flow from the expectation of a better life.

Such was the man, whose remains now lie before us, to teach us the most interesting lessons that mortals have to learn, the vanity of human things, the importance of eternity; the holiness of the divine law; the value of religion; and the certainty and rapid approach of death.[13]

I subscribe to the entire belief of the great and leading doctrines of the Christian religion, [and I exhort] that the course of life held up in the Christian system is calculated for the most complete happiness that can be enjoyed in this mortal state.[14]

Questions for Discussion

1. What evidence do we see that Stockton's patriotic vision was passed to his posterity?

2. What evidence do we have that Richard Stockton was a Christian?

3. What fellow signer of the Declaration did one of his daughters marry? What testimony did this groom give about his father-in-law?

4. From his own testimony, what would induce him to become involved in public service?

5. What incident shows that Richard Stockton had the quality of persuasiveness?

6. Name two instances in which God miraculously preserved Stockton's life from impending danger.

7. Did Richard Stockton have much to lose for supporting independence?

8. What qualities did he demonstrate when he separated himself from the royal council?

9. Who did Stockton call the Atlas of American Independence? To whom do we owe gratitude for remembering and making a record of this?

10. What was Stockton's report of the condition of the northern army? What shows him to be a man of generosity and self-sacrifice?

11. Tell the account of Stockton's capture and treatment while a prisoner of the British.

12. Recount the destruction of his home, personal library, possessions and writings.

13. How did the war affect his finances?

14. Give his "doctrinal statement" from his will and tell of his passion to record this for posterity.

15. What advice does he give his children?

16. List character qualities in Stockton's life as recounted in Dr. Samuel Smith's funeral sermon.

17. What does Dr. Smith attest to about Stockton's life as a Christian?

18. Tell Stockton's own words about his belief in Christianity as stated in his last will.

19. Look up the definition of "devoted." Tell how Stockton was not only devoted to his country but to the Lord as well.

20. Ask God how you can honor Him by a specific action of devotion.

John Witherspoon

Reverent Patriot

Hebrews 12:28-29

"A Beacon of Hope"

❧❧

BORN
February 5, 1723

BIRTHPLACE
Gifford, Scotland

EDUCATION
University of Edinburgh

OCCUPATION
Clergyman

MARRIED
Elizabeth Montgomery;
Mrs. Ann Dill, 1791

CHILDREN
12

AGE AT SIGNING
53

DIED
November 13, 1794; age 71

As a theological writer, Doctor Witherspoon had few superiors, and as a statesman he held the first rank. In him were centered the social elements of an upright citizen, a fond parent, a just tutor, and humble Christian.[1]

John Witherspoon was born in Edinburgh, Scotland in 1723 to a Presbyterian clergyman, and most sources claim he was a direct descendant of John Knox, the founder of Protestantism in Scotland. By age four, John Witherspoon could read the Bible. He attended public school in Haddington. The following was said of him:

> A precocious boy, endowed with a good mind and diligent in study, he was soon the best in his class. An important feature of Scottish university life outside of classrooms was the existence of literary clubs, which were common among the students and the professional men of Edinburgh. His activity in these societies made Witherspoon proficient in debate, which is valuable training for an alert mind, for clearness of expression, and for public speaking.[9]

Witherspoon entered the University of Edinburgh at 13 or 14 years of age, earning his Master of Arts at age 16, and a divinity degree in 1743. He continued his studies in theology until he was 21, when he became licensed to preach and was ordained a Presbyterian minister at Beith, Scotland.

In 1743, he accepted an invitation from the people of Beith to become their pastor. In the same year he became involved in the efforts of the Highlanders of Scotland to restore Charles Edward Stuart (Bonnie Prince Charlie) to the throne. Witherspoon was captured by the English at the Battle of Falkirk and taken prisoner, briefly imprisoned in a castle.

Two years later he married Elizabeth Montgomery. The couple had ten children, although only five survived infancy.

Shortly after entering the ministry, Witherspoon was involved in the controversy between the Moderate or liberal wing of the Scottish Kirk and the Popular or orthodox party, eventually becoming the leader of the Popular minority. His first publication, a satirical piece, *Ecclesiastical Characteristics* (1753), attracted the notice of the Reverend Samuel Davies, who, with Gilbert Tennent, was in Scotland the following year to raise funds for the College of New Jersey.

Witherspoon's many writings gained him wide recognition and in 1764 the University of Aberdeen gave him the degree of Doctor of Divinity. Two years later he was elected president of the College of New Jersey.[10]

Although he had previously declined, as his wife had serious reservations about moving to America, Richard Stockton was sent to persuade him, although it was eventually Benjamin Rush who sufficiently alleviated his wife's objections.

Of Witherspoon, Rush wrote:

His appearance in the pulpit is solemn and graceful. His sermons are loaded with good sense and adorned at the same time with all the elegance and beauty that language can give them. To Witherspoon, Rush wrote on March 25: "All America waits...with trembling impatience for your answer."[11]

It reflects no small honour upon Dr. Witherspoon, that he should consent to cross the ocean, and take charge of a college in a new country, leaving behind him a sphere of great respectability, comfort, and usefulness...It deserves also to be mentioned, that a little previous to his embarking for America, and while still in a state of suspense, respecting his duty, an unmarried gentleman of considerable fortune, and a relation of the family, offered to make him his heir, provided he would remain in Scotland.[12]

In August 1768, the Witherspoons reached Princeton. John Witherspoon loved his new home, claiming that he had "become an American the moment he landed."

The students at Nassau Hall lit candles in every window to give the Witherspoons a warm welcome. Dr. Witherspoon brought 300 books

*I*t was a distinguished feature in the American revolution that religious feeling was closely connected with political action. The persecutions which compelled our forefathers to seek the unshackled enjoyment of those feelings in the wilderness of the western world, were still fresh on the recollection of their descendants, and they continued, both by public and private acts, to appeal to the Supreme Judge of the world for the rectitude of their intentions, and to place a firm reliance on the protection of divine providence.[2]

*W*hile he was engaged in serving his country in the character of a civilian, he did not lay aside his ministry. He eagerly embraced every opportunity of preaching, and of discharging the carious duties of his station as a gospel minister, which he considered as his highest honor. Nor would he ever consent, as some other clerical members of congress did, to change, in any particular, the dress which distinguished his order...

*H*is powers of memory were of vast importance to him in congress: he often remarked that he could precisely repeat a speech, or sermon, written by himself, by reading it over only three times.[3]

*W*itherspoon served on more than 100 committees. To remind people that he believed God was on America's side, he always wore his minister's clothes to Congress. Even when America's prospects looked bleak, Witherspoon remained a beacon of hope, despite his personal sufferings. In 1777, John and Elizabeth's son James was killed at the Battle of Germantown in what is now Philadelphia. The British wrecked the Witherspoon farm near Princeton, and part of the Battle of Princeton in 1777 was fought right on the college campus. The college was damaged so extensively that it had to close for a time.[4]

for the college library and set about rearranging the college. He revised the grammar school, put finances in order, and began raising funds. The school, which was dedicated to educating Presbyterian ministers, now began to implement lectures, increase mathematics study, improve the teaching of science, and instruct students in French and history, as well as government, politics, and international law.

Witherspoon served as minister in the Princeton church. As problems with Britain began to increase, Witherspoon had great political influence As Moses Coit Tyler says in his *Literary History of the American Revolution:* "He seems to have come at the right moment, to the right place, in the right way."

Witherspoon was greatly criticized for his friendship with Patriot leaders:

> "He is as high a son of liberty as any man in America," John Adams wrote of Witherspoon in his diary... "After prayers the President attended us to the balcony of the college, where we have a prospect of an horizon of about eighty miles diameter." The doctor visited the Massachusetts men at their lodgings and took "a dish of coffee. He is one of the committee of correspondence, and was upon the Provincial Congress for Appointing delegates from this Province to

❧ Public Service ❧

1745–1757	**Presbyterian minister at Beith, Scotland**
1745–1746	**Took part in the Highlander's revolt in support of the Bonnie Prince Charlie and was captured by the British**
1757–1768	**Presbyterian pastor at Paisley, Scotland**
1768–1794	**President of the College of New Jersey (now Princeton University)**
1776	**Member of the New Jersey provincial congress that imprisoned Governor William Franklin**
1776	**Member of the state constitutional convention**
1776–1782	**Delegate from New Jersey to the Continental Congress; signed the Declaration of Independence and the Articles of Confederation**
1789	**Moderator of the first General Assembly of the Presbyterian Church in the United States**

Owing to a sort of nervous dizziness, he kept his Oratory well under restraint, but his eloquence was described as having made blood "shiver along the arteries." His religious devotions were constant in all his life and he was a firm believer in family prayer. Excepting Washington, he is said to have possessed more "presence" than any other man of his time.[5]

the General Congress." On Sunday, Adams reported, "Heard Dr. Witherspoon all day; a clear, sensible preacher."[14]

On May 17, declared a day of Fasting by Congress, Witherspoon delivered at Princeton a sermon on "The Dominion of Providence over the Passions of Men." For the Colonies to depend on the legislature of Great Britain would be, he said, "injury to the master, and ruin to the slave...If on account of their distance and ignorance of our situation, they could not conduct their own quarrel with propriety for one year, how can they give direction and vigour to every department of our civil constitutions, from age to age? There are fixed bounds to every human thing. When the branches of a tree grow very large and weighty, they fall off from the trunk. The sharpest sword will not pierce when it cannot reach. And there is a certain distance from the seat of government where an attempt to rule will either produce tyranny and helpless subjection, or provoke resistance and effect a separation." Dedicated to John Hancock, this sermon was published in America. It was reprinted in Glasgow, with notes denouncing him [the author] as a rebel and traitor. [15]

John Witherspoon and Richard Stockton were both elected delegates to the Continental Congress in June of 1776. They arrived in time to hear the debate over independence between John Adams and John Dickinson. When it was remarked that the colonies were "not yet ripe for a declaration of independence," Witherspoon is said to have declared, "In my judgment, sir, we are not only ripe,

but rotting." Witherspoon affixed his signature to the Declaration on August 2, having declared,

Although these gray hairs must soon descend into the sepulcher, I would infinitely rather that they should descend thither by the hand of the public executioner than desert at this crisis the sacred cause of my country.[16]

At this time Witherspoon shared lodgings in Philadelphia with two other New Jersey Signers, Abraham Clark and John Hart. Clark wrote from that city to Colonel Dayton: 'As to my Title — I know not yet whether it will be honourable or dishonourable, the issue of the War must Settle it — Perhaps our Congress will be Exalted on a high Gallows...Dr. Witherspoon Mr. Hart and my Self quarter together...P.S. You'll please to Accept this on Plain Paper, our dignity don't afford Gilt, and our pay scarcely any.

As the British invaders approached Princeton in November, 1776, President Witherspoon announced on the twenty-ninth that the college could no longer continue in peace, and classes were suspended. Work was not resumed until August, 1777. On December 2, 1776, General Washington hurried through the town and the British arrived five days later, billeting

One of Dr. Witherspoon's early biographers said: "It was a distinguished feature in the American Revolution that religious feeling was closely connected with political action." Although he was only in this country a little less than eight years before independence was declared, this man of God stood up to be counted as an American not long after his arrival — proud and unafraid, he signed the Declaration on oath, on August 2, 1776, risking irretrievably his cherished literary possessions, his honor and his standing in the Church to establish the American Republic under God.[6]

*I*t was his constant advice to young preach-ers, never to enter the pulpit without the most careful preparation; and it was his ambition, and his hope, to render the sacred ministry, the most learned, as well as the most pious and exemplary body of men in the republic. His known punctual-ity and exactness were most sacredly observed in the devotional exercises of the Christian life: be-sides the daily devotions of the closet, and the fam-ily, it was his established practice to observe the last day of every year, with his family, as a day of fasting, humiliation, and prayer; and he was also accustomed to set apart days for secret fasting and prayer, as occasion suggested. He maintained that family religion, and the careful discharge of relative duties, were an excellent incentive to the growth of religion in a man's own soul.

"How," said he, "can any person bend his knees in prayer every day with his family, without its be-ing a powerful restraint upon him from the indul-gence of any sin which is visible to them? Will such a one, think you, dare to indulge himself in anger, or choose to be seen by them, when he comes home staggering with drunkenness, unfit to perform any duty, or ready to sin still more by the manner of performance? But besides being a restraint from gross crimes, I cannot help saying, that speaking of the things of God with the concern of a parent, or the humanity of a master, must give a solemnity of spirit, and a sense of their moment, even greater than before.

"Let me, therefore, earnestly recommend the faith-ful discharge and careful management of family duties, as you regard the glory of God, the interest of his church, the advantage of your posterity, and your own final acceptance in the day of judgment."
7

themselves in Nassau Hall and in most of the houses. They were driven out by Washington at the Battle of Princeton, on January 3, 1777.

Thomas Nelson, Jr., wrote to Jefferson about the damage wrought by the enemy: "Old Witherspoon has not escap't their fury. They have burnt his Library. It grieves him much that he has lost his controversial Tracts." Also bring-ing grief to the Patriot minister was the damage done to the college he had worked so hard to build up. The library of two thousand books was scattered and the Rittenhouse orrery or planetarium was broken up.[17]

During the war, Witherspoon served on the provincial Congress that wrote a constitution for the state of New Jer-sey, and was one of the most influential members of Con-gress. He served on the board of war, and on a secret com-mittee that managed foreign relations.

When his colleague and friend, Richard Stockton, was captured and subjected to unusually cruel punishment, With-erspoon is believed to have authored the following resolution of Congress that declared:

While the shadow of hope remained that our enemies could be taught by our example, to respect those laws which are held sacred among civilized nations, and to comply with the dictates of a religion which they pre-tend, in common with us, to believe and revere, they have been left to the influence of that religion and that example. But since their incorrigible dispositions cannot be touched by kindness and compassion, it becomes our duty, by other means, to vindicate the rights of human-ity — We, therefore, the congress of the United States of America, do solemnly declare and proclaim, that if our enemies presume to execute their threats, or persist in their present career of barbarity, we will take such exem-plary vengeance as shall deter others from a like conduct.

*W*itherspoon published several books of Gospel sermons, and played major roles in two American editions of the Bible, including one from 1791, considered to be America's first family Bible."[8]

We appeal to that God who searcheth the hearts of men, for the rectitude of our intentions; and in his holy presence declare, that as we are not moved by any light and hasty suggestions of anger or revenge, so, through every possible change of fortune, we will adhere to this our determination.[18]

During this time Witherspoon wrote many papers and proclamations for prayer and fasting on days appointed by Congress. When he retired from Congress in 1782, Dr. Witherspoon gave himself to the task of rebuilding the college, although Princeton didn't recover from the war's disastrous effects during his lifetime. Nassau Hall had been used by American troops during the war. The British had burned his personal library and the college's 2,000 books were scattered everywhere. In May 1789, he was moderator of the American General Assembly; his wife died that year. Less than two years later he married Mrs. Ann Dill, a widow. They had two daughters.

Returning from a trip to England to attempt to raise funds for Princeton, Dr. Witherspoon was thrown against the side of the ship in a severe storm, causing injury to one eye. Later, the other eye was bruised when he was thrown by a horse while riding over land he had purchased in Vermont.

Consequently, Dr. Witherspoon was blind the last two years of his life, although he still enjoyed the outdoors and gardening at his farm, "Tusculum." Blindness did not prevent him from preaching. Aided by the guiding hand of another, he would ascend the pulpit and preach with all

Residence of John Witherspoon
Mercer County, New Jersey

the fervor of his youth and witness his listeners responding to the message of life in Jesus Christ.

He died on November 15, 1794, at 73 years of age at his home and was buried in the president's lot at Princeton. Thus ended his long and useful life, which had influenced so greatly the establishment of this new country.

John Witherspoon urged:

I entreat you in the most earnest manner to believe in Jesus Christ, for "there is no salvation in any other." [Acts 4:12] …If you are not reconciled to God through Jesus Christ, if you are not clothed with the spotless robe of His righteousness, you must forever perish.[9]

Questions for Discussion

1. Did Witherspoon lay aside his ministry and call to preach the gospel while serving his country?

2. What do we know about his incredible memory?

3. Why did he always wear his clerical robes to Congress? How did this reflect his reverent posture before God and dedication to promulgate the Gospel?

4. Give evidence that God used Witherspoon's persuasiveness to influence others.

5. What personal sacrifices did Witherspoon make regarding his family and possessions?

6. What spiritual disciplines did Witherspoon and his family practice?

7. What was his constant advice to young preachers?

8. What character qualities do we see exemplified in his personal life?

9. How did he describe family disciplines as being a safeguard in one's personal life?

10. What do we know of his life as a young boy?

11. How did he train his mind?

12. At what age was he licensed to preach?

13. What persuasive writing attracted the notice of Rev. Samuel Davies and led to his invitation to become president of the College of New Jersey?

14. What does Benjamin Rush attest of the manner in which Witherspoon delivered God's Word?

15. What character is reflected in Witherspoon's being willing to personally sacrifice to move to America?

16. What evidence do we have of Witherspoon being a visionary?

17. How does Tyler attest to Witherspoon's being used by God to influence men and nations?

18. What does Adams say of Witherspoon?

Pennsylvania

George Clymer
Benjamin Franklin
Robert Morris
John Morton
George Ross
Benjamin Rush
James Smith
George Taylor
James Wilson

George Clymer

Honorable Patriot

Proverbs 29:23

"My dearest wish is for my country to become independent"

✿✿

BORN
March 16, 1739

BIRTHPLACE
Philadelphia, Pennsylvania

EDUCATION
Tutored by his great-uncle

OCCUPATION
Merchant

MARRIED
Elizabeth Meredith

CHILDREN
9

AGE AT SIGNING
31

DIED
January 24, 1813; age 73

An extremely honest man, Clymer always spoke the truth and kept his word, even when it might have profited him not to do so. "He who justly estimates the value of a punctual promise," he said, "will not, without very good reason, disregard it, whether it be to sign a contract or walk with a friend; to pay a debt, or present a toy to a child."[1]

Born on March 16, 1739, in Philadelphia, George Clymer was orphaned at the age of seven. He was raised by his mother's uncle, a successful merchant named William Coleman, who instilled in the boy a love for reading. He taught the boy at home, making use of his extensive library, and later sent him to the College of Philadelphia, where, upon graduation, Clymer became an apprentice to his uncle.

> He was well versed in history, but his mind entertained, from the earliest period, a strong bias towards politics and agriculture, as those branches of science which he supposed would more materially conduce to the happiness and prosperity of his country, to the promotion of which his mind was undeviatingly directed.[6]

When Clymer was 26 years old, he married Elizabeth Meredith and entered into a partnership with her father as a merchant. George and Elizabeth had nine children, four of whom died as infants.

While yet a young man, General Washington had occasion to visit Philadelphia, where he was an entire stranger. Happening at the public house where Washington lodged, Mr. Meredith [Clymer's father-in-law] observed him, inquired his name, and finding him to be a stranger in the place, invited him to the hospitalities of his house, and kindly insisted upon his continuance with his family while he remained in the city. This accidental acquaintance led to a friendship of many years continuance, and at Mr. Meredith's, Washington ever after made it his home when he visited Philadelphia.[7]

Clymer was a zealous participant in meetings in Philadelphia for the patriots' cause following the Stamp Act. He became a captain in the militia to prepare for the colonies' defense and persuaded Philadelphia merchants to refuse to sell British tea. He served on the Committee of Safety, Pennsylvania's unofficial patriotic governing body. He was elected to go to the First Continental Congress in 1775, and diligently worked to raise money for the support of George Washington's troops who were then besieging Boston. Clymer exchanged all his personal funds for Continental currency and persuaded many wealthy friends to do the same.

In 1776, when two of Pennsylvania's delegates to Congress declined voting for independence and withdrew, George Clymer and Benjamin Rush were appointed to fill their seats. Clymer had said it was "his dearest wish" to sign the Declaration of Independence, and he did so on August 2, 1776.

When British troops marched into New Jersey and threatened Philadelphia in December 1776, Congress fled to Baltimore leaving Clymer, Robert Morris and George Walton with unusual powers to conduct and execute important business of the government since the rest of the ruling body had fled.

FROM CLYMER'S WRITINGS:

Mere swearing in conversation is nothing but powder without ball.

A habit must be a practice, but a practice may not be a habit.

The bow loses its spring, that is always bent; and the mind will never do much, unless it sometimes does nothing.

Some men's minds are like looking glasses; for having no images or impressions of their own, they can but reflect those of other people.

It is a hard condition of society where a man's duties seem to lie one way, and his reason another.

Some people may be compared to sieves, so fully does every thing they hear pass through them; but, unlike common sieves, they sift larger instead of smaller.

To make a lawyer, a subtle understanding is required; to make a legislator, a great mind.

A printer publishes a lie; for which he ought to stand in the pillory. The people believe in the lie and act upon it; and "the voice of the people is the voice of God"— and so the saying ends in blasphemy. It is less difficult to impose upon a whole million than upon one of the million: you can attempt the one only by something like sense; but the million are always to be moved by sound.

Old clothes have so far the advantage of old wit, that they may be used at second hand.

Politeness is more ceremonious; has a constant respect for your opinions; contradicts with the utmost deference; and gives place to you upon all occasions.

Good breeding is ever guarded in its address, and discreetly keeps free from subjects that might be in the slightest degree unwelcome.

The civil man may be of gross manners, without either politeness or good breeding. The polite man may not fall upon any of the common topics of civility, and may stumble upon things which good breeding avoids. The well-bred man is of a higher order: the former two are made by disposition; —he, by sense; he must be polite, but may not run too much upon civilities.[5]

Clymer served on both the Board of War and the Board of the Treasury, working tirelessly to raise support for the Continental Army.

At this period, the family of Mr. Clymer resided in Chester County, twenty-five miles distant from Philadelphia; but so strictly did he devote his time to the objects of his appointment, that when he paid them a visit, he left the city late in the afternoon, and returned in the morning.[8]

Due to Washington's victories in New Jersey, Congress returned to Philadelphia in March, 1777. Clymer requested a leave of absence two months later to recover his health from the great stresses he'd been under while performing his duties.

In July, he was appointed to investigate a report from General Washington, that "this Army was [to] be disbanded" this unless provision could be sent for the men.

When Clymer and the other members of the committee visited Washington's headquarters at Morristown, N.J., they were told by the commander-in-chief that "our soldiers have scarcely tasted any kind of vegetables" since Congress had changed the regulations applying to the Army's commissary department. Clymer reported back to Congress the necessary steps that had to be taken to insure the delivery of more food to the hungry soldiers.[9]

In September of 1777, the British capture of Philadelphia brought further hardship to Clymer. His home was in Chester County, outside Philadelphia, right in the path of the British march. His family managed to escape, but British sympathizers pointed out his house to British troops, "and the British soldiers sacked the house, destroyed the furniture, and wasted every sort of property which they could find."[4] They also surrounded the house of his aunt with intent to destroy it, but spared it when informed it didn't belong to him after all.

In 1778, Clymer was sent to endeavor to negotiate with the Indians in western Pennsylvania, who, inspired and financed by the British, were involved in massacres around Fort Pitt (now Pittsburgh). It was a difficult mission, as shown by a letter he wrote from Pittsburgh:

Many a melancholy moment have I had in reflecting that I was at so great a distance from those so dear to me: I do not, indeed, repent my coming here, because I have been in the discharge of my duty, although, after all, little good, I believe, will proceed from it. If others

⚭ Public Service ⚭

1775–1776	Served as one of the first Continental treasurers for the United Colonies
1776–1777	Delegate to the Continental Congress from Pennsylvania; signed the Declaration of Independence
1780–1782	Member of Congress of Confederation from Pennsylvania
1784–1788	Representative in Pennsylvania state legislature
1787	Delegate to Constitutional Convention; signed United States Constitution
1789–1791	U.S. representative from Pennsylvania; first United States Congress
1791–1794	Chief U.S. collector in Pennsylvania for excise tax on alcoholic beverages during period of Whiskey Rebellion
1795–1796	Member of commission appointed by President Washington that negotiated a peace treaty with Creek Indians in Georgia

had shown the same readiness, there would possibly have been a very different scene of things from the present. The Indians have broke out again, and about sixty miles from hence, have done considerable mischief, and there is no present remedy to apply, — the inhabitants being too spiritless or too sullen to assemble to oppose them.[10]

He nonetheless persisted in his duties.

While Mr. Clymer resided in Pittsburgh, he experienced a narrow escape from the tomahawk of the enemy. He was riding to the house of general Neville, situated at some distance from the town. There was a division in the road, both branches of which led to his place of destination, but his good fortune prevailing, he selected that which conducted him in safety to it; for on the same day, and at the same period of it, a white man was murdered by an Indian on the road which Mr. Clymer had rejected.[11]

He was thanked by Congress for his efforts in this dangerous mission.

In the autumn of 1780, he was elected to Congress for the third time. During that year, he worked with Robert Morris to establish a bank in Philadelphia to help alleviate the financial problems resulting from the war. He was also sent by Congress to tour the southern states to attempt to obtain financial aid in the war effort.

On his return, Clymer's term in Congress ended and with the war being nearly over, he decided he must turn his attention to his family that he'd neglected while so involved in public service. He moved to Princeton, New Jersey to allow his sons to attend the College of New Jersey.

Robert Morris persuaded him to return to Philadelphia in 1784 to oppose a group in the state government that was determined to destroy the Bank of America that Clymer and Morris had worked so hard to establish. He was elected to the state legislature again, and finally they were successful in renewing the bank's charter. He also worked to revise the state's penal code to end harsh treatment of criminals.

Clymer was chosen as a delegate to attend the Constitutional Congress of 1787.

> He particularly opposed a plan that was submitted by which the Senate would have been given the power to appoint all federal officials; and he joined Roger Sherman in holding out against the use of the word "slaves" in the Constitution, because he felt that the term was too degrading to use in a document intended to stand the test of time. When the Constitution finally was approved by the Convention, Clymer signed it with the other delegates from Pennsylvania.[12]

> It was a saying of Mr. Clymer's that "a representative of the people is appointed to think for and not with his constituents," and it is his duty to sacrifice his repose, his pleasures, his satisfactions, to theirs; and, above all, ever, and in all cases, to prefer their interest to his own. But his unbiased opinion, his mature judgment, his enlightened conscience, he ought not to sacrifice to you, to any man, or to any set of men living. These he does not derive from your pleasure; no, more from the law nor the constitution. They are a trust from Providence, for the abuse of which he is deeply answerable. Your representative owes you not his industry only, but his judgment; and he betrays, instead of serving, you, if he sacrifices it to your opinion.[13]

Clymer was chosen as one of Pennsylvania's U.S. Representatives in 1788. Upon completion of his term, George Washington appointed him chief collector in Pennsylvania for the excise tax on alcoholic beverages. Thomas Jefferson's Anti-Federalist Party strongly opposed it as an unfair tax, akin to those levied by the British. The Anti-Federalist farmers were in open rebellion to Clymer's attempts to collect the tax. Finally, President Washington called an army of 12,000 troops to squelch the Whiskey Rebellion in 1794. Clymer, in addition to suffering much abuse as chief tax collector, also lost a son who had joined the militia and was killed in one of the skirmishes.

In 1795, President Washington again asked for Clymer's assistance to work to bring peace with the Indian settlers in Georgia. Clymer took his wife, who was still grieving over the loss of their son, with him on the sea voyage to Georgia. Clymer sympathized with the Indians when he found settlers taking land without paying for it. He writes on June 30, 1796:

Residence of George Clymer
Philadelphia, Pennsylvania

> Our treaty was finished yesterday at noon, and the last signing is just published by our cannon. I am sure it is an honest treaty, for it was negotiated without artifice or threats; it is honest because it will greatly benefit each of the contracting parties; it is honest because it is protested against the Georgia Commissioners, who found all the customary avenues to the Indian lands barred by the principles we had laid down in conducting it.[14]

In his remaining years of life, he was elected President of the Philadelphia Bank, president of the Academy of Fine Arts, and Vice President of Philadelphia Agricultural Society.

Clymer died at age 74 on January 23, 1813, at the home of one of his sons in Morrisville, Pennsylvania. Joseph Hopkinson, son of signer Francis Hopkinson, said in his eulogy of Clymer:

> In this most useful virtue, Mr. Clymer was preeminent. During the seven years he held the presidency of this academy, his attention to the duties of the station were without remission. He excused himself from nothing that belonged to his office; he neglected nothing. He never once omitted to attend a meeting of the

directors, unless prevented by sickness or absence from the city; and these exceptions were of very rare occurrence. He was indeed the first to come; so that the board never waited a moment for their president. With other public bodies to which he was attached, I understand, he observed the same punctual and conscientious discharge of his duty. It is thus that men make themselves useful, and evince that they do not occupy places of this kind merely as empty and undeserved compliments, but for the purpose of rendering all the services which the place requires of them.[15]

Though he was given so little formal education as a boy, he was the man who proposed and helped organize the Pennsylvania Academy because he felt that his province should have a college. He also helped to organize the Pennsylvania Hospital, the first fire insurance company, the first voyage — or one of the first voyages — for Arctic exploration.[16]

Questions for Discussion

1. What did Clymer say about the value of a punctual promise?

2. What wonderful character trait was observed in Clymer regarding his words about others?

3. What was Clymer's dearest wish?

4. What do Clymer's sayings reveal about his character?

5. What was William Coleman able to instill in Clymer that served him his entire life?

6. What character trait did Clymer's father-in-law show to George Washington before he even knew who he was? What was the lifelong result of it?

7. What character trait did Clymer display in the political arena?

8. How did Clymer both use persuasiveness and set a good example in influencing others regarding their finances?

9. What unusual responsibility was assigned to Clymer and Robert Morris?

10. What character trait did Clymer demonstrate on the Board of War & Treasury? What was his responsibility on that board?

11. What quality did Clymer demonstrate regarding his appointments with others?

12. What character quality did Clymer demonstrate when he got the report of the plight of the soldiers?

13. What happened to Clymer's house and property?

14. Tell of Clymer's duties with the Indians. Although an act of God's Providence, what character trait did Clymer demonstrate in his narrow escape from the Indians?

15. What character trait would induce Clymer to relocate his family to obtain an education for his sons?

16. How did Clymer view his duty as a representative of the people?

17. Tell about Clymer's difficulties as tax collector.

18. What character trait was reflected in the treaty with the Indians?

19. Look up the quality "honorable" and tell why Clymer fits the description.

20. Purpose to live a life of honor and to honor others with your words. Think of a specific thing you could hope to do now or in the future to help achieve this goal.

Benjamin Franklin

Productive Patriot

Proverbs 10:4

"The Father of Our First Excellent Constitution"

❧❧

BORN
Boston, Massachusetts

EDUCATION
Self-taught

OCCUPATION
Printer, Statesman, Scientist

MARRIED
Deborah Read

CHILDREN
3

AGE AT SIGNING
70

DIED
April 17, 1790; age 84

He spent almost a third of his life representing America in the courts of Europe; there, he won France's crucial aid in the Revolutionary War with a treaty of alliance, and he negotiated the peace treaty that forced Great Britain to recognize American independence. Thomas Jefferson lauded him as "the greatest man and ornament of the age and country in which he lived."[1]

Born in Boston on January 17, 1706, Ben Franklin was the youngest son in a family of 17 children. His father, a staunch Puritan, wished to prepare Ben for the ministry, but couldn't afford to send him to school beyond the time he learned to read and write.

Benjamin was, of course, the favorite nephew of the English uncle for whom he had been named. Eight years older than his brother in Boston, the lonely uncle, who had lost his wife and all nine children, began to write letters in verse to his nephew Benjamin when the child was only four years old. At seven, the boy was writing verses in answer. Two years later, Uncle Benjamin came to visit the Boston Franklins, and he was much pleased with his namesake, for there was something about young Benjamin that usually drew marked attention from older men. Perhaps it was because he learned so easily and grasped ideas so quickly — more easily than the average child of his years. He could read at a very early age.[14]

At the age of ten, Ben went to work in his father's shop making soap and candles. When he was twelve years old, his father apprenticed him to his older brother, James, to learn the printing trade.

An example of Benjamin's early wisdom was his recognition of the value of his own time. He liked people — if they were not boring — and made friends easily. He liked certain games and boating; he was an expert swimmer. But he never had any use for loafing around taverns, drinking, or gambling. At fifteen, he couldn't get enough time to read. With any money he could save he bought books, and when he finished these books, he sold them to buy others. He read history, travel, fiction, science, and biography — Plutarch's Lives, essays by Defoe, Cotton Mather, and Locke. By himself, he now mastered the arithmetic he had failed a few years before. He read to learn, not just to pass the time. He studied prose style, argument, and discussion. When he came upon a volume of The Spectator, *he was delighted. This, he decided, was a style he wished to emulate; and he went about it cleverly, choosing one essay for study, jotting down the hints contained in each sentence, then rewriting it himself to compare his own work with the original.²*

The youth also educated himself, reading every book that he could borrow or buy from his small wages.¹⁵

Ben used to write articles for the newspaper which he signed, "Mrs. Silence Do Good" and slipped under the door of his brother's print shop, knowing James would not print them if he knew Ben had written them. They became very popular and well read.

Wanting a little money to buy books (we must remember that there were no public libraries), he conceived

the idea of asking his brother to give him half the money that his board cost and let him feed himself. Then he saved money by not eating meat. He found he could save half of the amount his brother paid him by making a meal of a biscuit or a slice of bread and some raisins. This gave him three advantages: he could have his light snacks alone in the office while the others went out for their meals and thereby have time to study; he discovered that he had a clearer head after one of his light meals than after a hearty one; he had more money to buy books and so feed his hunger for knowledge.¹⁶

When James was arrested because of criticisms from Massachusetts authorities, Ben, then 16, carried on the business in his absence. James had a strong temper and would mistreat Ben and the other apprentices. Ben sold his small collection of books and bought passage on a ship to New York, unwilling to stay with his brother any longer.

Unable to find work in New York City, he ventured to Philadelphia, arriving in October, 1723.

In his *Autobiography* written many years later, Franklin described how he walked from New Jersey to Philadelphia. He bought three loaves of bread for a Sunday morning breakfast, walked about town, met his future wife, Deborah Read, and eventually went to sleep in a Quaker meeting. He soon found work as a printer's helper, and moved into the house of his future wife as a boarder.¹⁷

When Benjamin was a boy, Josiah Franklin had often repeated to his son a proverb of Solomon: "Seest thou a man diligent in his calling, he shall stand before kings…" The son wrote in his autobiography, "I from thence considered industry as a means of obtaining wealth and distinction, which encouraged me…"⁵

Benjamin arrived in the Quaker City on a sunny September morning, tired, hungry, and dirty. The first thing he needed was food. Inquiring of a passing boy who was carrying bread, he learned where to find the baker. Unaware of the differences in the price of bread between Boston and Philadelphia, he simply asked for three pennyworth and was surprised to be given "three great puffy" rolls. With one under each arm while nibbling the third, he walked on up the street. As he passed a house where a young girl was standing at the door, she watched him go by, amused because he looked "most awkward" and ridiculous. He found this out some years later when this same girl, Deborah Read, became his wife.¹³

By this time Benjamin Franklin had grown to be a well-built, vigorous young man, about five-feet nine or ten inches tall, with a large head (which accommodated a good brain), and strong, deft hands. His hair was light brown, his eyes gray, and his regard steady and honest. His unfailing sense of humor was revealed by a humorous mouth and easy smile. He could be quick and prompt to act, but his speech was hesitant and slow. He was at his best in small groups of chosen friends in the clubs he formed, or others which he joined.[18]

The Governor of Pennsylvania took an interest in Ben and suggested to Ben's father that he set him up in business as a printer. When his father declined, Governor Keith suggested Ben go to London to buy printing equipment with letters of credit Keith promised to send ahead. Ben asked Deborah to marry him, promising to return, and sailed for England, only to find upon his arrival that Governor Keith hadn't sent the letters of credit. He had to go to work as a printer's helper and began to make many friends.

> Unfortunately he was thrown in the way of some distinguished infidels while he was in London, (among whom was Lord Mandeville,) and received flattering attentions from them. His mind became tinctured with their views, and he was induced to write a pamphlet upon deistical metaphysics, a performance which he afterward regretted, and candidly condemned.[19] Franklin received an offer from a merchant friend, Thomas Denham, on business in London, to return to America, as his clerk. With plenty of time for reflection during the long voyage, Benjamin drew up a plan for his future conduct in life. His first aim, he decided, was to be extremely frugal, pay his debts and save money "for some time."

Second, he must:

> endeavor to speak truth in every instance, to give nobody expectations that are not likely to be answered, but aim at sincerity in every word and action; the most amiable excellence in a rational being.

Third, he must apply himself industriously:

THE HOUSE IN WHICH BENJ. FRANKLIN WAS BORN
Milk Street House, Boston

The house in which Bemjamin Franklin was born
Milk Street House, Boston

> to whatever business I take in hand, and not divert my mind from my business by any foolish project of growing suddenly rich; for industry and patience are the surest means of plenty.

Fourth, he decided:

> to speak ill of no man whatever, not even in a matter of truth; but rather by some means excuse the faults I hear charged upon others, and upon proper occasions speak all the good I know of everybody. In his autobiography, the old Franklin wrote that he followed these resolutions, on the whole, "quite through to old age."[20]

His situation looked promising until Mr. Denham died a short time later and Franklin resorted to life as a journeyman with his former employer. He also had found that Deborah, having not heard from Ben but once during his long absence, had married another man.

Ben formed a partnership with another printer to start their own printing firm in Philadelphia where his character and talents won him public confidence, and he soon had a successful business. In 1730, Deborah Read's husband died and she and Ben married. They had two children, a son who died as an infant, and a daughter. They also raised William, his son from a previous relationship.

❧ Public Service ☙

1729	Began publishing the newspaper *The Pennsylvania Gazette*
1731	Founded the first subscription library, the Library Company of Philadelphia
1733–1758	Published *Poor Richard's Almanac*
1736–1751	Clerk of the Pennsylvania colonial legislature
1737–1753	Deputy postmaster of Philadelphia
1744–1754	Representative in the Pennsylvania colonial legislature
1740	Invented the Franklin stove
1747	Discovered positive and negative electricity
1749	Invented the lightning rod
1749	Helped found the Academy of Philadelphia (later the University of Pennsylvania)
1752	Used a kite to prove that lightning is electricity
1753–1774	Deputy postmaster general of the American colonies
1753	Received honorary masters degrees from Harvard and Yale
1754	Represented Pennsylvania in the Albany Congress; wrote the Albany Plan of Union for the colonies
1757–1762	Represented the Pennsylvania colonial legislature in London
1762	Awarded honorary degree of doctor of civil law by Oxford University
1763	Made a 1,600-mile tour of the American colonies inspecting post offices
1764–1775	Represented Pennsylvania, Georgia, New Jersey, and Massachusetts in London
1775	Appointed postmaster general by the Continental Congress
1775–1776	Member of the Pennsylvania Committee of Safety; delegate from Pennsylvania to the Continental Congress; signed the Declaration of Independence
1776	President of the Pennsylvania state constitutional convention
1776–1785	Represented the Continental Congress in Paris; negotiated and signed the treaty of alliance with France in 1778; negotiated and signed the treaty of peace with Great Britain in 1783
1785–1788	President of the State of Pennsylvania
1787	Delegate from Pennsylvania to the Constitutional Convention; signed the United States Constitution
1788	Elected president of the first antislavery society in the United States

*Benjamin Franklin had a goal. While still young, he had considered the kind of man he wanted to be. He felt he must refine his taste constantly, and this led him to copy the literary masters. Like most adolescents, he loved to take part in serious discussion, but after reading Plato's accounts of Socrates, he "gave up the disputatious habits" he had formed when engaged in discussion, and assumed a manner more persuasive, agreeable, and modest in argument. Aiming constantly to improve his mind, he also considered his manners. All these were useful and most desirable achievements for a boy who was to become in later life his country's ablest diplomat.*³

Franklin set up shop in a part of his house where his wife helped in selling books and stationery. Franklin began to write *Poor Richard's Almanac* in December, 1732. This sold 10,000 copies in a year — a huge volume for that time. It was full of thoughtful proverbs and witty sayings such as:

"God helps them that help themselves."
"A penny saved is a penny earned."
"He's a fool that makes a doctor his heir."
"Early to bed and early to rise, makes a man healthy, wealthy and wise."
"Men and melons are hard to know."
"He that can have patience can have what he will."
"The family of fools is ancient."
"The rotten apple spoils his companions."

Franklin conceived the idea of a lending library, worked out the details with friends and The Library Company was formed and is still operating in Philadelphia today.

In December, 1736, Franklin formed the town's first volunteer fire department and established "City Watch," providing better police protection. He served as clerk of the Pennsylvania Assembly, and postmaster for Philadelphia.

By the ago of 40, through diligence, planning, and working six days a week, Franklin had attained great wealth, but instead of indulging in leisure time, he turned to experimentation. He invented the "Franklin rod" — the lightning rod. One writer says that Franklin "found electricity a curiosity and left it a science."²¹

In June 1752 Ben and his son William performed a famous but risky experiment. They flew a kite in a storm. Lightning hit the kite and zoomed down the string to a key, where it ignited a spark. This proved that lightning was electricity. Another time, while riding through Maryland, Ben and William spotted a tornado and galloped toward it, backing away only when tree branches nearly hit them. Ben's observations provided people with a better understanding of tornadoes. "What good is science that does not apply to some use?" Ben once asked. He invented many devices to help people.²²

In 1740, he invented the Franklin stove to conserve fuel and heat homes efficiently.

Franklin's inquiring mind led him to make countless other scientific discoveries in the course of his life. He discovered that ocean waves could be calmed by pouring oil on the water. He invented bifocal glasses for reading. Franklin did not patent any of his inventions or discoveries, feeling that his best reward would be their widespread use by mankind.²³

To scientific men…he appeared to be a master; and though he had never attended college, both Harvard and Yale gave him the honorary degree of Master of Arts.²⁴

*In November, 1726, Benjamin Franklin composed his Articles of Belief and Acts of Religion, to serve as his creed and private religious service. In the Petition, asking for help in many ways, he prays —"That I may be preserved from atheism and infidelity, impiety and profaneness…and in my address, O to Thee carefully avoid irreverence and ostentation, formality and odious hypocrisy, Help me, O Father! That I may be loyal to my prince and faithful to my country, careful for its good, valiant in its defence, and obedient to its laws, abhorring treason as much as tyranny, Help me, O Father!"*⁷

BENJAMIN DESCRIBES DEBORAH, HIS WIFE, AS FOLLOWS:

"As much dispos'd to industry and frugality as myself. She assisted me cheerfully in my business…We kept no idle servants, our table was plain and simple." But one day he found his breakfast of bread and milk served in a china bowl, with a spoon of silver, instead of the accustomed two penny earthen porringer and pewter spoon. Deborah thought that her husband deserved these marks of luxury as well as any of his neighbors![8]

At 42 years of age, Franklin turned the management of the printing house over to his partner, David Hall. The firm continued to bring them steady income for many years. Franklin was elected delegate from Pennsylvania to attend a Congress to determine how the seven northern colonies could best protect themselves from attack when the French and Indian Wars broke out in 1754. The British sent General Braddock and two British regiments to America. Franklin was assigned the job of aiding Braddock in securing horses, wagons and supplies for a march on French Fort Duquesne (now Pittsburgh); Franklin gave a large part of his personal fortune to obtain the supplies. Franklin and George Washington both warned Braddock to be careful of ambush attacks, but Braddock ignored the warnings and was ambushed and fatally wounded. Franklin began organizing western defenses using colonial forces, and was elected colonel of a militia company.

Franklin represented the Pennsylvania legislature in London from 1757 until 1762. Upon his return in 1762, he was greeted as a hero, and the next year went on a tour

On meeting Franklin at dinner, Abigail Adams, wife of John Adams, wrote: "I thought I could read in his countenance the virtues of his hearts; among which patriotism shone in its full luster, and with that is blended every virtue of a Christian: for a true patriot must be a religious man."[9]

of the American colonies inspecting post offices in his position of deputy postmaster. He was then commissioned to raise troops to defend western Pennsylvania from Indian attacks.

Franklin was again in London about the time of the declaration of the Stamp Act. Franklin misjudged the response from the colonies, recommending a close friend as tax collector, and ordering stamps delivered to his printing firm in Philadelphia. His wife informed him of the response of the colonies; she had to arm herself to defend their house! Franklin began working to have the Stamp Act repealed, appearing before the Parliament to answer 174 questions which helped to give the British legislators a clear picture of the feelings of the colonists. Franklin was considered responsible for the repeal of the Stamp Act, and his reputation at home was restored.

In 1749, Franklin authored the famous piece entitled, "Proposals Relating to the Education of Youth in Pennsylvania," in which he discussed the content of the academic curriculum of the State's new university, noting that in its history classes: "History will…afford frequent opportunities of showing the necessity of a public religion from its usefulness to the public [and] the advantage of a religious character among private persons…and the excellency of the Christian religion above all others, ancient or modern."[11]

Franklin worked tirelessly to persuade British government leaders to reconsider the measures they were taking against the colonies. Franklin was in an awkward position. He had to remain on friendly terms with the British in order to influence them, but that caused suspicion to some in the colonies. Franklin published his views on "the bumbling course" the British government was taking as well as letters written by Thomas Hutchinson, governor of Massachusetts. As a result, the British government dismissed him as postmaster general of the American colonies. When the British government closed Boston Harbor in response to the Boston Tea Party, Ben Franklin offered to pay for the tea that had been destroyed from his own

Pennsylvania

ONE MERCHANT OBSERVED:

For the industry of that Franklin is superior to any thing I ever saw of the kind; I see him still at work when I go home from the club, and he is at work again before his neighbors are out of bed.[4]

pocket if Parliament repealed the order. When they refused, Franklin, realizing war was likely, set sail for home on March 21, 1775.

Upon arriving home, Franklin heard of the uprising at Lexington and Concord. He was elected as delegate to the Continental Congress and became a member of the Committee of Safety. The Continental Congress appointed him as postmaster general. He wrote a Plan of Union which he submitted to Congress, and it later became the basis for the Articles of Confederation. Franklin was seventy years old when he signed the Declaration of Independence, the oldest of all the signers.

The story is told that at the signing ceremony, John Hancock, the president of the Continental Congress, remarked: "We must be unanimous; there must be no pulling different ways; we must all hang together." To this, Franklin is said to have quipped, "Yes, we must indeed all hang together, or most assuredly we shall all hang separately."[25]

The following autumn he was sent to France to get help in funding soldiers and arms.

Before setting sail in October, Franklin, as a demonstration of his loyalty, turned over his entire fortune of 3,000 to 4,000 pounds to the Congress for its use in fighting the war.[26]

It was a perilous voyage. Had the American-armed sloop *Reprisal*, on which he traveled, been captured, Franklin would surely have been hanged for high treason, or perhaps beheaded. Yet the indomitable traveler took two grandsons with him: Temple Franklin, almost seventeen, the son of Franklin's Tory son,

William, and seven-year-old Benjamin F. Bache, the son of Franklin's daughter Sally.[27]

The French greeted Franklin with open arms and much enthusiasm.

Having lived thirty years in the society of scientists, scholars, politicians, clergymen, merchants and men of fashion, Dr. Franklin was no backwoods philosopher…He could speak French, though not always correctly. But he retained his simple dress — almost Quakerish, though he was not a Quaker. The French were charmed to see the stocky figure in the long brown coat, wearing the fur cap he had brought along to keep his head warm on the cold November voyage. His spectacles were the only ones to be seen in Paris. His long hair, straight and gray, was a contrast to the powdered wigs of fashion. The very plainness of his appearance made him conspicuous in a Parisian salon of Louis XIV's reign, when men dressed in lace-trimmed silks and satins of all colors. The Parisians regarded him as a kind of hero, "a combination of Voltaire and Rousseau, in a plain American package." Soon it became the fashion to have a medal or an engraving of his likeness on every French mantelpiece. He wrote his daughter Sally that his portrait was appearing on the lids of snuffboxes, even tiny ones in the finger-rings "and the numbers sold are incredible." These and other busts and prints "have made your father's face as well known as that of the moon," he told her. [28]

At first Franklin thought his efforts were in vain, but when the French heard of the American defeat of British general Burgoyne at Saratoga, New York in October of 1777, negotiations were bolstered. On February 6, 1778, Franklin signed a treaty of alliance with France.

The British, alarmed at the aid France was offering, endeavored to negotiate a peace treaty that did not include a guarantee of independence, and Franklin replied: "I never think of your ministry and their abettors, but with the image strongly painted in my view, of their hands red, and dripping with the blood of my countrymen, friends and relations: *No peace can be signed with those hands.*"[29]

When Washington, with France's aid, defeated the British, Franklin and other peace commissioners signed a peace treaty on September 3, 1783.

152

After the age of seventy, Benjamin Franklin had decided that he wanted to get younger, so he had begun counting backward with each new birthday. By the usual counting system he was eighty-four, but by his own method he was only fifty-six years old when he died in 1790![10]

It was on this occasion, that Doctor Franklin again put on a suit of clothes which ten years before, on the occasion of his being insulted before the English Privy Council, he declared he would never wear again until he had "signed England's degradation and America's independence." [30]

Franklin spent the next two years in Paris enjoying the respect and admiration as a representative of America. He wrote to Washington:

How happy should I be to see you in Europe, to accompany you, if my age and strength would permit, in visiting some of its ancient and famous kingdoms. You would on this side of the sea enjoy the great reputation you have acquired, free from those shades that the jealousy and envy of a man's countrymen and contemporaries are ever endeavouring to cast upon living merit. Here you would know and enjoy what posterity will say of Washington; for a thousand leagues have nearly the same effect as a thousand years. The feeble voice of those groveling passions cannot extend so far in time or distance. At present I enjoy that pleasure for you, as I frequently hear the old generals of this martial country, who study the maps of America, and mark upon them all your operations, speak with sincere approbation and great applause of your conduct, and join in giving you the character of one of the greatest captains of your age. [31]

Thomas Jefferson arrived to relieve Franklin of his duties, as he was 80 years old by that time.

Jefferson wrote: "There appeared to me more respect and veneration attached to the character of Dr. Franklin, in France, than to that of any other person in the same country, foreigner or native." [32]

Franklin was greeted at home in Philadelphia by bells, bonfires, and artillery salutes.

Dr. Franklin's landing was announced by a boom of cannon at the Market Street wharf — the very wharf where, as a runaway from Boston, he had first set foot in the city fifty years before. Bells rang as he moved up the four blocks to Franklin Court, his house which the British had plundered, where his daughter and grandchildren, those he had never seen, now lived. [33]

He was elected to succeed John Dickinson as president of the state of Pennsylvania, an office he held until 1788. He now, finally, was able to enjoy being at home after relentlessly working for freedom.

As he described it: "I am now in the bosom of my family, and find four new little prattlers, who cling about the knees of their grandpapa, and afford me great pleasure. I am surrounded by my friends, and have an affectionate, good daughter and son-in-law to take care of me. I have got into my *niche,* a very good house which I built twenty-four years ago, and out of which I have been ever since kept by foreign employments." [34]

His work on drafting the U.S. Constitution was invaluable. He was the oldest man to sign the Constitution, and he was called the "father of our free and excellent constitution."

Whilst the last members were signing, Doctor Franklin looking towards the President's chair, at the back of which a rising sun happened to be painted, observed to a few members near him, that painters had found it difficult to distinguish in their art, a rising, from a setting, sun. "I have," said he, "often and often, in the course of the sessions, and the vicissitudes of my hopes and fears as to its issue, looked at that behind the President, without being able to tell whether it was rising or setting; but now at length, I have the happiness to know, that it is a rising, and not a setting sun." [35]

Even though he'd been absent for almost 30 years in Europe, Franklin returned to find his estate had more than tripled in value since the war. As payment for his

After all, Benjamin Franklin not only drafted a statewide prayer proclamation for his own State of Pennsylvania but he also recommended Christianity in the State's public schools and worked to raise church attendance in the state. He also desired to start a colony in Ohio with the Rev. George Whitefield to "facilitate the introduction of pure religion among the heathen" in order to show the Indians "a better sample of Christians than they commonly see in our Indian traders." He enthused, "In such an enterprise I could spend the remainder of life with pleasure, and I firmly believe God would bless us with success."[6]

services in Europe, he was given an estate of 3,000 acres in Georgia, in addition to a large portion of land on the Ohio River, and several properties in Philadelphia he already owned. He now enjoyed designing gardens with gravel walks, building houses, and planting flowering shrubs on his estates.

His old ailment — gout, or "the stone'" as he called it, flared up again and he had to take aspirin for the pain, which caused a loss of appetite. He wrote to his sister, describing himself: "little remains of me but a skeleton covered with skin."[36]

He had to be carried through the streets in a specially designed chair he'd created, carried by four poles. The last years of his life were spent mostly in his bedroom. Pain did not dim, however, his cheerfulness and wit, or memory. He continued to work some, composed the inscription for the corner stone of the Library Company's new building, and listened to recitations by his nine-year-old granddaughter Deborah, of her next day's lesson from

Having emerged from poverty and obscurity in which I was born and bred, to a state of affluence and some degree of reputation in the world. . . with the blessing of God. . .[12]

Webster's spelling book. He never stopped writing delightful letters.

Ezra Stiles, the president of Yale and an old friend to Franklin wrote to him concerned about his welfare and asked him of his relationship with Jesus Christ. This is Franklin's reply, a letter written on March 9, 1790, just a little more than a month before Franklin's death:

Reverend and dear Sir,

You desire to know something of my Religion. It is the first time I have been questioned upon it. But I cannot take your Curiosity amiss, and shall endeavour in a few Words to gratify it. Here is my Creed. I believe in one God, Creator of the Universe. That he governs it by his Providence. That he ought to be worshipped. That the most acceptable Service we render to him is doing good to his other Children. That the soul of Man is immortal, and will be treated with Justice in another Life respecting its Conduct is this. These I take to be fundamental Principles of all sound Religion, and I regard them as you do in whatever Sect I meet with them.

As to Jesus of Nazareth, my Opinion of whom you particularly desire, I think the System of Morals and his Religion, as he left them to us, the best the World ever saw or is likely to see: but I apprehend it has received various corrupting Changes, and I have, with most of the present Dissenters in England, some Doubts as to his Divinity: tho' it is a question I do not dogmatize upon, having never studied it, and think it needless to busy myself with it now, when I expect soon an Opportunity of knowing the Truth with less Trouble. I see no harm, however, in its being believed, if that Belief has the good Consequence, as probably it has, of making his Doctrines more respected and better observed; especially as I do not perceive, that the Supreme takes it amiss, by distinguishing the Unbelievers in his Government of the World with any peculiar Marks of his Displeasure.

I shall only add, respecting myself, that, having experienced the Goodness of that Being in conducting me prosperously thro' a long life, I have no doubt of its Continuance of meriting such Goodness. My Sentiments on this Head you will see in the Copy of an old Letter enclosed, which I wrote in answer to one from a zealous Religionist, whom I relieved in a paralytic case by electricity, and who, being afraid I should grow proud upon it, sent me his serious though rather impertinent Caution. I send you also this Copy of another Letter, which will shew something of my Disposition relating to Religion. With great and sincere Esteem and Affection, I am, Your obliged old Friend and most obedient humble servant.

B. Franklin[37]

Jefferson stopped by to visit Franklin on his return from France and found him in bed. He called him the "venerable and beloved Franklin." Franklin wrote his last letter to Jefferson nine days before his death, which occurred on April 17, 1790, at the age of 84. Franklin's life had touched many. James Madison moved that the House of Representatives wear mourning for one month.

In his will he designated himself: "I, Benjamin Franklin, Printer, late Minister Plenipotentiary from the United States to the COURT OF France, now President of Pennsylvania." He never forgot what he owed to his trade. As an indentured printer's apprentice, little did he think that he "should ever literally *stand before kings.*" He continues with satisfaction to point out that this has since happened, for he has "stood before *five.*"[38]

Near the close of his life he told a friend: "Death is as necessary to the constitution as sleep; we shall rise refreshed in the morning. The course of nature must soon put a period to my present mode of existence. This I shall submit to with the less regret, as having seen, during a long life, a good deal of this world, I feel a growing curiosity to become acquainted with some other; and can cheerfully, with filial confidence, resign my spirit to the conduct of that great and good

Parent of mankind, who created it, and who has so graciously protected and preserved me from my birth to the present hour."[39]

He is buried next to his wife, Deborah, in Christ Church cemetery in Philadelphia.

In the early part of his life, he acknowledged himself to have been skeptical in religion, but he became in maturer years, according to the testimony of his intimate friend, Dr. William Smith, a believer in divine revelation. The following extract from his memoirs, written by himself, deserves to be recorded: "And here let me with all humility acknowledge, that to Divine Providence I am indebted for the felicity I have hitherto enjoyed. It is that power alone which has furnished me with the means I have employed, and that has crowned them with success. My faith in this respect leads me to hope, though I cannot count upon it, that the divine goodness will still be exercised towards me, either by prolonging the duration of my happiness to the close of life, or by giving me fortitude to support any melancholy reverse which may happen to me as well as to many others. My future fortune is unknown but to Him, in whose hand is our destiny, and who can make our very afflictions subservient to our benefit.[40]

This is his epitaph, which he wrote himself:

The body of BENJAMIN FRANKLIN, PRINTER,

Like the cover of an old book, its contents torn out, and stript of its lettering and guilding, lies here food for worms; Yet the work itself shall not be lost, For it will (as he believed) appear once more in a new and more beautiful edition, Corrected and amended by the Author.[41]

Questions for Discussion

1. How did Franklin feel about the use of time? What quality does this reflect?

2. What quality is reflected by how Franklin found time to read as a young man?

3. What achievements did he accomplish as a boy that prepared him to be a diplomat?

4. Tell the report of his industry as related by a neighbor.

5. How did the Scripture regarding industry, learned as a boy, influence Franklin for life?

6. For what was Franklin responsible that promoted the spread of Christianity?

7. What was Franklin's own personal creed and prayer?

8. How did Franklin promote Christian education?

9. Tell about Franklin's self-education.

10. What were Ben's first literary works?

11. What quality is seen in Ben's proposal to his brother which enabled him to buy books?

12. What were the resolutions for life Franklin drew up on his voyage to London as a young man?

13. Tell what character qualities are revealed in some of Franklin's sayings from *Poor Richard's Almanac.*

14. Tell how he started the first library.

15. Tell what community offices Franklin served in and those which he created.

16. From what qualities did Franklin attain great wealth by the time he was 40?

17. List some of Franklin's inventions.

18. What were Franklin's duties in the French & Indian War?

19. What quality did he demonstrate to fulfill his duties?

20. How was Franklin considered responsible for the repeal of the Stamp Act?

21. Why was Franklin dismissed from the position of Postmaster General?

❧ Questions for Discussion ❧

22. What quality did Franklin display in his negotiations with the British over the Boston Tea Party?

23. What did Franklin say at the time of the signing of the Declaration? What quality is reflected in his statement?

24. What demonstration do we know of generosity to the Patriot cause?

25. What quality made Franklin willing to risk the trip to France to attempt to get funding?

26. What was the French people's response to Franklin's arrival?

27. At what turning point did the French agree to help the Americans?

28. What was Franklin's response to the British "peace treaty" that didn't guarantee independence?

29. Tell the story of Franklin's suit of clothes he wore to sign the peace treaty in 1783.

30. What was Thomas Jefferson's observation of the French people's admiration of Franklin?

31. How did the American people welcome Franklin home?

32. What further services did Franklin perform after his return home?

33. Tell of Franklin's account of the rising sun on the chair.

34. What was the state of Franklin's finances upon his return home from Europe at the end of the war?

36. What was Franklin's belief in God? How do we know he had a respect for things of God? What did he believe about Jesus Christ?

37. What did he choose to be his epitaph?

38. Look up the quality "productive." Tell how this epitomizes Mr. Franklin's life.

39. What would be a specific way you can be more productive this week? Check on each other's progress at the end of the week.

35. What character quality characterized his final days?

Robert Morris

Benevolent Patriot

Luke 6:38,
Proverbs 11:25

"The Financier of the
Revolution"

BORN
January 31, 1734

BIRTHPLACE
Liverpool, England

EDUCATION
Common schools

OCCUPATION
Merchant

MARRIED
Mary White, 1769

CHILDREN
7

AGE AT SIGNING
42

DIED
May 8, 1806; age 87

When he entered business life at fifteen, Robert Morris was a tall, strong boy with a round fair face under a thatch of sandy red hair. Good-humored, with a pleasant personality, he was also a diligent and conscientious worker, whose industry, integrity, and common sense won him the high respect of his employers.[2]

Robert Morris was born in Liverpool, England, on January 31, 1734. His father, a rich merchant, moved to America and established himself in the tobacco trade in Oxford, Maryland, when Robert was only four years old. He sent for Robert to join him in America when Robert was thirteen years old. After traveling by himself to the colonies, he began studying under a tutor. After a year, Robert wrote to his father telling him that he had learned all the tutor could teach him. Before he was able to respond, his father was accidentally killed by a cannon shot celebrating the arrival of one of his ships.

Robert became an apprentice clerk to Charles Willing, one of Philadelphia's leading merchants. Through diligence in his assigned tasks, Robert soon earned the respect of his employer.

Once, while Mr. Willing was away, Robert learned that the price of flour was about to skyrocket. The teenage clerk bought up all the flour he could find in the Philadelphia area. The price of flour rose sharply the next day, netting large profits for the Willing company.[1]

At the age of 20, Robert was offered a partnership in the firm which became known as Willing, Morris & Co. (The other partner was

Thomas Willing, the owner's son.) During one of the voyages he made to the firm's ships, Morris was captured by the French.

> The brig on which he was traveling was captured by French privateers, who robbed the passengers of everything. But Morris, the captain, and the American crew escaped and managed to reach the shore of Cuba. Here they wandered through fields and forests, half-starved, until they finally reached Havana, a city ruined by the French three years before.
>
> They had saved their lives, but they had lost their money and baggage and were stranded. One day Morris, seeing a man trying unsuccessfully to make his watch run, suggested that he might be able to repair it. He did, and this first customer not only paid the stranded American boy, but sent him other customers who wanted repair work done. In this way, Morris managed to buy food and necessities until an American vessel arrived and took him home.[3]

By the time of the American Revolution, Willing, Morris & Co. had prospered greatly and was a leading mercantile enterprise in Philadelphia. The partnership lasted 39 years, until 1793.

> Prosperous though they were, however, the merchants and ship-owners were soon to find themselves in serious trouble. After the French and Indian war (1754-1763), the British government, in an effort to "regulate trade," began to pass laws that seriously hampered colonial businessmen. At first these laws may have been mere emergency measures, but the British government found these so-called "regulatory acts" so profitable that they were kept permanently. Most annoying of all was the law that required ships returning home with cargoes from Europe and Africa to stop in an English port on the way. This roundabout route meant needlessly long voyages, cost time and money, and encouraged smuggling to escape English import duties. Customs officials, knowing that smuggling was going on, began annoying investigations of merchants and shipping, and British naval vessels began prowling about to enforce the revenue acts.[4]

Though the firm of Willing, Morris & Co., with its huge foreign shipments, remained above reproach, all this governmental interference made trouble for them. Any financial or other business difficulty worried the senior partner, Willing, a timorous man who became very gloomy and pessimistic at such times. But Robert Morris rose to meet these problems with such optimism and determination that, as time went on, Willing, with ever-increasing trust, began to place greater responsibilities upon his partner. The two were great friends as well as partners. Finally, when Willing was elected Mayor of Philadelphia in 1763 at the end of the French and Indian War, Morris took over management of the business alone and remained the active head for almost twenty years.

When Parliament passed the Stamp Act, twenty-nine-year-old Morris took part in a meeting in Davenport's Tavern at which four hundred Philadelphia merchants, including Willing, Morris & Co., signed the Non-Importation Resolutions. Though this was a serious blow to their business, it seemed a patriotic duty to resist British encroachments on American rights. The next year Morris entered public life as Warden of the Port of Philadelphia.

An eligible young bachelor, a wealthy and successful merchant, a dashing man-about-town, Morris was invited everywhere. The most elegant social events were the Assembly dances, managed by Willing for some years, to which only Philadelphia's elect were invited. When thirty-five-year-old Robert Morris met the charming nineteen-year-old Mary White at one of these balls, his bachelor days were soon to end. Though he had no "family," he had achieved a position in society by his own ability and personal charm. Mary's father consented, and the wedding took place in Christ Church under crystal chandeliers sparkling with candles.

> Mary Morris was to prove her husband's greatest blessing, the perfect partner. She was the gracious hostess for Robert Morris's generous hospitality in their fine house on Front Street, facing the river in Philadelphia, and later at "The Hills," their three-hundred-acre estate overlooking the Schuylkill River, eight miles from Lancaster, Pennsylvania. Here, in the years to come, they would entertain the most important Americans and Frenchmen of revolutionary times, General Washington and the Marquis de Lafayette among them.[5]

The couple were to have seven children, five sons and two daughters.

In early summer of 1774, Paul Revere rode to Philadelphia with news of the closing of the Port of Boston and the quartering of British troops that had been imposed on Boston's citizens. Businessmen in Philadelphia, showing support of Bostonians, closed their business on June 1, and flew flags at half mast. The bells of Christ Church tolled in mourning of freedom.

On June 18, Thomas Willing presided over a meeting in the Philadelphia State House where a resolution was passed declaring the Boston Port Act unconstitutional and that the cause of Massachusetts was a cause common to all the colonies. A Continental Congress was called, as members from the Committees of Correspondence dispersed riders in all directions from colony to colony.

In September 1774, the First Continental Congress met at City Tavern in Philadelphia and walked to Carpenter's Hall to begin deliberation. The colonies ordered "meatless days" and for infantry artillery and cavalry units to be formed and trained. Benjamin Franklin served as President and Robert Morris as Vice President, and they met each morning at 6:00 AM.

> Their tasks were heavy. They must devise plans for the fortification of the Delaware river, which still lay open to attack, organize militia, issue bills of credit, purchase arms and ammunition, create defenses for the city and port of Philadelphia, and raise funds. And who could know better than Morris, long-experienced businessman and ship-owner, how to manage all these practical matters? [6]

Morris' diligence in his labors for defense led to his appointment to the Second Continental Congress in November of 1775. He was given the task of finding two sailing vessels to carry dispatches and also placed on a committee for naval armaments. He was on the committee that gave instructions to Silas Deane, American envoy to France and also served on the "Ways and Means" committee to help raise funds and fortify seaports.

Willing, Morris & Co. imported supplies for the army and sometimes did banking for the Congress, charging commissions for their services. Enemies accused Morris of "conflict of interests," but John Adams, well acquainted with him, declared that Morris "no doubt pursues

> *Herculean was this task, in the existing derangement of the American finances, he entered upon it with courage, and if not completely successful, certainly did more than could have been supposed practicable with the means placed in his hands. Incited by a penetrating and indefatigable mind, and supported by the confidence which his probity and punctuality, through the various grades of commercial results, had established, he discarded, in this threatening conjuncture, considerations applying forcibly to his own reputation, and devoted his entire attention to the resuscitation of public credit. Promulgating his determination to meet every engagement with punctuality, he was sought with eagerness by all who had the means of supplying the public wants.*
>
> *The scene suddenly changed: faithfully performing his promise, the public deficiencies began to disappear, and military operations no longer were necessary means. Strong in his personal credit, and true to his engagements, the superintendent became every day stronger in the public confidence, and unassisted, except by a small loan of six million of livres tournois, granted by the court of Versailles to the United States, this individual citizen gave food and motion to the main army; proving by his conduct, that credit is the offspring of integrity, economy, system, and punctuality.[8]*

mercantile ends, but thought him an excellent Member of our Body, a man with an honest Heart."[7]

On July 1 of 1776, Morris was not in favor of independence:

> He considered the vote premature. Benjamin Rush later explained Morris's stand. Morris, he wrote, "was opposed to the *time* (not to the *act*) of the Declaration of Independence, but he yielded to no man in his exertions to support it, and a year after it took place he publickly acknowledged on the floor of Congress that he had been mistaken in his former opinion as to its

Such was the instrumentality of Robert Morris, in the victory of Trenton; and it may truly be remarked, that although his own house was unadorned with the laurels of the warrior, it was his hand which crowned the heroes who triumphed on that day.[9]

time, and said that it would have been better for our country if it had been declared sooner."[10]

Morris had no hesitancy in signing the Declaration the next month, and he always worked for the American cause, living his belief that it was "the duty of every individual to act his part in whatever station his country may call him to in hours of difficulty, danger and distress. This, he said, was the only thing a gentleman could do."[11]

During the winter of 1777, when Congress was slow in supplying food and money for the army, it was to Robert Morris that George Washington appealed, and not in vain. He told Morris he was considering an offensive move, but without increased financial assistance could not do it. On Christmas night, when Washington crossed the Delaware and captured over 1,000 Hessian soldiers, it was Robert Morris working day and night who raised funds to pay the soldiers and to purchase food, clothing, and ammunition. This was Morris' reply to General Washington:

> I am up very early this morning to dispatch a supply of $50,000 to your Excellency… but it will not be got away so early as I could wish, for none concerned in this movement except myself are up.…if further occasional supplies of money are necessary, you may depend on my exertions either in a public or private capacity.[12]

George Washington never forgot how he relied on the financier.

The story is told that Morris was walking home from his counting house with Washington's problem on his mind when he met a wealthy Quaker friend who asked him what news there was. "The most important news,"

Public Service

1754–1793	Partner of Thomas Willing as a Philadelphia merchant
1775	Appointed member of Pennsylvania's committee of safety
1775–1778	Delegate from Pennsylvania to the Continental Congress; signed the Declaration of Independence and the Articles of Confederation
1779–1780	Member of the Pennsylvania legislature
1781–1784	Superintendent of finance and agent of marine for the Congress of the Confederation
1781	Founded the Bank of America at Philadelphia
1785–1786	Member of the Pennsylvania legislature
1786	Delegate of Pennsylvania to the Annapolis Convention
1787	Member of Pennsylvania delegation to the Constitutional Convention; signed the United States Constitution
1789–1795	United States senator from Pennsylvania

Morris is said to have replied, "is that I require a certain sum in specie, and that you must let me have it. Your security is to be my note and my honour." The friend replied, "Robert, thou shalt have it."[13] The money from this loan is said to have been used by Washington in winning his important surprise victory over the Hessian soldiers on the day after Christmas, 1776.

Morris labored hard and long on the Committee of Commerce and Committee of Finance. When the British occupied Philadelphia in the fall of 1777 and Congress had to move, Morris stayed in the city with British General Howe's permission. He sent Mrs. Morris with the children to Maryland to stay with her step-sister Mrs. Hall.

> "Having got my family and books removed to a place of safety," he wrote, "my mind is more at ease, and my time is now given up to the public, although I have many thousand pounds worth of effects here without any prospect of saving them."[14]

> *Robert Morris said: "Religion is the only solid basis of good morals; therefore, education should teach the precepts of religion and the duties of man towards God."*[15]

His estate was partially destroyed at the hand of the British. Richard Peters, a member of the congressional board of war, described an incident by which Morris secured a much needed supply of lead for bullets:

> In 1779 or 1780, two of the most distressing years of the war, General Washington wrote to me a most alarming account of the prostrate condition of the military stores, and enjoined my immediate exertions to supply the deficiencies. There were no musket-cartridges but those in the men's boxes, and they were wet; of course, if attacked, a retreat, or a rout, was inevitable. We (the board of war) had exhausted all the lead accessible to us, having caused even the spouts of houses to be melted, and had offered, abortively, the equivalent in paper of two shillings specie per pound for lead. I went, in the evening of the day on which I received this letter, to a splendid entertainment, given by Don Juan Mirailles, the Spanish minister. My heart was sad, but I had the faculty of brightening my countenance, even under gloomy disasters; yet it seems then not sufficiently adroitly. Mr. Morris, who was one of the guests, and knew me well, discovered some casual traits of depression. He accosted me in his usual blunt manner: "I see some clouds passing across the sunny countenance you assume; what is the matter?" After some hesitation, I showed him the general's letter which I had brought from the office, with the intention of placing it at home in a private cabinet. He played with my anxiety, which he did not relieve for some time. At length, however, with great and sincere delight, he called me aside, and told me that the Holkar privateer had just arrived at his wharf, with ninety tons of lead, which she had brought as ballast. It had been landed at Martinique, and stone ballast had supplied its place; but this had been put on shore, and the lead again taken in. "You shall have my half of this fortunate supply; there are the owners of the other half" (indicating gentlemen in the apartment). "Yes, but I am already under heavy personal engagements, as guarantee for the department, to those, and other gentlemen." "Well," rejoined Mr. Morris, "they will take your assumption with my guarantee." I, instantly, on these terms, secured the lead, left the entertainment, sent for the proper officers, and set more than one hundred people to work, during the night. Before morning, a supply of cartridges was ready, and sent off to the army. I could relate many more such occurrences.[17]

The year 1780 saw the American cause at its lowest point. Credit was gone; paper money was not worth the cost of printing it. The condition of the army was deplorable. Congress, having exhausted its own resources, failed to meet the soldiers' needs and now turned to Robert Morris, whom they appointed Superintendent of Finance. On his shoulders was placed the responsibility for America's finances.

> *Amidst his severest trials, he maintained a firmness and an independence of character, which in similar circumstances might belong to but few.*[16]

Instead of having magazines filled with provisions, we have a scanty pittance scattered here and there in the several states: Instead of having the various articles of field equipage ready to deliver, the quarter-master-general is but now applying to the several states to provide these things for their troops respectively: Instead of having a regular system of transportation established upon credit, or funds in the quartermaster's hand to defray the contingent expenses of it, we have neither the one nor the other; and all that business, or a great part of it, being done by military impressment, we are daily and hourly oppressing the people, souring their tempers, and alienating their affections: Instead of having the regiments completed to the new establishments, scarce any state in the union has, at this hour, one eighth part of its quota in the field; and there is little prospect that I can see, of ever getting more than one half. In a word, instead of having every thing in readiness to take to the field, we have nothing; and, instead of having the prospect of a glorious offensive campaign before us, we have a bewildered and gloomy prospect of a defensive one unless we should receive a powerful aid of ships, land troops, and money, from our generous allies and these at present are too contingent to build upon.[18]

The job before Morris was almost impossible. God had prospered this man to shoulder the weight of an entire country. His appointment served as a boost of encouragement to many, as he sought to pull the country out of its financial doldrums.

The necessary supplies of every thing required for the important and decisive enterprise, were chiefly furnished by means of Mr. Morris' credit, to an immense amount, and Mr. Peters superintended their provision and preparation. From seventy to eighty battering cannon, and one hundred pieces of field artillery, were completely fitted and furnished, with ammunition, although, on the return of the committee to Philadelphia, there was not a field-carriage put together, and but a small quantity of fixed ammunition in the magazines: the train was progressively sent on in three or four weeks, to the great honour of the officers and men employed in that meritorious service. All this, together with the expense of provision for, and pay of the troops, was accomplished on the personal credit of Robert Morris, who issued his notes to the amount of ONE MILLION FOUR HUNDRED THOUSAND DOLLARS, which were finally all paid.[19]

His own salary was only $6,000 a year and of his own private fortune he had given two million: one million alone for the Yorktown campaign, and half a million for mustering out the army.

Often, when the credit of the nation was almost gone, it was Robert Morris's signature alone — which stood for business integrity, stability, and commercial honor — that made it possible to borrow money for the public cause.[20]

In concluding a circular letter to the governors of the several states, dated the nineteenth of October, 1781, he makes the following feeling and eloquent remarks: "By the bounty of the Almighty, we are placed in a situation where our future fate depends upon our present conduct."[21]

Typical of the actions that he immediately embarked upon was a letter that he wrote to a New Jersey merchant on May 29, 1781, in which he said:

It seems that General Washington is now in the utmost necessity for some immediate supplies of flour, and I must either undertake to procure them, or the laws of necessity must be put in force (a threat to seize the provisions), which I shall ever study to avoid and prevent. I must therefore request that you will immediately use your best skill, judgment, and industry in purchasing, on the lowest terms you can, one thousand barrels of sweet, sound flour, and in sending it forward to camp in the most expeditious and least expensive manner that you can contrive. To obtain this flour readily and on good terms, I know you must pledge your private credit, and as I have not the money ready, although the means of raising it are in my power, I must also pledge myself to you, which I do most solemnly, as an officer of the public; but lest you should, like some others, believe more in private than

In accepting the office bestowed on me [superintendent of finance], I sacrifice much of my interest, my ease, my domestic enjoyments, and internal tranquility. If I know my own heart, I make these sacrifices with a disinterested view to the service of my country. I am ready to go still further; and the United States may command every thing I have, except my integrity, and the loss of that would effectually disable me from serving them more.[22]

in public credit, I hereby pledge myself to pay you the cost and charges of this flour in hard money. I will enable you most honourably to fulfill your engagements. My character, utility, and the public good, are much more deeply concerned in doing so than yours is.[23]

In August, 1781, Morris met with Washington at his headquarters to discuss a proposed attack against the British forces in New York City. He was there when Washington received the disappointing news that the French fleet would be unable to aid in the attack on New York, and instead planned to put into Chesapeake Bay. Washington then devised the plan to attack Cornwallis in Virginia; and Morris agreed to support the campaign with his personal credit. In the next several weeks he issued notes of more than a million dollars for the purchase of guns, ammunition,

On the twentieth of September, 1781, he makes the ensuing observations to the President of Pennsylvania, which serve to convey some idea of the invaluable services, and disinterested sacrifices of Robert Morris: "The late movements of the army have so entirely drained me of money, that I have been obliged to pledge my personal credit very deeply, in a variety of instances, besides borrowing money from my friends, and advancing, to promote the public service, every shilling of my own."[24]

and supplies. He also negotiated a $200,000 loan of hard money from the French. Washington made Morris' Philadelphia home his headquarters in September when his troops marched through the capital on the way to Yorktown and the victory that in effect concluded the Revolutionary War.[25]

Morris succeeded in establishing the Bank of North America, which acted as a lending agent to the new government. In October 1782, he wrote, pleading to the states:

It is a mighty fashionable thing to declaim on the virtue and sufferings of the army, and it is a very common thing for those very declaimers to evade, by one artifice or another, the payment of those taxes which alone can remove every source of complaint. Now, sir, it is a matter of perfect indifference by what subterfuge this evasion is effected, whether by voting against taxes, or, what is more usual, agreeing to them in the first instance, but taking care, in the second, to provide no competent means to compel a collection; which cunning device leaves the army at last, as a kind of pensionary upon the voluntary contributions of good whigs, and suffers those of a different complexion to skulk and screen themselves entirely from the weight and inconvenience... my credit has already been on the brink of ruin; if that goes, all is gone.[27]

Robert Morris, financier of the American Revolution, pledged his personal credit to the Republic, making possible the Yorktown Campaign in 1781, which ended the military operations of the war with the surrender of Lord Cornwallis.[26]

In the meantime the exertions of the financier were unremitting. He addressed a circular letter to the most influential men in the country, appealing to their characters and zeal, for their support, and requesting them in the most earnest manner to urge their friends and fellow citizens to become proprietors of the bank stock:

Robert Morris' mansion
S.E 6th and Market Street, Philadelphia

"Every subscriber," he observed, "will find his own interest benefited in proportion to the capital he deposits, and at the same time they will have the satisfaction to be considered, for ever, as the promoters of an institution that has been found beneficial to other countries, and inevitably must be so, in the highest degree, to this; — an institution that most probably will continue as long as the United States, and that will probably become as useful to commerce and agriculture, in the days of peace, as it must be to government during the war.

"I ask you to devote some of your time to promote this infant plan; which, as it gathers strength, may in the end prove the means of saving the liberties, lives, and property, of the virtuous part of America." [28]

In January, 1783, Morris wrote a letter of resignation to Congress, stating that as an honest man, he could no longer constantly pile up debt on which efforts were not being made to repay. He wrote to General Nathaniel Greene:

I felt the consequences of my resignation on public credit; I felt the probably derangement of our affairs; I felt the difficulties my successor would have to encounter; but still I felt, above all things, that it was my duty to be honest. This first and highest principle has been obeyed. I do not hold myself answerable for consequences. These are to be attributed to the opposers of just measures, let their rank and station be what it may. I expect much

obloquy for my conduct, because this is what I know to be the reward for any conduct whatever, which is right. To the slander I am indifferent, and still more indifferent about the attempts to question the services I have rendered. [29]

Congress, however, persuaded him to stay on through 1783 and most of 1784, until the army was paid and demobilized. The states, during this time, made little effort to pay their obligations to the national treasury, and America's credit fell to zero in European countries.

Upon his resignation he wrote:

The inhabitant of a little hamlet may feel pride in the sense of separate independence. But if there be not one government, which can draw forth and direct the efforts, the combined efforts of United America, our independence is but a name, our freedom a shadow, and our dignity a dream. To you, fellow citizens, these sentiments are addressed by one who has felt their force. In descending from that eminence on which your representatives had placed him, he avoids the shafts which calumny had aimed. He has no longer, therefore, any personal interest in those jealousies and distrusts which have embarrassed his administration, and may prove your ruin. He no longer asks confidence in himself. But it is his duty to declare his sincere opinion, that if you will not repose in the members of that general federal government which you yourselves have chosen, that confidence and those powers which are necessary, you must, and you will, (in no very distant period,) become the dupes of European politics. What may be the final event, time can only discover; but the probability is, that, first divided, then governed, our children may lament, in chains, the folly of their fathers. May heaven avert these evils, and endow us with

George Washington said:

"The abilities of the present financier have done wonders." [30]

wisdom so to act, as may best promote the present and future peace, prosperity, and happiness, of our country.

On the retirement of this eminent man from office, it was affirmed by two members of the Massachusetts delegation, "that it cost Congress at the rate of 18 millions per annum, hard dollars, to carry on the war, till he was appointed financier, and then it cost them but about 4 millions.[31]

Morris served as agent of marine for the Congress for 1781-1784 and was in charge of the affairs of the Continental Navy. He was a friend of John Paul Jones whose family later presented Morris with a gold-mounted sword that John Paul Jones had received from Louis XVI of France.

Morris' expertise as financier was even recognized internationally:

A minister at the court of Versailles, in a letter to Mr. Morris, dated the twelfth of August, 1782, said, "As a financier and provider for the exigencies of the state, is much admired and praised here; its good consequence being so evident, particularly with regard to the rising credit of our country, and the value of bills."[32]

After Morris retired from the financier position, in 1784, he served in the Constitutional Convention in 1787. He declined the position of Secretary-ship of the Treasury, but did serve as Senator from 1788–1795.

Struggling to rebuild his personal finances, Morris speculated heavily in Western lands. When the Napoleonic Wars paralyzed Europe, immigration diminished and so did sale of land. He tried selling to meet costs, but was sent to debtors' prison by a small creditor.

He lost everything, including his favorite residence, The Hills on the Schuylkill River, and his town houses, and was sent to the Prune Street Jail in Philadelphia in 1798 for three years. Mary Morris, who had been a gracious hostess for years in hospitable entertaining, proved a strong support in her husband's days of poverty and disgrace. She obtained an amnesty from Holland Land Company, through Governeur Morris (no relation), which supported her and her husband in his final days.

General Washington, who had written Morris that

"My hand and heart shall be with you" on his becoming Superintendent of Finance, even came to dine with Morris late in 1798 at the "hotel with grated doors," in Prune Street.[33]

In 1799, while visiting at Winchester, Virginia, she [Mary Morris] received a letter from George and Martha Washington which said:

We hope it is unnecessary to repeat in this place how happy we should be to see you and Miss Morris under our roof for so long a stay as you shall find convenient before you return to Philadelphia, for be assured we ever have and still to retain the most affectionate regard for you, Mr. Morris, and the family.[34]

Ironically enough, while confined for debt and thereby denied a chance to earn money to pay his debts, Morris had to pay a high price for the rent of his room in prison. Courageously, he said, "A man that cannot bear and face misfortune should never run risks, but I have been too adventurous and therefore it is a duty to meet my fate with fortitude."[35]

Released at age 66, a penniless man who had sacrificed a wealthy man's fortune for the cost of freedom, he never complained or blamed his country for never repaying his fortune. He tried several times to find work to earn money, enjoyed a bit of social life with President Thomas Jefferson, and ex-President George Washington at Mount Vernon, and lived modestly in a small house on Twelfth Street, the house in which he died in May of 1806. He was buried at Christ Church graveyard in the family vault. Years later, in 1939, his will was found along with wills of six other Signers, in a forgotten vault near the furnaces in the cellar of Philadelphia City Hall.

In his last will and testament, this shrewd man left a message to "the inhabitants of the United States of America," written about the time he retired as Superintendent of Finance. In stressing the need for a sound economy, he wrote,

How soon we may be plunged into another, a longer or more expensive contest, is known only to Him from whom no secrets are hidden... The only moral

surety for peace is a state of constant preparation for hostilities. [36]

Every sacrifice that could be made, he offered up on the altar of patriotism. He abandoned the ease and enjoyments of domestic life, and devoted his time, his talents, and his fortune, to the public benefit. It may be said of him, that like the Roman Curtius, he sacrificed himself for the good of the commonwealth. He discarded all attention to his private business, and consigned it to other hands, being resolved not to mingle his own affairs with those of the public, or suffer his mind to be, for a moment, diverted from his high official duties. He never permitted himself, or his private concerns, to interfere with the business of the nation: so far, in fact, did he carry this refined idea of duty, that he inflexibly adhered to a rule which he had laid down on his installation as financier, never to recommend any individual to office. He introduced into the department, every reform which the most judicious and rigid economy could devise. His sole system of finance, was that which resulted from the plain self-evident dictates of moral honesty. Taxation and economy were the two great pillars by which that system could alone be supported; "and," said Mr. Morris, "if the states will provide the former, I will pledge myself for the latter, so far as my abilities will permit." [37]

The Americans certainly owed, and still owe, as much acknowledgement to the financial operations of Robert Morris, as to the negotiations of Franklin, or even the arms of Washington. [38]

Questions for Discussion

1. Robert Morris, in providing food and munitions to the entire army, proved by his conduct that credit is the offspring of what four character qualities?

2. List the items supplied by Robert Morris' personal finances and distributed for the army's use by Mr. Peters. What was the total cost of these provisions?

3. What was the reason Morris gave for stating that education should teach religion and the duties of man towards God?

4. As a boy, what character qualities won him the respect of his employers?

5. What did Morris say he had long since learned to sacrifice to public service? To what extent was he willing to sacrifice — all but what?

6. Define disinterested. Would you say this was a quality Morris possessed? Give a couple of examples of this in his life.

7. What did George Washington say about Robert Morris?

8. What declaration concerning his finances did Morris make on September 20, 1781?

9. What was Morris' involvement in the Yorktown Campaign?

10. What character traits were evident in Morris while stranded in Cuba?

11. With what two qualities did Morris meet problems?

12. What character qualities did Morris have which led him to support the Non-Importation Resolutions? How did this affect his own income?

13. What two qualities can be seen in Morris by the way he treated guests?

14. How had Morris been prepared to manage all the practical affairs of preparing the artillery and cavalry units?

15. How did diligence in menial tasks cause Robert to rise to positions of influence?

16. What did John Adams say of Morris' character?

17. Look up the definition of "benevolent" in the appendix and explain how it characterizes the life of Robert Morris.

18. Think of someone in need you can give to this week, with either a gift of time, money, or service.

John Morton

John Morton

Responsible Patriot

Luke 16:10

"The most glorious service that I ever rendered to my Country"

❧❧

Born
1724

Birthplace
Ridley, Pennsylvania

Education
Home educated

Occupation
Surveyor, farmer

Married
Ann Justis, 1754

Children
8

Age at Signing
52

Died
April 1777; age 53

John Morton, the first signer to die, didn't live to witness the liberty he sacrificed for. His sacrifice was in his friendships and reputation. There were many supporters of reconciliation with Great Britain living in Pennsylvania, and many of his close friends turned against him for his stand for the patriots' cause. On his death bed Morton cried out,"Tell them they will live to see the hour, when they shall acknowledge it to have been the most glorious service that I ever rendered to my country."[1]

John was born in 1724 in Ridley township near Chester, Pennsylvania. His father died before John was born. Mary, John's mother, remarried a man named John Sketchley who became very attached to young John and took it upon himself to teach and train him as if he were his own son. Sketchley was a surveyor and taught young John the trade and skill in mathematics. John Morton had no formal schooling, just the dedicated teaching of his stepfather.

> The space of three months comprehended all the advantages that John Morton ever acquired from instruction in a public school. His education was superintended and directed, at home, by Mr. Sketchley, and what he acquired from that source, was improved and expanded, through the agency of talents which ranked among the first in the county. [2]

John became a farmer and surveyor. He married Ann Justis of Delaware, and together they raised three sons and five daughters. In 1764, John received the commission of justice of the peace and also became a representative in Pennsylvania's general assembly, where he was, for quite some time, the speaker.

Morton was elected by the legislature as a member to the Stamp Act Congress which met in New York City in 1765. When the sheriff of his county died around 1766, he was elected to replace him and remained in that office for three years.

Soon after the Battle of Lexington, he was appointed as a judge of the supreme court of Pennsylvania. He was a delegate to the First Continental Congress, held in Philadelphia. He was on the committee to form and adopt a plan to obtain redress of American grievances with Great Britain.

> The meeting was awfully solemn. The object which had called them together, was of incalculable magnitude. The liberties of no less than three millions of people, with that of all their posterity, were staked on the wisdom and energy of their councils. [3]

It is interesting to read passages from a letter he wrote to Thomas Powell, a merchant in London and a friend to whom Morton felt able to speak freely. As early as June 8, 1775, Morton was writing that:

> we are really preparing for the worst that can happen, viz. a Civil War. We have nearly 2000 Troops now under Arms in this City, and very well disciplined. I suppose the Province will raise 20,000 effective Men determined to support the Noble Cause of Liberty. [4]

Congress had turned out in a body on June 8 to see soldiers drilling and Morton had been impressed by the spectacle. He pointed out that General Gage was now so closely besieged in Boston that "he cannot penetrate 500 Yards into the Country, were he supported by all the troops now in England." The letter concludes:

> You have declared the New England people Rebels, and the other Provinces Aiders and Abettors. This is putting the Halter about our Necks, and we may as well have died by the Sword as be hang'd like Rebels. This has made the People desperate. [4]

This gives an idea of the determination with which Congress was meeting its problems.

Mr. Morton was re-elected to the Second Continental Congress. In debate, John Dickinson of Pennsylvania led the opposition to a complete break with Great Britain and was supported by three other members: Robert Morris, Charles Humphreys, and Thomas Willing. On July 2, when the resolution for independence came to vote, Morris and Dickinson were absent. Willing and Humphreys opposed independence. Ben Franklin and James Wilson supported it. The deciding vote was left to John Morton. Pennsylvania had a high percentage of Quakers, who opposed any military action.

> No wonder, then, that Mr. Morton experienced the most intense anxiety of mind, when he was required to give the casting vote of the Pennsylvania delegation; a vote which would either confirm or destroy the unanimity of the Declaration of Independence; — a vote upon which hung the important decision, whether the great state of Pennsylvania should, or should not, be included in the league which bound her sister colonies together. [5]

The opportune arrival of Caesar Rodney, which secured Delaware's vote for independence, left only

❧ Public Service ❧

1756–1776	Representative in the Pennsylvania legislature; speaker of the house from 1772–1776
1765	Delegate from Pennsylvania to the Stamp Act Congress
1766–1769	Sheriff of Delaware County, Pennsylvania
1774–1777	Delegate from Pennsylvania to the Continental Congress; signed the Declaration of Independence

Pennsylvania that would cast the determining vote of unanimity.

He controlled his vote in favour of independence; but the mental anxiety which he experienced in so novel and solemn a situation, and the great responsibility which he had incurred in case the measure should be attended with disastrous results, preyed upon his peace, and is confidently said to have accelerated, if it did not cause, his dissolution.[6]

In April 1777, a violent inflammatory fever caused his death at 54 years of age. He was the first of the signers to die. He was buried in the cemetery of St. James Church in Chester, of which he was a member.

Mr. Morton was a professor of religion, and a truly excellent man. To the poor he was ever kind; and to an affectionate family, consisting of wife, three sons, and five daughters, he was an affectionate husband and father.[7]

Residence of John Morton
Delaware County, Pennsylvania

✿ Questions for Discussion ✿

1. What was John Morton's biggest sacrifice to his country?

2. What did he cry out on his death bed?

3. What caused his death? Did he live to see independence procured?

4. Tell of the dedication of John's stepfather.

5. What public offices did John hold?

6. Tell what Morton relates in his letter to Thomas Powell. Explain his view of the dilemma.

7. Tell of Morton's personal struggle to vote for independence.

8. How did many of his friends and neighbors react to his signing the Declaration of Independence?

9. Do we have any evidence that suggests Morton may have been a Christian?

George Ross

Dutiful Patriot

Romans 13:6,7

"It is the duty of every man to contribute to the welfare of his country."

❧ ❧

BORN
May 10, 1730

BIRTHPLACE
New Castle, Delaware

EDUCATION
at home

OCCUPATION
Lawyer, Jurist

MARRIED
Anne Lawler, 1751

CHILDREN
3

AGE AT SIGNING
46

DIED
July 14, 1779; age 49

A portrait of George Ross in his legal robes shows him as an attractive young man, and he is described as being handsome, good-humored, and popular."[1]

George Ross was born in New Castle, Delaware, in 1730, the son of an Episcopal minister who took much care in teaching his son well. George became proficient in Latin and Greek, and at age 18 entered the law office of his brother in Philadelphia. He was admitted to the bar at age 21. He married Anne Lawler of Lancaster; they had two sons and a daughter.

> Among his first clients was beautiful young Anne Lawler, whom he soon married. At twenty-one, with a good practice, a beautiful wife, an attractive personality, a cordial manner, a love of dining and wining among congenial companions, George Ross was on his way up.[3]

In 1768 he was elected to the Pennsylvania legislature and remained in that position until the early years of the Revolutionary War. He was a delegate to the first Constitutional Convention in 1774. There he supported John Dickinson's conservative views. He worked to raise up the militia and planned defense measures. Although he was not on the legislature to vote for independence, he was there to sign it on August 2, 1776. He served his country without monetary reward:

Resolved, that the sum of one hundred and fifty pounds, out of the county stock, be forthwith transmitted to George Ross, one of the members of assembly for this county, and one of the delegates for this colony in the continental congress; and that he be requested to accept the same, as a testimony from this county, of their sense of his attendance on the public business, to his great private loss, and of their approbation of his conduct. Resolved, that if it be more agreeable, Mr. Ross purchase with part of the said money, a genteel piece of plate, ornamented as he thinks proper, to remain with him, as a testimony of the esteem this country has for him, by reason of his patriotic conduct, in the great struggle of American liberty." Such a testimony of respect and affection, on the part of his constituents, must have been not a little gratifying to the feelings of Mr. Ross. He felt it his duty, however, to decline accepting the present, offering as an apology for so doing, that he considered it as the duty of every man, and especially of every representative of the people, to contribute, by every means within his power, to the welfare of his country, without expecting pecuniary rewards.[4]

In 1776 Ross was elected vice president to serve with Benjamin Franklin at the state Constitutional Convention. Ross played an important role in drawing up the Pennsylvania state constitution.

RES. OF GEORGE ROSS.
Lancaster Pa.

Residence of George Ross
Lancaster, Pennsylvania

⤶ Public Service ⤷

1750	Admitted to the bar to practice law in Pennsylvania
1768–1776	Member of the Pennsylvania legislature
1774	Delegate from Pennsylvania to the first Continental Congress
1776	Vice president of the Pennsylvania state Constitutional convention
1776–1777	Delegate from Pennsylvania to the Continental Congress; signed the Declaration of Independence
1779	Admiralty judge of the State of Pennsylvania

In January, 1777, he became ill with gout and retired from public office. He recovered enough by spring to accept an appointment as admiralty judge for Pennsylvania for a few months, but at the age of 49, died on July 14, 1779, in Philadelphia.

In his domestic habits he was kind, generous, beloved; in his professional career zealous and able; as a politician always active and patriotic he seems to have well deserved the praise bestowed on him by one who knew him, as honest man and upright judge.[5]

As a lawyer, even before the revolution, he was among the first of his profession, a rank which he continued to hold, while he practiced at the bar. As a politician, he was zealous, patriotic, and consistent. As a judge, he was learned and upright, and uncommonly skillful in the dispatch of business. He comprehended with ease causes of the greatest intricacy, and formed his decisions, which often displayed much legal knowledge, with great promptness. It is to be added to his honour, that while he was thus distinguished abroad, he was characterized in the fulfillment of his domestic duties, by an uncommonly kind and affectionate disposition.[2]

❧ Questions for Discussion ❧

1. How is George Ross described?

2. List his character qualities.

3. How did Ross show hospitality?

4. How did Ross help to prepare for the Revolution?

5. How did Ross show selfless duty to his country? Why did he refuse monetary payment?

6. Ross helped to write the Pennsylvania constitution. Look it up in the appendix and comment on its Christian nature.

7. Look up the word "dutiful." To what did Ross have a sense of duty?

8. Ask God to develop a respect for duty in your life. To whom or what should you feel a sense of duty?

Benjamin Rush *(signature)*

Benjamin Rush

Confident and Dedicated Patriot

Philippians 1:6

"All will end well"

❧❧

BORN
December 24, 1745
BIRTHPLACE
Byberry, Pennsylvania
EDUCATION
Princeton College, Harvard,
Edinburgh
OCCUPATION
Physician
MARRIED
Julia Stockton, 1776
CHILDREN
13
AGE AT SIGNING
30
DIED
April 19, 1813; age 67

Dr. Rush's private virtues were not eclipsed by his public virtues; he was virtuous in all aspects of his life. He had once defined integrity as a strict coincidence between thought, words, and actions, and his life epitomized that consistency — he was the paragon of integrity. As demonstrated by his remarkable achievements, Dr. Rush fulfilled the life purpose he had set for himself:"to spend, and be spent, for the good of mankind."[23]

Piety to God was an eminent trait in the character of Dr. Rush. In all his printed works, and in all his private transactions, he expressed the most profound respect and veneration for the great Eternal.[30]

Benjamin Rush was born on Christmas Eve of 1745, in Byberry Township, northeast of Philadelphia, Pennsylvania. His great-grandfather had been a cavalry officer in Oliver Cromwell's army before emigrating to Pennsylvania. Benjamin's father, a farmer, died when the boy was six years old. His mother moved to Philadelphia and opened up a grocery store to provide for Benjamin and his siblings. Intent on providing a good education for her sons, she placed Benjamin, at the age of nine, under the care of Rev. Dr. Findlay, the principal of an academy at Nottingdam, Maryland, and also his uncle.

In this retired spot, and at this early age, he is said to have been deeply impressed with a reverence for religion, with the importance of a regular life, and of diligence, industry, and a punctual attention to business; an din genera, of such steady habits, as stamped a value on his character through life. The solid foundation which was thus laid for correct principles and an upright conduct, was chiefly the work of the learned and pious Dr. Finley. He was an accomplished instructor of youth. He trained his pupils for both worlds, having respect in all his intercourse with them, to their future, as well as present state of existence.[35]

Rush then attended the College of New Jersey and graduated at the age of 14. Later, he placed himself under the celebrated Dr. Redman of Philadelphia to learn medicine for the next six years. In 1766 he went to England for two years to obtain more training in medicine. While he was there, the trustees of the College of New Jersey where his uncle was president asked Rush to try to persuade John Witherspoon, then a Presbyterian minister in Scotland, to accept the presidency of the College. Rush convinced Mrs. Witherspoon, who was fearful of Indian attacks, and was successful in the mission of getting the Witherspoons to move to America.

The story is told that during this period, when the movement toward revolt was growing in the American colonies, Rush attended a debate in which a British orator declared "if the Americans possessed cannon, they had not even a ball to fire," causing Rush to retort that "if the Americans possessed no cannon balls, they could supply the deficiency by digging up the skulls of those ancestors who had courted expatriation from the old hemisphere, under the vivid hope of enjoying more ample freedom in the new." [36]

After returning to Philadelphia in 1769, Dr. Rush treated poor people at first, often for free. [37] He later began the first free medical clinic for the poor in Philadelphia. He also became known as the Father of American Psychiatry for his work on behalf of mental illness, and he helped establish the practice of veterinary medicine to provide proper medical care for animals.

Rush married Julia Stockton, 16-year-old daughter of Robert Stockton, fellow signer, in 1776. The couple had 13 children.

Dr. Rush encouraged Thomas Paine to write *Common Sense*, (and even suggested the title), which was used to spark patriotism in many prior to the Revolution.

Rush rode on horseback to meet the Massachusetts delegates to the First Continental Convention and developed a lasting friendship with John Adams. Along with Thomas McKean and James Smith, he helped to draft a declaration for Pennsylvania urging the delegates to vote for independence. He signed the Declaration of Independence on August 2.

Dr. Rush later described the signing that took place on August 2: "Awful silence pervaded the house when we were called up, one after another, to the table of the President of Congress to subscribe (sign) what was believed by many at that time to be our own death warrants." [38]

During the war, Rush served as surgeon general in the Continental Army and was nearly captured by the British while

While attending school under his uncle, Benjamin was not only instructed in classical literature, he also acquired what was of no less importance and which characterized him through life: a habit of study and observation, a reverence for the Christian religion and the habitual performance of the duties it inculcates. [1]

In the two years that Benjamin was at Princeton, then President Rev. Dr. Samuel Davies was directly responsible for instilling in Benjamin two traits which were visible throughout the remainder of his life. The first was an insatiable love for knowledge (perhaps the greatest effect a teacher can have upon a student), and the second was the habit of keeping a notebook to write down specific thoughts or facts he discovered during his reading. It was especially this latter habit which resulted in Benjamin's recording so many of the unique facts, observations, and anecdotes which make his works so interesting and enlightening. [2]

Dr. Finley, understanding the confusion facing his nephew, wisely advised him, "Before you determine on anything, set apart a day for fasting and prayer, and ask of God to direct you in the choice of a major decision. [3]

Dr. Rush's chaste behavior as an adult may be attributed to the truth of the ancient proverb that, "Just as the twig is bent, the tree's inclined." The early influence of his home was truly felt throughout his life. As he himself noted, his loving mother had paid strict "attention to the morals and religious principles of her children." In fact, the "reading of the word of God, and the offering up of family prayers generally recurred every day." [4]

tending to the wounded. He later wrote his observations on hospitals, army diseases, and the effects of the revolution on the army and people. He attended the American wounded in the battles of Princeton and Brandywine, after which the British, not being able to care for the American wounded, permitted Rush and other doctors to cross their lines and provide care to the wounded men.

In 1787, he became a member of the convention of Pennsylvania for the adoption of the Federal Constitution.

He pronounced the federal government a masterpiece of human wisdom.

In August of 1793, the yellow fever epidemic broke out in Philadelphia and resulted in the death of 4,000 people. Rush identified the first case of it on August 19. The Philadelphia College of Physicians asked him to devise a plan to contend with the disease. When his rules warning against the visiting of sick persons were printed in Philadelphia newspapers on August 28, the frightened public began fleeing from the capital city. Rush wrote to

Public Service

1769	Became professor of chemistry at the College of Philadelphia (now the University of Pennsylvania)
1776	Member of Pennsylvania patriotic congress; helped write a declaration of independence which the meeting urged the Continental Congress to adopt
1776	Elected to Pennsylvania legislature as delegate to the Continental Congress; signed the Declaration of Independence
1777	Appointed physician-general of military hospitals for the middle department of the Continental Army
1783	Became a staff member of the Pennsylvania Hospital
1786	Established the first free medical clinic in the United States
1787	Member of the Pennsylvania convention that ratified the United States Constitution
1789	Appointed professor of the theory and practice of medicine at the College of Philadelphia
1789–1790	Member of Pennsylvania state constitutional convention
1791	Appointed professor of medicine at the University of Pennsylvania
1793	Worked tirelessly in the yellow fever epidemic that killed about 4,000 persons in Philadelphia
1797–1813	Served as treasurer of the United States Mint
1798	One of few physicians who remained in Philadelphia during another severe yellow fever epidemic

In a letter which I had the pleasure to receive from Dr. Rush. . . he thus expresses the obligation he felt for the early impressions of piety he had received from his parents:"I have acquired and received nothing from the world which I prize so highly as the religious principles I inherited from them; and I possess nothing that I value so much as the innocence and purity of their characters."[5]

That Dr. Rush was easily encouraged by words from the Scriptures was not surprising, for he venerated the Scriptures as a final authority on any subject, and from neither his public nor his private writings did he ever exclude the spiritual.[6]

The weight of that folly and those vices [from the early part of his life] has been felt in my mind ever since. They have often been deplored in tears and sighs before God. It was from a deep and affecting sense of one of them that I was first led to seek the favor of God in His Son in the 21st year of my age. The religious impressions that were made upon my mind at this time were far from issuing in a complete union to God by His Son Jesus Christ, but they left my mind more tender to sin of every kind and begat in me constant desires for a new heart and a sense of God's mercy in the way of His Gospel. Religious company now became most agreeable to me, and I delighted in public worship and particularly in hearing evangelical ministers of all denominations. I made conscience of secret prayer from that time, nor do I recollect to have passed a day without it while in health to the present year.[7]

his wife the next day saying: "I have advised all the families that I attend, that can move, to quit the city. There is but one preventative that is certain, and that is to fly from it."[39]

The disease baffled even the oldest, most skilled physicians. There was a huge shortage of physicians because many fled from the city. At one time, there were only three physicians left to care for almost 6,000 people.

> A cheerful countenance was scarcely to be seen for six weeks. The streets every where discovered marks of the distress that pervaded the city. In walking for many hundred yards, few persons were met, except such as were in quest of a physician, a nurse, a bleeder, or the men who buried the dead. The hearse alone kept up the remembrance of the noise of carriages, or carts, in the streets. A black man leading or driving a horse, with a corpse, on a pair of chair wheels, met the eye in most of the streets of the city, at every hour of the day; while the noise of the same wheels passing slowly over the pavement kept alive anguish and fear in the sick and well, every hour of the night.[40]

Rush researched his library, poring over every book that might shed some light. He found a manuscript written by a Dr. Mitchell of Virginia in 1741 and adapted a plan to administer calomel and jalap and had the joy of seeing four out of the first five patients cured. He also used blood letting, cool air, cold drinks, low diets and application of cold water to the body.

> The conquest of this formidable disease was not the effect of accident, nor of the application of a single remedy; but it was the triumph of a principle in medicine. In this joyful state of mind, he entered in his note book, dated the 10th of September, "Thank God, out of one hundred patients whom I have visited or prescribed for this day, I have lost none."[41]

He supplied apothecaries with directions for making his purging powder, unable to keep up the demands on him. He sent a letter to the College of Physicians defending his methods of treatment, hoping to help in saving the thousands afflicted. Dr. Rush and his pupils were constantly helping patients. Between September 8 and 15, Dr. Rush visited and prescribed for between 100 to 120 patients a day. For many weeks he seldom sat down to eat, and continued prescribing for patients while he ate. His sister counted 47 people he had to turn away before 11:00 AM. People swarmed him in the streets for help. Friends tried to persuade him to leave the city for his own preservation.

> To their solicitations and urgent importunities he replied, "that he would not abandon the post which Providence had assigned him";

The Gospel of Jesus Christ prescribes the wisest rules for just conduct in every situation of life. Happy they who are enabled to obey them in all situations! …My only hope of salvation is in the infinite transcendent love of God manifested to the world by the death of His Son upon the Cross. Nothing but His blood will wash away my sins. I rely exclusively upon it. Come Lord Jesus! Come quickly! And take home Thy lost but redeemed Creature! I will believe and I will hope in Thy salvation! Amen, and amen! This attendance to religious matters was not merely superficial. As one of Dr. Rush's first biographers observed: It was his usual practice to close the day by reading to his collected family a chapter in the Bible, and afterwards by addressing his Maker in prayer, devoutly acknowledging His goodness for favors received and humbly imploring His continued protection and blessing. In fact, so cognizant was Dr. Rush of his relationship to God that he not only recognized but also acknowledged God's mercy amidst what many would consider the mundane routines of daily life: *"However trifling it may appear, I cannot help adding an acknowledgment of the good providence of God in having preserved me from falls in climbing and descending stairs and from insults in the streets in the most lonely places at all hours of the night during the course of [my life]."*[8]

Benjamin Rush completely fulfilled the life purpose which he had set for himself: "To spend, and be spent, for the good of mankind is what I chiefly aim at."[10]

"Shippen Mansion" Residence of Dr. Benjamin Rush
At the time of his death No. 98 South 4th Street, Philadelphia

that he thought it his duty to sacrifice not only his pleasures and repose, but his life, should it be necessary, for the safety of his patients.[42]

Rush himself became ill from the disease. The story is told that while he was recovering, he had a dream that a crowd of poor persons had gathered in front of his house asking him to help their friends and families and that he was about to turn away when a poor woman ran forward, crying out: "Oh, Doctor! Don't turn away from the poor! You were doomed to die of the yellow fever; but the prayers of the poor were heard by heaven, and have saved your life!"[43]

Five years later, the yellow fever struck again in Philadelphia and again Rush stayed and performed his duty as a doctor while many other prominent physicians fled. He was later sent gifts from the King of Prussia and Czar of Russia to acknowledge his sacrificial service.

In the month of January, we buried our youngest son with a pleurisy. On the 2nd of March I was seized with the same disorder [pleurisy] and lay for nine days in such a situation that my recovery is thought the next thing to a miracle. For my own part, I had taken leave of life. I not only settled all my worldly affairs but gave the most minute directions with respect to everything that related to my funeral. It pleased God to enable me to do this with an uncommon degree of composure, for the promises of the Gospel bore up my soul above the fear of death and the horrors of the grave. O! my friend, the religion of Jesus Christ is indeed a reality. It is comfortable in life, but in a near view of the last enemy [death] its value cannot be measured or estimated by the pen or tongue of a mortal.[20]

Rush continued to be involved in service to his country. In 1787, he wrote newspaper articles in support of the U.S. Constitution and was made a member of the Pennsylvania Convention, ratifying the state Constitution. He and James Wilson wrote a new Constitution for Pennsylvania. Rush was a leader in the fight against slavery. He helped found two Pennsylvania colleges, Dickinson College and Franklin and Marshall College. He also served as Treasurer of the U.S. Mint. In addition to all of this, Rush taught at the University of Pennsylvania and was responsible for educating over 3,000 medical students in his lifetime. He taught his students:

> Medicine without principles is an humble art, and a degrading profession. It reduces the physician to a level with the cook and the nurse, who administer to the appetites and the weaknesses of sick people. But directed by principles, it imparts the highest elevation to the intellectual and moral condition of man. In spite, therefore, of the obloquy with which they have been treated, let us resolve to cultivate them as long as we live. This, gentlemen, is my determination as long as I am able to totter to this chair; and if a tombstone be afforded after my death to rescue my humble name for a few years from oblivion, I ask no further addition to it, than that I was an advocate for principles in medicine. [44]

At the age of 67, after an illness of only a few days, his useful life ended on April 19, 1813. That day happened to be the thirty-eighth anniversary of the first battle of the Revolution. He was deeply mourned by the whole city, as well as in all parts of the country. A favorite phrase he often used to predict the war's outcome was "All will end well." It did end well and so did the life of a man who dedicated himself to be spent for the good of mankind.

When Dr. Benjamin Rush died in 1813, he was considered one of America's three most notable Founders, ranking in prominence along with George Washington and Benjamin Franklin. In 1791, this signer of the Declaration of Independence founded the First Day Society which grew into today's Sunday Schools. He also helped start America's first Bible society: the Bible Society of Philadelphia. The original constitution for that society was authored by Dr. Rush. In looking for ways to print Bibles faster and more economically, Dr. Rush and the Society came across what was called stereotyped printing — an early form of mass production. The result was America's first stereotyped, or mass-produced Bible — and it came about through the efforts of Dr. Benjamin Rush, signer of the Declaration. [25]

America's preeminent statesmen especially lamented his departure. For example, Thomas Jefferson wrote John Adams: "Another of our friends of seventy-six is gone, my dear sir; another of the co-signers of the independence of our country. And a better man than Rush could not have left us, more benevolent, more learned, of finer genius, or more honest." John Adams similarly lamented: "As a man of science, letters, taste, sense, philosophy, patriotism, religion, morality, merit, usefulness, taken all together, Rush has not left his equal in America; nor, that I know, in the world. In him is taken away, and in a manner most sudden and unexpected, a main prop of my life." [9]

It was not only by words, but in deeds, that he expressed his reverence for the Divine character. It was his usual practice to close the day by reading to his collected family a chapter in the Bible, and afterwards by addressing his Maker in prayer, devoutly acknowledging his goodness for favours received, and humbly imploring his continued protection and blessing. His respect for Jehovah, led him to respect his ministers, who acted consistently with their high calling. He considered their office of the greatest importance to society, both in this world and that which is to come. He strengthened their hand, and was always ready and willing to promote and encourage arrangements for their comfortable support, and for building churches, and for propagating the gospel. [31]

My only hope of salvation is in the infinite transcendent love of God manifested to the world by the death of His Son upon the Cross. Nothing but His blood will wash away my sins [Acts 22:16]. I rely exclusively upon it. Come, Lord Jesus! Come quickly![45]

Of schools and education:

Dr. Rush noted that the classes at Princeton. . . were usually closed by delivering in a plain way some of the most striking and intelligible evidences of the truth of the Christian religion. . . [T]o the impressions they made upon my understanding, I ascribe my not having at any time of my life ever entertained a doubt of the Divine origin of the Bible. I wish this mode of fortifying the reason of young people in the principles of Christianity were more general. The impressions which are made upon their fears or their faith by sermons and creeds soon wear away, but arguments fixed in the understanding are indelible.[11]

Dr. Rush happily recorded several of the religious declarations announced over the new Franklin College, including: "Come and visit, thou Savior of men, They dedicated to Thee today. All in the glorious work assisting, we build on Christ, the Corner-Stone."[12]

He took so lively an interest in every thing that concerned his pupils, that each of them believed himself a favourite, while his kind offices to all proved that he was the common friend and father of them all.[28]

Such is my veneration for every religion that reveals the attributes of the Deity, or a future state of rewards and punishments, that I had rather see the opinions of Confucius or Mahomed inculcated upon our youth than see them grow up wholly devoid of a system of religious principles. But the religion I mean to recommend in this place is that of the New Testament. [A]ll its doctrines and precepts are calculated to promote the happiness of society and the safety and well being of civil government. A Christian cannot fail of being a republican.[13]

The occupation of the schoolmaster is truly dignified. He is, next to mothers, the most important member of civil society. . .We are grossly mistaken in looking up wholly to our governments, and even to ministers of the Gospel, to promote public and private order in society. Mothers and schoolmasters plant the seeds of nearly all the good and evil which exists in our world. Its reformation must therefore be begun in nurseries and in schools. . . Let us establish schools for this purpose in every township in the United States.[14]

In an educational policy paper he authored in 1791, Dr. Rush offered compelling reasons why the Bible should never be taken out of American schools, even predicting that if the Bible were removed from the classroom, there would be an explosion of crime. He explained: "In contemplating the political institutions of the United States, [if we remove the Bible from schools,] I lament that we waste so much time and money in punishing crimes and take so little pains to prevent them."[24]

To Dr. Rush, every place was a school, every one with whom he conversed was a tutor. He was never without a book, for, when he had no other, the book of nature was before him, and engaged his attention. In his lectures to his pupils, he advised them, "to lay every person they met with, whether in a packet boat, a stage wagon, or a public road, under contribution for facts on physical subjects." What the professor recommended to them, he practiced himself. His eyes and ears were open to see, hear, and profit by every occurrence.[26]

Dr. Rush was firm in his belief that education, to be successful, must infuse the principles of Christianity throughout all of its academic disciplines. In fact, when he presented his plan for universal public education on March 28, 1787, he explained: Let the children who are sent to those schools be taught to read and write. . . [and] above all, let both sexes be carefully instructed in the principles and obligations of the Christian religion. This is the most essential part of education — this will make them dutiful children, teachable scholars, and, afterwards, good apprentices, good husbands, good wives, honest mechanics, industrious farmers, peaceable sailors, and, in everything that relates to this country, good citizens. In a separate educational proposal, he again declared: It will be necessary to connect all these [academic] branches of education with regular instruction in the Christian religion.[15]

HE OBSERVED:

I believe that the greatest discoveries in science have been made by Christian philosophers, and that there is the most knowledge in those countries where there is the most Christianity. . . [T]hose Christians, whether parents or schoolmasters, who neglect the religious instruction of their children and pupils, reject and neglect the most effectual means of promoting knowledge in our country. With this conviction at the core of his educational beliefs, it is not surprising that he believed that the Bible was the essential academic textbook. In fact, one of his most often reprinted works was A Defense of the Use of the Bible as a Schoolbook (1791). Almost two years before the first public release of that writing, he was already speaking on the subject. For example, in a July 13, 1789, letter, Dr. Rush told a friend: I am now preparing an address to be delivered . . ."upon the necessity and advantages of teaching children to read by means of the Bible. I consider this as a matter of more importance in the world than keeping up a regular Gospel ministry and yet, strange to tell! There are religious men and even ministers of the Gospel who disapprove of it. The great enemy of the salvation of man, in my opinion, never invented a more effectual means of extirpating [extinguishing] Christianity from the world than by persuading mankind that it was improper to read the Bible at schools. . ."[16]

It may be useful to students to be informed, that Dr. Rush constantly kept by him a note book, consisting of two parts, in one of which he entered facts as they occurred; in the other, ideas and observations, as they arose in his own mind, or were suggested by others in conversation. His mind was under such complete discipline, that he could read or write with perfect composure in the midst of the noise of his children, the conversation of his family, and the common interrogatories of his visiting patients.[27]

His correspondence was extensive, and his letters numerous; but every one of them, as far as can be known to an individual, contained something original, pleasant, and sprightly. I can truly say, remarks Dr. Ramsay, that in the course of thirty-five years' correspondence and friendly intercourse, I never received a letter from him without being delighted and improved; nor left his company without learning something.[29]

[A]s a Christian, zealous and consistent; and in his domestic relations, he was the center of a circle of love and true affection. Through life the Bible was a "lamp to his feet" [Psalm 119:105] — his guide in all things appertaining to his duty toward God and man. Amid all his close and arduous pursuit of human knowledge, he never neglected to "search the scriptures" [John 5:39] for that knowledge which points the soul aright in its journey to the Spirit Land. His belief in revealed religion and in the Divine inspiration of the Sacred Writers is manifested in many of his scientific productions.[34]

In an address to ministers of every denomination, on subjects interesting to morals, he remarks, "If there were no hereafter, individuals and societies would be great gainers by attending public worship every Sunday. Rest from labour in the house of God winds up the machine of both soul and body better than anything else, and thereby invigorates it for the labour and duties of the ensuing week."[32]

Students came even from Europe, to attend his lectures; and in 1812, the year before he died, those in the class who attended his lectures, amounted to four hundred and thirty. Within the last nine years of his life, the number of his private pupils exceeded fifty. It is stated by his biographer, that during his life he gave instruction to more than two thousand pupils.[33]

Dr. Rush was especially concerned that he transmit these same values to his children, and consequently he did not hesitate to instruct his children accordingly. For example, just before John (the firstborn of Dr. Rush's thirteen children) departed for an overseas trip in 1796, Dr. Rush reminded his 21-year-old son:

1. Be punctual in committing your soul and body to the protection of your Creator every morning and evening. Implore, at the same time, His mercy in the name of His Son, our Lord and Savior Jesus Christ.
2. Read in your Bible frequently, more especially on Sundays.
3. Avoid swearing and even an irreverent use of your Creator's name. Flee youthful lusts.
4. Be courteous and gentle in your behavior to your fellow passengers, and respectful and obedient to the captain of the vessel.
5. Attend public worship regularly every Sunday when you arrive at Calcutta.

James (the seventh of Dr. Rush's children) received his medical degree from the University of Pennsylvania in 1809 and, like his father, sought to pursue further medical studies in Edinburgh. Just before the twenty-three year old James departed for Edinburgh, Dr. Rush similarly reminded him: "Commit yourself, and all that you are interested in, daily to the protection of your Maker, Preserver, and bountiful Benefactor. Keep a journal from the day you leave Philadelphia, in which insert subjects of sermons, speeches, etc. Remember, thou hast a character to lose."[22]

In fact, Dr. Rush really believed that those duties actually intertwined and overlapped. For example, by serving his country, he believed that he was protecting his family; therefore, performing his duty to his country was part of doing his duty to his family. It was quite simple for Dr. Rush to determine what was a duty; for according to his strongly developed moral sense, duty was simply doing what was right. As he explained to his wife, Julia, on the eve of the approaching American Revolution, it was his sense of right and wrong — his sense of duty — which caused him to contend so zealously for his country:

"Our cause prospers in every county of the province. The hand of heaven is with us. Did I not think so, I would not have embarked in it. You have everything to hope and nothing to fear from the part which duty to God, to my country, and to my conscience have led me to take in our affairs. The measures which I have proposed have hitherto been so successful that I am constrained to believe I act under the direction of Providence. God knows I seek His honor and the best interests of my fellow creatures supremely in all I am doing for my country."

A few months later, the Declaration of Independence signed and the Revolution officially commenced, he reaffirmed to Julia that his duty to God and his family still superseded all others, including any fame he might receive: "I shall be better satisfied if the same can be said of me as was said of the prophet of old, 'That I walked in the fear of the Lord, and begat sons and daughters' [Genesis 5:22], than if it were inscribed upon my tombstone that I governed the councils or commanded the arms of the whole continent of America."[21]

BIBLE SOCIETIES

Having taken into consideration the inestimable value of the revelation which it hath pleased God to make to our world of His existence, character, will, works, and grace in Jesus Christ in the Bible, and of the great benefits to be expected from the distribution of it among persons who are unable or not disposed to purchase it, [we] have agreed to form . . . a Society for that purpose, to be called "The Bible Society." The Philadelphia Society was determined to distribute the Bible freely. Why? As Dr. Rush explained: "[T]o furnish . . . Bibles gratuitously [freely] will have a happy tendency to induce many to appreciate the sacred Scriptures more highly than they have been wont to do; and may dispose those who possess Bibles, but have suffered them to lie neglected in their houses, to peruse them with serious attention." How successful was the Philadelphia Society in reaching its goal? At the end of its first year, it reported: "Some hundreds of families are now in possession of a Bible . . . which never had one before. . . . The institution of a Bible Society in this place, therefore, must be considered an auspicious event. And the Managers . . . conclude this report by declaring it to be not only the object of their prayers, but their hopes, that before the present generation shall have passed away, the Holy Scriptures will be read by all the principal nations under heaven: And thus the way be opened for the fulfillment of the prediction of the prophet, 'The earth shall be full of the knowledge of the Lord as the waters cover the sea.'" [Habakkuk 2:14] It had also been the desire of the Philadelphia Bible Society to see similar societies established across the country. As Dr. Rush had explained in their original constitution: "The first object . . . was to draw the attention of the public, not only in this state but through the United States, to the great importance of [Bible Societies]; and to stimulate the friends of the Bible in the other large cities on this continent, to exert themselves to establish societies similar to the one organized in this city."[17]

Bible Societies had been formed in Maryland, Massachusetts, New York, New Jersey, New Hampshire, Connecticut, and South Carolina. As he himself declared: "The Gospel of Jesus Christ prescribes the wisest rules for just conduct in every situation of life. Happy they who are enabled to obey them in all situations!"[18]

Let every family in the United States be furnished at the public expense, by the Secretary of this office, with a copy of an American edition of the Bible. . .

Let the following sentence be inscribed in letters of gold over the doors of every State and Court house in the United States: "The Son of Man came into the world not to destroy men's lives, but to save them." [Luke 9:56][19]

❧ Questions for Discussion ❧

1. For what does Rush praise his parents for teaching him as a child?

2. How did Rush view the Scriptures?

3. What two traits was Rev. Samuel Davies responsible for inculcating in young Rush?

4. What was Rush's uncle, Dr. Findlay's advice to him concerning decision making?

5. At what age was Rush saved and what led to his making that decision?

6. Tell Rush's personal statement of faith of his belief in Jesus Christ.

7. What was Rush's usual practice at the end of each day?

8. What did Jefferson write to John Adams at the time of Rush's death?

9. What was Rush's stated purpose in life? Did he achieve it?

10. Tell how classes at Princeton usually closed each day.

11. What religious declaration did Rush place over the new Franklin College?

12. What religion did Rush recommend to everyone?

13. What two people most greatly influence a child's life, according to Benjamin Rush?

14. What did Rush believe to be the purpose of schools?

15. What did Rush attribute to be the success of schools?

16. To what did Rush observe as to the belief of most inventors or great scientists?

17. What did Rush believe to be the essential textbook?

18. How did Rush believe children should be taught to read?

19. Why did Rush establish Bible societies?

20. How successful was their goal?

21. What did Rush as Secretary of the Peace decide that each family of the U.S. must have?

22. What sentence was to be inscribed over every State and Court house in the U.S.?

Questions for Discussion

23. When extremely ill, thinking perhaps he would die, what declaration did Rush make?

24. What did Rush believe concerning his duty to family and country?

25. Tell Rush's words which proved his confidence in the patriotic cause.

26. Tell what values Dr. Rush reminded his son to implement before his son left for an overseas trip.

27. Tell Dr. Rush's practices in going to church.

28. For what type of printing is Dr. Rush responsible? Why did he develop it?

29. How do we know Dr. Rush had a love for learning?

30. What extraordinary trait did Dr. Rush have that caused each of his pupils to believe he was Dr. Rush's favorite student?

31. How many students did Rush influence over his lifetime?

32. How did Rush describe the atmosphere in the room on the day of the signing of the Declaration of Independence?

33. Tell of Rush's duties during the Revolution, his capture, and his observations during that time.

34. What quality drove Rush to treat wounded British as well as wounded American soldiers?

35. What accomplishments did Rush achieve after the Revolution?

36. Tell of Rush's work and outstanding qualities during the outbreak of yellow fever.

37. What have you learned from studying this man's life. Name two qualities from this man's life you can ask God to help develop in your life.

38. Look up the word "confident" in the character quality appendix. Tell how it describes Rush's life.

39. Look up the word "devoted" and give proof of it in Rush's life.

40. Ask God to give you a special vision in which you can learn to display confidence and dedicate your life to fulfilling it.

James Smith

Cheerful Patriot

Proverbs 15:13

"A Professor of Religion"

☙❧

BORN
1719

BIRTHPLACE
Ireland

EDUCATION
Philadelphia Academy

OCCUPATION
Lawyer,
Manufacturer

MARRIED
Eleanor Armor

CHILDREN
5

AGE AT SIGNING
57

DIED
July 11, 1806; age 87

He was for many years a professor of religion, and very regular in his attendance on public worship. Notwithstanding his fondness for jest, he was more than most men ready to frown upon every expression which seemed to reflect on sacred subjects.[1]

No one knows exactly when James Smith was born, except that it was around 1719 in Ireland. His parents moved to America when he was ten years old and James attended school in nearby Philadelphia that was taught by Reverend Francis Alison.

"In those early days in America, when congregations were not large enough to be able to pay their pastors an adequate salary, nor to require all of a pastor's time, it was common for a minister to 'keep school.' In most communities, he was the best educated man and so the man best equipped for teaching."[4]

James therefore learned proficiency in Latin and Greek. He also studied surveying, after which he read law in his brother's law office in Lancaster. He was admitted to the bar when he was 26 and soon set up practice in York, where he was the only resident lawyer in town. He married Eleanor Armor of New Castle, Delaware and they had three sons and two daughters.

Smith was elected as a delegate from York to the convention in Philadelphia in 1774 to decide what to do about the Coercive Acts in Boston. Smith was elected colonel of a regiment he assembled for the protection of Pennsylvania.

In July 1776, he was at the convention to draft a state constitution from Pennsylvania, and on July 20 he was selected to replace one of the Pennsylvanians who opposed the Declaration of Independence. He signed on August 2nd with the rest of the delegates. He continued to serve in Congress until 1778, when he retired.

He served one term in the assembly and for a few months was judge of Pennsylvania High Court of Errors and Appeals. In 1782 he was Brigadier General of the militia and counselor for the Pennsylvania-Connecticut-Wyoming Valley controversy.

He was again elected to Congress by the assembly in 1785, but declined due to his age. He continued to practice law. In 1805, a fire destroyed his office and all his papers, including his collection of letters from Benjamin Franklin and Samuel Adams and others, which is why we don't have more information about him now. James died at the age of 87, thirty years and one week after the adoption of the Declaration of Independence.

An early biographer described him during this period as "social, jocular, and friendly…the life of all conviviality…with a store of rich and diverting anecdote that was inexhaustible and unequalled."[5]

Colonel Smith had been appointed one of a very important committee, charged with the duty of collecting testimony concerning the barbarous treatment of prisoners by the enemy, and the unjustifiable destruction of private property committed by the British armies… [Here are excerpts of his report:] That in every place where the enemy has been, there are heavy complaints of oppressions, injury and insults suffered by the inhabitants from officers, soldiers and Americans disaffected to their country's cause.

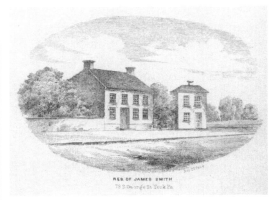

Residence of James Smith
78 South George Street, York, Pennsylvania

First, The wanton and oppressive devastation of the country and destruction of property. Second, The inhuman treatment of those who were so unhappy as to become prisoners. Third, The savage butchery of many who had submitted or were incapable of resistance. Fourth, The lust and brutality of the soldiers in the abusing of women. The committee had authentic information of many instances of the most indecent treatment, and actual ravishment of married and single women; but such is the nature of that most irreparable injury, that the persons

Public Service

1774	Delegate to the convention of patriots in Philadelphia
1774	Raised the first company of volunteer soldiers in Pennsylvania for defense against the British.
1775–1776	Member of the Pennsylvania patriotic conferences; helped write a declaration calling for the independence of Pennsylvania
1776	Member of the Pennsylvania state constitutional convention
1776–1778	Delegate to the Continental Congress; signed the Declaration of Independence
1780	Member of the Pennsylvania state legislature
1781	Judge of the Pennsylvania high court of errors and appeals
1782	Appointed brigadier general of Pennsylvania volunteers

*I*t was a singular trait in the character of Mr. Smith, that he should so obstinately refuse to inform his friends of his age.[2]

His memory was remarkably retentive of anecdotes, and his perception of the ridiculous quick and unerring. With these powers, a well-regulated temper and great benevolence, it is not to be wondered at that he should have been the delight of the social circle, should have inclined to the company of younger persons, and should frequently have set the court house as well as the tavern bar room in a roar of laughter.[3]

suffering it, and their relations, though perfectly innocent, look upon it as a kind of reproach to have the facts related and their names known. They have, however, procured some affidavits, which will be published in the appendix. The originals are lodged with the secretary of congress. The fences destroyed, the houses deserted, pulled in pieces or consumed by fire, and the general face of waste and devastation spread over a rich and once well cultivated and well inhabited country.

But above all, places of worship, ministers and religious persons of some particular protestant denominations seem to have been treated with the most rancorous hatred, and at the same time with the highest contempt.

The prisoners, instead of that humane treatment which those taken by the United States experienced, were in general treated with the greatest barbarity. Many of them were near four days kept without food altogether: when they received a supply, it was both insufficient in point of quantity and often of the worst kind: they suffered the utmost distress from cold, nakedness and close confinement: freemen and men of substance suffered all

that a generous mind could suffer from the contempt and mockery of British and foreign mercenaries: multitudes died in prison; and when others were sent out, several died in the boats while carrying ashore, or upon the road attempting to go home.

The savage butchery of those who had submitted and were incapable of resistance. The committee found it to be the general opinion of the people in the neighbourhood of Princeton and Trenton, that the enemy the day before the battle of Princeton had determined to give no quarter. They did not, however, obtain any clear proof, that there were any general orders for that purpose; but the treatment of several particular persons at and since that time, has been of the most shocking kind, and gives too much countenance to the supposition. Officers wounded and disabled, some of them of the first rank, were barbarously mangled or put to death. A minister of the gospel in Trenton, who neither was nor had been in arms, was massacred in cold blood, though humbly supplicating for mercy.[6]

✌Questions for Discussion✌

1. What evidences do we have of James Smith being a Christian?

2. What qualities made Smith a delight socially?

3. What type of early education did Smith receive?

4. What useful services did Smith perform for his country?

5. Smith helped draft Pennsylvania's State Constitution. What is its Christian nature?

6. Tell of Smith's report of the treatment of prisoners by the British.

7. Look up the meaning of "cheerfulness." How did this characterize Smith's life?

8. Think of a way you can be a cheerful influence in someone's life this week.

George Taylor

Industrious Patriot

Proverbs 13:4

"From indentured servant
to Signer"

❧❧

BORN
1716
Birthplace: Ireland

EDUCATION
no information

MARRIED
Mrs. Anne Savage, 1742

OCCUPATION
Ironmaster

CHILDREN
2

AGE AT SIGNING
60

DIED
February 23, 1781; age 65

George Taylor is one of the two signers about whom least is known. He was born in Ireland, son of a minister, in 1716. Desiring as a young man to come to America, but not having money for passage, he gave himself as an indentured servant, working for five years to pay for his passage. He was 20 years old when he sailed to Pennsylvania, indentured to Mr. Savage in his iron foundry near Philadelphia. When Mr. Savage learned George had received some education, he promoted him to clerk. Mr. Savage died a few years later, and George married his widow Anne. They had two children. George became owner of the foundry, and by hard work increased the size of his business and attained a good fortune. They built a large home in Northampton, Pennsylvania.

In 1764, he was elected to the Provincial Assembly. He participated in debates over the Stamp Act and drew up an address to King George, thanking him for the repeal of the Stamp Act. In 1775, he was elected as a colonel in the militia, and also appointed delegate to the Provincial Congress. When the provincial legislature decided to replace the five delegates that opposed independence, George Taylor was chosen to replace one of them, and therefore was not present to vote for independence, but was there to sign on August 2.

Mr. Taylor resigned from Congress in 1777, and settled in Easton, where he managed his affairs with much success, repairing his fortune, which had greatly suffered because of his service to his country.

George Taylor spent his last two years in poor health, and died on February 23, 1878, at 65 years of age.

Residence of George Taylor
North East Corner of Ferry & 4th Streets, Easton, Pennsylvania

ॐ Public Service ॐ

1764–1770   Member of the Pennsylvania colonial legislature

1775–1776   Member of the Pennsylvania provincial congress

1776–1777   Delegate from Pennsylvania to the Continental Congress; signed the Declaration of Independence

1777   Member of Pennsylvania's first Supreme Executive Council

ॐ Questions for Discussion ॐ

1. What was an indentured servant? What quality can be said of a man who would leave his home, place himself in servitude to pay for his passage to the Colonies and work to earn back his freedom?

2. By what quality did George acquire a large fortune?

3. In what offices did he serve?

4. What do we know of any sacrifice he made for his country?

5. How was Taylor an industrious man?

6. To what areas of your life do you need to apply diligence? Set a specific goal to achieve this week.

James Wilson

Precise Patriot

Proverbs 9:9

"All power is derived from the people"

❧

BORN
September 14, 1742

BIRTHPLACE
Carskerde, Scotland

EDUCATION
University of St. Andrews;
Glasgow, and Edinburgh

OCCUPATION
Lawyer

MARRIED
Rachel Bird, 1771;
Hannah Gray, 1793

CHILDREN
7

AGE AT SIGNING
33

DIED
August 21, 1798; age 55

As a patriot none was firmer; as a Christian none sincerer; and as a husband, father, neighbor, and friend, he was beloved and esteemed in the highest degree.[1]

James Wilson was born at Carskerde, near St. Andrews, Scotland, on September 14, 1742. He received his education at the University of St. Andrews, Glasgow, and Edinburgh. He emigrated to the colonies in 1765, living in New York for a year before moving to Pennsylvania with a letter of introduction to Dr. Peters, an Episcopal minister. Peters helped him get a position as a Latin tutor at the College of Philadelphia. In a few months, he entered the law office of John Dickinson and was admitted to the bar in 1767. He set up a practice in Carlisle, Pennsylvania, dealing often in land dispute cases. He began buying land himself and bought a farm.

He married Rachel Bird, a daughter of a wealthy ironworks owner, and they had six children before she died in 1786. He later married Hannah Gray, daughter of a Boston merchant, with whom he had one child.

James was an early believer in the colonies' cause and in less than 10 years after coming to America, became a member of the Pennsylvania provincial meeting in July 1774, and headed up the Committees of Correspondence at Carlisle. He used his pen to influence others.

A fellow delegate to the Convention observes that "in his opinion, the most able and useful members of it, were James Wilson, and James Madison; that he is in doubt which of these deserved the preference, but was inclined to give it to the former." [2]

His pamphlet, "Considerations on the Nature and Extent of the Legislative Authority of the British Parliament," was published. In this he maintained that Parliament had no constitutional right to make laws for the colonies. This was an advanced position to take in 1774 and not many Pennsylvanians held it, but Wilson had already been arguing his points for four years. Of course, this was the opinion of the Adamses and Hancock of Massachusetts. His pamphlet was distributed among the first Continental Congressmen when they met and it made a considerable impression. [8]

He was elected to the Second Continental Congress and served on various committees, including the Board of War.

Dr. Benjamin Rush, to whom we are indebted for reporting his impressions of so many of the congressmen of 1776, regarded Wilson as an eminent lawyer, an enlightened statesman, a profound and accurate scholar. "Wilson," he said, "spoke often in Congress and his eloquence was of the most commanding kind.

Mr. Wilson was about six feet in height; erect; or, rather, if the expression may be allowed, stooping backward. His person was dignified and respectable; and his manner a little constrained, but not ungraceful. His features could not be called handsome, although they were far from disagreeable; and they sometimes bore the appearance of sternness, owing to his extreme nearness of sight. His voice was powerful, but its cadence perfectly modulated. [4]

At an early day, Mr. Wilson entered with patriotic zeal into the cause of American liberty. He was an American in principle from the time that he landed on the American shore; and at no period in the revolutionary struggle, did he for a single hour swerve from his attachment to the principles which he had adopted. [5]

He reasoned, declaimed, and persuaded according to circumstances with equal effect. His mind, while he spoke, was a blaze of light. Not a word ever fell from his lips out of time, or out of place, nor could a word be taken from or added to his speeches without injuring them. He rendered great and essential services to his country in every stage of the Revolution." [9]

In a pamphlet published in 1774 [Wilson] declared that "all power is derived from the people." [3]

Thanks to Wilson, Franklin and Morton, Pennsylvania chose independence by a 3–2 vote on July 2, 1776. Wilson was instrumental in helping to create the U.S. Constitution, next only to James Madison. Wilson insisted that government should serve the people and that the people should elect their lawmakers directly. He firmly stated, "All power is derived from the people."

In May, 1784, James Wilson was one of eight Pennsylvania delegates to the Philadelphia convention to adopt a constitution for the United States, held in Independence Hall with George Washington as President. Only six of the thirty-nine members had been Signers of the Declaration of Independence: Benjamin Franklin, James Wilson, Robert Morris, and George Clymer of Pennsylvania; Robert Sherman of Connecticut; George Read of Delaware. The total number was small "but the quality was excellent." Students of constitutional history consider this "to have been as wise and capable a deliberative body as ever assembled in this country, perhaps the wisest."[10]

Throughout the convention, he acted as a spokesman for the aged and feeble Benjamin Franklin, reading Franklin's speeches for him.[11]

Wilson served later in the Pennsylvania Convention which ratified the Constitution. He made a long speech in favor of its adoption and concluded his argument:

> If there are errors, it should be remembered, that the seeds of reformation are sown in the work itself, and the concurrence of two-thirds of the congress, may, at any time, introduce alterations and amendments...Regarding it, then, in every point of view, with a candid and disinterested mind, I am bold to assert, that it is the BEST FORM OF GOVERNMENT WHICH HAS EVER BEEN OFFERED TO THE WORLD.[12]

In the selection of persons for high judicial offices, Washington consulted public opinion, as well as intrinsic worth; and a high degree of character was blended with real talent. In a letter, written on the occasion to John Rutledge, [Washington] makes the following remarks: "Regarding the due administration of justice as the strongest cement of good government, I have considered the first organization of the judicial department, as essential to the happiness of the people, and to the stability of the political system. Under this impression, it has been with me an invariable object of anxious solicitude, to select the fittest characters to expound the laws, and to dispense justice." At the head of a department, deemed by himself so important, he placed Mr. John Jay; and nominated, as associate justice, James Wilson of Pennsylvania.[7]

❧ Public Service ❧

1766	Taught Latin at the College of Philadelphia
1766–1767	Studied law under John Dickinson and admitted to the bar
1774–1775	Member of the Pennsylvania provincial convention
1775–1777	Delegate to the second Continental Congress; signed the Declaration of Independence
1779–1782	Advocate general of France in the United States
1781	Appointed a director of the Bank of North America
1782–1783	Delegate from Pennsylvania to the Constitutional Convention; signed the U.S. Constitution
1787	Member of Pennsylvania state ratification convention
1789–1798	Member of the Pennsylvania state constitutional convention; helped write the new state constitution
1789–1798	Associate justice of the Supreme Court of the United States
1790–1791	First professor of law at the College of Philadelphia (now the University of Pennsylvania)

RES. OF JAS WILSON "FORT WILSON"
SW cor Third & Walnut St. Phila.

Residence of James Wilson "Fort Wilson"
SW Corner of Third & Walnut Street, Philadelphia

After the death of his father, his mother again remarried, and must have been in straightened circumstances, as Mr. Wilson frequently sent her pecuniary aid from this country, even when he himself was much embarrassed.[6]

In 1779, during a period of rioting over food shortages and high prices in Philadelphia, Wilson and some friends were attacked in his house by those opposed to his acting as counsel for Tories. There was a loss of life on both sides. The City Troop intervened but Wilson was obliged to leave the city for a while.[13]

President George Washington appointed Wilson as one of the first jurists of the U.S. Supreme Court in 1789. The same year he was appointed first professor of law at the College of Philadelphia, the same school where he had taught Latin upon his arrival to America 24 years earlier. One of his students at this time was Bushrod Washington, nephew of George Washington.

Like Robert Morris, Wilson became deeply involved in land speculation, buying thousands of acres of western land, borrowing huge sums of money to do so.

Much of this land was purchased for him by the Blount brothers, the most famous of whom was William Blount, a fellow-signer of the United States Constitution who was impeached by the House of Representatives and was expelled from the United States Senate in 1797. With the collapse of land values, Wilson fell into serious debt, and only his office as an associate justice of the Supreme Court saved him from total disgrace.[14]

While serving as a circuit judge, Wilson died at the age of 55 at the home of an associate, Justice James Iredell. His vacancy on the Supreme Court was filled by his student, Bushrod Washington.

Mr. Wilson was more a man of books, than of the world; and always possessed a simplicity, in this respect, which afforded frequent cause of good-humoured merriment to his friends. In private life, he was friendly, interesting, and hospitable; amiable and benevolent in his deportment; of strict truth and integrity; and affectionate and indulgent as a husband and a father. In a word, his domestic character and conduct were such, as uniformly to secure the reverence and affection of his family and friends.[15]

<small>❧</small> Questions for Discussion <small>❧</small>

1. What did Benjamin Rush say of Wilson?

2. What is said about Wilson's Christianity?

3. What character trait did Wilson show in sending money to his mother, even when he was struggling financially?

4. What qualification did Washington look for in a judge?

5. What type of influence did Wilson use to help persuade the people toward independence?

6. What offices did Wilson hold?

7. What was Wilson's role in the writing of the Constitution?

8. What quality is demonstrated in Wilson acting as Franklin's spokesman?

9. What was Wilson's declaration about the Constitution?

10. Who was one of Wilson's students and what office did this student later hold?

11. List qualities seen in this man's life.

12. How did Wilson employ preciseness in his speech?

13. How can you become a person of fitly spoken words? List some ways your words need improvement. Set specific goals.

Delaware

Thomas McKean
George Read
Caesar Rodney

Thomas McKean

Patriot of Integrity

I Timothy 2:1–3

"Man of Many Offices"

✧✧

BORN
March 19, 1734

BIRTHPLACE
New London Township, Pennsylvania

EDUCATION
Philadelphia Academy

OCCUPATION
Lawyer, Judge

MARRIED
Mary Borden, 1763;
Sarah Armitage, 1774

CHILDREN
11

AGE AT SIGNING
42

DIED
June 24, 1817; age 83

No act of my public life was ever done from a corrupt motive; nor without a deliberate opinion that the act was lawful and proper in itself.[1]

Thomas McKean was born in New London Township, Pennsylvania in 1734. By age eight, Thomas was learning Latin and Greek in school. After the usual elementary education, he studied for seven years under Reverend Francis Allison, during which time George Read (later to be a fellow signer), was also a pupil. He then read law with his cousin David Finney at New Castle, Delaware. In 1754, at the age of 20, he was admitted to the Delaware bar and permitted to practice in Delaware, Pennsylvania and New Jersey. In 1763 he married Mary Borden, sister of Francis Hopkinson's wife, Ann. They had six children.

During the next two and a half decades, McKean occupied an array of appointive and elective offices in Delaware, some simultaneously: high sheriff of Kent County; militia captain; trustee of the loan office of New Castle Country; customs collector and judge at New Castle; deputy attorney general of Sussex Country; chief notary officer for the province; and clerk (1757–59) and member (1762–79) of the legislature, including the speakership of the lower house (1772–73). In 1762, he had also helped compile the colony's laws.[5]

Mr. McKean was a delegate to the Stamp Act Congress in 1765 and chosen along with Caesar Rodney to prepare an address to the British House of Commons. McKean zealously opposed the encroachments of British power upon American freedom and was elected as a member of the Continental Congress.

Thomas McKean was instrumental in assuring that Delaware voted for independence. The Delaware Assembly met on June 10 at New Castle, and on June 13, McKean wrote to Congress in Philadelphia:

> The Assembly here have information this moment by express that there are a thousand Tories under arms in Sussex country…but we expect soon to give a good Account of these misguided people. That same day, at seven in the evening, he reported that the Insurgents in Sussex country have dispersed…[6]

On July 1, as indicated in Jefferson's notes, the Lee independence motion was about to be voted on. Delaware was divided. McKean was for it and Read against. Caesar Rodney was involved in military duties.

Thomas McKean described what followed in a letter that he wrote to a nephew of Rodney in 1813: "Whereupon, without delay I sent an Express (at my private expence) for your honored Uncle Caesar Rodney Esquire, the remaining member for Delaware, whom I met at the State-house door in his boots

He was the last to pen his signature to the Declaration, sometime after January 18, 1777… and he figured prominently in not one but two States, Delaware and Pennsylvania. He was also the only signer to be the chief executive of and concurrent officeholder in two States. Furthermore, he numbered among those who also subscribed to the Articles of Confederation, and he served a long tour in Congress.[3]

and spurs, as the members were assembling; after a friendly salutation (without a word on the business) we went into the Hall of Congress together, and found we were among the latest: proceedings immediately commenced, and after a few minutes the great question was put; when the vote for Delaware was called, your uncle arose and said: 'As I believe the voice of my constituents and of all sensible and honest men is in favor of Independence and my own judgment concurs with them, I vote for Independence,' or in words to the same effect."[7]

Delaware's vote for independence made it unanimous. A few days after the Declaration of Independence had been adopted, McKean led his battalion of militia to Perth Amboy, New Jersey to support General George Washington's army.

He was sometimes exposed to considerable danger, in the skirmishes, or rather cannonading, which occurred. An instance of this nature is related by himself…The lines of the enemy were about six hundred yards distant. Several shallops were spied sailing along the opposite shore towards the enemy's men-of-war. Colonel M'Kean had received orders to hold his battalion in readiness to march into town at a minute's warning, and the men were immediately under arms. "I left them," he remarks, "under lieutenant-colonel Dean, to be marched to town, whilst I mounted my horse, and waited on the ground for orders. On the road, which is a straight and wide lane, (something like Market Street,) all the way from the camp to the Sound, and in a line with the enemy's batteries, about twenty cannon balls flew close to me, sometimes just on one side, sometimes on the other, and some just over my head. I confess, I was not a little alarmed, being the first time that I had ever heard a cannon ball, but clapped spurs to my horse, and rode on amidst the balls for the general's, where orders had just been issued to halt the battalion: I was going to execute them, when, on turning round, I saw a horse shot through the neck with a four-pounder, within much less distance than the width of Market Street, from me. The fire was so incessant, and so direct on the street that I had to return, that some gentlemen entreated me to wait a short time; but, as the troops under my care were in full march, and colonel Miles's battalion close behind them, I thought it my duty to stop them, as some of them otherwise would probably be killed, without a chance of effecting any beneficial service. On my return, I found the fire hotter than before, the enemy then playing from three batteries of three or four guns each; but, through God's favor, I escaped unhurt, and marched the troops to the camp."[8]

Immediately after this tour of duty, he was called to Dover, Delaware as a member of the convention to adopt a constitution for Delaware. Upon his arrival, a committee called upon McKean and asked him to write the constitution. He agreed and stayed up all night writing the document, and presented it at ten o'clock the next morning. He became speaker of the Delaware house of representatives under the new constitution.

McKean was not present on August 2, 1776, when most of the other delegates signed the Declaration of Independence, as he was leading troops in New Jersey. He later returned to Congress, where he signed the Declaration, probably sometime in 1777.

During his lifetime, some raised the question as to whether he had actually signed the document. In September of 1796, he wrote this reply:

> Modesty should not rob any man of his just honour, when by that honour, his modesty cannot be offended. My name is not in the printed journals of congress, as a party to the Declaration of Independence, and this,

A letter from John Adams (his friend of many years) to McKean's son also concerned in the charges, ends with this tribute: "I, Your father and Caesar Rodney, were among the Patrick Henrys, the Christopher Gadsdens, the Thomas Jeffersons, the Samuel Adamses, the Roger Shermans — the best tried, firmest pillars of the revolution."[4]

❧ Public Service ❧

1754	Began practicing law in Delaware and Pennsylvania
1756–1757	Deputy attorney general in Sussex County, Delaware
1757–1758	Clerk of the lower house of the Delaware legislature
1762–1779	Member of the Delaware legislature
1765–1773	Speaker of the house of representatives of the Delaware legislature
1774–1783	Delegate from Delaware to the Continental Congress: signed the Declaration of Independence and the Articles of Confederation
1776	Chairman of the Committee of Safety for Pennsylvania
1777	Acting president of Delaware
1777–1799	Chief justice of the State of Pennsylvania
1781	President of the Congress of the Confederation
1799–1808	Governor of Pennsylvania

On the occasion of being elected governor of Pennsylvania, he said to the people, that "he trusted, that under his administration, their happy system of government, raised on the sole authority of the people, would, by the favour of God, be continued inviolate; and that neither foreign nor domestic enemies, neither intrigue, menace, nor seductions, should prevail against it. The constitution of the United Sates, and of Pennsylvania," said he, "shall be the rule of my government; the security of persons, property, liberty, and reputation, my chiefest care; and my best endeavours shall be exerted to fulfill all your reasonable and just expectations."[8]

like an error in the first concoction, has vitiated most of the subsequent publications, and yet the fact is, that I was then a member of congress for the state of Delaware, was personally present in congress, and voted in favour of independence on the fourth of July, 1776, and signed the Declaration after it had been engrossed on parchment, where my name, in my own handwriting, still appears.[9]

McKean held so many positions both before and after the war that at times it seemed impossible that he was one man. In July of 1777, the executive council of Pennsylvania appointed McKean as chief justice of that state; a position he held for the next 22 years. He was, however, still heavily occupied with duties in Delaware. One of the cases over which he presided was *Republican v. John Roberts.* In that case, John Roberts was sentenced to death after a jury found him guilty of treason. Chief Justice McKean then delivered a Gospel message to John Roberts in the courtroom, admonishing him to accept Christ before his death, so that he could spend eternity in heaven rather than in hell.[10]

On September 13, 1777, Britain's troops captured President John McKinley of Delaware, and McKean was made acting president for the next several months. Later, McKean wrote to John Adams about this period of his life:

I have had my full share of the anxieties, cares and troubles of the present war. For some time, I was obliged to act as president of the Delaware state, and as chief justice of this: General Howe had just landed, at the head of the Elk river, when I undertook to discharge these two important trusts. The consequence was, to be hunted like a fox by the enemy, and envied by those who ought to have been my friends. I was compelled to remove my family five times in a few months, and, at last, fixed them in a little log-house on the banks of the Susquehanna, more than a hundred miles from this place: but safety was not to be found there, for they were soon obliged to remove again, on account of the incursions of the Indians.[11]

McKean had been on the committee that drafted the Articles of Confederation. He was the first man to be elected President of the Congress under the Articles of Confederation, on June 10, 1781.

While serving as president, he had the honor of receiving from General Washington the news of the surrender of Cornwallis, at Yorktown:

The dispatch was delivered to him about three o'clock in the morning of October 22, 1781, and the night-watchman who had guided Washington's messenger to McKean's residence began crying through the streets: "Past three o'clock and Cornwallis is taken!"[12]

While serving as Chief Justice of Pennsylvania, he had many difficult decisions to make. He presided at the trial of Loyalists and upheld their death sentences.

…the justice of the supreme court of Pennsylvania who served after McKean had retired from the bench said of him: 'Chief Justice McKean was a great man: his merit in the profession of the law, and as a judge, has never been sufficiently appreciated. It is only since I have been upon the bench, that I have been able to conceive a just idea of the greatness of his merit. His legal learning was profound and accurate…[13]

McKean was elected to the Pennsylvania state ratification convention and approved the U.S. Constitution. He told the convention:

I have gone through the circle of office, in the Legislature, Executive, and Judicial departments of government; and from all my study, observation, and experience, I must declare, that from a full examination and due consideration of this system, it appears to me the best the world has yet seen. I congratulate you on the fair prospect of its being adopted, and am happy in the expectation of seeing accomplished what has long been my ardent wish, that you will hereafter have a salutary permanency in magistracy and stability in the laws.[14]

McKean's first wife, Mary, died in 1773, leaving two sons and four daughters, the baby only two weeks old. On September 3, 1774, he married Sarah Armitage of New Castle, with whom he had five more children.

At the age of 65, McKean was elected governor of Pennsylvania and resigned as chief justice. He received considerable criticism for removing from appointed offices everyone who was not a member of his political party.

He mentioned this in a letter to Thomas Jefferson, saying, "It is, at least, imprudent to foster spies continually about oneself. I am only sorry that I did not displace ten or eleven more; for it is not right to put a dagger in the hands of an assassin." [15]

Some tried to convince him to run for Vice-President in 1803, but he declined.

At the age of seventy-four, McKean retired to private life in 1808. In a letter to John Adams a few years later he described his retirement: "Three years ago I shook hands with the world, and we said farewell to each other: the toys and rattles of childhood, would, in a few years more, be, probably, as suitably to me, as office, honour, or wealth; but (thank God,) the faculties of my mind are, as yet, little, if any thing impaired, and

"Duches House"-Residence of Thomas McKean
South Third Street, Philadelphia

my affections and friendships remain unshaken. Since my exemption from official and professional duties, I have enjoyed a tranquility, never (during a long, protracted life,) heretofore experienced; and my health and comforts are sufficient for a moderate man." [16]

He made one more public appearance at a meeting in Philadelphia, called to discuss preparations for a defense against a possible invasion of the city by the British in the War of 1812.

McKean called upon the citizens to lay aside personal differences warning them 'that there were then but two parties, our country and its invaders.[17]

McKean died at 83 years old in Philadelphia, on June 24, 1817. He was buried in the cemetery of Philadelphia's Presbyterian Church.

❧Questions for Discussion❧

1. What declaration does McKean himself make concerning his motive for being in public service? Read the definition of "integrity" and tell how McKean exemplifies this quality.

2. Read information in the appendix on the Christian nature of the Constitution of Pennsylvania.

3. List the offices Thomas McKean held in service to his country, some concurrently.

4. What was John Adams' tribute to Thomas McKean?

5. Under whom did both Thomas McKean and George Read study?

6. Whose sister did Thomas McKean marry?

7. How was Thomas McKean instrumental in assuring that Delaware voted for independence?

8. What service did McKean render to his country just days after the vote?

9. Retell of McKean's narrow escape.

10. To what did he attribute his protection?

11. What qualities did McKean demonstrate while writing the Constitution of Delaware?

12. Read the Constitution of Delaware. Tell what it says concerning Christians in leadership.

13. Why wasn't McKean present on August 2 at the actual signing of the Declaration?

14. Tell of McKean's account of his family's many moves to avoid capture by the British.

15. What did the supreme court justice of Pennsylvania say about McKean, his predecessor?

George Read

An Honest Lawyer

I Thessalonians 4:11–12

"First and foremost he wanted what was best for Delaware"

ᕽᕽ

BORN
September 18, 1783

BIRTHPLACE
Cecil County, Maryland

EDUCATION
Philadelphia Academy

OCCUPATION
Lawyer

MARRIED
Gertrude Ross

CHILDREN
5

AGE AT SIGNING
42

DIED
September 21, 1798; age 65

As a lawyer, a patriot, a senator, and a judge, he was alike unpretending, consistent, dignified, and impartial. His other peculiar characteristics were an inflexible integrity of motive; a cool determination of purpose; and an invincible perseverance in the conclusions of his judgment.[1]

George Read, one of only six men who signed both the Declaration of Independence and the United States Constitution, was born in Cecil County, Maryland, on September 18, 1733. His father was born into a wealthy Irish family. As a young boy, his family moved to New Castle County, Delaware and he later was educated at a school at Chester, Pennsylvania. He then went to New London, Pennsylvania to be educated under the Reverend Francis Allison, who also instructed several others who would be future Signers of the Declaration and Constitution.

At age 17, he went to Philadelphia to study law under John Moland, and there developed a close friendship with John Dickinson, who later was called "the Penman of the Revolution."

At age 19, Read was admitted to the bar to practice law. He established his practice in New Castle, Delaware, and built up an excellent practice where he became known as an "honest lawyer."

In 1763 he married Mrs. Gertrude Ross Till, a widow and daughter of the pastor of the Anglican church in New Castle. His wife's

His manners were dignified, and his dignity may sometimes have bordered upon austerity. He avoided trifling occupations, disliked familiarity, and could not tolerate the slightest violation of good manners, for which he was himself distinguished. A strict and consistent moralist, he granted no indulgence to laxity of principle in others; and he was remarkably adverse to that qualified dependence which an obligation necessarily produces. Notwithstanding an exact attention to his expenditure, which he never permitted to exceed his income, his pecuniary liberality was very extensive. Mr. Read was above the middle size, erect, and dignified in his demeanour; and he was remarkable for attention to personal arrangements. He was an excellent husband, a good father, and indulgent master, and upright judge, a just man, and a fearless patriot.[2]

brother, John Ross, arranged for Read to replace him as Delaware's attorney general. Also by this marriage, he became brother-in-law of George Ross, who was to become a fellow signer of the Declaration of Independence. George and Gertrude Read had five children.

In 1765, Read was elected a representative from New Castle County to the general assembly of Delaware, a position he occupied for 12 years.

On August 1, 1774, Mr. Read was chosen a member of the Continental Congress and served there till 1777.

First and foremost, he wanted what was best for Delaware. Convinced that most Delawareans weren't ready to separate from England, he voted against independence on July 2, 1776. Yet once independence was declared, Read thought it best for Delaware to unite with the rest of the country, so he shifted gears and signed the Declaration.[5]

The following September, the British captured Wilmington, Delaware, seizing the first governor of the state, John McKinley. Delaware asked George Read to replace him as governor until McKinley's release.

In attempting to move his family safely across the Delaware River, he looked for a safe place to cross, as the shore was almost covered with ships of the enemy. The tide was low and their boat became grounded. The British dispatched an armed barge in their pursuit. Mr. Read presented himself as a country gentleman, returning to his home. The presence of his wife, mother and infant children gave probability to his story, and the Royal Navy, with good humor, actually assisted him. The sailors offered to carry their baggage and his wife, mother and children up the bank. It wasn't until months later they discovered they had let one of the most hunted Americans in the Middle Colonies slip through their fingers.

His exhausting duties affected his health, and in August 1779, he resigned his seat in the Assembly of Delaware. He was re-elected, though, the following year. In 1782, he was appointed Judge of the Court of Appeals. In 1785 he was appointed Judge of a special court by Congress to handle a dispute about land between Massachusetts and New York. He was a member of the Convention of 1786, to work on changes in the Articles of Confederation. The following year he was elected a member of the Senate of Delaware under the new Constitution, of which he was a signer.

George Read and Thomas McKean, both responsible for writing Delaware's constitution and wanting to maintain integrity in the office, placed in it,

> Every person who shall be chosen a member of either house, or appointed to any office or place of trust…shall…make and subscribe the following declaration, to wit: "I do profess faith in God the father and in Jesus Christ, his only Son, and in the Holy Ghost, one God, blessed forever more, and I do acknowledge the Holy scriptures of the Old and New Testament to be given by divine inspiration."[6]

In 1793, he was elevated to the position of Chief Justice of the Supreme Court of Delaware, where he remained until a sudden illness caused his death in 1798, at 64 years of age.

In all the offices which Mr. Read was entrusted by his fellow citizens, he appeared with distinguished ability; but it was as a judge that he stood pre-eminent. For this station he was peculiarly fitted, not only by his unusual legal attainments, but by his singular patience in hearing all that the council might deem important to bring forward, and by a cool and dispassionate deliberation of every circumstance which would bear upon the point in question. To this day his decisions are much respected in Delaware, and are often referred to, as precedents of no doubtful authority.

In private life, the character of Mr. Read was not less estimable and respectable. He was consistent

RES. OF GEORGE READ.
Wilmington Del.

*Residence of George Read
Wilmington, Delaware*

By an adherence to the royal cause, he had reason to anticipate office, honour, and wealth. But his patriotism and integrity were of too pure a character to be influenced by worldly preferment, or pecuniary reward. The question with him was, not what a worldly policy might dictate, but what reason and justice and religion would approve.[3]

❧ Public Service ❧

1753	**Admitted to the bar to practice law**
1763–1744	**Attorney general for the crown for Delaware**
1765–1780	**Member of the Delaware Legislature**
1774–1779	**Delegate from Delaware to the Continental Congress; signed the Declaration of Independence**
1776	**President of the Delaware state constitutional convention**
1777–1778	**Acting president of Delaware**
1782–1789	**Judge of the court of appeals in admiralty cases**
1786	**Delegate from Delaware to the Annapolis Convention**
1787	**Member of the Constitutional Convention; signed the United States Constitution**
1789–1793	**United States senator from Delaware**
1793–1798	**Chief justice of Delaware**

For five years Read presided over the highest court in Delaware. His experience and ability were respected by the lawyers of the state, and his decisions were regarded as landmarks in the development of law and order in the post-revolutionary period.[4]

in all the relations of life, strict in the observance of his moral duties, and characterized by an expanded benevolence towards all around him.[7]

His children, grandchildren, and great grandchildren were prominent in the service of the United States.

On the fifth of December, 1782, Mr. Read was appointed one of the judges of the court of appeals in admiralty cases. This appointment was announced to him in the most flattering manner, by Mr. Boudinot, then president of Congress, and afterwards the venerable president of the Bible Society:

Sir, It gives me very particular satisfaction to have the honour of presenting you the commission of the United States in congress assembled, whereby you are constituted one of the judges of the court of appeals in all cases of capture on the water.

Your established character as a gentleman, lawyer, and man of integrity, leave me no room to doubt but this appointment will do honour to congress, produce the happiest consequences to the good citizens of these states, and, I hope, real satisfaction to yourself, from the consciousness of serving your country with fidelity.

I have the honour to be, with every sentiment of esteem and respect,

Sir, your obedient, And very humble servant, Elias Boudinot.

Hon .George Read.[8]

His acceptance of this appointment was conveyed to Mr. Boudinot, in the following letter:

Newcastle December 10th, 1782

Sir, I had the honour to receive your excellency's letter of the sixth instant, enclosing under its cover a commission to me from the United States of America in congress assembled, for a judge's place of their court of appeals. This unlooked for mark of confidence from that honourable body, impresses me with the strongest sense of gratitude, and I can only say that under this impression, I accept of this appointment with the fullest intention to discharge the duties thereof to the best of my poor abilities, and I hope with an integrity that may become the station. I am persuaded that in doing so, I shall make the best return in my power, for the honour conferred, and the trust reposed in me by the great council of America.

I beg leave to return your excellency my particular thanks for the very flattering and polite manner in which you have been pleased to communicate to me this appointment.

I have the honour to be, with great respect, Your excellency's most obedient And very humble servant,
GEORGE READ
His Excellency, Elias Boudinot, President of Congress.[9]

We have now seen this eminent individual distinguishing himself at the bar as a lawyer, — animating his fellow-citizens against oppression as a patriot, — taking his seat on the national council as a sage, — and presiding on the bench, as one of the judges of the land. In all these lofty stations, exposed to that strict and merciless scrutiny, to which, we trust, republicans will ever subject men in office, no blemish was discovered in his conduct. Applause at the bar did not, in him, generate vanity; success in political life, ambition; nor the dignity of the bench, dogmatism. As a lawyer, a patriot, a senator, and a judge, he was alike unpretending, consistent, dignified, and impartial. His other peculiar characteristics, were an inflexible integrity of motive, a slow and calm deliberation of his subject, a cool determination of purpose; and an invincible perseverance in the conclusions of his judgment.[10]

Questions for Discussion

1. What are we told were Read's characteristics as a lawyer, patriot, senator, and judge?

2. List the many character qualities of George Read as related by his great-grandson.

3. What governed Reed's decision of whether to side with the royal cause or the Patriots?

4. What could he have expected to gain to adhere to the royal cause?

5. What precedents did Read's decisions set while presiding over the Delaware Supreme Court?

6. How many men signed both the Declaration and the Constitution?

7. For what character trait did Read become known?

8. What caused Read to vote against independence, but then change his mind in support of it?

9. Tell of the near escape of George Read and his family while crossing the Delaware River.

10. What character qualities did he employ while handling this sticky situation?

11. Read was a signer of Delaware's state constitution. How did he write it so as to assure that the integrity of office would be preserved?

12. Tell what character qualities Elias Boudinot, president of Congress and later president of the Bible Society, saw in Read's life.

13. Read the definition of "honesty." Set a specific step of action to apply honesty in every area of your life.

Caesar Rodney

The Sacrificial Patriot

John 15:13

"I vote for Independence"

❧❧

BORN
October 7, 1728

BIRTHPLACE
Dover, Delaware

EDUCATION
Self-Educated

OCCUPATION
Landowner

MARRIAGE/CHILDREN
Bachelor; no children

AGE AT SIGNING
47

DIED
June 28, 1784; age 55

John Adams wrote this description after meeting him: "Caesar Rodney is the oddest-looking man in the world; he is tall, thin and slender as a reed, pale; his face is not bigger than a large apple, yet there is some sense and fire, spirit, wit, and a humour in his countenance."[1]

Caesar Rodney, one of eight children, was born near Dover, Delaware on October 7, 1728. He was taught at home by his mother. When Caesar was 17, his father died; at which time he took over the 800-acre family farm and helped his mother raise his six younger brothers and sisters. It was when he was in his late twenties that he completed his child-raising responsibilities and entered public service.

In 1775, he was chosen sheriff of Kent County. Following his term as sheriff he was made a justice of the peace and judge of the lower courts. In 1762, he represented Delaware in the provincial legislature.

In 1765, the first general congress assembled to decide what to do about the Stamp Act. When King George later repealed it, Rodney, along with Thomas McKean and George Read were chosen to express thanks to the king. They drafted the following letter:

> We cannot help but glorying in being the subjects of a king, that has made the preservation of the civil and religious foundation and constant rule of his government, and the safety, ease, and prosperity

of his people, his chiefest care; of a king, whose mild and equal administration is sensibly felt and enjoyed in the remotest parts of his dominion. The clouds which lately hung over America are dissipated. Our complaints have been heard, and our grievances redressed; trade and commerce again flourish. Our hearts are animated with the warmest wishes for the prosperity of the mother country, for which our affection is unbounded, and your faithful subjects here are transported with joy and gratitude. Such are the blessings we may justly expect will ever attend the measures of your majesty, pursuing steadily throughout your wide extended empire, assisted with the advice and support of a British parliament, and a virtuous and wise ministry. We most humbly beseech your majesty, graciously to accept the strongest assurances, that having the justest sense of the many favours we have received from your royal benevolence, during the course of your majesty's reign, and how much our present happiness is owing to your paternal love and care for your people; we will at all times most cheerfully contribute to your majesty's service, to the utmost of our abilities, when your royal requisitions, as heretofore, shall be made known; that your majesty will always find such returns of duty and gratitude from us, as the best of kings may expect from the most loyal subjects, and that you will demonstrate to all the world, that the support of your majesty's government, and the honour and interests of the British nation, are our chief care and concern, desiring nothing more than the continuance of our wise and excellent constitution, in the same happy, firm, and envied situation, in which it was delivered down to us from our ancestors, and your majesty's predecessors.[5]

It was reported that the letter delighted King George, who read it over twice. Unfortunately, the Stamp Act was followed by other oppressive measures. The citizens of Delaware wanted reconciliation with the Mother country, but also had a high regard for their inalienable rights. These same three men drafted another letter in an effort to appeal to King George.

If our fellow-subjects of Great Britain, who derive no authority from us, who cannot in our humble opinion represent us, and to whom we will not yield in loyalty and affection to your majesty, can at their will and

pleasure, of right, give and grant away our property; if they enforce an implicit obedience to every order or act of theirs for that purpose, and deprive all, or any of the assemblies on this continent, of the power of legislation, for differing with them in opinion in matters which intimately affect their rights and interests, and every thing that is dear and valuable to Englishmen, we cannot imagine a case more miserable; we cannot think that we shall have even the shadow of liberty left. We conceive it to be an inherent right in your majesty's subjects, derived to them from God and nature, handed down from their ancestors, and confirmed by your royal predecessors and the constitution, in person, or by their representatives, to give and grant to their own cares have acquired and saved, and in such proportions and at such times, as the national honour and interest may require. Your majesty's faithful subjects of this government have enjoyed this inestimable privilege uninterrupted from its first existence, till of late. They have at all times cheerfully contributed to the utmost of their abilities for your majesty's service, as often as your royal requisitions were made known and they cannot now, but with the greatest uneasiness and distress of mind, part with the power of demonstrating their loyalty and affection to their beloved king [6]

Caesar Rodney suffered from poor health. Asthma often made breathing difficult, and gout sometimes left him unable to walk, but worse yet was a skin cancer that plagued him from his youth. It began to spread to cover one side of his face, and in 1768, part of a tumor was removed from his face, leaving a deep gash across his cheek

He was, as our biographical notice of him clearly indicates, a man of great integrity, and of pure patriotic feeling. He delighted, when necessary, to sacrifice his private interests for the public good. He was remarkably distinguished for a degree of good humour and vivacity; and in generosity of character was an ornament to human nature.[2]

that he kept covered with a green scarf. Unfortunately, the operation did not rid him of the cancer. It was strongly recommended to him by a Philadelphia physician to seek treatment in England, as his best chance. Although his family entreated him to go, his dedication to the American cause prevented him from seeking the only possible cure to his disease. Mr. Rodney was elected speaker of the Provincial Assembly in 1769. He later became chairman of the Committee of Correspondence. Rodney, McKean and Read were sent as delegates to the first Continental Congress in 1774. John Adams said this upon meeting Rodney:

> In 1774 I became acquainted with McKean, Rodney, and Henry [Patrick]. Those three appeared to me to see more clearly to the end of the business than any others of the whole body. At least they were more candid and explicit with me than any others…[7]

While attending to his duties in Congress, he was appointed Brigadier General of his province in 1775. Because of this appointment, he alternated between duties in Congress and duties in his military appointment. After being absent from Congress in an effort to squelch a Loyalist uprising that threatened his home territory, he returned home tired and feeling quite ill. He received an urgent request from Thomas McKean urging him to be present at the State House in the morning to break a deadlock vote for independence. The state house was 80 miles away, and a violent rainstorm was brewing.

On June 7, Richard Henry Lee, delegate from Virginia, had introduced the following resolution in Congress:

> That these United Colonies are, and of right ought to be, free and independent States, that they are absolved from all allegiance to the British Crown, and that all political connection between them and the State of Great Britain is, and ought to be, totally dissolved.

It had become clear that a unanimous vote was imperative. Each colony had only one vote, determined by the majority in its delegation. Delaware had three representatives, Rodney, McKean, and Read. Read felt the move premature. Many delegates faced anguish over which way to vote, but on the morning of the vote, July 2, it looked like the fate of the resolution fell on Delaware. A chain of events had helped sway some delegates. General Washington had just reported that British vessels were gathering in

🐏 Public Service 🐏

1758	Elected high sheriff of Kent County, Delaware
1761–1776	Member of the Delaware colonial legislature; for several years speaker of the house
1765	Delegate to the Stamp Act Congress
1774	Chairman of Delaware's first patriotic convention of delegates
1774–1776	Delegate from Delaware to the Continental Congress; signed the Declaration of Independence
1775–1777	Brigadier general in command of Delaware's militia
1778–1781	President of Delaware
1782–1783	Elected to Congress, but did not serve because of ill health

New Jersey harbor by the threes and fours, and an attack looked imminent.

Delegates began arriving at the State House, whose tall steeple bore this inscription from Leviticus: "Proclaim liberty throughout all the land unto all the inhabitants thereof."

The air was humid that morning after the previous night's tumultuous rains and heavy clouds threatened to break loose again. Thomas McKean paced the hall peering anxiously from one of the tall windows. Proceedings would start in just a few minutes. To him, it seemed that the fate of the resolution rested on one sick man — his friend and colleague, Caesar Rodney.

John Hancock, the President, began taking his seat, as did his secretary. Suddenly, the pounding of horses hooves sounded on the cobblestone streets. Here came Caesar Rodney in his three-cornered hat up Chestnut Street. He was mud-splattered and bedraggled, a picture of fatigue and suffering. McKean greeted him with grateful fervor. Rodney had departed from Dover within ten minutes of receiving McKean's message the previous evening. He hadn't even stopped to change clothing, but mounted his horse and rode through a swift thunderstorm. He stopped along the way only to change horses, and continued through the night. As he strode into the Assembly Chamber, arm-in-arm with McKean, President Hancock called the assembly to order.

> When Delaware was called, Caesar Rodney pulled himself to his feet. He said, "As I believe the voice of my constituents and of all sensible and honest men is in favor of Independence, and my own judgment concurs, I vote for Independence!" Then he sank exhausted into his seat.[8]

> The twelve colonies participating had voted unanimously for Freedom! Each man present fully realized what his vote meant in terms of personal danger should this rebellion fail. King George III had declared every rebel in the land a traitor. The penalty for treason was death by hanging. Caesar Rodney, who had ridden from Dover all though a stormy night to turn the vote of Delaware to independence, selflessly relinquished any chance left to him of going to England for treatment of the ailment said to have eventually caused his death.[9]

> *Of the personal character of Mr. Rodney, we have few opportunities of obtaining information, beyond the materials which have formed the subject of this notice. As a politician, he displayed at all times great integrity and high-mindedness, never yielding his deliberate opinions to the prevailing sentiments of the day, and sacrificing his present interest to his sense of honour and justice. This course in a few instances, was for a time injurious to his political aims, but it eventually gained for him, what an honourable course always gains for a statesman in the end, the unbounded confidence and esteem of his countrymen.[3]*

Rodney signed his name to the Declaration of Independence on August 2, with most of the other delegates. William Ellery of Rhode Island sat where he could observe each signer.

> William Ellery, his chin on his hand, was studying the countenance of the next signer. Caesar Rodney, the first of the Delaware delegation to come to the table, had won the eternal admiration of his Congressional associates with his wild ride from Dover, Delaware, on the night of July 1. Ellery found this man's appearance fascinating. Rodney was tall and thin. His small, wrinkled face seemed even smaller because of the green scarf he used to cover the left cheek that was afflicted by an advanced case of skin cancer. Despite his ill health, his eyes blazed with an indomitable spirit and a keen sense of humor.[10]

In September, when the British advanced into Delaware, Rodney collected troops, and by the direction of General Washington:

> placed his forces south of the main army to observe the movements of the British at the head of Elk River, Maryland, and, if possible, to cut the enemy off from their fleet. He wrote to General Washington, telling

The private character of Mr. Rodney is chiefly remarkable for its good humour and vivacity. He was fond of society, and not averse to the pleasures of the table, never exceeding, however, the boundaries of propriety and good manners. He was particularly fond of associating with persons younger than himself, to whom his easy manners, long knowledge of the world, and fund of wit and anecdote, afforded a never failing pleasure.[4]

of his difficulties in getting the militia to turn out, and saying that, "As soon as I can set forward I shall advise you. God send you a complete victory." Mr. Rodney remained with the army for nearly two months, and during a great part of the time entered into the most active and laborious services, which his station as brigadier general required. Even after the period for which the troops under him had enlisted was expired, he offered to remain with the army, and perform the duties of a soldier, wherever the commander in chief might think he could be useful. Sensible of the patriotic spirit by which this officer was dictated, general Washington wrote him the following highly flattering letter, the original of which now lies before us, dated at Morris-Town, on the eighteenth of February, 1777.

Sir — Lord Stirling did me the favour of sending to me your letter of the eighth instant to him, mentioning your cheerfulness to continue in service, (though your brigade had returned home,) and waiting my determination on that head. The readiness with which you took the field at the period most critical to our affairs — the industry you used in bringing the militia of the Delaware state — and the alertness observed by you in forwarding on the troops from Trenton — reflect the highest honour on your character, and place your attachment to the cause in the most distinguished point of view. They claim my sincerest thanks, and I am happy in this opportunity of giving them to you. Circumstanced as you are, I see no necessity in detaining you longer from your family and affairs, which no doubt demand your presence and attention. You have therefore my leave to return.[11]

As president of the state, Caesar Rodney received alarming appeals from General Washington for relief of the of the army's desperate need for supplies. In the spring of 1780 the General informed him that, "...the army is again reduced to an extremity of distress, for want of provision...we have *this* day but *one* day's supply [of flour] in the camp." Rodney worked constantly to help. In a letter to John Dickinson (elected a Delaware delegate in November, 1776), he asked his colleagues to assure the committee appointed to procure flour that he would do everything in his power, but he feared the flour would "come high;" as those termed speculators are as thick and as industrious as bees, and as active and wicked as the devil himself.[12]

Loved by the people of Delaware, who wanted to re-elect him, Rodney declined in 1782 because of his failing health. They still elected him to Congress, but he was never able to take his seat. His cancer continued to spread, and took his life on June 28, 1784.

Questions for Discussion

1. What do we learn of Caesar Rodney's character from John Adams' description?

2. What do we know about his character as a politician, which gained him esteem from his countrymen?

3. What do we know about his private Christianity?

4. Where was Caesar Rodney educated? By whom?

5. What circumstances helped to teach him responsibility at an early age?

6. What was his first public office?

7. Reading the appeal made by Rodney and McKean to King George, what qualities does it reveal Rodney to have?

8. Tell about his second appeal to King George.

9. How was Rodney, in fact, signing his own death warrant by signing the Declaration of Independence?

10. Would you use the word "disinterested" to describe his character? Why?

11. What insight does John Adams give us of Rodney's foresight and vision?

12. Why was Rodney not present to hear Richard Henry Lee's proposal for independence?

13. Why did McKean say that the fate of the nation rested upon one sick man?

14. Describe the account of Rodney's famous horseback ride.

15. What does it reveal about Rodney's character and sacrifice?

16. What was the penalty for treason?

17. What character trait did William Ellery note in Rodney's countenance at the time of the signing?

18. In what position did Rodney serve his country, though sick himself?

19. What character quality do we find in this account of his service?

20. Tell of George Washington's appeal to Rodney for provisions. What was Rodney's response? What character does this reveal about him?

21. Ask God if there is something you can sacrifice (like time, money, service) in order to have influence in leading this country back to its godly roots.

Maryland

Charles Carroll
Samuel Chase
William Paca
Thomas Stone

Charles Carroll

Courageous Patriot

Joshua 1:9

"On fire for religious freedom"
"The best and most
glorious cause"

❧❧

BORN
September 19, 1737

BIRTHPLACE
Annapolis, Maryland

EDUCATION
Catholic and foreign schools

OCCUPATION
Landowner

MARRIED
Mary Darnall, 1768

CHILDREN
7

AGE AT SIGNING
38

DIED
November 14, 1832; age 95

His mind was highly cultivated. He was always a model of regularity of conduct, and sedateness of judgment. In natural sagacity, in refinement of taste and pleasures, in unaffected and habitual courtesy, in vigilant observation, vivacity of spirit, and true susceptibility of domestic and social happiness, in the best forms, he had but few equals during the greater part of his long and bright existence.[1]

Charles Carroll of Carrollton

C harles Carroll was the only Catholic to sign the Declaration of Independence, and also was reputed to be the wealthiest man in America at the time. He was born in Annapolis, Maryland on September 20, 1737, the son of a tobacco planter. As a child he suffered from fevers, and it was thought that he wouldn't live past childhood. When he was eight years old, his father took him to France to receive a Catholic education, as Catholics in Maryland at the time were denied all political, religious and educational freedom. Young Charles attended a school run by English Jurists at St. Omer for six years, along with two of his cousins.

He then attended six more years in college-level studies in France. He went to London in 1757, where he studied law for another six years.

At the age of 26, Carroll returned home to Maryland. He spoke French fluently, was an accomplished horseman, and had the manners of an aristocrat. His father gave him Carrollton Manor, a 10,000-acre estate in Frederick County, Maryland, and he was known from then on as Charles Carroll of Carrollton.

Mr. Carroll, as a politician was quick to decide, and prompt to execute. His measures were open and energetic, and he was more inclined to exceed than to fall short of the end which he proposed. As a speaker he was concise and animated; the advantages of travel and society made him graceful; books, habits of stuffy and acute observation made him impressive and instructive. As a writer he was remarkably dignified; his arrangement was regular, his style was full, without being diffuse, and, though highly argumentative, was prevented from being dull by the vein of polite learning which was visible throughout. In person Mr. Carroll is slight, and rather below the middle size. His face is strongly marked, his eye is quick and piercing, and his whole countenance expressive of energy and determination. His manners are easy, affable, and graceful; and in all the elegancies and observances of polite society, few men are his superiors.[2]

He married his cousin, Mary "Molly" Darnall in June, 1768, when he was 30 years old. The couple had seven children.

Though some thought Carroll would side with Great Britain, he was a fervent patriot. He resented Great Britain for oppression of Catholics, both in the colonies and in Ireland. In writing to George Washington, he called the struggle for independence, "the best and most glorious cause."[5]

Charles wrote anti-British newspaper articles for the Maryland gazette which he signed using the name "Second Citizen." When the governor of Maryland proclaimed in 1771 that civil officers of the colony must collect specific fees, Carroll argued the legality of such a proclamation being issued without the approval of the legislature. The proclamation was hung upon a gallows by the public hangmen, and the people of Annapolis went to Carroll as a group thanking him for defending their rights, and made him their "First Citizen."

The following letter was sent by William Paca, a fellow signer, to commend him:

Sir, your manly and spirited opposition to the arbitrary attempt of government, to establish the fees of office by proclamation, justly entitles you to the exalted character of a distinguished advocate for the rights of your country. The proclamation needed only to be thoroughly understood, to be generally detested: and you have had the happiness to please, to instruct, to convince your countrymen. It is the public voice, sir, that the establishment of fees, by the sole authority of prerogative, is an act of usurpation, and act of tyranny, *which in a land of freedom, must not, cannot, be endured.* The free and independent citizens of Annapolis, the metropolis of Maryland, who have lately honoured us with the public character of representatives, impressed with a just sense of the signal services which you have done your country, instructed us, on the day of our election, to return you their hearty thanks. Public gratitude, sir, for public services, is the patriot's due; and we are proud to observe the generous feelings of our fellow citizens toward an advocate for liberty. With pleasure we comply with the instructions of our constituents, and in their names we thank you for the spirited exertion of your abilities. We are, sir, most respectfully, your very humble servants, William Paca, Matthews Hammond.[6]

Carroll became convinced early on that independence was necessary. He had the following conversation with Samuel Chase, later to be a fellow signer:

Carroll already had made up his mind that revolution was the only likely way by which the dispute with Britain could ultimately be settled. He is said to have disclosed this in the following conversation with Samuel Chase, who also later signed the Declaration of Independence:

Chase: "We have the better of our opponents; we have completely written them down."
Carroll: "And do you think that writing will settle the question between us?"
Chase: "To be sure, what else can we resort to?"
Carroll: "The bayonet! Our arguments will only raise the feeling of the people to that pitch, when open war will be looked to as the arbiter of the dispute."[7]

When a member of the British parliament wrote to Carroll mocking the idea of resistance by the colonies and stating that 6,000 British soldiers could march from one end of the colonies to the others, Carroll wrote the following reply:

So they may, but they will be masters of the spot only on which they encamp. They will find nought but enemies before and around them. If we are beaten on the plains, we will retreat to our mountains and defy them. Our resources will increase with our difficulties. Necessity will force us to exertion; until, tired of combating, in vain, against a spirit which victory after victory cannot subdue, your armies will evacuate our soil, and your country retire, an immense loser, from the contest. – No, sire. – We have made up our minds to abide the issue of the approaching struggle, and though much blood may be spilt, we have no doubt of ultimate success.[8]

In 1774, Carroll had much influence in Maryland's version of the "Boston Tea Party." The colonies' patriots had resolved not to allow tea to be imported. The ship *Peggy Stewart* arrived in Annapolis loaded with tea, and an angry mob of colonists gathered, threatening violence. Friends of the owner, Anthony Stewart, turned to Carroll for advice and protection.

Carroll is said to have replied: "Whatever may be my personal esteem for Mr. Stewart, and my wish to prevent violence, it will not be in my power to protect him, unless he consents to pursue a decisive course of conduct. My advice is, that he set fire to the vessel, and burn her, together with the tea she contains, to the water's edge." Within a few hours, the ship was burned, and mob violence was averted.[9]

Carroll influenced the Maryland legislature to reverse their instructions to the Maryland delegation to oppose independence.

After reciting the wrongs suffered from the king of Great Britain, the declaration continues, "We, the delegates of Maryland, in convention assembled, do declare, that the king of Great Britain has violated his contract with this people, and that they owe no allegiance to him. We have therefore thought it just and necessary to empower our deputies in congress, to join with a majority of the United Provinces in declaring them free and independent states, in framing such further confederation, in making foreign alliances, and in adopting such other measures as shall be judge necessary for the preservation of their liberties. No ambitious views, no desire of independence, induced the people of Maryland to form a union with

❧ Public Service ❧

1775–1776	**Delegate to Maryland's patriotic convention; helped write Maryland's state constitution**
1776	**Appointed by Continental Congress to a commission to urge Canadians to support the United Colonies against Great Britain**
1776–1778	**Delegate from Maryland to the Continental Congress; signed the Declaration of Independence**
1777–1894	**State senator in Maryland legislature**
1789–1792	**Represented Maryland as U.S. senator in Congress**

the other provinces. To procure an exemption from parliamentary taxation, and to continue to the legislatures of these colonies the sole and exclusive right of regulating their internal polity, was our original and only motive. To maintain inviolate our liberties, and to transmit them unimpaired to posterity, was our duty and first wish; our next to continue connected with, and dependent on Great Britain. For the truth of these assertions we appeal to that Almighty Being, who is emphatically styled the Searcher of hearts, and from whose omniscience nothing is concealed. Relying on his divine protection, and trusting to the justice of our cause, we exhort and conjure every virtuous citizen, to join cordially in defence of our common rights, and in maintenance of the freedom of this and her sister colonies."[10]

He then returned to Congress in time to sign the Declaration of Independence. He signed, *Charles Carroll of Carrollton.*

 The question naturally arises, Why did Mr. Carroll append to his signature the place of his residence, "Carrollton?" It is said that when he wrote his name, a delegate near him suggested, that as he had a cousin of the name of Charles Carroll, in Maryland, the latter might be taken for him, and he (the signer) escape attainder, or any other punishment that might fall upon the heads of the patriots. Mr. Carroll immediately seized the pen and wrote, "of Carrolton," at the end of his name, exclaiming, "They cannot mistake me now!"[11]

A signature to the declaration, was an important step for every individual member of congress. It exposed the signers of it to the confiscation of their estates, and the loss of life, should the British arms prove victorious. Few men had more at stake in respect to property than Mr. Carroll, he being considered the richest individual in the colonies. But wealth was of secondary value in his estimation, in comparison with the rights and liberties of his country. When asked whether he would annex his name, he replied, "most willingly," and seizing a pen, instantly subscribed "to this record of glory."

*B*etter known to William Ellery and to others in the hall was Charles Carroll, thirty-eight, who now accepted the quill pen from Thomas Stone. Carroll was the sole Roman Catholic in the Congress, a fact that intrigued Ellery, who knew that according to Maryland law, Catholics were not permitted to enter politics. Consequently, Carroll's desire for independence and freedom from the old regime had been stirred not only by the usual motives but by a personal determination to bring genuine religious freedom to Maryland. As Carroll came forward, William Ellery heard someone remark, "There goes another fortune!" Carroll smiled and inscribed with a flourish, "Charles Carroll of Carrollton."[3]

"There go a few millions," said someone who watched the pen as it traced the name of Charles Carroll, of Carrollton, on the parchment.[12]

Also in 1776, Carroll helped frame Maryland's first state constitution, and later served as one of Maryland's

CHARLES CARROLL OF CARROLLTON
Baltimore Md

Residence of Charles Carroll of Carrollton
Baltimore, Maryland

first two senators. Once owning hundreds of slaves, he eventually turned against slavery and freed many of them, including 30 when he turned 80 years old.

Although Charles Carroll had been sickly in his youth, he rode his horse ten miles a day at age ninety-three. He was one of the last three signers to die. People would drop by to visit him, just to shake his hand.

The following is an excerpt from his biography, written while he was still living:

> We have now reached the termination of Mr. Carroll's public life, in his sixty-third year, and see him retiring among his fellow citizens to the quiet enjoyments of his family circle. His life, from 1801, up to the present time, affords few materials for a biography. It has glided along, in that tranquil happiness which the full enjoyment of every faculty, the recollection of past honours, the possession of a large fortune, the affection and attention of children and grand-children, and the respect of his countrymen, could bestow; and in his ninetieth year, Charles Carroll of Carrollton finds his activity undiminished, his faculties unimpaired, and his feelings and affections buoyant and warm… On the third of July, 1826, there only remained — John Adams, Thomas Jefferson, and Charles Carroll of Carrollton.[13]

He fought continually to ensure that the State of Maryland upheld freedom of religion. In 1832, the last of the signers died in his daughter's home in Baltimore. He was ninety-five years old.

> He seemed to have been born for the occasion and the crisis; and his fine intellect, undaunted courage, and fervid temperament, all ministered to the glorious result. He arrived at manhood just as the disputes between the colonies and the mother country began; and from that time till the declaration of independence, he moved about unceasingly like a flame, casting warmth and light around him. His contagious ardour and powerful rhetoric, made proselytes of his wealthy and less sanguine friends, who having much to lose, were timorous and lukewarm in the cause; and thus were some recruits enlisted that afterwards sustained their parts efficiently and nobly. His influence over the less considerate was unbounded; he was described as moving perpetually "with a mob at his heels." This was in the very commencement of the troubles, when he was the torch that lighted up the revolutionary flame in Maryland. …The vehemence of his feelings on the subject of party politics was to be expected in a man who never had been lukewarm in his life. He could not separate his feelings from his judgment; and though he may have been mistaken, he was unquestionably sincere and firmly patriotic. "Yes, sir," said he to a son-in-law, a few years before his death, "you are a democrat; and you are right to be one, for you are a young man; but an old man, Mr. _____, would be a fool to be a democrat."[14]

> On the mercy of my Redeemer I rely for salvation and on His merits; not the works I have done in obedience to His precepts.[15]

❧☙

Charles Carroll and Samuel Adams both cited religious freedom as reason they became involved in the American Revolution.[4]

☙ Questions for Discussion ☙

1.   What was Charles Carroll's driving passion to be involved in the struggle for independence?

2.   What was Charles Carroll's personal declaration about his belief in Jesus Christ?

3.   What character qualities attributed to the success of his social influence? (Why did others seem to be around him?)

4.   What examples of decisiveness do we see in Mr. Carroll's life?

5.   What hardships had his family faced which God used to motivate him to be an advocate for religious liberty?

6.   What qualities that he possessed led others to trust in his leadership?

7.   Describe qualities revealed by his conversation with Samuel Chase.

8.   What qualities do we see shine forth in his reply to the member of the British parliament who mocked him?

9.   How did Carroll use his power of influence in Maryland's version of the "Boston Tea Party"?

10. Tell how Carroll's persuasiveness influenced the Maryland legislature to change their position on independence.

11. What character quality motivated Carroll to add "of Carrollton" to his signature on the Declaration?

12. The fact that Carroll was putting his "millions" in jeopardy, tells us what about his character?

Samuel Chase

Bold Patriot

Philippians 1:20

"Bulldog for Freedom"

BORN
April 17, 1741

BIRTHPLACE
Somerset County, Maryland

EDUCATION
Self-taught

OCCUPATION
Lawyer

MARRIED
Anne Baldwin, 1762
Hannah Kitty Giles, 1784

CHILDREN
6

AGE AT SIGNING
35

DIED
June 19, 1811; age 70

One colleague said that he had "more learning than knowledge, and more of both than judgment." But though radical in his opinions and aggressive in action, the enthusiasm and vitality of his devotion to the cause of independence were invaluable during the Revolution and the early years of the new nation.[2]

Samuel Chase was born on April 17, 1741, in Somerset County, Maryland, the son of an Episcopal clergyman who had emigrated from England. Samuel was taught at home by his father who had been a professor of Latin and Hebrew. His mother died during his birth, which may account for his lack of training in gentlemanly manners.

At 18, Samuel went to Annapolis, Maryland, where he studied law. He learned quickly and was admitted to the bar at the age of 20. In 1762, he married Anne Baldwin of Annapolis. They had six children, although only four survived infancy.

Chase was elected to the colonial legislature at age 23, and held that position for the next 20 years. Chase was a man of strong beliefs. In a surprising decision, he helped pass regulations opposed by the royal governor, that reduced the amount of payment to the church and cut in half the income of the clergy, including that of his own father.

When the British Parliament passed the Stamp Act, Chase instigated mob actions to show the people's displeasure of "taxation without representation." Proud of his actions when the Stamp Act was repealed, Chase wrote:

I admit, gentlemen, that I was one of those who committed to the flames, in effigy, the stamp distributor of this province, and who openly disputed the parliamentary right to tax the colonies, while you skulked in your houses, some of you asserting the parliamentary right, and esteeming the stamp act as a beneficial law. Others of you meanly grumbled in your corners, not daring to speak out your sentiments.[5]

Chase helped organize Maryland's Committee of Correspondence and was sent to the first Continental Congress in 1774. He was sent again to the Continental Congress in 1775 and supported the appointment of George Washington as commander-in-chief of the Continental Army.

Because of his florid oratory, Chase became known as the "Demosthenes of Maryland." Long before Congress was ready to declare the colonies independent, Chase made speeches in Congress in which he declared "by the God of heaven he owed no allegiance to the king of Great Britain" – shocking words to the more conservative delegates. Chase discovered in the autumn of 1775 that one of the delegates from Georgia, a Presbyterian clergyman by the name of John Joachim Zubly, had been writing to the royal governor of Georgia disclosing that the Continental Congress was discussing the likelihood of declaring the colonies independent. Chase took the floor of Congress to denounce Zubly as a traitor; but before the Georgia delegate could be arrested for treason Zubly admitted his guilt by fleeing back to Georgia and the protection of the royal governor. There Zubly became an active Tory, siding with the British until his death late in the Revolutionary War. Chase won many friends and admirers for his fearless exposure of the traitor.[6]

Chase was sent on a mission to Canada along with Benjamin Franklin, Charles Carroll, and John Carroll, to encourage people there to join the colonies. They failed in their attempt, and returning to Congress found the

❧ Public Service ❧

1761	Admitted to the bar in Annapolis, Maryland
1764–1775	Represented Maryland in the Continental Congress; signed the Declaration of Independence
1776–1784	Member of the Maryland state legislature
1783–1784	Emissary to London seeking to recover money for Bank of England stock owned by Maryland
1788	Delegate to the Maryland convention that ratified the United States Constitution
1788–1795	Judge of the criminal court of Baltimore County
1791–1794	Chief justice of the general court of Maryland
1796–1811	Associate justice of the Supreme Court of the U.S.
1804	Impeached by the U.S. House of Representatives for malfeasance in office
1805	Acquitted of charges of malfeasance by the U.S. Senate

delegates in serious deliberation over independence. Finding the orders given to the Maryland delegates was a major obstacle, he returned to Maryland hurriedly and made a whirlwind tour around the state, making speeches on stumps or wherever possible, to any groups of farmers and villagers who would listen. He forcefully urged citizens to let their voices be heard to the Maryland convention of Annapolis.

The tide of patriotism that Chase and others stirred, swayed the conservative members of the Maryland convention. On June 28, 1776, Chase wrote to John Adams in Philadelphia: "Friday evening, nine o'clock. I am just this moment from the house to procure an  express to follow the post, with an unanimous vote of our convention for independence. See the glorious effect of country instructions. The people have fire, if it is not smothered." Riding horseback, Chase hurried back to Philadelphia, arriving in time to vote with the rest of the Maryland delegation on July 2 in support of Richard Henry Lee's resolutions for independence, to approve the Declaration of Independence on July 4, and to sign it on August 2.[7]

Chase continued in Congress until 1778, serving on various committees. One committee looked for ways to restrict the activity of Tories and enemies of the patriotic cause. Another was responsible for the arrest and imprisonment of Quakers in Pennsylvania and New Jersey who published articles accusing the Continental Congress of giving information to the British forces.

About this time his wife died, leaving him to raise the children, so he returned to Annapolis to continue serving in the state legislature and worked to rebuild his law practice. It was during this time, on a trip to Baltimore, that he attended a debate and noticed the potential of William Pinkney, who was a pharmacy apprentice as he had no money for law school. Chase invited Pinkney to move to Annapolis, funding and guiding his law study. Pinkney had a distinguished career as U.S. representative, diplomat, attorney general of the United States, and U.S. senator.

After the peace treaty was signed with Great Britain in 1783, Chase was chosen by the governor of Massachusetts to go to London in order to collect $800,000 owed

Associate Justice Joseph Story, who was appointed to the Supreme Court after Chase's death, described Chase in his last years: "His manners are coarse, and in appearance harsh; but in reality he abounds with good humor…In person, in manners, unwieldly strength, in severity of reproof, in real tenderness of heart, and above all in intellect, he is the living, I had almost said the exact, image of Samuel Johnson." More than twenty years later, Chief Justice John Marshall wrote of his former colleague: "He possessed a strong mind, great legal knowledge, and was a valuable judge, whose loss was seriously felt by his survivors. He was remarkable also for his vivacity and his companionable qualities. He said many things which were much admired at the time, but I have not treasured them in my memory so as to be able to communicate them."[1]

to the state by the bank of England. He was unsuccessful in negotiating, but Pinkney was able to collect the money 13 years later while serving as U.S. Commissioner in England. While in London, Chase married Hannah Kitty Giles on March 3, 1784. The couple had two daughters.

In 1786, John Edward Howard, a Revolutionary War hero and later governor of Maryland, offered Chase a large tract of land in Baltimore in exchange for Chase

Chase was only thirty-five when he signed the Declaration. He looked older. Ellery was amused by the angry expression on the Maryland delegate's face as he picked up the quill. Unlike the calm deliberation of the majority of the signers, Chase wrote his name as though he wished the ink were pure venom that could somehow bring death to King George.[3]

RES. OF JUDGE SAMUEL CHASE
Baltimore, Md.

Residence of Judge Samuel Chase
Baltimore, Maryland

moving there and helping build the future of the town. Chase accepted, and Baltimore became his home for the rest of his life.

In 1788, Chase was appointed judge of the criminal court of Baltimore County. He continued to practice law until, in 1791, he was appointed chief justice of Maryland's general court.

An incident occurred in 1794 that showed Chase's unswerving belief in the supremacy of the law. A riot had taken place in which a mob had tarred and feathered some men who had spoken out against the ruling party in Baltimore. The two leaders of the mob had been arrested, and when they were brought to court many members of the mob appeared in their support. The prisoners refused to give bond for their further appearance in court, and the sheriff was afraid to take them to jail against the wishes of the mob. Chase then asked the sheriff to swear him in as an

officer so that he personally could take the men to jail. On hearing this, a fellow-lawyer warned him that he would endanger his life and property by such an action. "God forbid," he replied, "that my countrymen should ever be guilty of so daring an outrage; but, sire, with the blessing of God, I will do my duty — they may destroy my property, they may pull down my house over my head, yea, they may make a widow of my wife, and my children fatherless — the life of one man is of little consequence compared to the prostration of the laws of the land — with the blessing of God, I will do my duty, be the consequences what they may." Chase carried his point, and bond was provided for the accused leaders of the mob.[8]

On January 27, 1796, George Washington commissioned Chase as an associate justice of the Supreme Court of the U.S., in which position he remained for the rest of his life. Afflicted with severe gout, he died in Baltimore two months after celebrating his seventieth birthday.

Judge Chase was a man of great benevolence of feeling and in all his walks he exemplified the beauties of Christianity, of which he was a sincere professor.[9]

*H*e was a firm believer in Christianity, and but a short time before his death, having partaken of the sacrament, he declared himself to be in peace with all mankind.[4]

Questions for Discussion

1. Give an example of determination in Samuel Chase's life.

2. What character quality was demonstrated when Chase helped pass regulations to reduce income to the clergy?

3. What character traits were demonstrated by the burning in effigy of a stamp collector?

4. Why was Chase known as the "Demosthenes of Maryland"?

5. What character qualities are demonstrated in Chase's life by the way in which he dealt with John Zubly?

6. When Chase returned from Canada and found that Maryland delegates were held back from voting for independence by previous orders, how did he, one man, change the course of events? What character is shown by a man who would do this?

7. Tell of Chase's horseback ride in the nick of time to vote for freedom.

8. Tell how Chase influenced William Pinkney's life and what character he possessed that led him to do this. What is one great accomplishment that Pinkney later achieved?

9. What character did John Edward Howard recognize to be in Chase's life when he gave him land in exchange for expertise?

10. What character quality was exemplified by Chase's defending the law of the land in 1794?

11. Do we have any evidence that Samuel Chase was a Christian?

12. List the character in Chase's life reported to us by Justice Joseph Story and Chief Justice John Marshall.

13. How did Chase demonstrate the quality of boldness?

14. Is there a righteous cause for which God wants to empower you with boldness to defend or fight?

William Paca

Zealous for Religious Freedom

Galatians 4:18

"Gospel Preacher's Advocate"

∿∿

BORN
October 31, 1740
BIRTHPLACE
Abingdon, Maryland
EDUCATION
College of Philadelphia;
Inner Temple, London
OCCUPATION
Lawyer, jurist
MARRIED
Mary Chew, 1763;
Anne Harrison, 1777
CHILDREN
6
AGE AT SIGNING
35
DIED
October 13, 1799; age 58

He was a pure and active patriot, a consistent Christian, and a valuable citizen, in every sense of the word. His death was mourned as a public calamity; and his life, pure and spotless, active and useful, exhibited a bright exemplar for the imitation of the young men of America.[1]

William Paca, a son of a prominent planter-landowner was born in 1740, at Chilbury Hall, near Abingdon, Maryland. He received his early education from private tutors, and at age 15, he attended the College of Philadelphia. Upon graduating, he studied with an attorney in Annapolis and read law in London.

In 1763, he married Mary Chew and set up practice in Annapolis. They had five children, but only three lived to adulthood. His wife died when she was 38, and he remarried, to Anne Harrison. He and Anne had one child; Anne died at age 23. Their child died before his third birthday.

In 1767, Paca was elected to a seat in the Maryland legislature, and in 1773 became a member of the Maryland Committee of Correspondence. He received an appointment to the first Continental Congress at which time he signed the Declaration of Independence. As a member of the council of safety, he spent thousands of dollars of his own funds to supply American troops. He served as governor of Maryland from 1782-1785. Paca was instrumental in working on the Bill of Rights.

After his first wife died, he sold his home in Annapolis and moved to Wye Plantation. In later life, he had rebuilt his fortune, and Wye Hall was said to be the nation's most magnificent mansion. He aided in establishing Washington College at Chesterton, Maryland.

As governor, he was known for his correctness and integrity, for dignity and simplicity. He zealously defended religion, to which he gave personal donations. He made the following recommendation to the general assembly:

> "It is far from our intention," said he, "to embarrass your deliberations with a variety of objects; but we cannot pass over matters of so high concernment as religion and learning. The sufferings of the ministers of the gospel of all denominations, during the war, have been very considerable; and the perseverance and firmness of those, who discharged their sacred functions under many discouraging circumstances, claim our acknowledgements and thanks. The bill of rights and form of government recognize the principle of public support for the ministers of the gospel, and ascertain the mode. Anxiously solicitous for the blessings of government, and the welfare and happiness of our citizens, and thoroughly convinced of the powerful influence of religion, when

Paca and Chase both sided with America against the Mother Country, but their styles were different. While Chase stirred up crowds with his fiery speeches, Paca, a quiet man, preferred to write newspaper articles and work behind the scenes. Together, they were a great team that helped lead Maryland toward independence.[3]

RES. OF Wᵐ PACA
Queenstown Mᵈ

*Residence of William Paca
Queenstown, Maryland*

❧ Public Service ❧

1764	Admitted to the bar to practice law in Maryland
1768–1774	Member of the colonial legislature of Maryland
1774–1779	Delegate from Maryland to the Continental Congress; signed the Declaration of Independence
1777–1779	Member of the Maryland state senate
1778–1780	Chief judge of the circuit court of appeals in admiralty
1782–1785	Governor of Maryland
1789–1799	Federal district judge for Maryland

diffused by its respectable teachers we beg leave most seriously and warmly to recommend, among the first objects of your attention, on the return of peace, the making such provision as the constitution, in this case, authorizes and approves."[5]

Governor Paca's recommendation was warmly received by the assembly which passed several rulings in aid of several denominations of Christians, numerous at that time in Maryland.

The interest which he manifested in favour of religion, met the warm approbation of the various sects; and from the Episcopalians, in particular, it elicited, through their convention, a formal expression of thanks.[6]

Paca accepted an appointment from President George Washington in 1789 as a federal district judge for Maryland.

Before making this appointment, Washington wrote to James McHenry for his opinion of Paca, and received McHenry's reply that Paca would 'carry much respectability and legal dignity into the office.[7]

William Paca remained in the office of judge of the district court of Maryland until he died at the age of 58 at Wye Hall.

In his address he was unusually graceful, and in his social powers was excelled by few. His attention to the young was not the least excellent trait in his character. He sought their company, and took a deep interest in their moral and intellectual improvement. Even after he became governor of the state, he was in the habit of attending a club at Annapolis, composed of young men and gentlemen of science. In this school, many were trained, who afterwards became highly distinguished both as statesmen and lawyers. It was here that the celebrated orator, William Pinkney, first attracted the attention of Judge Chase, an account of whose particularly kind conduct towards him, we have given in the life of that gentleman. We shall only add to this notice of Mr. Paca, that as he lived a life of distinguished usefulness, so he died regretted by all who knew how to estimate moral worth, intellectual elevation, and political integrity.[4]

<svg> Questions for Discussion <svg>

1. Paca and Chase made a good team in working for Maryland's independence. What qualities, although very different from Chase's, did God use in Paca's life to influence the people of Maryland?

2. What qualities compelled Paca to train young men?

3. What character qualities do you see in Paca's life?

4. What is an example of generous self-sacrifice in Paca's life?

5. What characterized Paca's duties as governor?

6. What evidence do we have that Paca was a Christian?

7. Tell evidence of William Paca having lived a useful life.

8. How can you exercise zealousness in defending Jesus Christ? Or religious freedom?

Thos. Stone

Thomas Stone

Patriot of Initiative

Colossians 3:17

"A Professor of Religion"

BORN
1743
BIRTHPLACE
Charles County, Maryland
EDUCATION
Self-taught
OCCUPATION
Lawyer
MARRIED
Margaret Brown, 1768
CHILDREN
3
AGE AT SIGNING
33
DIED
October 5, 1787; age 44

Mr. Stone was a professor of religion, and distinguished for a sincere and fervent piety. To strangers, he had the appearance of austerity; but among his intimate friends, he was affable, cheerful, and familiar. In his disposition he was uncommonly amiable, and well disposed. In person, he was tall, but well-proportioned. [1]

Thomas Stone was born to a wealthy landowner at his family's plantation in Charles County, Maryland. As a boy, young Thomas rode twenty miles on horseback to and from school each day, and by his early teens, he had obtained a good education in the Latin and Greek languages. When his father died, his estate went to Thomas' elder brother. Thomas had a thirst for learning, though, and borrowed money to go to Annapolis, Maryland in order to study law under Thomas Johnson, who later became Maryland's first state governor. He was admitted to the bar at 21 years old and began practicing the following year in Frederick, Maryland. Two years later, he moved back to Charles County and continued to practice law.

At 25 years of age, he married Margaret Brown with whom he had at least three children. In 1771, they purchased a farm in Charles County, Maryland, with his wife's dowry. They built Habre-de-Venture, which would be his home for the rest of his life.

Stone was elected to the Second Continental Congress of 1775. He rarely spoke in Congress, and dreaded the prospect of a long, bloody war with the Mother Country. He did sign the Declaration of Independence, but hoped for some way of reconciliation with Great Britain.

While in Congress, he served on many committees, including the one that created the Articles of Confederation, which held the colonies together during the Revolution.

Upon his retirement from Congress, he was elected to represent Maryland in the state senate. About the time the U.S. Constitution was being created, his wife became ill. She had been inoculated for smallpox while visiting Thomas in Philadelphia in 1776. At that time, inoculation was a risky process and she became quite ill, remaining an invalid until she died in June, 1787, at the age of 34 years. Stone retired to his farm in Charles County. Four months later, Thomas, still grief-stricken over the loss of his wife, accepted the advice of his doctor to take a trip abroad to recover his spirits. On October 5, 1787, while awaiting a ship at Alexandria, Virginia, he suddenly died at the age of 44.

Residence of Thomas Stone
Port Tobacco, Maryland

*I*t seems essential to our very existence as a free people, and without it we may soon be constrained to bid adieu to independence, to liberty, and safety — blessings, which from the justice of our cause, and the favour of our Almighty Creator, visibly manifested in our protection, we have reason to expect, if, in an humble dependence on his divine providence, we strenuously exert the means which are placed in our power.[3]

❧ Public Service ❧

1764	Admitted to the bar to practice law in Maryland
1775–1777	Represented Maryland in the Continental Congress; signed the Declaration of Independence
1777–1778	Member of the Maryland state senate
1783–1784	Delegate to the Congress of the Confederation; acting president of the Congress for several days

He was most truly a perfect man of business; he would often take the pen and commit to paper, all the necessary writings of the senate, and this he would do cheerfully while the other men were amusing themselves with desultory conversation; he appeared to be naturally of an irritable temper, still he was mild and courteous in his general deportment, fond of society and conversation, and universally a favourite from his great good humour and intelligence; he thought and wrote much as a professional man, and as a statesman, on the business before him in those characters. He had no leisure for other subjects; not that he was unequal to the task, for there were few men who would commit their thoughts to paper with more facility or greater strength of argument. There was a severe trial of skill between the senate and the house of delegates, on the subject of confiscating British property. The senate for several sessions unanimously rejected bills passed by the house of delegates for that purpose; many, very long and tart, were the messages from one to the other body, on this subject; the whole of which, were on the part of the senate, the work of Mr. Stone, and his close friend and equal in all respects, the venerable Charles Carroll of Carrollton. [2]

The situation of many of our fathers, during those trying times, was similar to that of Mr. Stone. They had small patrimonies; business was in a great measure suspended; and, added to this, their time and talents were imperiously demanded by their suffering country. Yet, amidst all these difficulties and trials, a pure patriotism continued to burn within their breasts, and enabled them most cheerfully to make any and every sacrifice to which they were called by the cause of freedom. Nor should it be forgotten, that in these sacrifices the families of our fathers joyfully participated. They received without a murmur "the spoiling of their goods," being elevated by the reflection, that this was necessary for the achievement of that independence to which they considered themselves and their posterity as entitled. [4]

❧Questions for Discussion❧

1. How did Thomas Stone make himself available to the Senate?

2. What are some qualities you see in Mr. Stone's life that distinguish a true statesman from a politician?

3. What proof do we have that Thomas Stone showed much determination to learn as a young boy?

4. Our founding fathers had a compelling drive to leave liberty for their posterity. What can you do to help restore this for your posterity?

5. Do we have testimony which bears witness that Thomas Stone was a Christian? Give examples.

6. How did Stone show initiative while in the Senate?

7. Plan to do something this week on your own to help someone else.

Virginia

Carter Braxton
Benjamin Harrison
Thomas Jefferson
Francis Lightfoot Lee
Richard Henry Lee
Thomas Nelson, Jr.
George Wythe

Carter Braxton

Hospitable Patriot

I Peter 4: 9–10

"Advocate for Religious Liberty"

◦◦◦

BORN
September 10, 1736

BIRTHPLACE
King and Queen County, Virginia

EDUCATION
College of William and Mary

OCCUPATION
Planter, merchant

MARRIED
Judith Robinson, 1755;
Elizabeth Corbin, 1761

CHILDREN
18

AGE AT SIGNING
39

DIED
October 10, 1797; age 61

His marriage to the daughter of a British official made it difficult for him to accept the idea of a complete break with Great Britain despite his patriotism.[1]

Carter Braxton

C arter Braxton was born on September 10, 1706, son of a wealthy planter in Newington, Virginia. His mother died when he was seven days old, and his father died when Carter was but a teenager. At his father's death, he inherited an estate that included five plantations and many slaves in King William County. He studied at William and Mary College.

He married at 19 years of age to Judith Robinson, daughter of a wealthy planter, whose dowry added to his fortune. Sadly, Judith died two years later while giving birth to their second child.

Carter sailed to England, and remained there for a couple of years, enjoying himself in British society. Upon returning home, he found that his brother had built him a beautiful brick Georgian-style mansion on the Pamunkey River, named Elsing Green. Carter happily made it his home and was remarried to Elizabeth Corbin, whose father was the king's receiver-general of customs in the Virginia colony. With his second wife he had 16 children.

Braxton has been described as an "affectionate and obliging" husband, father, friend, and neighbor. He enjoyed entertaining his friends

*Residence of Carter Braxton
Newington, Virginia*

who included the wealthiest members of Virginia society. His home was noted for the richness and beauty of its furniture and silverware, and his wine cellar was filled with the best wines.[4]

He built another mansion, Chericoke, also on the Pamunkey River. This building was destroyed by fire during the revolution, along with many of his valuable papers. It is said that he lived in considerable splendor at both mansions. He was very hospitable and generous, and entertained much.

In 1761, Braxton entered the House of Burgesses as a representative of King William County. He signed the non-importation agreement which protested the Townshend's Act taxing glass, paper, paint and tea.

In 1772 he was elected sheriff of King William County, and was elected a delegate to the First Continental Congress. Governor Dunmore seized all the colony's gunpowder and took it aboard the British warship to which he had fled. Patrick Henry demanded either payment for the munitions or the return of it. The governor refused to do either, and prepared to meet Henry in battle. Braxton volunteered to mediate the situation, and succeeded in getting his father-in-law to pay Henry for the gunpowder.

Braxton sat in on the last session of the Virginia House of Burgesses. The representatives were enraged at the news of the fighting in Boston. Governor Dunmore, fearing for his life, fled to a British warship on the night of June 7 and refused to return to Williamsburg.

The captain of the *Fowey* had declared his intention to fire upon and destroy the town, if the governor should experience any personal violence, and he placed the broadside of his vessel parallel with the shore, and shotted his guns for the purpose.[5]

A convention was called at Richmond in July for the purpose of setting up a government for the colony. Braxton was elected as delegate, and took an active part in its many duties. They set about the task of raising men, money, and munitions for their defense. Meanwhile, Dunmore began raiding up and down the Virginia coast, attacking towns and plantations from his ship of war.

In December of 1775, when Peyton Randolph, a Virginia delegate, died suddenly, Braxton was elected to the Constitutional Convention to replace him. Braxton was still hoping for reconciliation with Great Britain:

as late as April 14, 1776, he wrote a letter to an uncle saying that America was not ready for independence. Just a month later, on May 17, he wrote his uncle that "America with one united Voice" should seek independence.[6]

More likely he felt it would hurt the country if Congress appeared to be divided.[7]

Braxton signed the Declaration of Independence on August 2, 1776. His term was up nine days later, and he returned home.

Virginia had decided to reduce the number of delegates they sent to the Constitutional Convention, so Braxton did not return. Instead, he represented King William County in the new Virginia legislature in October of 1776. He worked diligently on many committees, but is most known for his achievements on freedom of religion.

From this time, he continued to be a delegate in the house for several years, where

*L*ast of the Virginia delegates to sign on August 2 was Carter Braxton. William Ellery observed that this was the first of the signers who showed no enthusiasm for the task. Braxton's expression was dull, resigned, without emotion, as he lifted the quill pen. Searching his memory, Ellery thought he understood something of the man's feelings, for after the early death of his Virginia-born wife, Judith Robinson, Carter Braxton had gone to England where he made many friends among the leaders of British society. In 1761, he married again, this time to Elizabeth Corbin, daughter of a British Colonel who held the post of Receiver of Customs in Virginia for the King. Braxton's magnificent home became a center of social activity where officials from England as well as leading citizens of Virginia were lavishly entertained.[3]

he proved himself to be faithful to his constituents, and a zealous advocate for civil and religious liberty.[8]

He was described by an acquaintance as "an agreeable, though not a remarkably forcible, public speaker. His eloquence was easy and gentlemanly; his language good; and his manner agreeable." For the rest of his life, Braxton served almost continuously as a delegate to the legislature.[9]

He presented a plan to help win the war: Slaves should be recruited to defend Virginia and granted their freedom in return, he said. Virginia rejected the idea, but eventually about 5,000 African-American men, many of them slaves, served in the patriot forces.[10]

Braxton helped supply salt, uniforms, and blankets for the American forces, though the War brought Braxton many hardships. Some of his plantations and land holdings were ravaged by the British. His mansion, Chericoke, was destroyed by fire. At the beginning of the war, Braxton had heavily invested in shipping to carry American cargo to the other colonies, but the British captured most of his ships. His debt could only be collected in depreciated currency; therefore, he went deeper and deeper into debt, selling his plantation, mortgaging his

❦ Public Service ❧

1761–1771	Member of the Virginia House of Burgesses
1772–1773	Sheriff of King William County, Virginia
1774–1775	Member of the Virginia Convention that chose delegates to the Continental Congress; member of the Virginia House of Burgesses
1775–1776	Delegate to the Continental Congress; signed the Declaration of Independence
1776–1797	Member of the Virginia state legislature
1786–1791, 1794–1797	Member of Virginia's executive council

slaves and furniture, and borrowing from relatives and friends. When he couldn't pay his debts, his estates were seized. Finally Braxton and his family were forced to move to Richmond in 1786, giving up the rich country life to which they were accustomed.

The people of Henrico County, where he moved, elected him as a representative in the legislature, where he served on the executive council until his death. On October 16, 1797, he suffered a stroke and died.

His venerable widow, by the exertions of her friends, and the operation of a beneficent law, saved from the wreck of his estate, enough to protect her declining years from absolute want.[2]

Questions for Discussion

1. What do we know about Carter's education from the appendix about William & Mary College?

2. What evidence do we have that Carter had the quality of hospitality? Generosity?

3. Why was signing the Declaration especially difficult for Carter?

4. Give an instance in which God used Carter Braxton's influence to avert conflict between the American and British.

5. What was Mr. Braxton's plan for freeing the slaves?

6. To what duties did Mr. Braxton apply himself during wartimes?

7. What personal sacrifices did Carter Braxton make for our liberty?

8. What goal can you set to promote hospitality in your life? Psalm 101:6, 7 gives us a key as to what type of people to invite into our homes. What is it?

Benjamin Harrison

Joyful Patriot

Proverbs 15:23

"Father of one president and great-grandfather of another"

❧❧

BORN
1726

BIRTHPLACE
Charles City
County, Virginia

EDUCATION
College of William and Mary

OCCUPATION
Planter

MARRIED
Elizabeth Bassett, 1745

CHILDREN
7

AGE AT SIGNING
50

DIED
April 24, 1791, age 65

Benjamin Harrison the signer was the father of one president and the great-grandfather of another. William Henry Harrison, the youngest of Benjamin and Elizabeth's seven children, grew up to become the nation's ninth president. The signer's great-grandson, also named Benjamin Harrison, was our twenty-third president.[1]

Benjamin Harrison was born in Charles City County, Virginia in 1726 at Berkeley, his parent's estate. He attended William and Mary, but never graduated due to a misunderstanding with an officer of the college. After his father was struck by lightning and died, Benjamin returned to manage the estate. Soon after, he married Elizabeth Bassett. They had many children, but only seven lived past childhood.

At 23 years of age, he was elected to the House of Burgesses, where he served for 25 years. In 1764 he was on a committee of the house that wrote a petition to the King of England protesting the Stamp Act. In 1773, he became a member of the committees of correspondence. He was a member of the provincial Congress and attended the first Continental Congress, where he served as chairman, and also of the board of war and ordinance responsible for supervising the Continental Congress. "Harrison told John Adams that he would have walked the 200 miles to get to Congress, if need be."[3]

While in Philadelphia, he shared the same house as George Washington and Peyton Randolph, president of the Continental Congress.

Residence of Benjamin Harrison
Berkley, Virginia

After Washington left for Boston as commander-in-chief of the army, and Randolph died, Harrison lived alone and did a great deal of entertaining other delegates, incurring debts that took him years to pay.

At the time John Hancock was elected president of Congress in May 1775, the British were especially enraged at Hancock's home colony, Massachusetts, which they felt had led the thirteen colonies into war. Harrison, who was six-feet-four and weighed 240 pounds, reportedly picked up Hancock and set him down in the president's chair while commenting, "We will show Mother Britain how little we care for her by making a Massachusetts man our president!"⁴

Harrison, as chairman, presided over the debates about independence on July 1 and 2, 1776.

An anecdote has been preserved that illustrates Harrison's joviality, even in so serious a matter as the adoption of the Declaration of Independence. The story tells that the delegates were discussing the grim possibility that those who signed the document might well end up being hanged by the British when the corpulent Harrison turned to the short, slender Elbridge Gerry and said, 'When the hanging scene comes to be exhibited, I shall have all the advantage over you. It will

be over with me in a minute, but you will be kicking in the air half an hour after I am gone.⁵

While in Congress, Harrison helped establish three major governmental departments — what we now call the Defense, Navy, and State Departments.⁶

He retired from Congress in 1777, returning to his seat in the Virginia house of delegates, where he was elected speaker of the house, and remained in that post for four years. During this period, the British raided and plundered their way through Virginia and the legislature, with Harrison as its head, was forced to flee from town to town to keep from being captured.

Near the end of the war, his quip about the hangman's rope nearly came true. He had to flee into the interior of Virginia to avoid being captured by the English.⁷

Harrison was elected governor in 1781 when Thomas Nelson resigned. He was re-elected twice, serving until 1784. During his governorship, the Battle of Yorktown occurred, and independence was won. After his term, he again became speaker of the state legislature. He was an opponent of the

As a member of the board of war, and as chairman of that board, an office which he retained until he left congress, he particularly distinguished himself. According to the testimony of a gentleman who was contemporary with him in congress, he was characterized for great firmness, good sense, and peculiar sagacity in difficult and critical situations. In seasons of uncommon trial and anxiety, he was always steady, cheerful, and undaunted.²

ratification of the U.S. Constitution without first having a Bill of Rights.

His financial state suffered, and in 1789, he wrote to Governor William Livingston of New Jersey, asking for help in obtaining a federal appointment:

> The friendship you formerly honoured me with, and the confidence I still have in it, will I hope excuse me to you, for asking the favour of you to assist me with your interest, with the senatorial delegates of your State in Congress, for the appointment of a naval officer for the district of Norfolk and Portsmouth in this State. The being a placeman is a line I never expected to walk in, but the distresses brought on me by the ravages and plunderings of the British, have reduced me so low that some prop is necessary, for the comfort of a numerous and valuable family. That I have some claims on the American States, you, my friend, know, as many of my long services were familiar to you; which services, together with my strong attachment to the American cause after my return from Congress marked me out as a peculiar object of British vengeance; and which they did not fail to execute in the most outrageous manner, when the fortune of war put my whole estate in their power. I take the liberty to enclose you a letter to the gentlemen, which you'll be so obliging as to forward to them in any manner you shall please.[8]

In the spring of 1791, Mr. Harrison was attacked by a severe fit of gout. He partially recovered. In April, he was re-elected a member of the legislature, and he and his friends celebrated, feeling sure he'd be elected governor again soon. On the day after the election, Harrison threw a party at his home with much eating and drinking. It aggravated his gout, and during the night he became quite ill.

> Before the family physician arrived, he directed some medicine to be prepared for him; as an old and faithful domestic brought it to his bedside, she said, "Here, sir, is the medicine you asked for." "And here, Molly," he calmly replied, "will soon be a dead man." On the following day he died, with perfect resignation and composure.[9]

❧ Public Service ❧

1749–1774	Member of the Virginia provincial congress
1774–1777	Delegate from Virginia to the Continental Congress; signed the Declaration of Independence
1778–1781	Speaker of the Virginia House of Delegates
1781–1784	Governor of the Commonwealth of Virginia
1785–1791	Speaker of the Virginia House of Delegates

Questions for Discussion

1. As reported by a fellow Congressman, what qualities did Benjamin Harrison show by his service on the board of war?

2. Read the qualifications to enter The College of William and Mary and the doctrinal statement of the school. What type of training does this show Harrison to have obtained?

3. What qualities are demonstrated in Harrison's life by the statement he made to John Adams?

4. What quality did Harrison demonstrate by carrying on the duties of Peyton Randolph when he died?

5. Give instances to show that Harrison had a spirit of joyfulness. How did this help to relieve others during tense times?

6. What personal sacrifices did Harrison make in behalf of our freedom? What dangers did he encounter?

7. Write a definition of "joyfulness." Find a Bible verse to commit to memory and try to internalize this quality into your life. Others like to be around a joyful person.

Thomas Jefferson

Loyal Patriot

Hebrews 3:5–6

"Penman of the Declaration"

❧❧

BORN
April 13, 1743

BIRTHPLACE
Albemarle County, Virginia

EDUCATION
Tutors; College of William & Mary

OCCUPATION
Planter

MARRIED
Martha Wayles Skelton

CHILDREN
6

AGE AT SIGNING
33

DIED
July 4, 1826; age 83

Mr. Jefferson's manner was simple but dignified, and his conversational powers were of the rarest value. He was exceedingly kind and benevolent, an indulgent master to his servants, liberal and friendly to his neighbors. He possessed remarkable equanimity of temper, and it is said that he was never seen in a passion. His friendship was lasting and ardent; and he was confiding and never distrustful. In religion he was a freethinker; in morals, pure and unspotted; in politics, patriotic, honest, ardent and benevolent.[3]

Thomas Jefferson was born on April 13, 1743, at his parents' plantation in Albermarle County, Virginia. Thomas entered a grammar school at age five. When he was nine, he was sent to a nearby private school to learn the classical languages under the tutelage of a Scottish clergyman. His father died when he was 14, and he inherited an estate of 2,000 acres along with 30 slaves. He continued his education at another private school near Charlottesville until he was 16 years old, at which time he entered the College of William and Mary in Williamsburg, Virginia. There he spent two years, graduating in 1762. He later wrote of his time there:

> It was my great good fortune, and what probably fixed the destinies of my life, that Dr. William Small, of Scotland, was then professor of mathematics, a man profound in most of the useful branches of science, with a happy talent of communication, correct and gentlemanly manners, and an enlarged and liberal mind.[8]

Jefferson then began to study law at the office of George Wythe, later to be a fellow-signer. While a student, Jefferson heard the famous speech of Patrick Henry against the Stamp Act. It aroused a fire within him.

> Jefferson later wrote of this speech by Henry: "He appeared to me to speak as Homer wrote." He adds, "torrents of sublime eloquence from Henry, backed by the solid reasoning of Johnson, prevailed; and the resolution was carried by a single vote."
>
> "I well remember," he continues, "the cry of treason by the speaker, echoed from every part of the house, against Mr. Henry: I well remember his pause, and the admirable address with which he recovered himself, and baffled the charge thus vociferated. Henry now [became] almost too familiar for quotation: 'Caesar had his Brutus, Charles the First his Cromwell, and George the Third ("treason!" cried the speaker; "treason! Treason!" echoed the house;) may profit by their example. If this be treason, make the most of it.' " [9]

At this time, Mr. Jefferson commenced his political career, and has himself given us, in few words, an outline of the reasons which powerfully impelled him to enter the lists, with other American patriots, against the parent country. "The colonies," says he, "were taxed internally and externally; their essential interests sacrificed to individuals in Great Britain; their legislatures suspended; charters annulled; trials by jurors taken away; their persons subjected to transportation across the Atlantic, and to trial by foreign judicatories; their supplications for redress thought beneath answer, themselves published as cowards in the councils of their mother country, and courts of Europe; armed troops sent amongst them, to enforce submission to these violences; and actual hostilities commenced against them. No alternative was presented, but resistance or unconditional submission. Between these there could be no hesitation. They closed in the appeal to arms."[5]

Jefferson was admitted to the bar in 1767 and practiced law for the next seven years. In 1769 he was elected a member of the Virginia House of Burgesses where he remained until the outbreak of the Revolutionary War. Jefferson earned a reputation as a good writer early in his career.

On January 1, 1772, Thomas married a widow, Martha Wayles Skelton, daughter of a well-to-do lawyer. By their marriage, his land holdings doubled. He began construction on Monticello in 1770 and when his home in Shadwell burned, the couple moved to Monticello, although it was still under construction. He and his wife had six children, though only two daughters survived childhood. Martha died in 1782, and Jefferson never remarried.

Jefferson was asked to present the resolutions drawn up by the committee of correspondence, meeting in Raleigh Tavern, but he deferred it to Dabney Carr (who was husband of Jefferson's sister, Martha). The resolutions were approved, and Jefferson was appointed to the committee of correspondence, along with ten other legislators.

> When Carr died only a month later leaving a widow and six children, Jefferson took the entire family to Monticello and reared and educated the children as his own.[10]

When news reached Virginia of the closing of the port of Boston in response to the Boston Tea Party, Jefferson, Patrick Henry, the two Lees, and several others "cooked up a resolution," as Jefferson said, to set aside June 1 as a day of fasting and prayer in Virginia:

> This House, being deeply impressed with apprehension of the great dangers to be derived to British America from the hostile invasion of the city of Boston in our Sister Colony of Massachusetts Bay, whose commerce and harbor are, on the first day of June next, to be stopped by an armed force, deem it highly necessary that the said first day of June be set apart, by the members of this House, as a day of fasting, humiliation and prayer, devoutly to implore the divine interposition, for adverting the heavy calamity which threatens destruction to our civil rights and the evils of civil war; to give us one heart and one mind firmly to oppose, by all just and proper means, every injury

ONE OF THE BEST DESCRIPTIONS OF JEFFERSON
WAS WRITTEN BY HIS GRANDSON, THOMAS
JEFFERSON RANDOLPH:

*M*r. Jefferson's hair, when young, was of
a reddish cast, sandy as he advanced
in years — his eye, hazel — dying in his
84th year, he had not lost a tooth, or had one
defective; his skin, thin, peeling from his face
on exposure to the sun, and giving it a tettered
appearance, the superficial veins so weak, as
upon the slightest blow, to cause extensive
suffusions of blood, in early life, upon standing
to write for any length of time, bursting
beneath the skin: it, however, gave him no
inconvenience. His countenance was mild and
benignant, and attractive to strangers...

Mr. Jefferson's stature was commanding, six feet
two and a half inches in height, well formed,
indicating strength, activity, and robust health;
his carriage, erect; step firm and elastic,
which he preserved to his death; his temper,
naturally strong, under perfect control — his
courage, cool and impassive — no one ever
knew him exhibit trepidation — his moral
courage of the highest order — his will, firm
and inflexible — it was remarked of him that
he never abandoned a plan, a principle, or a
friend...

His habits were regular and systematic. He was
a miser of his time, rose always at dawn, wrote
and read until breakfast, breakfasted early, and
dined from three to four — after breakfast
read for half an hour in his public rooms or
portico, in summer — visited his garden and
workshops — returned to his writing and
reading till one, when he rode on horseback
to three of half past — dined, and gave the
evening to his family and company — retired
at nine, and to bed from ten to eleven. He said
in his last illness, that the sun had not caught
him in bed for fifty years.

RES. OF THOMAS JEFFERSON, MONTICELLO.
Vᴬ

Residence of Thomas Jefferson
Monticello, Virginia

*H*e always made his own fire. He drank water but once a day, a single
glass, when he returned from his ride. He ate heartily, and much vegetable
food, preferring French cookery, because it made the meats more tender.
He never drank ardent spirits or strong wines — such was his aversion
to ardent spirits that when, in his last illness, his physician desired him
to use brandy as an astringent, he could not induce him to take it strong
enough...

His manner was dignified, reserved with strangers, but frank and cordial
with his friends; his conversation always cheerful, often sportive, and
illustrated by anecdotes. He spoke only of the good qualities of men, which
induced the belief that he knew little of them, but no one knew them
better. I had formed this opinion, and on hearing him speak very favorably
of men with defects known to myself, stated them to him, when he asked if
I supposed he had not observed them, adding others not noted by me, and
evincing much more accurate knowledge of the individual character than
I possessed, observing, "My habit is to speak only of men's good qualities."
When he believed that either men or measures were adverse to Republican
institutions, he spoke of them with open and unqualified condemnation...

His manners were of that polished school of the Colonial Government, so
remarkable in its day — under no circumstances violating any of those
minor conventional observances which constitute the well-bred gentleman,
courteous and considerate to all persons. On riding with him, when a lad,
we met a Negro who bowed to us; he returned his bow, I did not; turning
to me he asked, "Do you permit a Negro to be more of a gentleman than
yourself?"[1]

In 1775, Mr. Jefferson was selected by the Virginia legislature to answer Lord North's famous "Conciliatory Proposition," called, In the language of the day, his "Olive branch"; but it was an olive branch that concealed a serpent; or, as the former President Adams observed, "it was an asp, in a basket of flowers." The task assigned him, was performed by Mr. Jefferson in a manner the most happy and satisfactory. The reply was cool and calm and close — marked with uncommon energy and keen sagacity. The document may be found in most of the histories of that period, and is manifestly one of the most nervous and manly productions of that day. It concluded with the following strong and independent language:

These, my lord, are our sentiments, on this important subject, which we offer only as an individual part of the whole empire. Final determination we leave to the general congress, now sitting, before whom we shall lay the papers your lordship has communicated to us. For ourselves, we have exhausted every mode of application, which our invention could suggest, as proper and promising. We have decently remonstrated with parliament — they have added new injuries to the old; we have wearied our king with supplications — he has not deigned to answer us; we have appealed to the native honour and justice of the British nation — their efforts in our favour have hitherto been ineffectual. What then remains to be done? That we commit our injuries to the even handing justice of that Being, who doth no wrong, earnestly beseeching Him to illuminate the councils, and prosper the endeavours of those to whom America hath confided her hopes; that through their wise discretions, we may again see reunited the blessings of liberty, prosperity, and harmony with Great Britain.[6]

to American rights; and that the minds of his Majesty and his Parliament, may be inspired from above with wisdom, moderation and justice, to remove from the loyal people of America all cause of danger from a continued pursuit of measures pregnant with their ruin.[11]

It was two days later that the governor, in anger, dissolved the House of Burgesses, and again the legislators resorted to meeting in Raleigh Tavern. They decided to urge the other colonies to call a general Congress — the First Continental Congress.

Jefferson was ill when a convention of Virginia legislators met in August 1774, but he sent along a paper, "A Summary View of the Rights of British America Intended for the Inspection of the Present Delegate of the People of Virginia, Now in Convention." It soon became known as "Jefferson's Bill of Rights." It was addressed to King George and made the following appeal:

Open your breast, sire, to liberal and expanded thought. It behooves you to think and act for your people. The great principles of right and wrong are legible to every reader; to peruse them, requires not the aid of many counselors. The whole art of government consists in the art of being honest.[12]

Jefferson wrote the Declaration of Independence on a portable writing desk he had invented, while sitting in the parlor of his apartment that he'd rented on the second floor of a brick house at Market and Seventh Streets. Commenting on the writing, Jefferson said:

I turned to neither the book nor pamphlet while writing it. I did not consider it as any part of my charge to invent new ideas altogether and to offer no sentiment which had ever been expressed before." He said that he saw his task of writing as: "Not to find out new principles or new arguments, never before thought of, not merely to say things which had never been said before; but to place before mankind the common sense of the subject, terms so plain and firm as to command their assent, and to justify ourselves in the independent stand we impelled to take. Neither aiming at originality of principle or sentiment, nor yet copied from any particular and previous writing, it was intended to be an expression of the American mind.... All its authority rests then on the harmonizing sentiments of the day, whether expressed in conversation, in letters, printed essays, or the elementary books of public right, as Aristotle, Cicero, Locke, Sidney, etc.[13]

Because of ill health and the need to care for his family, Jefferson resigned from Congress in the fall of 1776. In October, he took his seat in the Virginia legislature. Although Jefferson influenced the making of many laws, the one he said he wanted to be remembered for was the statute for religious freedom:

> Well aware that the opinions and beliefs of men depend not on their own will, but follow involuntarily the evidence proposed to their minds; that Almighty God hath created the mind free, and manifested his will that free it shall remain by making it altogether insusceptible of restraint; — that our civil rights

I have sworn upon the altar of God, eternal hostility against every form of tyranny over the mind of man.
— *Thomas Jefferson*[2]

have no dependence on our religious opinions any more than our opinions on physics or geometry; that therefore the proscribing any citizens as unworthy the public confidence by laying upon him an incapacity of being called to offices of trust and emolument unless he profess or renounce this or that religious opinion is depriving him injuriously of those privileges and advantages to which, in common with this fellow-citizens, he has a natural right; — that the opinions of men are not the subject of civil government nor under its jurisdiction; — and finally that truth is

❧ Public Service ❧

1767	Admitted to the bar to practice law
1769–1775	Member of the Virginia House of Burgesses
1775–1776	Delegate from Virginia to the Continental Congress; wrote and signed the Declaration of Independence
1779–1781	Governor of Virginia
1783–1784	Delegate from Virginia to the Congress of the Confederation
1784–1785	Representative of Congress in Europe to help negotiate trade treaties
1785–1789	Minister to France
1789–1793	Secretary of state of the United States
1797–1801	Vice president of the United States
1901–1809	President of the United States
1817–1825	One of the founders of the University of Virginia

great and will prevail if she is left to herself; that she is the proper and sufficient antagonist to error, and has nothing to fear from the conflict unless by human interposition disarmed of her natural weapons, free argument and debate; errors ceasing to be dangerous when it is permitted freely to contradict them. We, the General Assembly, do enact, That no man shall be compelled to frequent or support any religious worship, place or ministry whatsoever, nor shall be enforced, restrained, molested or burdened in his body or goods, nor shall otherwise suffer, on account of his religious opinions or beliefs; but that all men shall be free to profess and by argument to maintain their opinions in matters of religion, and that the same shall in no wise diminish, enlarge or affect their civil capacities.[14]

Jefferson also worked to pass laws providing for a free public school system, and limitations on the death penalty and laws forbidding the importation of slaves. He succeeded

command of General Tarlton was rapidly hastening to Charlottesville, for the purpose of surprising and capturing the members of the assembly. They had only time, after the alarm was given, to adjourn to meet at Staunton, and to disperse, before the enemy entered the village. Another party had directed their course to Monticello to capture the ex-governor. Scarcely had the family time to make arrangements, indispensable for their departure, and to effect their escape, before the enemy were seen ascending the hill, leading to the mansion-house. Mr. Jefferson himself, mounting his horse, narrowly escaped, by taking a course through the woods. This flight of Mr. Jefferson, eminently proper, and upon which his safety depended, has unwarrantably excited in times gone by the ridicule and censure of his enemies.[15]

Later, in 1781, Jefferson was injured in a fall from his horse, and he took advantage of his convalescence to write a book of natural history and philosophy called

Not only did he recommend that the Great Seal of the United States depict a Bible story and include the word "God" in the national motto, but President Jefferson also negotiated a federal treaty with the Kaskaskia Indians in which he included direct federal funding to pay for Christian ministers to work with the Indians and for the building of a church in which Indians could worship — and this treaty was ratified by the U.S. Senate.[8]

Patrick Henry as governor of Virginia in 1779. Much of his energy was spent in collecting money and supplies for the Continental Army. Virginia soon became the theatre for war. Benedict Arnold entered it with British troops and Tory troops, and began spreading desolation with fire and sword along the James River. Richmond, the capitol, was partly destroyed.

On the twenty-fourth of May, the legislature was to meet at Charlottesville. They were not formed for business, however, until the twenty-eighth. A few days following which, the term for which Mr. Jefferson had been elected expired, when he again found himself a private citizen. On leaving the chair of state, Mr. Jefferson retired to Monticello, when intelligence was received, two days after, that a body of troops under

Notes on Virginia. In it he set forth his ideas that the best future for America lay in becoming a nation of farmers, and that manufacturing should be left to the European countries.[16]

Jefferson stayed out of public life for two years, during which time his wife died. In 1783, he returned to Congress and was sent, along with Benjamin Franklin and John Adams, to negotiate commercial treaties with Europe. He took his daughter with him and stayed for five years, and, as minister to France, strengthened relations with the French and gained commercial concessions as well.

In the following years, Jefferson interspersed pleasant interludes at Monticello with filling offices in service to his country. George Washington asked him to be Secretary of State in his cabinet. Jefferson and Alexander Hamilton became leaders of opposing thought that grew into the American two-party system of politics.

> Jefferson's party supported the Southern States, farm interests, state's rights, a strict interpretation of the Constitution, and a strong belief in democracy. On the other hand, Hamilton's Federalist party supported the Northern States, banking and manufacturing interests, a strong central government, a loose interpretation of the Constitution, and a belief that the voice of the people could not be entirely trusted.[17]

Jefferson grew weary of politics and resigned on December 31, 1793, succeeded by his cousin, Edmund Randolph. Jefferson vowed never to "meddle with politics more." He returned home to Monticello to supervise his now more than 10,000 acres. About this period of his retirement he wrote,

> From 1793 to 1797, I remained closely at home, saw no one but those who came there, and at length became very sensible of the ill effect it had upon my own mind, and of its direct and irresistible tendency to render me unfit for society and uneasy when necessarily engaged in it. I felt enough of the effect of withdrawing from the world then, to see that it led to an anti-social and misanthropic state of mind, which severely punishes him who gives into it; and it will be a lesson I shall never forget as to myself.[18]

Jefferson's supporters rallied to get him to run for President when George Washington decided not to run for a third term. He lost by three electoral votes to John Adams, and became his vice-president. As time wore on, the two became opposed to each other's beliefs, especially over Alien and Sedition Acts, which dealt with freedom of speech.

In 1800, the election was a hard-fought battle between Jefferson and Adams. A falling out between Adams and Aaron Burr, Jefferson's running mate, split the Federalist party. Finally Jefferson was declared President by the House of Representatives with Burr as Vice President.

> Jefferson called for a healing of the political antagonism engendered by the election. "Every difference of opinion," he said, "is not a difference of principle. We have called by different names brethren of the same principle. We are all Republicans — we are

*O*ne of Jefferson's favorite sayings was, "It is wonderful how much may be done if we are always doing." He lived by that motto, achieving much in an incredible number of fields.[5]

all Federalists. If there be any among us who would wish to dissolve this Union, or to change its republican form, let them stand undisturbed as monuments of the safety with which error of opinion may be tolerated where reason is left free to combat it." Jefferson also stated his concept of the best government as that which governs least: "A wise and frugal government, which shall restrain men from injuring one another, which shall leave them otherwise free to regulate their own pursuits of industry and improvement, and shall not take from the mouth of labor the bread it has earned. This is the sum of good government, and this is necessary to close the circle of our felicities."[19]

During Jefferson's first term, the United States more than doubled in size when he purchased the Louisiana territory from France for $15 million. He also sent Meriweather Lewis and William Clark on an expedition that learned information about the land stretching from the Mississippi River to the Pacific Coast. Jefferson was overwhelmingly re-elected in 1804. He stated in his inaugural address:

> I do not fear that any motives of interest may lead me astray; I am sensible of no passion which could seduce me knowingly from the path of justice; but the weakness of human nature, and the limits of my own understanding, will produce errors of judgment sometimes injurious to your interests; I shall need, therefore, all the indulgence I have heretofore experienced; the want of it will certainly not lessen with increasing years. I shall need, too, the favour of that Being in whose hands we are, who led our forefathers, as Israel of old, from their native land, and planted them in a country flowing with all the necessaries and comforts of life; who has covered our infancy with his

providence, and our riper years with his wisdom and power.[20]

Jefferson declined to run for a third term, but supported James Madison. In a farewell address to Congress, he said,

> Availing myself of this, the last occasion which will occur of addressing the two houses of the legislature at their meeting, I cannot omit the expression of my sincere gratitude for the repeated proofs of confidence manifested to me by themselves, and their predecessors, since my call to the administration, and the many indulgences experienced at their hands. The same grateful acknowledgements are due to my fellow-citizens generally, whose support has been my great encouragement, under all embarrassments. In the transactions of their business, I cannot have escaped error. It is incident of our imperfect nature. But I may say with truth, my errors have been of the understanding, not of intention; and that the advancement of their rights and interests has been the constant motive of every measure. On these considerations, I solicit their indulgence. Looking forward with anxiety to their future destinies, I trust, that in their steady character, unshaken by difficulties, in their love of liberty, obedience to law, and support of public authorities, I see a sure guarantee of the permanence of our republic; and retiring from the charge of their affairs, I carry with me the consolation of a firm persuasion, that heaven has in store for our beloved country, long ages to come of prosperity and happiness.[21]

> …later writing of his feelings that "never did a prisoner released from his chains feel such relief."[22]

Jefferson retired to Monticello and retreated to Poplar Forest, near Lynchburg, when life grew too hectic. He retained his health and entertained statesmen, politicians, scientists, explorers, scholars, and Indian chiefs. He also achieved another one of the things he wished to be remembered for: the founding of the University of Virginia in Charlottesville. He chose the curriculum, planned the buildings, supervised construction, and chose professors. In 1825 it began to hold classes with over 100 students.

Toward the end of his life, his pecuniary affairs became embarrassed, and he was obliged to sell his library, which

Congress purchased for $30,000. A short time previous to his death, he received permission from the Legislature of Virginia to dispose of his estate by lottery, to prevent it being sacrificed to pay his debts. He did not live to see it consummated.[23]

Jefferson and John Adams resumed their friendship, laying aside political differences. They corresponded often, and interestingly, they both died on the fiftieth anniversary of the signing of the Declaration of Independence, July 4, 1826, at nearly the same hour.

> In the spring of 1826, his bodily infirmities greatly increased, and in June he was confined wholly to his bed. About the first of July he seemed free from disease, and his friends had hopes of his recovery; but it was his own conviction that he should die, and he gave directions accordingly. On the third, he inquired the day of the month. On being told, he expressed ardent desire to live until the next day, to breathe the air of the fiftieth anniversary of his country's independence. His wish was granted: and on the morning of the fourth, after having expressed his gratitude to his friends and servants for their care, he said with a distinct voice, "I resign myself to my God, and my child [The University of Virginia] to my country."[24]

Jefferson's achievements rank him as one of the greatest Americans, but he himself wished to be remembered for three works, which he directed to be listed on his tombstone: Here was buried Thomas Jefferson / author of the Declaration of American Independence / of the Statute of Virginia for religious freedom / and Father of the University of Virginia.[25]

The citizens of Washington, D.C. had extended an invitation to Jefferson, as one of the surviving signers, to attend the grand celebration of our country's 50th anniversary. Being too ill, he had declined, but on June 24, responded with this letter:

> Respected Sir: The kind invitation I received from you, on the part of the citizens of the city of Washington, to be present with them at their celebration of the fiftieth anniversary of American independence, as one of the surviving signers of an instrument, pregnant with our own and the fate of the world, is most flattering to myself, and heightened by the honourable

accompaniment proposed for the comfort of such a journey. It adds sensibly to the sufferings of sickness, to be deprived by it of a personal participation in the rejoicings of that day; but acquiescence under circumstances is a duty not placed among those we are permitted to control. I should, indeed, with peculiar delight, have met and exchanged there congratulations personally, with the small band, the remnant of the host of worthies who joined with us, on that day, in the bold and doubtful election we were to make for our country, between submission and the sword; and to have enjoyed with them the consolatory fact that our fellow citizens, after half a century of experience and prosperity, continue to approve the choice we made. May it be to the world, what I believe it will be, (to some parts sooner, to others later, but finally to all,) the signal of arousing men to burst the chains, under which monkish ignorance and superstition had persuaded them to bind themselves, and to assume the blessings and security of self-government. The form which we have substituted restores the free right to the unbounded exercise of reason and freedom of opinion. All eyes are opened or opening to the rights of man. The general spread of the lights of science has already laid open to every view the palpable truth, that the mass of mankind has not been born with saddles on their backs, nor a favoured few, booted and spurred, ready to ride them legitimately, by the grace of God. These are the grounds of hope for others; for ourselves, let the annual return of this day forever refresh our recollections of these rights, and an undiminished devotion to them. I will ask permission here, to express the pleasure with which I should have met my ancient neighbours of the city of Washington and its vicinities, with whom I passed so many years of a pleasing social intercourse — an intercourse which so much relieved the anxieties of the public cares, and left impressions so deeply engraved in my affections, as never to be forgotten. With my regret that ill health forbids me the gratification of an acceptance, be pleased to receive for yourself, and those for whom you write, the assurance of my highest respect and friendly attachments.[26]

[He] called his family around him and conversed separately with each of them; to his beloved daughter, Mrs. Randolph, he presented a small morocco case, which he requested her not to open until after his death — when the sad limitation had expired, it was found to contain an elegant and affectionate strain of poetry, on the virtues of her from whom he was thus torn away.[27]

*M*r. Jefferson's manner was simple but dignified, and his conversational powers were of the rarest value. He was exceedingly kind and benevolent, an indulgent master to his servants, liberal and friendly to his neighbors. He possessed remarkable equanimity of temper, and it is said that he was never seen in a passion. His friendship was lasting and ardent; and he was confiding and never distrustful. In religion he was a freethinker; in morals, pure and unspotted; in politics, patriotic, honest, ardent and benevolent.[3]

Questions for Discussion

1. What character qualities are seen in Jefferson's life by his grandson?

2. What were Jefferson's reasons for fighting for independence?

3. Read through each paragraph of the information on Jefferson separately, listing character qualities you observe in this man's life.

4. What can we learn from Thomas Jefferson's favorite motto?

5. Discuss Jefferson's answer to Lord North's conciliatory proposition.

6. How does he show a respect for God in his answer?

7. Look up William & Mary College in the appendix. To what type of teaching was Jefferson exposed? What helped to shape his frame of reference?

8. Under whom did Jefferson study law?

9. Tell what Jefferson thought about Patrick Henry's famous speech.

10. What character qualities did Jefferson show by caring for his brother-in-law's family?

11. Jefferson was partially responsible for calling for a day of prayer and fasting upon the closing of the port of Boston. What can we deduce of his view of God?

12. Explain how, what became known as Jefferson's Bill of Rights shows that he understood the principle of making a proper appeal.

13. How did Jefferson view his task of writing the Declaration of Independence?

14. What three things did Jefferson want to be remembered for? What was his view on religious liberty?

15. Tell about Jefferson's near escape from Charlottesville.

16. What can we learn about the use of our time from Jefferson when he was recovering from a fall off his horse? What quality did he display?

❧ Questions for Discussion ❧

17. What lesson did he learn from his sense of wanting to withdraw from engaging in life?

18. What was Jefferson's view of education?

19. What actions did Jefferson take that demonstrated his respect for inculcating Christian principles into society?

20. How did Jefferson demonstrate loyalty?

21. List those you serve. Write down one way you could demonstrate loyalty to each person you serve.

Francis Lightfoot Lee

Francis Lightfoot Lee

Friendly Patriot

Proverbs 18:24

"Friend to
General Washington"

☙❧

BORN
October 14, 1734
BIRTHPLACE
Westmoreland County, Virginia
EDUCATION
Private tutors
OCCUPATION
Planter
MARRIED
Rebecca Taylor, 1769
CHILDREN
None
AGE AT SIGNING
41
DIED
January 11, 1797; age 62

*Possessed of ample wealth, he used it
like a philosopher and a Christian in
dispensing its blessing for the benefit
of his country and his fellow men.[1]*

Francis Lightfoot Lee was born on October 14, 1734, at the Lee's estate, Stratford, in Westmoreland County, Virginia. Francis was the fourth oldest of six brothers. He grew up enjoying the pleasures of life on a plantation rather than the rigorous studies his other brothers pursued. His parents died when he was in his middle teens. His entire education came from private tutors at his family's estate.

The elder sons of the family, having finished the usual course of instruction at home, prior to the death of their father, were sent away to English colleges; but Francis, being too young, at the period of occurrence, to leave home, never enjoyed that advantage. His classical and literary acquirements were, therefore, entirely derived from his domestic tutor, a Scotch clergyman of the name of Craig, who, being a man of science, not only made him a good scholar, but gave him an early fondness for reading and mental investigation, which, in a mind so apt and vigorous by nature, prepared him for those scenes of usefulness and honour, in which he was afterwards engaged. This partiality for books was cherished and aided, in a great measure, by the valuable library collected by his father: in which were to be found the

He was placed at an early age under the care of the Reverend Doctor Craig, a Scotch clergyman of eminent piety and learning. His excellent tutor not only educated his head but his heart, and laid the foundation of character, upon which the noble superstructure, which his useful life exhibited, was reared.[3]

BIRTH PLACE OF R.H.LEE & FRANCIS LIGHTFOOT LEE.
Stratford House Westmoreland

*Birthplace of Francis Lightfoot Lee and Richard Henry Lee
Stratford House, Westmoreland, Virginia*

best editions of all the great British writers, in every branch of science, poetry, and belles-lettres.[6]

Francis was elected to Virginia's House of Burgesses in 1758, the same year his brother, Richard Henry Lee, took his seat. He married a cousin, Rebecca Taylor, the daughter of a wealthy plantation owner and race horse fancier, in 1769. The couple had no children, but helped raise two of their nieces. They made their estate, Menokin, in Richmond County, their home.

Francis and Richard Lee were quite different. Richard was a captivating speaker and often the center of attention. Francis preferred to stay in the background, working quietly in Congressional committees. He served on the Board of War, obtaining necessary supplies for the army. "Fellow delegates remarked on his wit and strength of argument in small group discussions."[7]

On July 2, 1776, Francis Lightfoot Lee voted in favor of his brother's resolution and signed the Declaration of Independence in August. The brothers resigned from Congress on the same day, May 15, 1779. Francis served briefly in the Virginia state legislature and then retired from public life.

The remainder of his life was spent in ease on his plantation. He was interested in agricultural experimentation, and devoted much time to developing ways to improve his crops and livestock. The winter of 1796–97 was extremely cold in Virginia, and Lee developed a case of pleurisy, as did his wife. He died on January 11, 1797 at Menokin, and Rebecca died a few days later.

It is said, that he had embraced the religion of the gospel, and that under its supporting hope and consolation, he made his exit in peace from the world.[8]

His last moments were those of a Christian, a good, an honest, and a virtuous man; and those who witnessed the scene were all ready to exclaim, "Let me die the death of the righteous, and let my last end be like his."[9]

When the Federal Constitution was being drafted in 1787, he differed from his brother in strongly supporting the new form of government. He also showed farsighted wisdom in helping to secure free navigation of the Mississippi for Americans.[2]

Francis Lightfoot Lee is well known to have been uniformly a great admirer of, and strongly attached to, general Washington, as a virtuous patriot; a great, a good, and an honest man; and it is a fact, which evinced this opinion as powerfully as possible, that he was the only one of his family who always avowed himself of a friend of our present system of federal government, principally upon the ground of its having been approved of, and sanctioned by one he so highly esteemed.[4]

He always possessed more of the gay, good humour, and pleasing wit of Atticus, than the sternness of Cicero. To the young, the old, the grave, the gay, he was alike a pleasing and interesting companion. None approached him with diffidence; no one left him but with regret. To the poor around him, he was a counselor, physician, and friend; to others, his conversation was at once agreeable and instructive, and his life a fine example for imitation.[5]

Public Service

1758–1776	Member of the House of Burgesses of Virginia
1775–1779	Delegate from Virginia to the Continental Congress; signed the Declaration of Independence and the Articles of Confederation

Questions for Discussion

1. What do we know of Francis' early training? How did his character, molded at an early age, affect his adult life?

2. Does Francis' life exhibit the fruit of early training in the Scriptures? What can we glean from this as parents or possible future parents?

3. What qualities did Francis demonstrate in his attitude toward George Washington?

4. What evidence do we have that Francis was an enjoyable person to be around?

5. What quality do we see regarding his use of resources?

6. Unlike his brother, Francis wasn't a gifted speaker. In what other ways did God gift him and use him?

7. What evidences do we have that Francis was a Christian?

8. What do we know about Francis, in his final years, that shows that he still had a desire to learn? What helped build a love for learning in Francis, while still a boy?

9. What are the characteristics of a good friend?

10. Proverbs gives us a key as to how to have friends. What is it? If you don't know, look it up in a concordance, under "friends."

11. Proverbs also gives a warning as to how to choose friends. Look it up to find out what it is.

Richard Henry Lee [signature]

Richard Henry Lee

Persuasive Patriot

Proverbs 15:23

"Resolute for Freedom"

BORN
January 20, 1732

BIRTHPLACE
Westmoreland County, Virginia

EDUCATION
Tutors, schools in England

OCCUPATION
Planter

MARRIED
Anne Aylet, 1757;
Anne Gaskins Pinckard, 1769

CHILDREN
9

AGE AT SIGNING
44

DIED
June 19, 1794, age 62

Richard Henry Lee was born on June 20, 1732, at his family's estate, Stratford, in Westmoreland County, Virginia, just a month before George Washington was born in the very same county. Lee was one of six brothers, one of whom, Francis Lightfoot Lee, also signed the Declaration of Independence. His family had their own schoolhouse on their estate where tutors taught their children. Richard went to England at the age of 11 to study for seven years.

> The story is told that his older brothers warned him that English schoolboys were likely to try to beat up a young American colonist, so Richard daily trained in boxing with a young slave before sailing to England.[7]

> He read with avidity, every scrap of history of that character, which fell in his way. Thus he was early indoctrinated with the ideas of re-publicanism, and before the season of adolescence had passed, he was warmly attached to those principles of civil liberty, which he after-ward so manfully contended for.[8]

In that Congress, Mr. Lee was one of the prime movers, and his convincing and persuasive eloquence nerved the timid to act and speak out boldly for the rights of the colonists. His con-duct there made a profound impression upon the public mind, and he stood before his countrymen as one of the brightest lights of the age.[2]

While still in England, his father, Thomas Lee, died, and at age 19 Richard returned home to manage the estate that he had inherited. He was commissioned as captain of the militia in Westmoreland at age 23, and led his troops to volunteer their services to British General Braddock in the expedition against the French.

> The haughty Braddock proudly refused to accept the services of those plain volunteers, deeming the disciplined troops whom he brought with him, quite sufficient to drive the invading Frenchman from the English domain. …Braddock did indeed accept the services of Major Washington and a force of Virginia militia, and had he listened to the advice of the young Virginia soldier, he might not only have avoided the disastrous defeat at the Great Meadows, but saved his own life. But when Washington, who was well acquainted with the Indian mode of warfare, modestly offered his advice, the haughty Braddock said: "What, an American buskin teach a British General how to fight!" The advice was unheeded, the day was lost, and Braddock was among the slain.[9]

Lee brought his troops home, disgusted at the British for their arrogance. Lee was married to Anne Aylett in his mid-twenties and they had four children. They lived in Chantilly, their estate on the Potomac River. In 1768, Lee suffered two serious blows: in the spring he had a hunting accident in which he lost four of his fingers; and in December, his beloved wife died. The following year he again married, to Anne Pinckard, with whom he had five more children.

Richard was elected justice of the peace in 1757 and the following year was re-elected to the House of Burgesses, where he held his position until it was dissolved at the beginning of the Revolutionary War.

Lee supported the abolition of slavery, as proved by his first speech in the House of Burgesses:

> As the consequences, sir, of the determination which we must make in the subject of this day's debate, will greatly affect posterity as well as ourselves, it surely merits our most serious attention. If this be bestowed, it will appear both from reason and experience, that the importation of slaves into this colony has been, and will be attended with effects dangerous to our

An early biographer described Lee's appearance thus: His person was tall and well proportioned; his face was on the Roman model; his nose Caesarian; the port and carriage of his head leaning persuasively forward; and the whole contour noble and fine. The eye which shed intelligence over such features, had softness and composure as its prevailing characteristic, till it glowed in debate or radiated in conversation. His voice was clear and melodious, and was modulated by the feeling which swayed his bosom. The progress of time was insensible to those who listened to his conversation, and he entwined himself around the minds of his hearers, fixing his memory on their hearts.[1]

political and moral interest. When it is observed that some of our neighbouring colonies, though much later than ourselves in point of settlement, are now far before us in improvement, to what, sir, can we attribute this strange but unhappy truth? The reason seems to be this, that with their whites, they import arts and agriculture, while we with our blacks, exclude both. Nature has not particularly favoured them with superior fertility of soil, nor do they enjoy more of the sun's cheering influence, yet greatly have they outstript us. Were not this sufficient, sir, let us reflect on our dangerous vicinity to a powerful neighbour; and that slaves, from the nature of their situation, can never feel an interest in our cause, because they see us enjoying every privilege and luxury, and find security established, not for them, but for others; and because they observe their masters in possession of liberty which is denied to them, they and their posterity being subject for ever to the most abject and mortifying slavery. Such people must be natural enemies, and consequently their increase dangerous to the society in which they live…

I have seen it observed by a great writer, that Christianity, by introducing into Europe the truest principles of humanity, universal benevolence, and brotherly love, had happily abolished civil slavery. Let us, who profess the same religion, practice its precepts, and by agreeing to this duty, convince the world that we know and practice our true interests, and that we pay a proper regard to the dictates of justice and humanity.[10]

Lee became known for his addresses and writings to the king and British Parliament opposing the Stamp Act and Townshend Acts.

To his brother in 1768, he writes, "that a change of men in the British Cabinet can produce no change of measures on the American question. So circumstanced here, the cause of American liberty will be desperate indeed, if it find not a firm support in the virtuous and determined resolution of the people of America. This is our last, our surest hope, this our trust and refuge." Another letter, written about the same time, concludes thus, "once more let me remind you that no confidence is to be reposed in the justice or mercy of Britain, and that American liberty must be entirely of American fabric."[11]

In 1774 the Virginia governor dissolved the House of Burgesses because of their opposition to the Coercive Acts against Boston. The Virginia legislators then met in Raleigh Tavern in Williamsburg, where they issued an address to the other colonies, prepared by Lee, to call a general Congress "to deliberate on those general measures which the united interests of America from time to time require."[12]

When the first Congress dissolved itself on the twenty-sixth of October, 1774, the impression which remained on the public mind, concerning Richard Henry Lee was, that in him elegance of manners was united with the strictest honour, and unshaken fidelity; that he was proof against temptation; firm, upright and void of ambition; that with great ardour of feeling, the boldness of his spirit was under the curb of reason and discretion.[5]

Richard Henry Lee and Patrick Henry were among the delegates chosen to attend the First Continental Congress in Philadelphia.

The majority of the delegates to the first Continental Congress of 1774 still were hopeful of placating the British king and parliament, and they refused to approve the following resolution offered by Lee:

Resolved, that, as we find the reason, declared in the preamble to the act of parliament for raising a revenue in America, to be for supplying the civil government, the administration of justice, and for protecting, defending and securing the colonies, that congress recommend it to those colonies, in which it is not already done, to provide constitutional, competent, and honourable support for the purposes of government and administration of justice; and that as it is quite unreasonable that the mother country should be at the expense of maintaining standing armies in North America for its defence, and that administration may be convinced that this is unnecessary and improper, as North America is able, willing, and, under providence, determined to defend, protect, and secure itself, the congress do most earnestly recommend to the several colonies, that a militia be forthwith appointed and well disciplined, and that it be well provided with proper arms.[13]

Lee was among those present at St. John's Church in Richmond when Patrick Henry gave his famous speech with his cry of "Give me liberty or give me death." Lee totally supported Henry's appeal to arm the militia. In a stirring speech, Lee proclaimed,

Admitting the probable calculations to be against us, we are assured in holy writ, that the race is not to the swift, nor the battle to the strong; and if the language of genius may be added to that of inspiration, I will say with our immortal bard: "Thrice is he armed, who hath his quarrel just, And he but naked, tho' locked up in steel, Whose conscience with injustice is oppressed."[14]

Lee was elected delegate to the Second Continental Congress in 1775 and was said to have liked its spirit of determination. When Washington was unanimously elected commander-in-chief, Lee was appointed chairman of the committee responsible to give Washington instructions.

About this time, Lee wrote a second address to the people of Great Britain:

> Yet we conclude not that we propose to surrender our property into the hands of your ministry, or vest your Parliament with a power which may terminate in our destruction. The great bulwarks of our Constitution we have desired to maintain by every temperate, by every peaceable means; but your ministers, equal foes to British and American freedom, have added to their former oppressions an attempt to reduce us by the sword to a base and abject submission. On the sword, therefore, we are compelled to rely for protection. Should victory declare in your favor, yet men trained to arms from their infancy and animated by the love of liberty, will afford neither a cheap nor easy conquest. Of this at least we are assured, that our struggle will be glorious, our success certain; since even in death we shall find that freedom which in life you forbid us to enjoy.[15]

Lee is perhaps most famous for his resolution on the floor of Congress urging delegates to declare independence from Great Britain, on June 7, 1776:

Resolved: That these United Colonies are, and of right ought to be, free and independent States, that they are absolved from all allegiance to the British Crown, and that all political connection between them and the State of Great Britain is, and ought to be, totally dissolved.

That it is expedient forthwith to take the most effectual measures for forming foreign Alliances.

That a plan of confederation be prepared and transmitted to the respective Colonies for their consideration and approbation. In concluding the speech in which he introduced this resolution, Lee eloquently said: "Why, then, sir, why do we longer delay? Why still deliberate? Let this happy day give birth to an American republic. Let her arise, not to devastate and to conquer, but to re-establish the reign of peace and law. The eyes of Europe are fixed upon us; she demands of us a living example of freedom, that may exhibit a contrast, in the felicity of the citizen, to the ever-increasing tyranny which desolates her polluted shores. She invites us to prepare an asylum, where the unhappy may find solace, and the persecuted repose. She entreats us to cultivate a propitious soil, where that generous plant which first sprung and grew in England, but is now

☙ Public Service ❧

1758–1775	Member of the Virginia House of Burgesses
1774–1775	Member of Virginia's patriotic provincial congress
1774–1779	Delegate to the Continental Congress; wrote the resolution that led to the Declaration of Independence; signed the Declaration of Independence and the Articles of Confederation
1780–1784	Member of the Virginia state legislature
1784–1785	President of the Congress of the Confederation
1785–1789	Delegate to the Congress of the Confederation
1789–1792	United States senator from Virginia

withered by the poisonous blasts of Scottish tyranny, may revive and flourish, sheltering under in salubrious and interminable shade all the unfortunate of the human race. It we are not this day wanting in our duty, the names of the American legislators of 1776 will be placed by posterity at the side of Theseus, Lycurgus, and Romulus — of the three Williams of Nassau, and of all those whose memory has been, and ever will be, dear to virtuous men and good citizens." [16]

His resolution was seconded by John Adams, but opposed by John Dickinson of Pennsylvania and Robert Livingston of New York, who were still hoping for reconciliation with Great Britain. On June 10, Congress voted to postpone the vote until July 1; but in the meantime, a committee was formed to begin writing the document. That same day, Richard Henry Lee received word from home that his wife was seriously ill and he immediately left, leaving his fellow delegate, Thomas Jefferson, to fill his place and thereby write the famous Declaration of Independence. Lee was absent from Congress on the day of the vote, and also the signing, but affixed his name to the document on September 4, 1776.

In consequence of his great exertions to procure a declaration of Independence, and his able support of the freedom of his country, Mr. Lee was exposed to the more immediate and implacable hatred of the king of England and his ministers. It is asserted that, had the arms of England prevailed, the surrender of Washington and Lee would have been demanded as a preliminary to any treaty. The rudeness of individuals cannot be charged upon their nation, yet, that men, in the garb and rank of gentlemen, could not refrain from expressing, to the sons of Mr. Lee, then at school in St. Bees, "the hope that their father's head might soon be seen on Tower hill," may serve to show the light in which he was viewed by the royalists of that day. The desire of the enemy to cut off by any means so able a supporter of the rights of America, was only equaled by the solicitude of his fellow citizens to secure his safety and happiness. During his absence from Congress, a British captain of marines, with a strong party of men from vessels of war then in the Potomac,

broke into his house at midnight, and by threats and bribes endeavoured to prevail on his domestics to betray their master, for, it was understood that Mr. Lee was in the vicinity. Honourably deceitful, the servants assured the party, that he had already set out for Philadelphia, although he was then only a few miles from his farm. The solicitude of his friends for his safety was evinced by their constraining him to forego the melancholy pleasure of a visit to General Charles Lee, then a prisoner in New York. Mr. Lee's reply to the invitation of the general, is marked with the brevity of deep feeling and with the language of manly grief, which swells the bosom, when it cannot serve a friend in the time of necessity.

"My dear friend, My feelings are not to be described. I would go to every extremity to serve my friend and the able friend of liberty and mankind. But here my power fails. I have not the smallest idea of personal danger, nor does this affect the present question. Farewell, my dear friend, may you be as happy as you deserve, then the cause of humanity will have nothing to fear for you." Richard Henry Lee. [17]

During a short recess in September, he was actively engaged in the Virginia Assembly where he effectually stripped the mask from the "conciliatory measures," so called, of Lord North, which were evidently arranged to deceive and divide the American people. By this annihilation of the last vestige of confidence in royalty, in the hearts of the people of Virginia, he became very obnoxious to Lord Dunmore, the royal governor of the province, and he tried many ways to silence the patriot. [6]

Mr. Lee was one of the first "Committee of Correspondence" appointed in Virginia in 1778, and he was greatly aided in the acquirement of knowledge and respecting the secret movements and opinions of the British Parliament, by frequent letters from his brother, Arthur Lee, who was a distinguished literary character in London, and an associate with the leading men of the realm. He furnished him with the earliest political intelligence, and it was generally so correct, that the Committees of Correspondence in other colonies always received without doubt, any information which came from the Virginia Committee. Through this secret channel of correct intelligence, Richard Henry Lee very early learned that nothing short of absolute political independence would probably arrest the progress of British oppression and misrule, in America. Hence, while other men thought timidly of independence, and regarded it merely as a possibility of the distant future, Mr. Lee looked upon it as a measure that must speedily be accomplished, and his mind and heart were prepared to propose it whenever expediency should favor the movement.[18]

Lee served on many important committees while in Congress and signed the Articles of Confederation. For a short while, he commanded the militia of Westmoreland, although he was hampered due to the previous hunting accident when he lost the use of one hand.

The testimony of Generals Weedon and Greene in favour of the military arrangements for defence made by Mr. Lee, are not more honourable to his fame than the complaints of the enemy, "that they could not set foot on Westmoreland without having the militia immediately upon them." Such was the language of Captain Grant, who at that time with a few British schooners and tenders kept possession of the Potomac, and ravaged the counties on both its banks. The nature of this command prevented any distinguished exploit, yet the frequent skirmishes with the enemy rendered it peculiarly dangerous. On one occasion, in an attempt to seize a tender of the enemy which had been driven ashore, Mr. Lee narrowly escaped; for while he was rallying his scattered company, which the long guns from the boats of the enemy and the small arms of a detachment on shore had thrown into confusion, his attention was so occupied that his horse fell

He possessed a rich store of political knowledge, with an activity of observation and a certainty of judgment, which turned that knowledge to the very best account. He was not a lawyer by profession, but he understood thoroughly the constitution both of the mother country and of her colonies, and the elements also of the civil and municipal law. Thus, while his eloquence was free from those stiff and technical restraints, which the habit of forensic speaking are so apt to generate, he had all the legal learning which is necessary to a statesman. He reasoned well and declaimed freely and splendidly. The note of his voice was deep and melodious. It was the canorous voice of Cicero. He had lost the use of one of his hands, which he kept constantly covered with a black silk bandage, neatly fitted to the palm of his hand, but leaving his thumb free; yet, notwithstanding this disadvantage, his gesture was so graceful and highly finished, that it was said he had acquired it by practicing before a mirror. Such was his promptitude, that he required no preparation for debate. He was ready for any subject as soon as it was announced, and his speech was so copious, so rich, so mellifluous, set off with such bewitching cadence of voice, and such captivating grace of action, that while you listened to him you desired to hear nothing superior; and indeed, thought him perfect. He had quick sensibility and a fervid imagination.[4]

BIRTH PLACE OF R.H. LEE & FRANCIS LIGHTFOOT LEE.
Stratford House Westmoreland.

*Birthplace of Francis Lightfoot Lee and Richard Henry Lee
Stratford House, Westmoreland, Virginia*

Mr. Lee was a sincere practical Christian, a kind and affectionate husband and parent, a generous neighbor, a constant friend, and in all the relations of life, he maintained a character above reproach. "His hospitable door," says Sanderson, "was open to all; the poor and destitute frequented it for relief, and consolation; the young for instruction; the old for happiness; while a numerous family of children, the offspring of two marriages, clustered around and clung to each other in fond affection, imbibing the wisdom of their father, while they were animated and delighted by the amiable serenity and captivating graces of his conversation. The necessities of his country occasioned frequent absence; but every return to his home was celebrated by the people as a festival; for he was their physician, their counselor, and the arbiter of their differences. The medicines which he imported were carefully and judiciously dispensed; and the equity of his decision was never controverted by a court of law."[3]

with him amid the broken and insecure ground on the beach, only a few yards from the advance of the British troops. His presence of mind did not forsake him in so untoward an accident and he was by great skill able to cover the retreat of his little party without considerable loss on his side.[19]

In 1784 he was elected president of the Congress. After about a year, he retired, but continued on as a delegate from Virginia until the Congress of the Confederation ended with the ratification of the U.S. Constitution.

Lee opposed the ratification of the Constitution, and wrote a series of articles called "Letter from the Federal Farmer." He thought the Constitution gave the federal government too much power.

These articles were written with restraint but firm conviction that the Constitution was not democratic enough. "Every man of reflection must see," he wrote, "that the change now proposed is a transfer of power from the many to the few."[20]

Lee was elected one of Virginia's first U.S. senators, defeating James Madison. He worked to secure amendments to the constitution to attain a more democratic government. He fought for freedom of religion, or "a general assessment for the support of the Christian religion."[21]

His sentiments on "the general assessment law," are thus stated in a letter to Mr. Madison, and are co-incident with those of Patrick Henry. "It is certainly comfortable to know, that the legislature of our country is engaged in beneficial pursuits; for I conceive that the general assessment, and a digest of the moral laws, are very important concerns; the one to secure our peace, and the other our morals. Refiners may weave reason into as fine a web as they please, but the experience of all times shows religion to be the guardian of morals; and he must be a very inattentive observer who cannot perceive, that in our country, avarice is accomplishing the destruction of religion, for want of a legal obligation to contribute something to its support. The declaration of rights, it seems to me, rather contends against forcing modes of faith and forms of worship, in religious matters, than against compelling contribution for the support of religion in general." To state the opinions of Mr. Lee on these subjects, seemed to be the duty of his biographer; but to discuss the merits of the questions involved in them, belongs to the philosophic historian.[22]

In 1792, Lee retired from his office to enjoy his family and friends. The Virginia senate sent him this note of thanks:

Resolved, unanimously, that the speaker be desired to convey to Richard Henry Lee, the respects of the senate; that they sincerely sympathize with him in those infirmities, which have deprived their country of his valuable services; and that they ardently wish he may, in his retirement, with uninterrupted happiness, close the evening of a life, in which he hath so conspicuously shone forth as a statesman and a patriot; that while mindful of his many exertions to promote the public interests, they are particularly thankful for his conduct as a member of the legislature of the United States.[23]

In 1792 he had the misfortune of experiencing a carriage accident, and sustained injuries from it.

Mr. Lee breathed his last on the nineteenth of June, 1794, in the sixty-fourth year of his age, at Chantilly, Westmoreland county, Virginia, a few weeks before the celebration of the day on which his eloquent tongue and intrepid mind, had given birth to the independence of his country.[24]

The following is a brief sketch of his life by an early biographer who wrote while some of the signers were still alive:

Enough has been said to show the extent of his acquirements and the refinement of his taste, the solidity of his judgment and the vividness of his imagination, but the personal appearance of such a man may be an object of curiosity to posterity…In the vigour of his mind, amid the honours of the world and its enjoyments, he had declared his belief in Jesus Christ as the Saviour of men.[25]

☙ Questions for Discussion ❧

1. How did God use the persuasiveness and eloquence of Richard Henry Lee to influence Congress?

2. What are some of the character traits that his countrymen admired in him? How did using manners help to win our country's freedom?

3. What did young Richard Henry Lee read about? How did God use this later to influence others?

4. What experience did Richard Henry Lee have that resulted in disgust for the arrogant attitude of the British General?

5. Name two reasons besides taxation without representation that we can deduce led Richard Henry Lee to favor independence?

6. List all evidences from this text that Richard Henry Lee was a Christian.

7. What character qualities could be said of Richard Henry Lee and his fellow legislators who met undercover in Raleigh Tavern?

8. Comment on Richard Henry Lee's discourse after he heard Patrick Henry's stirring speech.

9. What can we learn of Richard Henry Lee from his address to the people of Great Britain?

10. Read and discuss Richard Henry Lee's famous resolutions for independence.

11. Tell of Richard Henry Lee's narrow escape from capture by the British.

12. Comment on the remark made to Richard Henry Lee's two sons. Comment on the pressure on entire families of each signer.

13. Tell why Lee opposed ratification of the Constitution. Have his fears have been realized?

14. Tell how Richard Henry Lee was a defender of religious freedom and read his thoughts on it to James Madison.

15. Tell how Mr. Lee exhibited persuasiveness.

16. Think of an issue that affects our country. Write a persuasive letter to the editor of your newspaper to persuade others to a righteous view of the issue.

Thomas Nelson, Jr.

Sacrificial Patriot

Matthew 6:33

"Virginia's Favourite Soldier"

ᴄᴧ·ᴄᴧ

BORN
December 26, 1738

BIRTHPLACE
Yorktown, Virginia

EDUCATION
Cambridge University, England

OCCUPATION
Merchant and planter

MARRIED
Lucy Grymes, 1762

CHILDREN
13

AGE AT SIGNING
37

DIED
January 4, 1789; age 50

The 44th Signer of the Declaration was Thomas Nelson of Yorktown, Virginia, described by John Adams as "a fat man…alert and lively for his weight." [1]

Thomas Nelson was born at Yorktown in Virginia on December 26, 1738, the oldest of five sons. His father was a wealthy merchant and landowner. As was common in that time, he was sent to England at the age of 14 to continue his studies. He started at a private school not far from London, then went to Cambridge to Trinity College. He returned home at the age of 22.

The following year Thomas married Lucy Grymes, the daughter of a wealthy plantation owner. Nelson's father gave him valuable plantation lands and a house in Yorktown. Thomas and Lucy had 13 children.

By his long residence in England, he had acquired in a considerable degree, an attachment to the manners of its country gentlemen, and a fondness for their pursuits. These he somewhat adopted himself. He rode out daily to his plantation, a few miles from York, a servant generally attending him with his fowling piece, and he often amused himself in shooting. He kept a pack of hounds at a small farm near the town, and in the winter exercised himself in company with his friends and neighbours, once or twice a week in a fox chase. His house was a scene of the most genteel and liberal hospitality: no gentleman ever stopped an hour in York without receiving an invitation to it, unless a previous acquaintance with him, and his hospitable character and manners rendered such an invitation unnecessary, according to the general mode at that time of visiting among gentlemen in Virginia.[4]

At the age of 26, Nelson was elected to the Virginia House of Burgesses. He served there until it was dissolved by Governor Dunmore in 1774 for passing resolutions opposing the British parliament's closing of the port of Boston. The delegates immediately met in Raleigh Tavern and called for a meeting inciting the other colonies to join them in a Continental Congress.

Nelson performed a daring protest against the British Tea Act: He boarded the ship *Virginia*, anchored near his home in Yorktown, and dumped two chests of British tea into the York River. This was very risky in an age when destroying another person's property was a serious crime. Even Samuel Adams, the organizer of the Boston Tea Party, hadn't taken part in the actual tea dumping. Nelson seems to have escaped punishment for his bold act of defiance. [5]

In March 1775, Mr. Nelson took a prominent part in a very bold proposal:

This measure was no less than the organization of a military force in the province; a step which, passing the line that yet seemed to bind the colonies to the mother country, placed them in the prominent position of a nation determined to gain or hazard all.[6]

Many of the men thought the proposal too dangerous, and held hopes for reconciliation with the British. On the other hand, proponents of the resolution cautioned them against holding delusive hopes and urged at least a preparation for the dangers which threatened them. Mr. Nelson declared his firm support.

As his residence was in a part of the country, the most exposed of any to attack, this declaration was censured as imprudent by many of his friends; but such was the generous ardour of his feelings, that no private interest could induce him to suppress them, at a time when he believed their influence would be beneficial to the general cause.[7]

The resolution was approved and Virginia's course was set if the British government persisted in their oppressive measures.

When the Virginia legislators adopted his resolution, Nelson rode with it to Philadelphia. There it provided the basis of Richard Henry Lee's independence resolutions that led to the Declaration of Independence.[8]

Thomas Nelson was elected to the Continental Congress in the summer of 1775. In 1776, in a letter he wrote to Mr. Prye, (who later became governor of Virginia), he expressed his thoughts on independence.

I wish I knew the sentiments of our people upon the grand points of confederation and foreign alliance, or in other words, of independence; for we cannot expect to form a connexion with any foreign power, as long as we have a womanish hankering after Great Britain; and then to suppose we can have any affection for a people who are carrying on the most savage war against us.[9]

Extremely interesting was a letter he wrote to a personal friend in February 1776, that shows some of the thoughts that the delegates wrestled with in regards to independence or reconciliation.

Independence, confederation and foreign alliance are as formidable to some of the congress, I fear a majority, as an apparition to a weak, enervated woman… We are now carrying on a war and no war. They seize our property wherever they find it, either by land or sea; and we hesitate to retaliate, because we have a few friends in England who have ships. Away with such squeamishness, say I…One of them refused to ordain a young gentleman, who went from this country, because he was a rebellious American; so that unless we submit to parliamentary oppression, we shall not have the gospel of Christ preached among us, but let every man worship God under his own fig tree.[10]

While waiting for the other delegates to come around, he busied himself on various committees in Congress, including supervising the treasury, and framing the Articles of Confederation.

Nelson watched as all the delegates finally voted in favor of independence and enthusiastically signed the

Declaration of Independence on August 2, 1776. The following spring, while serving in Congress, Nelson experienced a stroke that affected his memory. The other delegates finally persuaded him to return home. His recovery was slow, and he had to resign his seat. It is believed that he suffered other strokes as well as periodic bouts of asthma. However, he still held a seat in Virginia's legislature during the war, and raised money, often using his own funds, to pay troops.

> The sudden call of the militia from their homes left many families in embarrassed circumstances, for a great part of the agricultural operations were suspended. General Nelson used the extent of his means in ameliorating the condition of their families, by having his own numerous servants till their land. He also distributed his money liberally among them, and thus more than a hundred families were kept from absolute want.[11]

In August, 1777, after being home only a short while, Nelson again was called to public duty. A large British fleet had been sighted off the coast of Virginia, and it was feared that an invasion was about to be launched. In preparation for the expected attack, Governor Patrick Henry appointed Nelson brigadier general and commander-in-chief of the Virginia militia. Only a few hundred militia-men had been mustered for the colony's defense, when the British fleet sailed off for an attack on Philadelphia, and Nelson was able to return to civilian life.[12]

In October, the Virginia legislatures passed a law confiscating British property. Nelson vehemently opposed it, calling it unfair to British merchants who had the extended credit to the colonists and were not to blame for the actions of the British government. "I hope this bill will be rejected," Nelson declared, "but whatever be its fate, by God, I will pay *my* debts like an honest man."[13]

Nelson rallied troops in March of 1778 to aid the war effort in Pennsylvania. He outfitted a troop of 70 horsemen at his own expense, and with himself as commanding officer, arrived in Philadelphia only to find the British had changed course and his unit wasn't needed.

> Having a plantation near York, he sent all his negroes and labourers, and even some of his domestic servants to work during their absence for the poor men of the neighbourhood, who had been called off from the support of their families to join the militia that had been suddenly assembled. The fact is mentioned on the personal knowledge and information of an old friend of general Nelson, who observes in communicating it, that he has reason to believe that the same generous and benevolent conduct was observed by him on some other occasions, both before and after it.[14]

❧ Public Service ❧

1765–1774	Member of the House of Burgesses of Virginia
1774–1776	Member of the provincial congress of Virginia
1775–1779	Delegate to the Continental Congress; signed the Declaration of Independence
1777–1781	Commander-in-chief of the militia of Virginia
1781	Governor of Virginia

Nelson sent the troops home, providing money from his own pocket for their trip. Interestingly enough, the outdoor activity he'd engaged in improved his health and in 1779, he accepted another term in the Continental Congress. He served from February to April, when his illness recurred and he was forced to return home.

At the urging of Congress, the Virginia legislature set out to borrow two million dollars in the spring of 1780 — the money to be given to the continental treasury to help buy provisions for the French fleet that was expected to help end the war. Nelson set about endeavoring to raise the money for the legislature, but on every hand he received the following reply from those he had asked for loans: "We will not lend the government a shilling — but we will lend you, Thomas Nelson, all that we can possibly raise." With that, Nelson made the loans in his own name, and turned the money over to the government, receiving in return securities that later turned out to be worthless.[15]

In 1781, Virginia became the chief theatre of war. The traitor Benedict Arnold and General Philips ravaged the coasts and rivers, causing destruction. In addition, Cornwallis waged battles in the south, and was successful.

It was about this time Thomas Jefferson's term as governor ended, and Thomas Nelson was elected to fill the office.

The active Colonel Tarleton, of the British army, made every effort to effect the capture of the legislature of

It also appears that in instances, finding he could not obtain money even on his own security, when the repayment was to be made in current money, he went so far as to give his bond for the amount to be repaid in tobacco at the price which it then brought. The price of this article afterwards rose to a great height, not only in paper currency, but in specie: he was obliged to redeem his obligations at a very great sacrifice, for which he never received any recompense from the public.[2]

Virginia. He succeeded in getting some into his custody, and so irregular became their meetings, in consequence of being frequently obliged to disperse and flee for personal safety, that they passed an act which placed the government of the State in the hands of the governor and his council. The council too, being scattered, General Nelson had the whole responsibility laid upon his shoulders, and in the exercise of his individual powers he was compelled, by the exigencies of the times, to do some things that were not strictly legal; but the legislature subsequently legalized all his acts.[16]

By placing himself as head of a force of men, Nelson managed to check Cornwallis' progress. Nelson, with his personal funds paid the men until the siege of Yorktown was accomplished.

At length every thing being prepared, they were ready to commence their march and join the main army under general Washington; their gallant and generous commander well knew, however, that many had embarked with him from the purest principles of patriotism, when their slender means ill warranted such an expedition. He called them together, therefore, on the eve of their departure; he explained to them his views; he encouraged them by his own animated confidence; and he held out to them the fair hope of remuneration at some more prosperous day. "If however," he concluded, "any one here is in want of money, let him repair to my quarters. I will myself supply him." Many accepted his offer as their wants became pressing and their means decreased. He was in fact the banker for the whole company; his generosity was displayed throughout the whole expedition; and as is unfortunately too often the result of such conduct, he finally suffered the loss of very considerable sums.[17]

Due to the situation of the British being in Virginia, the members of the ruling council were often scattered. During this time:

Mr. Nelson was driven by necessity to perform many measures on his own authority and at his own responsibility — a course of conduct infinitely painful to a man of his sound political principles, and strict views of public rights. On the one hand, he saw and felt that he was departing from the line of his duty, as defined and limited by the laws of the commonwealth: on the other, he knew that its salvation, and indeed that of all the Union, was at stake… He decided to risk censure, perhaps punishment, for his conduct, and pursue the disinterested course which promised the greatest general benefit to the whole community. This determination once formed, he promptly executed it. As soon as the allied army reached Virginia, every measure which his office, his public or personal influence, and his private wealth enabled him to adopt, was promptly done; and it was certainly owing, in no small degree, to his exertions, that the frail materials of the army were kept together until they secured the liberties of the country, by the glorious and final blow given to the enemy at Yorktown.[18]

Nelson led the Virginia brigades of about 3,000 militia men at Yorktown. Of this siege, Nelson commented: "This blow must be a decisive one, it being out of the power of Great Britain to replace such a number of good troops."[19]

British soldiers had taken refuge in Nelson's Yorktown home.

During the siege he observed that while the Americans poured their shot and shells thick and fast into every part of the town, they seemed carefully to avoid firing in the direction of his house. General Nelson inquired why his house was spared, and he was informed that it was out of personal regard for him. He at once begged them not to make any difference on that account, and at once a well directed fire was opened upon it. At that moment a number of British officers occupied it, and were at dinner enjoying a feast, and making merry with wine. The shots of the Americans entered the house, and killing two of the officers, effectively ended the conviviality of the party.[20]

RES. OF THOMAS NELSON Jʳ YORKTOWN VA

*Residence of Thomas Nelson Jr,
Yorktown, Virginia*

Nelson, whose devotion to the common cause was ardent and unbounded, requested that the artillerists would not spare his house more than any other, especially as he knew it to be occupied by the principal officers of the British army. Two pieces were accordingly pointed against it. The first shot went through the house and killed two of a large company of officers, then indulging in the pleasures of the table. Other balls soon dislodged the hostile tenants.[21]

The battle was won. Independence was achieved and General George Washington commended Nelson's service to his country:

The general would be guilty of the highest ingratitude, a crime of which he hopes he shall never be accused, if he forgot to return his sincere acknowledgements to his excellency governor Nelson, for the succours which he received from him and the militia under his command, to whose activity, emulation and bravery, the highest praises are due. The magnitude of the acquisition will be ample compensation for the difficulties and dangers which they met with so much firmness and patriotism.[22]

He was the favourite soldier of Virginia, and we hear of him in all directions, animating the troops by his energy and example, or planning expeditions to oppose the enemy.[3]

Governor Nelson's health began to decline due to the acute stresses of his war duties. In November of 1781, he wrote the following letter to the speaker of the house of delegates:

"The very low state of health," he says, "to which I am reduced, and from which I have little expectation of soon recovering, makes it my duty to resign the government, that the state may not suffer for want of an executive." His resignation was accepted, and a successor appointed.[23]

Shortly after his resignation, charges were brought to the legislature against some of the actions Nelson took during the time the council was scattered and he made executive decisions to stage the defense of Yorktown. He requested permission to present his case before the legislature and was acquitted of all charges publicly.

An act to indemnify Thomas Nelson, Junior, Esquire, late governor of this commonwealth, and to legalize certain acts of his administration. Whereas, upon examination it appears that previous to and during the siege of York, Thomas Nelson, Esquire, late governor of this commonwealth, was compelled by the peculiar circumstances of the state and army, to perform many acts of government without the advice of the council of state, for the purpose of procuring subsistence and other necessaries for the allied army under the command of his excellency general Washington; be it enacted that all such acts of government, evidently productive of general good, and warranted by necessity, be judged and held of the same validity, and the like proceedings be had on them as if they had been executed by and with the advice of the council, and with all the formalities prescribed by law. And be it further enacted that the said Thomas Nelson, Jr., Esquire, be

and he hereby is in the fullest manner indemnified and exonerated from all penalties and dangers which might have accrued to him from the same.[24]

Mr. Nelson retired from political life and resided at his pretty little estate, Offly, in Hanover County, as he lacked funds to renovate his Yorktown home. He delighted in his family and in entertaining many visitors, including Frenchmen with whom he'd joined forces at Yorktown. He died on January 4, 1789, just after his fiftieth birthday.

He descended into the grave honoured and beloved; and alas! of his once vast estates, that honour and love was almost all that he left behind him. He had spent a princely fortune in his country's service; his horses had been taken from the plough, and sent to drag the munitions of war; his granaries had been thrown open to a starving soldiery, and his ample purse had been drained to its last dollar, when the credit of Virginia could not bring a sixpence into her treasury. Yet it was the widow of this man who, beyond eighty years of age, blind, infirm and poor, had yet to learn whether republics can be grateful.[25]

A tribute by Colonel Innis:

As a man, a citizen, a legislator and a patriot, he exhibited a conduct untarnished and un-debased by sordid or selfish interests, and strongly marked with the genuine characteristics of true religion, sound benevolence and liberal policy. Entertaining the most ardent love for civil and religious liberty, he was among the first of that glorious band of patriots whose exertions dashed and defeated the machinations of British tyranny and gave to United America, freedom and independent empire.[26]

Questions for Discussion

1. In reading the account of Thomas Nelson, sacrifice shines through this man's life. Tell of all the sacrifices recorded here that this man made for you.

2. List the qualities that are demonstrated in his life by his great sacrifice of his home in the Battle of Yorktown.

3. List examples of the generosity of this man.

4. Look up the definition of "hospitality." Tell why "hospitable" could be used to describe this man.

5. What bold proposal did Nelson make which demonstrated his selfless patriotism?

6. From the letter he wrote to a friend in 1776, what information do we have to support the idea that the propagation of the gospel of Jesus Christ was a motivating factor in his support of independence?

7. List ways in which God used Thomas Nelson to achieve victory at Yorktown.

8. What evidences do we have that Thomas Nelson was a Christian?

9. What can you sacrifice for the good of someone else?

George Wythe

George Wythe

Truthful Patriot

Proverbs 3:3

"Defender of Truth"

BORN
1726

BIRTHPLACE
Elizabeth City County, Virginia

EDUCATION
Home-taught

OCCUPATION
Lawyer, jurist

MARRIED
Ann Lewis, 1747;
Elizabeth Taliafero, 1755

CHILDREN
1

AGE AT SIGNING
50

DIED
June 8, 1806; age 80

No man ever left behind him a character more venerated than George Wythe. His virtue was of the purest kind; his integrity inflexible, and his justice exact; of warm patriotism, and devoted as he was to liberty, and the natural and equal rights of men, he might truly be called the Cato of his country, without the avarice of the Roman; for a more disinterested person never lived.

(continued on next page)

George Wythe was born in 1726 at Back River in Elizabeth County, Virginia, near Yorktown. His father was a prosperous plantation owner and his mother, a well-educated Quaker woman, taught him Latin and Greek. By the time he was a teenager, he had an excellent education. His father died when George was three years old, his mother when he was 20. The estate was left to his older brother, as his father had died without a legal will.

Wythe attended William and Mary College and became a clerk in his uncle's law office. In 1750 he was admitted to the bar. He married Ann Lewis, the sister to his legal assistant, who lived only about a year after their marriage. Eight years later, he remarried to Elizabeth Taliafero of Williamsburg. Just prior to his remarriage his brother died, leaving George the family estate.

He chose, however, to live in Williamsburg in the house that his new father-in-law, an architect, designed and built for him and his betrothed, whom he married about 1755. Their only child died in infancy.[7]

His career actually began at the age of 30 when he began his law practice. Thomas Jefferson studied law under him and had great admiration for Wythe. Other prominent men who studied under him were John Marshall and Henry Clay.

Wythe sometimes paid for the schooling of needy law students and took them into his home to live. Thomas Jefferson, who had lost his father when he was just fourteen, called Wythe, "my second father." [8]

Wythe was a member of the House of Burgesses for several sessions, where he served until the Revolutionary War brought an end to that body. Wythe represented the College of William and Mary in the House of Burgesses and was personal advisor to the governor of the colony. By the time he was in his 40s, fellow lawyers in Williamsburg described Wythe as "second to none of the profession with us." [9]

Wythe was a member of the second Continental Congress and helped persuade others to vote for the Declaration of Independence. He then returned to Virginia to help draft the state constitution and therefore wasn't present on August 2 for the signing. He added his name, however, on August 27, 1776.

During the revolution, Mr. Wythe suffered greatly in respect to his property. His devotion to public services left him little opportunity to attend to his private affairs. The greater part of his slaves he lost by the dishonesty of his superintendent, who placed them in the hands of the British. By economy and judicious management, however, Mr. Wythe was enabled, with the residue of his estate, and with his salary as chancellor, to discharge his debts, and to preserve his independence. [10]

Wythe also held the distinguished seat of professor of law at William and Mary. Wythe was a member of the Virginia delegation headed by George Washington that was sent to the Constitutional Convention in Philadelphia in 1787. Wythe was appointed chairman of the committee on rules.

In 1791, the year after Wythe resigned his professorship, he was appointed chancellor of the courts of Virginia, which necessitated him having to move his home to Richmond, the capitol of the state. Wythe helped revise the Virginia constitution, was elected speaker of the house

Temperance and regularity in all his habits, gave him general good health, and his unaffected modesty and suavity of manners endeared him to every one. He possessed a way of easy elocution, his language chaste, methodical in the arrangement of his matter, learned and logical in the use of it, and of great urbanity in debate. Not quick of apprehension, but with a little time, profound in penetration, and sound in conclusion. In his philosophy he was firm, and neither troubling, nor perhaps trusting anyone with his religious creed, he left to the world the conclusion, that that religion must be good which could produce a life of such exemplary virtue. His stature was of the middle size, well formed and proportioned, and the features of his face, manly, comely, and engaging. Such was George Wythe, the honour of his own, and model of future times.

—Thomas Jefferson[1]

George Wythe won fame for his legal skill and honesty. He wouldn't take a case if he felt his client was in the wrong, and if he caught a client lying, he dropped the case and returned any fees he had been paid. Some people even poked fun at him because he preferred to lose a case than bend the truth.[3]

Chancellor Wythe," as he was now called, began his most important work when he accepted the professorship of law at the College of William and Mary — the first chair of law in any American college. With his profound knowledge of the law and his penetrating mind, he did much to map the future course of American jurisprudence.[5]

the constitution, will say to them here is the limit of your authority; and hither shall you go, but not further.[11]

Wythe established a private school, being devoted to teaching the young. During this time, one of his pupils was Henry Clay, then a teenager.

Among other pupils was a negro boy belonging to him, whom he taught Latin, and he was preparing to give him a thorough education, when both he and the boy died. This occurrence took place the eighth day of June, 1780, when Mr. Wythe was in the eighty-first year of his age. His death was sudden and was believed to have been caused by poison placed in his food by a near relative. That person was tried for the crime, but acquitted. The negro boy alluded to, partook of the same food, and died a short time previous to his master.[12]

In his old age he lived with two of his former slaves: his housekeeper, Lydia Broadnax, and a youth named Michael Brown. Wythe was very fond of Michael, and named him to inherit part of his estate. Also in the household was George Wythe Sweeney, the signer's

---

George Wythe had taken the stand that the only political link between the colonies and Great Britain was their common allegiance to the King; that "that nation and its Parliament had no more authority over us than we had over them."[4]

---

of delegates, and was appointed one of three judges of the high court of chancery of Virginia by Patrick Henry. In the court of appeals in Virginia, Wythe was responsible for setting the precedent (later used by the U.S. Supreme Court,) that a law could be held to be unconstitutional. His opinion stated:

Nay, more, if the whole legislature, an event to be deprecated, should attempt to overleap the bounds prescribed to them by the people, I, in administering the public justice of the country, will meet the united powers, at my seat in this tribunal; and, pointing to

---

❧ Public Service ❧

1752–1768	Member of the House of Burgesses of Virginia
1768–1775	Clerk of the House of Burgesses of Virginia
1775–1776	Delegate from Virginia to the second Continental Congress; signed the Declaration of Independence
1776	Helped write the constitution for the Commonwealth of Virginia; appointed to committee to revise the laws of Virginia
1777	Speaker of the House of Delegates of the Virginia legislature
1778–1786	Judge of the Virginia court of chancery
1779–1786	First professor of law in America, at the College of William and Mary
1786–1806	Chancellor of the Commonwealth of Virginia

great-nephew. Sweeney, who was in line to inherit most of Wythe's estate, ran up gambling debts. First he forged his uncle's name on checks. Then, to get the whole estate, he poured poison into the coffee that George Wythe, Michael Brown, and Lydia Broadnax drank. The signer and the young man died, but Lydia, although gravely ill, survived.[13]

A few days before Wythe died, he changed his will, mentioning the suspicious death of one of his freed slaves who would have benefited from his will, and cut Sweeney out of it altogether. There was plenty of evidence against Sweeney, but he was brought to trial and acquitted, as a black person at the time wasn't allowed to testify against a white person. Therefore, Lydia wasn't allowed to testify what she knew. How tragic that such a distinguished patriot should be murdered by a selfish relative.

By his last will and testament, he bequeathed his valuable library and philosophical apparatus to his friend, Mr. Jefferson, and distributed the remainder of his little property among the grandchildren of his sister, and the slaves whom he had set free.[14]

During his lifetime he manumitted all of his adult slaves, and he provided for the freedom of the younger ones, who were his property at the time of his death. He also made provision in his will for the support of a man, woman, and child whom he had given freedom.[15]

His manner of living was plain and abstemious. He found the means of suppressing the desires of wealth by limiting the number of his wants. An ardent desire to promote the happiness of his fellow men, by supporting the cause of justice, and maintaining and establishing their rights, appears to have been his ruling passion. As a judge, he was remarkable for his rigid impartiality, and sincere attachment to the principles of equity; for his vast and various learning,; and for his strict and unwearied attention to business. Superior to popular prejudices, and every corrupting influence, nothing could induce him to swerve from truth and right. In his decisions, he seemed to be a pure intelligence, untouched by human passions, and settling the disputes of men, according to the dictates of eternal and immutable justice. . . .he was prompted by his genuine patriotism and philanthropy, which induced him for many years to take great delight in educating such young persons as showed an inclination for improvement.[6]

Mr. Wythe was a man of great perseverance and industry, kind and benevolent to the utmost; was strict in his integrity, sincere in every word, faithful in every trust; and his life presents a striking example of the force of good resolution triumphing over the seductions of pleasure and vice, and the attainments which persevering and virtuous toil will bring to the practician of these necessary ingredients for the establishment of an honorable reputation, and in the labors of a useful life. Mr. Wythe was twice married, but he left no offspring, an only child, by his first wife, having died in infancy.[2]

⚘Questions for Discussion⚘

I.   As you read through the text, list character qualities you see in this man's life. (There are at least 30). List any specific blessings you see God bestowed on him or our country as a result of his character.

2.   For what outstanding character quality did George Wythe become known?

3.   How did his mother's early training in his life prepare him for God's plan for his future?

4.   How did God use this man to disciple others? Name some of the men he discipled.

5.   Tell what George Wythe personally sacrificed for our freedom.

6.   Explain how God used Wythe and his understanding of the proper position of authority to set a proper precedent for the U.S. Supreme Court.

7.   Explain the special relationship Wythe had with his slaves. How does this differ from what is commonly taught about master/slave relationships? (Understand, King George wouldn't allow for slavery to be abolished in the colonies — look it up in the Declaration of Independence as one of the grievances the colonists had against Britain.) What provision did he make in his will for former slaves?

8.   What evidence do we have that Wythe was a Christian?

9.   Wythe attended the College of William and Mary and later was made Chancellor of the school. Look up in the appendix the information about the College of William and Mary at the time.

10.   Choose one outstanding quality from the life of this man, such as honesty or truthfulness. Learn its definition and the corresponding Bible verse for the quality. List specific ways you can begin to implement this character trait in your life.

11.   It is so easy to bend the truth to fit our desires. Purpose to be honestly truthful. Commit a Bible verse on truthfulness to memory and begin to meditate on it.

North Carolina

Joseph Hewes
William Hooper
John Penn

Joseph Hewes

Ardent Patriot

Titus 2:14

"It is done and I will abide by it"

∾∾

BORN
January 23, 1730

BIRTHPLACE
Kingston, New Jersey

EDUCATION
Common schools

OCCUPATION
Merchant

AGE AT SIGNING
46

DIED
November 10, 1779; age 49

Although the events in the life of Mr. Hewes, which we have been able to collect, are few, they perhaps sufficiently speak his worth, as a man of integrity, firmness, and ardent patriotism. To this may be added, that in personal appearance he was prepossessing, and characterized in respect to his disposition for great benevolence, and in respect to his manners for great amenity. He left a large fortune, but no children to inherit it.[2]

Joseph Hewes,

Joseph Hewes was born in Kingston, New Jersey in 1730, to a Quaker family. As a boy, Joseph was apprenticed to a Philadelphia merchant and acquired a business of his own which he made quite prosperous.

A friend referred to Hewes as one of "the best and agreeable men in the world," but something happened to change his cheerful outlook. Just days before he was to marry a woman named Isabella Johnston, she died. Brokenhearted, Joseph Hewes never married.[5]

He moved to Edenton, North Carolina sometime before 1763 and set up a profitable shipping business. He was elected to the North Carolina legislature in 1766 and continued in that position until 1775. He was a member of the local Committee of Correspondence and was sent as delegate to the first meeting of the second Constitutional Congress. He strongly supported the non-importation agreements although it meant great personal loss to his own shipping business.

A peace-loving and friendly man, he hoped to avoid any violence. He wrote to an English friend: "...we want no revolution. But

Despite the fact that Hewes' fortune was dependent upon trade with Great Britain, he subscribed to the decision of the first Continental Congress to cut off all exports and imports in trade with the British if they did not recognize the rights of the colonists.[1]

every American is determined to a man to die or to be free." The next spring, he again was elected as a delegate to the Continental Congress. He traveled to Philadelphia, arriving there in May with news of the fighting at Lexington and Concord ringing in his ears. A convention of Pennsylvania and New Jersey Quakers had met early in 1775 to denounce the efforts of the Continental Congress, but Hewes broke with his Quaker background to support the war measures voted by the second Continental Congress.[6]

At the second Continental Congress, however, John Adams convinced him that independence was the will of the people in the states.

William Hooper was away, so if John Penn voted for independence and Joseph Hewes voted against it, North Carolina would be locked in a one-one tie. According to John Adams, in the midst of the debates on independence, Hewes suddenly rose from his chair and declared that he would vote for separation from England. Lifting his hands as if in prayer, Hewes cried out, "It is done, and I will abide by it!" Joseph Hewes and John Penn both voted for independence on July 2, and a month later they and William Hooper signed the Declaration.[7]

Once he signed the Declaration, he never wavered in working for the American cause. He would labor in Congress from dawn to dusk without even pausing to eat or drink. Because of his shipping experience, he was chosen to be chairman of the marine committee set up to establish the navy. We have Hewes to thank for appointing

During that session [during which he helped to draw up a Declaration of rights] he was actively engaged in maturing a plan for a general non-importation agreement throughout the Colonies, and he voted for and signed it. In this act his devoted patriotism was manifest, for it struck a deadly blow at the business in which he was engaged. It was a great sacrifice for him to make, yet he cheerfully laid it upon the altar of Freedom.[3]

❧ Public Service ❧

1766–1775	**Member of North Carolina's colonial legislature**
1773	**Member of the North Carolina committee of correspondence**
1774–1777	**Delegate from North Carolina to the Continental Congress; signed the Declaration of Independence**
1778	**Member of the North Carolina state legislature**
1779	**Delegate from North Carolina to the Continental Congress**

John Paul Jones as an officer of the Continental Navy in December, 1775. John Paul Jones became America's greatest naval war hero.

Hewes lived for just over three years after the signing. Illness forced him to leave Congress on October 29, 1779, and he died 12 days later at 49 years of age. It is believed that his death was caused by overwork and that he had sacrificed his health to help free his country. He is buried in Christ Church churchyard in Philadelphia.

Questions for Discussion

1. We don't have volumes of information on Joseph Hewes, but what character qualities can you discover by reading back through what we do know?

2. How was the signing of the non-importation agreement a particularly large sacrifice for Hughes?

3. What qualities did William Ellery see in this man?

4. What factors made joining in the fight for independence an especially courageous act for this man?

5. The account by John Adams of Hewes at the signing of the Declaration tells us what about his character?

6. The fact that Hewes would often labor in Congress, without stopping even to eat or drink points to what character quality?

7. How had God prepared Hewes to establish a navy? What great contribution did he make to the Continental Navy?

8. What is believed to have been a factor in Hewes' death? What does this tell us about his character?

9. How does this man's life inspire you?

10. What does "ardent" mean? How can you become more engaged in our struggle to preserve our freedom today?

William Hooper

Firm Patriot

Hebrews 3:5–6

"Prophet of Independence"

BORN
June 17, 1742
BIRTHPLACE
Boston, Massachusetts
EDUCATION
Harvard College
OCCUPATION
Lawyer
MARRIED
Anne Clark, 1767
CHILDREN
3
AGE AT SIGNING
34
DIED
October 14, 1790; age 48

He was an ardent friend to his country, zealously attached to her rights, and ready to make every required personal sacrifice for her good.[1]

William Hooper was born in Boston, Massachusetts in 1742, the son of a Congregationalist clergyman. He studied for the ministry, beginning with seven years of preparatory education at Boston Latin School. In 1757, he was able to enter Harvard in the sophomore class, at the age of 15. Upon graduating at age 18, he began the study of law under James Otis, the Boston lawyer who coined the slogan, "Taxation without representation is tyranny." Mr. Otis had great influence on young Hooper.

Upon completing his law studies, he moved to Wilmington, North Carolina to set up practice. Then, at age 25, he married Anne Clark of Wilmington, with whom he had a daughter and two sons. Hooper's parents and Anne's parents were Loyalists, as were many of their friends.

In 1773, Hooper was elected to North Carolina's colonial legislature. About this time his allegiance to Britain began to wane. In 1774, he was sent to the first Continental Congress. During the Second Continental Congress in 1775, he wrote to the people of Jamaica, explaining the situation in the American colonies:

That our petitions have been treated with disdain, is now become the smallest part of our complaint: ministerial insolence is lost in

In a letter dated April 1774 to his friend James Iredell, he prophesied the Colonies' break with Great Britain — the earliest known prediction of independence, which won for Hooper the epithet "Prophet of Independence."[2]

The thirteen colonies were "striding fast to independence, and ere long will build an empire upon the ruins of Great Britain," he wrote to a friend in 1774.[6]

while he was away on business, the city fell to the enemy. British raiders were sent to capture him, but he fled as a fugitive. For the next 10 months, he was separated from his loved ones, often destitute, and had to depend upon his friends in Edenton for shelter and food. During this time, he fell violently ill with malaria, and was nursed back to health by his friend Iredell's wife.

When the British evacuated in November, Hooper returned to discover most of his property in ruins. He rejoined his wife and family, who had fled to Hillsboro, which he made his home for the rest of his life. The hardships of war and the toll of malaria caused his health to decline. He died in 1790, at the age of only 48.

ministerial barbarity. It has, by an exertion peculiarly ingenious, procured those very measures, which it laid us under the hard necessity of pursuing, to be stigmatized in parliament as rebellious: it has employed additional fleets and armies for the infamous purpose of compelling us to abandon them: it has plunged us in all the horrors and calamities of civil war: it has caused the treasure and blood of Britons (formerly shed and expended for far other ends) to be spilt and wasted in the execrable design of spreading slavery over British America: it will not, however, accomplish its aim: in the worst of contingencies, a choice will still be left, which it never can prevent us from making. [8]

From 1774–1777, Hooper divided his time between Congress, where he gained a reputation as an orator, and the North Carolina provincial assembly, where he labored to set up a state government.

In 1777, financial responsibilities and a desire to be near his family forced him to resign from Congress and return to Wilmington. There, he was elected state legislator, in which capacity he served till 1786.

The British invaded North Carolina in 1780. Hooper moved his family from Finian, his home, to Wilmington for safety, but in January, 1781,

When he engaged in revolutionary measures, he was fully aware of the dangers to which he exposed his person and estate; yet in spite of untoward events, his enthusiasm never abated, his firmness never forsook him. In times the most disastrous he never desponded, but maintained the ground he had assumed with increased intrepidity.[7]

RES. OF W? HOOPER. WILMINGTON, N.C.

Residence of William Hooper
Wilmington, North Carolina

In his person, Mr. Hooper was of middle stature, well formed, but of delicate and slender appearance. He carried a pleasing and intelligent countenance. In his manners he was polite and engaging, although towards those with which he was not particularly acquainted, he was somewhat reserved. He was distinguished for his powers of conversation; in point of literary merit he had but few rivals in the neighbourhood in which he dwelt. As a lawyer, he was distinguished for his professional knowledge, and indefatigable zeal in respect to business with which he was entrusted. Towards his brethren he ever maintained a high and honourable course of conduct, and particularly towards the younger members of the bar. As a politician, he was characterized for judgment, ardour, and constancy. In times of the greatest political difficulty and danger, he was calm, but resolute. He never desponded; but trusting to the justice of his country's cause, he had an unshaken confidence that heaven would protect and deliver her.[3]

He was rated by John Adams as one of the leading orators. Dr. Rush, with more restraint, described him as a sprightly and sensible young lawyer, and a rapid but correct speaker.[4]

Like all the others who signed the Declaration of Independence, Mr. Hooper was peculiarly obnoxious to the British, and on all occasions, they used every means in their power to possess his person, harass his family, and destroy his estate.[5]

✍ Public Service ✍

c.1765	**Moved to North Carolina to practice law**
1770–1771	**As deputy attorney general, helped put down the rebellion of the "Regulators" in western North Carolina**
1773–1774	**Member of North Carolina's colonial legislature**
1774–1776	**Member of North Carolina's provincial congress**
1774–1777	**Delegate from North Carolina to the Continental Congress; signed the Declaration of Independence**
1777–1782	**Member of the North Carolina state legislature**
1786	**Appointed by Congress to help mediate border dispute between Massachusetts and New York**

Questions for Discussion

1. What was Hooper's attitude toward his country?

2. What won Hooper the title of "The Prophet of Independence"?

3. What did John Adams say of Hooper?

4. Tell what qualities Hooper was known for as a judge, as a lawyer, towards his brethren, as a politician, and in times of danger.

5. Tell how the British attempted to bring him to ruin.

6. Give evidence of his courageousness.

7. What did Hooper study at Boston Latin School?

8. How did Hooper and his wife Anne's parents feel about independence from Great Britain?

9. Why did Hooper's allegiance to Britain begin to wane?

10. In what two offices did Hooper serve from 1774–1777?

11. Why did Hooper resign from Congress? What was his next area of service?

12. Tell of his fate trying to evade capture by the British.

13. What became of his family? His property?

14. In what area of your life do you need more constancy?

John Penn

Peacemaker

James 3:17

"My first wish is that America may be free"

❧

BORN
May 6, 1740
BIRTHPLACE
Carolina County, Virginia
EDUCATION
Self-taught
OCCUPATION
Lawyer
MARRIED
Susannah Lyme, 1763
CHILDREN
3
AGE AT SIGNING
36
DIED
September 14, 1788; age 48

My first wish is that America may be free.[1]

John Penn was born in Carolina County, Virginia on May 17, 1741, the son of a small plantation owner. He had no formal education and was self-taught until, when he was 18, his father died. At that time, he decided to teach himself to become a lawyer, and so began studying law books in the personal library of a relative, Edmund Pendleton, then a local justice of the peace and later one of Virginia's leading statesman.

Penn worked so diligently that by the time he was 21, he was qualified to enter the bar and practice law in Virginia. The following year, he married Susannah Lyme, with whom he had three children. In 1774, they relocated to North Carolina. The provincial congress soon elected him as one of its delegates to the Continental Congress. He took his seat in Philadelphia in October, 1775, and served there until 1780.

Penn became convinced of the need for complete independence and urged his associates to "encourage and animate our people." He signed his name to the Declaration of Independence on August 2, 1776. Penn was a determined worker in Congress, sticking with the task even at great financial loss personally. In 1780, he returned to North Carolina to aid in its defense against the British invasion led by Cornwallis.

As a member of the state's board of war, Penn was given almost dictatorial powers to aid the state in the emergency. He used these powers with discretion, helping supply the militia and guerilla forces that defeated the British and forced them to retreat before the year was over.[3]

He was a tremendous help to the citizens of North Carolina, assisting in rebuilding the devastation caused by the war. He devoted his last years to his law practice and enjoying life with this family from whom he had endured separation during most of the war years. He died at his home near Stovall, North Carolina at the age of 47, and was buried on his own estate. About 100 years later, his body was moved to Guilford Courthouse National Military Park where it was buried with that of William Hooper, a fellow signer of the Declaration of Independence.

Unobtrusive and unassuming but remarkably efficient, likeable, and discreet, Penn quickly won the respect of his congressional colleagues. He rarely disputed with others, but when he did, his good humor and peaceful manner saved the day. On one occasion, he feuded with President of Congress Henry Laurens of South Carolina over a personal matter. He accepted Lauren's challenge to a duel, but en route to the proposed site convinced Laurens that they should bury their differences and drop the matter.[2]

Public Service

1762	**Admitted to the bar to practice law in North Carolina**
1774	**Moved to Granville County, North Carolina**
1775–1780	**Delegate to the Continental Congress from North Carolina; signed the Declaration of Independence and the Articles of Confederation**
1780	**Member of the board of war of North Carolina**

കെ Questions for Discussion കെ

1. How did John Penn handle a dueling challenge with wisdom and still retain his honor? What qualities did he demonstrate through this situation?

2. This man was self-taught and achieved a difficult goal. How can you apply this in your life? What quality must you apply yourself to strive for?

3. Give an example of determination in Penn's life and work in Congress.

4. What qualities did Penn demonstrate during the emergency situation while serving on the board of war?

5. How did Penn spend his final years? What qualities do we see demonstrated during this time?

6. Is there someone you are often tempted to argue with? Purpose to be a peacemaker and plan a good deed to do to surprise him.

South Carolina

Thomas Heyward, Jr.
Thomas Lynch, Jr.
Arthur Middleton
Edward Rutledge

Thomas Heyward, Jr.

Patriotic Statesman

II Timothy 2:14

"God Save the States"

❧❧

BORN
July 28, 1746

BIRTHPLACE
St. Helena's Parish, South Carolina

EDUCATION
Middle Temple, London

OCCUPATION
Lawyer

MARRIED
Elizabeth Matthewes 1774
Suzanne Savage, 1786

CHILDREN
8

AGE AT SIGNING
30

DIED
March 6, 1809; age 62

Dr. Benjamin Rush described him as a "firm republican," saying at the same time that he was a man of good education and most amiable manners who had "an elegant poetical genius."[1]

Thomas Heyward, Jr. was born in St. Luke's Parish, South Carolina in 1746, son of one of the wealthiest planters in the province. His father was determined to provide his son with a good education and placed him in the best classical school in the area. He became proficient in Greek and Latin, and was sent to London to study law in the Middle Temple. At age 19, he was admitted to the bar and then spent several years touring Europe.

Heyward was 25 years old when he began practicing law in South Carolina. Two years later, he married Elizabeth Matthewes, with whom he had five children.

Heyward was elected to the first provincial Congress in North Carolina, and was chosen as a delegate to the First Continental Congress, as well as being made a member of the Committee of Safety.

He warmly supported Richard Henry Lee's motion for independence, and signed his name to the Declaration of Independence just a few days after his thirtieth birthday. He remained in Congress until

In his public duties he was honest, firm, and intelligent, he conscientiously and fearlessly embarked in the revolution. He was neither blind to its dangers, nor indifferent to its morality. His life, estate, and reputation, he cast upon the waters of strife. A successful revolution could confer no more on him than on the humblest of his countrymen. Though the prize was common, his stake was among the largest. Of such a character, a stranger to public virtue can scarcely form a conception; and yet America produced thousands, in whom the promotion of the general zeal was the predominating motive, who ventured upon the most desperate hazards under the influence of a patriotism which stifled every selfish consideration; nobly grasping at an assured freedom, and a national independence for themselves and their posterity. The lesson they teach is the only preservative of freedom. It can neither be achieved nor maintained without patriotism.[3]

1778, when he was appointed Judge of the criminal and civil courts of South Carolina.

While the British were besieging Charleston, he presided at the trial and conviction of several Loyalists charged with carrying on treasonable correspondence with the British. Heyward became a particular object for British abuse when these prisoners were executed in view of the British forces.[4]

Heyward joined the militia in 1779 as a captain of the artillery, in the same battalion with Edward Rutledge, another signer. He fought in several battles and suffered a gunshot wound at the Battle of Beaufort, which scarred him for life. He and Rutledge were both captured by the British during the fall of Charleston. They were imprisoned at St. Augustine, Florida, in a prison reserved for rebels considered particularly dangerous. The British proceeded to plunder Heyward's plantation and carried away all of his slaves, many of whom were sold in Jamaica to sugar planters. He retrieved several of them some years later, but it was estimated that the loss of his sold slaves alone cost him $50,000. It was while he was imprisoned that he composed a song, "God Save the States," to the music of "God Save the King," and taught it to his fellow prisoners. It served to inspire the prisoners to new heights of patriotism.

After about a year in prison, Heyward and Rutledge were released in a prisoner exchange. On route to Philadelphia by ship, Heyward nearly lost his life when he fell overboard. He saved himself from drowning by hanging onto the ship's rudder until he was rescued. To add to his hardships, his wife died in his absence from home in 1782.

Upon return to South Carolina, Heyward resumed his judicial office, and was elected to the state legislature; he also was elected president of the Agricultural Society of South Carolina. Heyward served as one of the presidential electors after the U.S. Constitution was adopted. He helped prepare the new South Carolina state constitution.

He remarried in 1786 and had three children with his new wife, Suzanne Savage. At the age of 45, he retired to his plantation to enjoy his wife and children, and the liberty that his efforts helped to win. He died on March 6, 1809 on his family estate where he was born.

Like other wealthy planters, he maintained a fine town house in Charleston, and this was occupied by President Washington on a visit to that lovely city in his first administration.[2]

RES. OF THOMAS HAYWARD
Charlestown S.C.

Residence of Thomas Heyward
Charleston, South Carolina

❧ Public Service ❧

1771	Admitted to the bar to practice law in South Carolina
1774–1776	Member of the provincial congress
1775–1776	Member of South Carolina's committee of safety
1776–1778	Delegate from South Carolina to the Continental Congress; signed the Declaration of Independence
1778–1789	South Carolina state circuit judge
1779–1780	Served as captain of artillery in the militia
1780–1781	Imprisoned by the British in St. Augustine, Florida
1782–1784	Member of the state legislature
1785	First president of the Agricultural Society of South Carolina
1790	Member of the state constitutional convention

Questions for Discussion

1. Besides his signature on the Declaration, what event made Heyward a target for British abuse?

2. Was Heyward a man of great courage? Explain your answer.

3. List and discuss each loss Heyward experienced at the hand of the British.

4. How did God use Heyward's character to uplift and inspire fellow prisoners?

5. List examples of Heyward's usefulness to his country despite many losses.

6. How did he use his poetic abilities to inspire fellow prisoners to their patriotic mission?

7. We have a duty to our country. What can you and your family do to actively promote righteousness and involvement in civil government?

Thomas Lynch, Jr.

Meek Patriot

Psalm 25:9

"Lost at Sea"

❧❧.

BORN
August 5, 1749

BIRTHPLACE
Prince George's Parish
South Carolina

EDUCATION
Eton and Cambridge, England

OCCUPATION
Planter

MARRIED
Elizabeth Shubrich, 1772

AGE AT SIGNING
26

DIED
1779; age 30

He not only possessed that strict moral worth which is the only sure foundation of success in life, but exalted it by maxims and principles of the most refined delicacy and hour. His self-denial, evinced in a commendable control over his own passions, was as remarkable as the tenderness and ardour of his affection for his friends.[2]

Thomas Lynch, Jr., the next-to-youngest man to sign the Declaration of Independence, was born at his father's plantation, Hopsewee, on the Santee River in Prince George's Parish, South Carolina, on August 5, 1749. His father was one of the most influential leaders and wealthiest planters of the colony. His mother died when he was a young child, and his father placed him in the Indigo Society School in Georgetown for his basic education. At 12, he was sent to Eton School in England, his father wanting his son to follow in his footsteps as a political leader. From there he went on to Cambridge University and studied law at Middle Temple, London, although he really held no aspirations to be a lawyer.

Lynch returned to America about 1772, informing his father that he had no desire to be a lawyer. His father then gave him one of the largest plantations on the Santee River for a means of livelihood. He married Elizabeth Shubrich, whose sister later married Edward Rutledge, another one of South Carolina's signers.

Lynch soon caught the patriotic spirit of his father, who was then a delegate in the Continental Congress. Young Lynch was given commission as captain in the South Carolina militia. In July of 1775, he and Charles Cotesworth Pinkney, also a captain, set out on a recruiting campaign. Being unaccustomed to rough living, Lynch became ill with a fever which continued to plague him the rest of his life.

Late in 1775, Lynch got word that his father had been stricken with paralysis in Philadelphia, and consequently resigned as delegate to the Continental Congress. Although his commanding officer refused to grant him leave to go to his father's bedside, his father's friends were successful in winning him an appointment by the legislature as delegate to fill his father's place, and he was then excused from military duty.

Lynch began the 600-mile trip and arrived in Philadelphia in the spring of 1776, in time for the deliberations on independence. He and the other South Carolinians voted for independence.

Observing the pallor of this young delegate, William Ellery wondered if he would be able to serve in Congress much longer. As it was to turn out, Thomas Lynch, Jr.'s signing of the Declaration of Independence was the high point of his short life, for from that day he was destined to know only tragedy.[4]

Whether the fatigues of his journey had aggravated his malady, or the change of climate had been unpropitious, it is impossible to determine, but he had not been long in congress before his health began to decline with the most alarming rapidity. He was, however, enabled to give his full sanction to those measures which were tending, with irresistible efficacy, to the declaration of independence. One of the last acts of his political life was to affix his signature to this important manifesto.[5]

Upon signing, Thomas left immediately to go to his sick father, who was still in Philadelphia. Thomas, Sr. reportedly improved somewhat under Young Thomas's care, but soon had another stroke while in Annapolis on the way home with his son, that proved fatal.

Young Thomas was also suffering from ill health. Advised by doctors that a change in climate might help him, he and his wife set sail on an ocean voyage to England via the West Indies in late 1779. Their ship was lost at sea, believed to be sunk in a storm. Thomas, just 30 years old, died, leaving no children.

❧ Public Service ❧

1775	Commissioned a captain in the militia
1776	Delegate to the Continental Congress from South Carolina; signed the Declaration of Independence

Questions for Discussion

1. Tell what qualities Thomas Lynch possessed in regard to the care of his ailing father, while ill himself.

2. The comment that he caught the patriotic spirit from his father gives what insights to a parent or future parent?

3. What testimony do we have concerning the faith of this man?

4. What qualities did Thomas possess that endeared him to his friends?

5. Tell of William Ellery's observation of Thomas Lynch at the time of his signing the Declaration.

6. How is it believed that Thomas Lynch and his wife died?

7. How did Lynch bear his trials with meekness?

8. Are there expectations you harbor in your life that you must yield to God?

Arthur Middleton

Enduring Patriot

II Timothy 2:3

"Resolute for Freedom"

❧❧

BORN
June 26, 1742
BIRTHPLACE
Middleton Place, South Carolina
EDUCATION
At home and in England
OCCUPATION
Planter
MARRIED
Mary Izard, 1766
CHILDREN
9
AGE AT SIGNING
34
DIED
January 1, 1787; age 44

He left Cambridge in his twenty-second year, with the degree of bachelor of arts, and with the reputation of a profound scholar and a moral man.[1]

Arthur Middleton was born at his family's estate, Middleton Place, on June 26, 1742, near Charleston, South Carolina. He was the son of Henry Middleton, president of the Continental Congress in 1774. At 12 years of age, Arthur was sent to England for schooling at Hackney and Westminster, continuing at the University of Cambridge, when he was 18. Upon graduation, he took two years to tour Europe.

Upon returning to South Carolina in 1766, he married Mary Izard, whom he took on an extensive tour of Europe that lasted several years. Together, the couple had nine children. In 1773, the family returned to Middleton Place, South Carolina, the residence given to Arthur by his father. Middleton joined the patriots in the cause for independence. In April 1775, he was appointed by the provincial Congress to a committee of safety.

In the winter of 1776, Mr. Middleton was on a committee to form a government for South Carolina and was appointed a delegate to the Continental Congress at Philadelphia. He actively promoted independence from Great Britain.

> *Lord William Campbell had married a near relation of Mrs. Middleton, and the families were on good terms; but this did not prevent Mr. Middleton from making a motion "that the governor should be immediately taken into custody."[2]*

In that body he was firm and unyielding in principle, and when, soon afterward, Lord William Campbell was appointed governor, and it was discovered that he was acting with duplicity, Mr. Middleton laid aside all private feeling, and recommended his immediate arrest. This proposition was too bold to meet the views of the more timid majority of the committee, and the governor was allowed to flee from the state even though he was closely related to Middleton's wife, and their families were close to each other. Had the proposition of Mr. Middleton been carried into effect, much bloodshed might have been saved in South Carolina, for Lord Campbell, after his flight joined Sir Henry Clinton, and representing the Tory interest as very powerful in that state, induced that commander, in connection with the fleet of Sir Peter Parker, to ravage the coast and make an attack upon Charleston. In that engagement Lord Campbell was slain.[3]

In signing the Declaration of Independence, Arthur Middleton stood to lose much, as he was a man of great wealth.

By this patriotic act, he placed himself in a position to lose life and property, should the contest prove unsuccessful, but these considerations had no weight with him.[4]

Mr. Middleton remained in Congress until the end of 1777, when he returned to South Carolina. The British invaded that state in 1779 and Middleton's property was targeted. He joined Governor Rutledge in his attempt to defend the state, leaving his own property vulnerable. He wrote instructing his wife to relocate to a friend's house about a day's journey away. A large portion of his estate was sacrificed. His property was plundered and 200 of his slaves were captured and sold in the West Indies. His valuable collection of paintings was either stolen or rifled. Whatever they couldn't sell, the British mutilated. Arthur himself was taken captive after the surrender of Charleston a year later, and sent to St. Augustine, Florida. He remained in prison for approximately a year. It was reported

❧ Public Service ❧

1775–1776	**Member of the provincial congress of South Carolina**
1776–1777	**Member of the committee of safety of South Carolina**
1776–1777	**Delegate from South Carolina to the Continental Congress; signed the Declaration of Independence**
1778	**Declined election as governor of South Carolina**
1780–1781	**Captured by the British and held at St. Augustine, Florida**
1781, 1782	**Delegate from South Carolina to the Congress of the Confederation**

that his wife begged the British to help care for her children during her husband's imprisonment.

Mr. Middleton and his fellow prisoners, although not placed in close confinement, were subjected to mortifying and humiliating restraints by the petty tyranny of the officer commanding that garrison. Very far from having his spirit subdued by this gloomy and trying reverse, it was known to his companions in misfortune, that he had resolved to endure all the evils which it was in the power of a resentful foe to inflict, rather than to follow the example of too many of his countrymen, by claiming the "protection" of the British government. On the contrary, nothing appeared to give him so much pain as the accounts, which were sedulously communicated, of some individuals who had hitherto been regarded as firm friends of liberty, having consented to exchange their situation as prisoners of war, for that of British subjects.[5]

He was finally released as an exchange prisoner and then sent to Philadelphia. South Carolina at once elected him to represent them in Congress, and he served there until 1782, when he finally returned to his family.

Mr. Middleton had witnessed the distresses occasioned by the oppressive measures of lord Cornwallis, and his soul had revolted at the horrors which he beheld around him. Actuated by these feelings, after lord Cornwallis's surrender, he submitted to congress a motion to the following effect: "…that lord Cornwallis should be regarded in the light of a barbarian, who had violated all the rules of modern warfare, and had been guilty of innumerable cast of wanton cruelty and oppression; and further, that he, the said lord Cornwallis, should not be comprehended in any exchange of prisoners which should take place between the British government and that of the United States." This resolution, from considerations of a peculiar nature, was not adopted, but the motive which suggested it was duly appreciated.[6]

Middleton was a representative in the South Carolina legislature until 1787, when he developed a fever caused by exposure, which would not respond to treatment. He died on New Year's Day, 1787, at age 44, leaving his widow with eight children who later held honored positions in their free country.

To use the language of a writer of the times, he possessed "the plainest manners with the most refined taste: great reading and knowledge of the world, concealed under the reserve of the mildest and most modest nature; a complete philanthropist, but the firmest patriot; cool, steady, and unmoved, at the general wreck of property and fortune, as far as he was personally concerned, but with a heart melting for the sufferings and woes of others; a model of private worth and public virtue; a good citizen, a good father, and an exemplary husband; accomplished in letters, in the sciences, and fine arts; well acquainted with the manners of the courts of Europe, whence he has transplanted to his country nothing but their embellishments and virtues."[7]

Questions for Discussion

1. What was Middleton's reputation as a young man leaving Cambridge University?

2. How was Middleton related to Lord William Campbell? Recount the situation which led Middleton to ask for his removal and tell what character qualities motivated him to take this position.

3. What do we hear of Middleton's hospitality? Personal frugality?

4. Why did Middleton stand to lose much in signing the Declaration? What can we surmise about his character from his willingness to sign this document?

5. Arthur Middleton was called to sacrifice much. Tell of his personal sacrifices during this time at the hand of the British.

6. What was Arthur Middleton's resolve as a prisoner? What character trait motivated his resolution concerning Cornwallis' violation of the rules of warfare?

7. We are told that Arthur Middleton left eight children when he died. What are we told about his children that reflects on their father's character?

8. List qualities reported of Middleton in the final quote.

9. Choose one of the character qualities we've heard to be in the life of Arthur Middleton and set a specific goal or project to develop that quality in your life.

10. What is "endurance"? How did Middleton live this out while in prison?

11. What adverse circumstances might you be in now that you need to employ endurance to accomplish God's best?

Edward Rutledge

Cautious Patriot

Proverbs 19:2

"Dangerous Rebel"

ᴥ᛫ᴥ

BORN
November 23, 1749
BIRTHPLACE
Charleston, South Carolina
EDUCATION
Tutored at home,
Middle Temple, London
OCCUPATION
Lawyer, planter
MARRIED
Henrietta Middleton, 1774
Mary Eveleigh, 1792
CHILDREN
3
AGE AT SIGNING
26
DIED
January 23, 1800; age 50

Without arrogance or envy, and confiding with justice in his own sound judgment, he was a patient, candid, polite listener to the arguments of others.[3]

Edward Rutledge was born in Charles Town, South Carolina, on November 23, 1749, the youngest of seven children. His father, Dr. John Rutledge, a physician, died when he was only one year old. Tutors provided him with his early education, and when he was old enough he worked as a clerk in his brother's law office.

When he was 19 he was sent to study law in London at the Middle Temple, and was admitted to the bar in 1773 when he returned from England. He married Henrietta Middleton, a daughter of one of the wealthiest planters in South Carolina. Edward, by receiving a dowry, became the richest man in his family. The couple had three children.

Edward was elected to the colonial legislature in 1774 and later that year went to the First Continental Congress, along with his brother John and father-in-law Henry Middleton. All three men hoped for a reconciliation with Great Britain. In a letter to a friend in South Carolina, Edward expressed his cautious view:

> I long to tell you what we have done, but am prevented, from silence having been imposed upon us all, by consent, the first week in congress.

This, however, I must say, that the province will not be able to account for our conduct until we explain it, though it is justifiable upon the strictest principles of honour and policy. Don't be alarmed; we have done no mischief, though I am sure, if, Mr. _____ had had his way, we should. But you may thank your stars you sent prudent men; and I trust that the youngest is not the least so. The gentleman to whom you have alluded is, if possible, worse than ever; more violent, more wrong-headed. But I do not mean to censure others; sufficient for me if I pursue a right line, and meet with the approbation of my countrymen.[5]

"Rutledge," John Adams said of the wealthy South Carolinian, "was 'a peacock.'" He was referring to the fact that Ned dressed in fancy clothes and had a proud manner.[1]

Edward also attended the Second Continental Congress. He was still undecided when Richard Henry Lee presented his resolution for independence. He asked for the final vote to be delayed from June 7 until July 1. Rutledge and his fellow signers from South Carolina voted negatively, as he felt the colonies should confederate and strengthen themselves and nurture foreign alliances first.

He was warmly in favor of independence, and fearlessly voted for the Declaration, notwithstanding there were large numbers of people in his state opposed to it, some through timidity, some through self-interest, and some through decided attachment to the royal cause.[2]

When he saw that the rest of the colonies were in favor of independence, he persuaded the other South Carolina delegates to vote affirmatively for the sake of being unified, and South Carolina reversed its position. This meant that Henrietta Middleton Rutledge had a husband and brother who were both signers.

In August, 1776, Rutledge was appointed by Congress along with John Adams and Benjamin Franklin to meet with the British commander lord Howe in New York at his request to discuss the possibility of a peace settlement. The negotiations were fruitless, but in later years, Rutledge enjoyed telling an anecdote about Franklin that occurred at the time. According to the story, Franklin offered the British sailors who took them back from Howe's headquarters a handful of gold and silver coins for their trouble, but the

❧ Public Service ❧

1773	**Admitted to the bar to practice law in South Carolina**
1774–1777	**Delegate from South Carolina to the Continental Congress; signed the Declaration of Independence**
1779	**Served as captain of artillery in the Revolutionary War**
1780–1781	**Prisoner of the British**
1782–1798	**Served in South Carolina state legislature**
1798–1800	**Governor of South Carolina**

officer in charge would not let the soldiers accept it. When Rutledge later asked Franklin why he had done this, the witty old statesman replied, "As these people are under the impression that we have not a farthing of hard money in the country, I thought I would convince them of their mistake: I knew, at the same time, that I risked nothing by an offer which their regulations and discipline would not permit them to accept." [6]

Edward ("Ned") returned home in late 1776 to help defend the state. When the British seized Charleston in the spring of 1780, Rutledge was among the first captives. He had become a captain in an artillery battalion.

After the fall of Charleston, and the capture of Lincoln and the American army, Cornwallis became fearful of the influence of many citizens, and finally adopted a most cowardly measure. By his order, the Lieutenant Governor, (Gadden) most of the civil and military officers, and some others of the friends of the republicans, of character, were taken out of their beds and houses by armed parties, and collected at the Exchange, when they were conveyed on board a guard ship, and transported to St. Augustine. [7]

Residence of Edward Rutledge
Broad Street, Charleston, South Carolina

Rutledge was imprisoned in St. Augustine, Florida, where "dangerous" rebels were held. He was released about a year later in a prisoner exchange. Edward learned that his mother had also been held by the British.

She had endured some persecution from the British, not for her good will to the cause of America, for that could not be otherwise, but for her supposed power and capacity to aid that cause. The commander of Charleston had ordered her to be removed from her country residence, and confined to the limits of the town, upon the suggestion that much was to be apprehended from a woman like Mrs. Rutledge. He did not distinctly state the nature of his apprehensions, but they were a flattering testimonial that the talents, for which we have already given her credit, were peculiarly great. [8]

South Carolina elected Edward to the state legislature for many years. His wife, Henrietta, died in 1792, and later that year he married Mary Shubrich Everleigh. Rutledge held the position of governor of South Carolina from 1798 to 1800, when, afflicted with the gout, he asked to be replaced to go home; but he finished out the session.

On his way to Charleston, he suffered inconveniences from excessive rains and cold, which he was ill qualified to endure, and soon after he arrived at his house, was unable to rise from his bed. He bore his last illness with great fortitude, and expired on the twenty-third day of January, 1800. [9]

He died while still serving as governor at 50 years of age.

His constitution, never strong, was materially shattered by hereditary gout; and his increasing debility was apparent to all who saw him. He, nevertheless, continued to perform the duties of his station with his wonted activity and cheerfulness. [4]

Questions for Discussion

1. How did Edward Rutledge display courage in voting for independence?

2. Although suffering from a debilitating disease, what character qualities did Rutledge continue to maintain?

3. Explain Rutledge's cautious view of independence.

4. Why did he vote against independence on June 7?

5. What character quality could be said of Rutledge when he changed his mind in support of independence, and how did he then help the cause?

6. What personal sacrifice did Rutledge suffer? How about his family?

7. Is there something in your life you desire to accomplish, but wisdom would require waiting for the right timing?

Georgia

Button Gwinnett
Lyman Hall
George Walton

Button Gwinnett

Intemperate Patriot

Galatians 5:24–5

"Died in a Duel"

❧❧

BORN
1735
BIRTHPLACE
Gloucestershire, England
EDUCATION
Common Schools
OCCUPATION
Merchant, Planter
MARRIED
Anne Bourne, 1757
CHILDREN
3
AGE AT SIGNING
41
DIED
May 16, 1777; age 42

He was about six feet in height, and his person was properly proportioned, lofty, and commanding. Without possessing remarkable eloquence, his language was mild and persuasive. His manners were polite, and his deportment graceful. He was of an irritable temper, and impatient of contradiction. He left a widow and several children, who did not long survive him.[1]

Button Gwinnett

Button Gwinnett was born in Gloucestershire, England in 1735, named in honor of his godmother Barbara Button. After being taught by his father and the common schools, he learned trade finance from an uncle, a British merchant. He married Anne Bourne in 1757, and they had three girls.

In 1759, he entered the export shipping business and built up an extensive trade with the American colonies, which led to his emigration to the colony of Georgia, where he purchased a store. Not making a big success of it, he decided to try farming. He borrowed $3,000 and purchased St. Catherine's Island. It was located off the coast of Georgia, not far from Sunbury. He built a home and then purchased more coastal lands on credit and received grants of others from the colony. He bought large numbers of slaves to work his holdings. Poachers presented a problem by raiding his livestock.

In 1773, Gwinnett's creditors took over his land and slaves, letting him keep his house, where he lived the rest of his life, except for when he and his family were forced by the British to escape in their boat to Sunbury for temporary refuge. The British also raided his livestock.

Gwinnett entered politics in 1768 when he was designated as one of His Majesty's justices of the peace. The voters of St. John's Parish, where he lived, elected him to the colonial assembly at Savannah. He attended sporadically, due to his financial situation. He left public office for five years to try to straighten finances out.

Unlike Lyman Hall and George Walton, he entered the patriot cause belatedly. Hall persuaded him to reconsider. The provincial Congress appointed him to the Continental Congress just in time for him to sign the Declaration of Independence.

He was elected speaker of the Georgia legislature where he helped form the state constitution. Also, he briefly served as Georgia's governor. Gwinnett offered himself as a candidate for chief executive offices of the state, but was defeated.

Shortly after the close of the constitutional convention, Archibald Bulloch, president of the provincial congress, died, leaving the state without a chief executive; and a committee of the state's leaders appointed Gwinnett to act as president until a meeting of the legislature could be called. During his brief tenure as chief executive officer of Georgia, Gwinnett created considerable friction between himself and Brigadier General Lachlan McIntosh, who had been appointed by the Continental Congress to raise a brigade of the Continental Army in Georgia. Gwinnett claimed authority over McIntosh's troops because of his office as president of the state. McIntosh disputed the claim because his commission was authorized by Congress. Nevertheless, without

McIntosh's knowledge, Gwinnett ordered some of the militia forces to make an attack on East Florida. The defeat of this expedition seemed to prove Gwinnett's lack of military ability.[2]

When both Gwinnett and McIntosh appeared before the legislatures to explain the failed attack, Gwinnett outtalked McIntosh; and McIntosh, enraged at being blamed for the failure, called Gwinnett "a scoundrel and a lying rascal" in front of the Georgia legislators. Gwinnett challenged McIntosh to a pistol duel over the insult. The story of the duel is contained in sworn statement that George Wills made before John Wereat in a later investigation of the death of Gwinnett:

…late on the evening of Thursday, the fifteenth, May, Inst., a written challenge was brought to General McIntosh signed by Button Gwinnett, wherein the said Mr. Gwinnett charged the General with calling him a scoundrel in the public convention and desired he would give satisfaction for it, as a gentleman, before sunrise the next morning, in Sir James Wright's pasture behind Colonel Martin's house. To which the gentleman humorously sent answer to Mr. Gwinnett that the hour was rather earlier than his usual, but would assuredly meet him at the place and time appointed with a pair of pistols, as agreed upon with Mr. Gwinnett's second, who had brought the challenge. "Early the next morning Mr. Gwinnett and his second found the General and his second waiting on the ground, and after politely saluting each other the General drew his pistols to show he was loaded only with single balls, but avoided entering into any conversation but the business on hand. It was then

෴ Public Service ෴

1769	Member of the colonial legislature of Georgia
1776–1777	Delegate from Georgia to the Continental Congress; signed the Declaration of Independence
1777	President and commander in chief of the State of Georgia

proposed and agreed to that they should go a little lower down the hill, as a number of spectators appeared, and when the ground was chose the seconds asked the distance. Mr. Gwinnett replied whatever distance the General pleases. The General said he believed eight or ten feet would suffice, and they were immediately measured, to which the General desired another step might be added. It was then proposed to turn back to back. The General answered, 'By no means, let us see what we are about,' and immediately each made his stand and agreed to fire as they could. Both pistols went off nearly at the same time when Mr. Gwinnett fell, being shot above the knee and said his thigh was broke. The General was also shot through the thigh and stood still in his place and not thinking his antagonist was worse wounded than himself, as he immediately and afterward declared, asked if he had enough, or was for another shot. To which he objected and the seconds declaring they both behaved like gentlemen and men of honor, led the General up to Mr. Gwinnett and they shook hands.[3]

Gwinnett, however, died as a result of his wounds eleven days later on May 27, 1777, because of a gangrenous leg. He was the second signer to die. His wife and daughter also died before the war ended.

THE DUEL IN WHICH BUTTON GWINNETT WAS KILLED BY COL. LACHLAN McINTOSH.

The Duel in which Button Gwinnett was killed by Colonel Lachlan McIntosh

Because his public career was brief, his signature is rare and valuable. A document he signed has sold for as much as $100,000.

ᴧᴐQuestions for Discussionᴧᴐ

1.   Tell what the British did to Gwinnett and his family and possessions.

2.   What lack of character do we see in Gwinnett's life that led to his death?

3.   What positive character qualities can we find in his life from the narration?

4.   Find a verse in the Bible that would apply to the dueling situation and have been the godly answer to the dispute.

5.   Purpose to deal with your anger and master your emotions.

Lyman Hall
Enthusiastic Patriot

Phillipians 1:25-26

"He had the power of imparting
his energy to others"

❧

BORN
April 12, 1724

BIRTHPLACE
Wallingford, Connecticut

EDUCATION
Yale College

OCCUPATION
Physician

MARRIED
Abigail Burr, 1752;
Mary Osburn

CHILDREN
1

AGE AT SIGNING
52

DIED
October 19, 1790; age 66

*He was about six feet high, and finely
proportioned: his manners were easy and
polite, and his deportment affable and
dignified: the force of his enthusiasm was
tempered by discretion, and he was firm in all
his purposes and principles: the ascendancy
which he gained, sprung from his mild,
persuasive manner, and calm, unruffled temper.
Possessed of a strong, discriminating mind,
he had the power of imparting his energy to
others, and was peculiarly fitted to flourish
in the perplexing and perilous scenes of the
revolution.[2]*

Lyman Hall was born in Wallingford, Connecticut on April 12, 1724. He studied for the ministry at Yale College, and graduated at the age of 23, when he began preaching. He married Abigail Burr of Fairfield, Connecticut, who only lived one year after they were married. Two years later after Abigail died, he married Mary Osborn of Connecticut, with whom he had one son.

Hall began to study medicine, and set up practice in 1752 in Sunbury, Georgia. He became a successful doctor and rice planter. The residents of Georgia at this time were sparsely settled, and felt a great need for British protection; consequently, many were Loyalists. Hall resided in St. John's Parish, an area in Georgia where many New Englanders had settled. Hall did his best to stir up patriot sentiment among the people. When Georgia failed to elect any delegates to the Continental Congress, Hall called an independent convention, which elected him as its delegate. He attended the second Continental Congress, although at first he wasn't allowed to vote until Georgia finally sanctioned Hall's presence in Congress and appointed four other delegates. Hall served in this capacity until 1780.

A New England physician, Lyman Hall helped inspire the patriotism of Georgia by serving in the Continental Congress as the only representative from the colony. He signed the Declaration of Independence, and continued to serve in Congress through five years of the Revolutionary War, even though the British destroyed his home and plantation. After the War, the people of Georgia honored him by electing him to a term as the state's governor.

…John Adams referred to Hall and his fellow Georgian, Button Gwinnett, as "a powerful addition to our phalanx."[1]

In 1778, his home in Savannah and his rice plantation were ravaged by the British. They destroyed his Hall's Knoll and Sunbury residences, and confiscated his property. Hall managed to move his family to Connecticut until the British evacuated Savannah in 1782. He then moved back to attempt to mend his fortune.

St. John's Parish elected him to the state legislature where he helped institute programs to rebuild the war-damaged state. He also acted as judge of the inferior court of Chatham County and trustee of a proposed state university (later to be called Franklin College and University of Georgia).

In 1785, he sold his Hall's Knoll and purchased Shell Bluff Plantation on the Savannah River. Hall died in 1790 at the age of 66 and was greatly lamented by the people of Georgia.

❧ Public Service ❧

1775	**Represented St. John's Parish of Georgia in the second Continental Congress**
1775–1780	**Member of Georgia's delegation to Congress; signed the Declaration of Independence**
1783–1784	**Governor of Georgia**

Questions for Discussion

1. How did Hall help to inspire the patriotism of Georgians?

2. What happened to Hall's home and plantation? Describe all his losses.

3. List qualities observed in Hall's life.

4. What did Lyman study in college?

5. How did the people of Georgia honor Hall after the war?

6. Why were many Georgians loyalists?

7. What offices did he hold after the war?

8. Where did he move his family for safety during the war?

9. How can you inspire others by being more enthusiastic?

George Walton

Determined Learner

Colossians 3:23

"Shot and Imprisoned"

⚜

BORN
1741

BIRTHPLACE
Farmville,
Prince Edward County, Virginia

EDUCATION
Self-taught

OCCUPATION
Lawyer

MARRIED
Dorothy Camber, 1775

CHILDREN
2

AGE AT SIGNING
35

DIED
February 2, 1804; age 63

He was six times elected a representative to congress: twice, governor of the state; once, senator of the United States; and four times, judge of the superior courts: the latter office he held during fifteen years, and until the day of his death. He was one of the commissioners on the part of the United States, to negotiate a treaty with the Cherokee Indians in Tennessee, and several times a member of the state legislature.[1]

George Walton was born to a poor family near Farmville, Virginia in 1741. His parents both died when he was a boy, and he was brought up by his uncle and aunt, who apprenticed him to a carpenter when he was 15 years old. George had a deep thirst for knowledge, but his master forced him to work from sunrise to sunset and refused to give him a candle at night so he could read. George collected wood scraps from the carpentry work and burned them in the evening so he could read his borrowed books and spend his evenings in study. When his apprenticeship was ended, he moved to Georgia and began to study law in the office of Mr. Young; and in 1774 was admitted to the bar to practice law in Georgia. The following year, he married Dorothy Camber, with whom he would have at least two children. Although Mr. Young was a Loyalist, George chose friends who were patriots.

In 1774, Walton and three other patriots signed their names to a newspaper notice calling the citizens of Savannah to meet "at the Liberty Pole at Tondee's tavern" to discuss how to best support the people of

Boston who were under the burden of British tyranny. A committee of correspondence was established, of which Walton was a member.

In January 1775, Walton became secretary of the new provincial Congress. He was elected to replace one of the delegates to the Continental Congress who proved to be a Loyalist. He took his seat in time to vote for independence and sign his name to the Declaration of Independence.

He soon won the respect of his fellow Congressional members, though most were more wealthy and educated than he. When Congress, fearing a British attack, left Philadelphia for Baltimore in December, 1776, George Walton, George Clymer and Robert Morris were appointed to remain in Philadelphia and carry out executive functions.

His wife, Dorothy Camber, was the daughter of a British Loyalist, but she was as ardent in her support of the colonial cause as her husband. [2]

Walton continued his service in Congress until 1778, when he was appointed to be a colonel in the Georgia militia. In the battle for Savannah, while he was commanding a battalion on the right of General Howe's army, he was shot through the thigh and knocked off his horse. The British captured him and took him as a prisoner of war. After being held nine months, he was released by prisoner exchange for a British navy captain in September, 1779.

In October, he was elected governor of Georgia, and remained in that position until he returned to Congress in May of 1780 for two years. He was again elected governor of Georgia, chief justice of the state, and senator of the United States.

During the latter part of his life he became

afflicted with the gout, which caused him much suffering during his declining years. When severely tormented with this painful disease, he found in his library a solace and enjoyment for his mind, which had a tendency to soften its acuteness; and he frequently remarked to his physicians, that "a book was the most effectual remedy." [3]

He had only one son living at the time of his death, who was a great comfort to him. His son was secretary of state while his father was governor.

୶ Public Service ୬

1774	Admitted to the bar to practice law in Georgia
1775	President of the Georgia Committee of Safety
1776–1781	Member of Georgia's delegation to the Congress; signed the Declaration of Independence
1778–1779	Captured by the British while serving as a colonel in the Georgia militia
1783–1789	Chief justice of Georgia
1789–1790	Governor of Georgia
1795–1796	U.S. senator from Georgia
1799–1804	Judge of the superior court of Georgia

He died on February 2, 1804, at the age of 63, at his home in Augusta, Georgia. In the words of a biographer, who lived at the time of his death,

Judge Walton was universally beloved by those who knew him intimately, and the carpenter's apprentice became the most exalted citizen of the Commonwealth in which he resided. Even at this late day, the remembrance of his services and exalted character, is fresh in the hearts of the people.[4]

ᴄᴑ Questions for Discussion ᴄᴑ

1. List all the offices Walton held in service to his country and state.

2. How did Walton exhibit determination to be able to fulfill his burning desire for reading as a young apprentice? Tell what he had to do to be able to read.

3. Tell of George's choice of friends.

4. What committees did Walton serve on?

5. What office was Walton appointed to in the Georgia militia?

6. What happened to Walton at the Battle of Savannah?

7. What other offices did Walton hold after the Revolution?

8. What did Walton give his attention to while sick?

9. In what area in your life do you need to cultivate determination, in order to succeed and overcome deficiencies?

A Parting Charge

The 56 signers were just ordinary men like you and me, only they understood the meaning of duty and commitment to God, their country, family and the world. We desperately need such leaders today! God has given us the command in Luke 19:13 to "occupy until He comes." I pray that you and your family will be those leaders.

> My God! How little do my countrymen know what precious blessings they are in possession of, and which no other people on earth enjoy!
> —Thomas Jefferson[1]

It is our responsibility to spread God's truth and help it to infiltrate and affect society. Charles Finney proclaimed to Christians in the mid-1800's a lesson we need to learn from today.

> The Church must take right ground in regard to politics . . . [T]he time has come that Christians must vote for honest men and take consistent ground in politics…Christians have been exceedingly guilty in this matter. But the time has come when they must act differently…God cannot sustain this free and blessed country which we love and pray for unless the Church will take right ground…It seems sometimes as if the foundations of the nation are becoming rotten, and Christians seem to act as if they think God does not see what they do in politics. But I tell you He does see it, and He will bless or curse this nation according to the course [Christians] take [in politics]."[2]

The future we leave to our children depends on what we do today. In 1803, Rev. Mathias Burnett gave this charge:

> Finally, ye…whose high prerogative it is to…invest with office and authority or to withhold them and in whose power it is to save or destroy your country, consider well the important trust…which God…[has] put into your hands. To God and posterity you are accountable for them…Let not your children have reason to curse you for giving up those rights and prostrating those institutions which your fathers delivered to you.[3]

I have written this book with much prayer that as you read it God will inspire you with a vision for your life. One man (or woman) totally dedicated to the Lord can be used of God to impact the entire world. May God use you to bring about revival in our day!

Character Quality Definitions

ardent	Passionate, zealous, engaged
available	Making one's own schedule and priorities secondary to the wishes of those served
benevolent	Giving to others' basic needs without having as one's motive personal reward
bold	Confident that what one says or does is true, right, and just
cautious	Knowing how important right timing is in accomplishing right actions
cheerful	Having good spirits; uplifting to others
confident	Having full belief, trusting, relying, fully assured
consistent	Fixed, firm, durable
courageous	Bravery, intrepidity, the quality of mind which enables men to encounter danger and difficulties with firmness, or without fear
dedicated	Consecrated, devoted to God
determined	Purposing to accomplish God's goals in God's time regardless of the opposition
devoted	Consecrated or given wholly to
diligent	Visualizing each task as a special assignment from the Lord and using all one's energies to accomplish it
disinterested	The quality of having no personal interest or private advantage
dutiful	Respectful of that which a person owes to another person, government or God; submission to just authority
enduring	The inward strength to withstand stress to accomplish God's best
enthusiastic	Expressing with one's spirit the joy of the soul
fervent	Ardent, earnest, excited zeal
firm	Steady, constant, unshakable
friendly	Kind, favorable, disposed to promote the good of another
honest	Upright, just; fair in dealing with others
honorable	Possessing a scrupulous character; upright; without deceit
hospitable	Cheerfully sharing food, shelter, and spiritual refreshment with those God brings into one's life
industrious	Diligent in business or study; steady application of the mind or body

initiative	Recognizing and doing what needs to be done before being asked to do it
integrity	uprightness or purity; moral soundness; honesty in mutual dealings
intemperate	Not moderate or restrained; indulging to excess an appetite or passion
joyful	The exultation of one's inward being that results from genuine harmony with God and others
just	Honest, conforming exactly to laws; influenced by a regard to the laws of God; committed to truth
kind	Disposed to do good to others and to make them happy; tenderness or goodness of heart
loyal	Using difficult times to demonstrate commitment to those one serves
meek	Yielding personal rights and expectations to God
moral	Conformed to God's just laws in one's behavior
passionate	Highly excited and driven to action; highly zealous
patriotic	Inspired by the love of one's country; devoted to the welfare of one's country
peacemaker	One who makes peace by reconciling parties that are at variance
persuasive	Guiding vital truths around another's mental roadblocks
precise	Exact; well thought-out
productive	Having the power of producing achievements
resourceful	Finding practical uses for that which others would overlook or discard
responsible	Knowing and doing what both God and others expect
reverent	Esteemed veneration for God and humble submission to His will
sacrificial	To show devotion, although it requires personal loss
sincere	Eagerness to do what is right with transparent motives
steadfast	Firm in mind or purpose; fixed in principle
temperate	Habitual moderation in regard to indulgences of natural passion; patience
truthful	Purity from falsehood; honesty; sincerely committed to the true state of things
zealous	Warmly engaged in a righteous cause; passionate

Patrick Henry's Speech Delivered to Signers "Our Heritage of Freedom"

Patrick Henry, in his speech just before the signing of the Declaration of Independence on July 4, 1776. The copy from which this is taken is credited to the *Boston Journal,* but without date.

These words will go forth to the world when our bones are dust. To the slave in bondage they will speak hope; to the mechanic in his workshop, freedom.

That parchment will speak to kings in language sad and terrible as the trumpet of the archangel. You have trampled on the rights of mankind long enough. At last, the voice of human woe has pierced the ear of God, and called His judgment down.

Such is the message of the Declaration to the Kings of the world. And shall we falter now? And shall we start back appalled when our free people press the very threshold of freedom?

Sign! If the next moment the gibbet's rope is around your neck.

Sign! If the next moment this hall rings with the echo of the falling axe.

Sign! By all your hopes in life, or death, as husbands, fathers… as men with our names to the parchment, or be accursed forever!

Sign! Not only for yourselves, but for all ages, for that parchment will be the textbook of freedom, the Bible of the rights of man forever.

Sign! For the declaration will go forth to American hearts like the voice of God. And its work will not be done until throughout this wide continent not a single inch of ground owns the sway of privilege or power. It is not given to our poor human intellect to climb the skies, to pierce the councils of the Almighty One. But methinks I stand among the awful clouds which veil the brightness of Jehovah's throne. Methinks I see the recording angel—pale as an angel is pale—weeping as an angel can weep, come trembling up to the throne and speaking his dreadful message.

Father! The old world is baptized in blood.

Father! It is drenched with the blood of millions who have been executed, in slow and grinding oppression.

Father! Look! With one glance of thine eternal eye, look over Europe, Asia, Africa, and behold everywhere a terrible sight… man trodden down beneath the oppressor's feet, nations lost in blood, murder and superstition walking hand in hand over the graves of their victims, and not a single voice to whisper hope for man.

He stands there (the angel) his hand trembling with the human guilt. But hark! The voice of Jehovah speaks out from the awful cloud. "Let there be light again. Let there be a new world. Tell my people, the poor, downtrodden millions, to go out from the old world; tell them to go out from wrong, oppression and blood. Tell them to build up my altar in the new."

As God lives, my friends, I believe that to be His voice. Yes, were my soul trembling on the wing of eternity, were this hand freezing to death, were my voice choking with the last struggle, I would still, with the last gasp of that voice, implore you to remember the truth God has given America to be free. Yes, as I sank down into the gloomy shadows of the grave, with my last gasp I would beg you to sign that parchment. In the name of the One who made you, the Savior who redeemed you, in the name of the Millions whose very breath is now hushed as, in intense expectation, they look up to you for the awful words "YOU ARE FREE."[1]

The Christian Nature of State Constitutions

The Founding Fathers realized that the character of a lawmaker or ruler is the key to a good government. Just laws are crucial and the Founding Fathers based our system of law on Scripture (see *Keys to Good Government* by David Barton for more information). Yet, without men of character to implement these laws, the intended result will not be achieved. Consider how William Penn explained it:

I know some say, "Let us have good laws, and no matter for the men that execute them." But let them consider that though good laws do well, good men do better; for good laws may [lack] good men... but good men will never [lack] good laws, nor [allow bad] ones.[1]

Or, as John Adams explained:

We electors have an important constitutional power placed in our hands: we have a check upon two branches of legislature... It becomes necessary to every [citizen] then, to be in some degree a statesman: and to examine and judge for himself... the... political principles and measures. Let us examine them with a sober...Christian spirit.[2]

This belief is reflected in the state constitutions that many of the signers of the Declaration returned home to write.

Delaware State Constitution (written in part by Thomas McKean and George Read):

Every person, who shall be chosen a member of either house, or appointed to any office or place of trust...shall...make and subscribe to the following declaration, to wit: "I do profess faith in God the father, and in Jesus Christ, his only Son, and in the Holy Ghost, one God, blessed forever more, and I do acknowledge the Holy scriptures of the Old and New Testament to be given by divine inspiration." [3]

Pennsylvania State Constitution authored by Benjamin Rush and James Wilson:

And each member [of the legislature], before he takes his seat, shall make and subscribe the following declaration, viz: "I do believe in one God, the Creator and Governor of the universe, the rewarder of the good and the punisher of the wicked, and I do acknowledge the Scriptures of the Old and New Testament to be given by Divine Inspiration."[4]

North Carolina's State Constitution required that:

No person, who shall deny the being of God, or the truth of the [Christian] religion, or the divine authority either of the Old or New Testaments, or who shall hold religious principles incompatible with the freedom and safety of this State, shall be capable of holding any office, or place of trust or profit in the civil department, within this State.[5]

The Massachusetts State Constitution, authored by Samuel Adams and John Adams, stated:

[All persons elected must] make and subscribe the following declaration, viz. "I do declare that I believe the Christian religion and have firm persuasion of its truth." [6]

NOTE: For further information on the Christian nature of state constitutions, see *Original Intent: The Courts, the Constitution, and Religion* by David Barton.

The Christian Nature of America's Universities

Harvard College

Students who became signers:

> John Adams
> John Hancock
> Samuel Adams
> William Ellery
> William Hooper
> Robert Treat Paine
> William Williams
> Elbridge Gerry

Harvard was established to train ministers of the gospel, as revealed in its two mottoes:

> "For Christ and the Church"
> "For the Glory of Christ"

As a further example, the 1636 Rules of Harvard declared:

Let every student be plainly instructed and earnestly pressed to consider well the main end of his life and studies is to know God and Jesus Christ which is eternal life (John 17.3) and therefore to lay Christ in the bottom as the only foundation of all sound knowledge and learning. And seeing the Lord only giveth wisdom, let every one seriously set himself by prayer in secret to seek it of Him (Prov. 2,3). Every one shall so exercise himself in reading the Scriptures twice a day that he shall be ready to give such an account of his proficiency therein.[1]

By 1790 the rules had changed little:

All persons of what degree forever residing at the College, and all undergraduates…shall constantly and seasonably attend the worship of God in the chapel, morning and evening…All the scholars shall, at sunset in the evening preceding the Lord's Day, lay aside their diversions and…it is enjoined upon every scholar carefully to apply himself to the duties of religion on said day.[2]

Yale College

Students who became signers:

> Lyman Hall
> Philip Livingston
> Lewis Morris
> Oliver Wolcott

In 1699, Yale was founded by ten ministers in order: "[T]o plant, and under the Divine blessing, to propagate in this wilderness the blessed reformed Protestant religion."[3]

When classes began in 1701, Yale required: "[T]he Scriptures…morning and evening [are] to be read by the students at the times of prayer in the school…studiously endeavor[ing] in the education of said students to promote the power and purity of religion." [4]

In 1720, Yale admonished its students: "Above all, have an eye to the great end of all your studies, which is to obtain the clearest conceptions of Divine things and to lead you to a saving knowledge of God in his Son Jesus Christ." [5]

In pursuit of this goal, Yale stipulated: "All the scholars are required to live a religious and blameless life according to the rules of God's Word, diligently reading the holy Scriptures, that fountain of Divine light and truth, and constantly attending all the duties of religion." [6]

"…All the scholars are obliged to attend Divine worship in the College Chapel on the Lord's Day and on Days of Fasting and Thanksgiving appointed by public Authority." [7]

Princeton College

Students who became signers:

    Richard Stockton

    Benjamin Rush

    Joseph Hewes

Princeton University was founded by Presbyterians in 1746 with Rev. Jonathan Dickinson as President, followed by a long line of preachers influential in the Great Awakening, such as Jonathan Edwards, Samuel Davies, Samuel Finley, and then Rev. Dr. John Witherspoon himself, a signer of the Declaration.

Its requirements under Dr. Witherspoon included:

> Every student shall attend worship in the college hall morning and evening in the hours appointed and shall behave with gravity and reverence during the whole service. Every student shall attend public worship on the Sabbath… Besides the public exercises of religious worship on the Sabbath, there shall be assigned to each class certain exercises for their religious instruction suited to the age and standing of the pupils… and no student belonging to any class shall neglect them. [8]

Witherspoon personally instructed students:

> [H]e is the best friend to American liberty who is most sincere and active in promoting true and undefiled religion and who sets himself with the greatest firmness to bear down profanity and immorality of every kind. Whoever is an avowed enemy of God, I scruple [hesitate] not to call him an enemy to his country. [9]

John Witherspoon, being the president of Princeton,

> …may have trained more influential early American leaders than any other individual, for of the students that he personally instructed, one became a U.S. President, one a Vice President, three became Supreme Court Justices, 13 were governors, and at least 20 became senators and 30 more became congressmen—not to mention several presidential cabinet members as well. Dr. Witherspoon may rightly be called the educational father of many Founding Fathers. [10]

Appendix D

The College of William and Mary

Students who became signers:

       Thomas Jefferson

       Carter Braxton

       Benjamin Harrison

       George Wythe

The College of William and Mary was founded 1692, "that the youth may be piously educated in good letters and manners and that the Christian faith may be propagated … to the glory of Almighty God." [11]

A century later, it was still pursuing this goal. Its requirements in 1792 stipulated: "The students shall attend prayers in chapel at the time appointed and there demean themselves with that decorum which the sacred duty of public worship requires." [12]

In fact, at the university level in 1860, 262 out of the 288 college presidents since William and Mary's founding were ministers of the Gospel—as were more than a third of all university faculty members. [13]

In 1890, James Angell, President of the University of Michigan, reported that over 90 percent of the state universities conducted chapel services; at half, chapel attendance was compulsory; and a quarter required regular church attendance *in addition* to chapel attendance. [14]

Preface

1. David Barton, *The Role of Pastors & Christians in Civil Government* (Aledo, TX: Wallbuilder Press, 2003), quoting *The Works of John Adams, Second President of the United States* by John Adams; Charles Francis Adams, editor (Boston, MA: Little, Brown & Co., 1856), Vol. X, p. 284 to Hezekiah Niles on Feb.13, 1818), p. 8.

2. Barton, *The Role of Pastors & Christians,* quoting *John Adams, Works* (1856) Vol. X, p. 45, to Thomas Jefferson on June 28, 1813, p. 18.

3. Barton, *The Role of Pastors & Christians,* quoting *Reports of Committees of the House of Representatives made During the First Session of the Thirty-Third Congress* (Washington, DC: A.O.P. Nicholson, 1854), p. 6, 8–9), p. 21.

4. Darlene Stoker and B. Elaine Clegg, *Our Heritage of Freedom* (Idaho Falls, ID: GCS Distribution, 1998), p. 84.

5. Ibid., p. 84.

6. Ibid., p. 48.

7. David Barton, *The Spirit of the American Revolution* (Aledo, TX: Wallbuilder Press, 1994.)

8. Barton, *The Spirit of the American Revolution,* quoting Hezekiah Niles, *Principles & Acts of the Revolution in America* (Baltimore, MD: William Ogden Niles, 1822), p. 189; debate in the House of Commons, April 26, 1774), p. 12.

9. Charles A. Goodrich, *Lives of the Signers to the Declaration of Independence* (New York: Thomas Mather), p. 381.

10. Barton, *The Spirit of the American Revolution,* p. 6.

11. Jared Sparks, editor, *The Writings of George Washington* (Boston, MA: American Stationers' Co., 1838), Vol. VI, p. 36, to Brigadier Gen. Nelson on August 20, 1778.

12. Donald E. Cooke, *Our Nation's Great Heritage: The Story of the Declaration of Independence and the Constitution* (Maplewood, NJ: Hammond Incorporated, 1972), p. 55.

13. Barton, *The Spirit of the American Revolution,* p. 9, quoting George Washington, *The Writings of George Washington,* John C. Fitzpatrick, editor (Washington DC: US Government Printing Office, 1932), Vol. V, p. 245, from his General Orders of July 9, 1776.

14. Barton, *The Spirit of the American Revolution,* p. 9, quoting George Washington, *Writings,* Vol. XI, p. 343, from his General Orders of May 2, 1778.

15. Barton, *The Spirit of the American Revolution,* p. 9, quoting *Journals of Each Provincial Congress of Massachusetts in 1774 and 1775,* William Lincoln, editor (Boston, MA: Dutton & Wentworth, 1838), p. 70, Dec. 10, 1774.

16. Barton, *The Spirit of the American Revolution,* quoting *Journals of the American Congress from 1774 to 1778* (Washington: Way & Gideon, 1823), Vol. II, p. 107–111).

17. Barton, *The Spirit of the American Revolution,* quoting de Tocqueville, *The Republic of the United States of America and Its Political Institutions, Reviewed and Examined,* Henry Reeves, translator (New York: A.S. Barnes & Co., 1851), Vol. I, p. 337.

18. Barton, *The Role of Pastors & Christians in Civil Government,* quoting John M. Taylor, *Garfield of Ohio: The Available Man* (New York: W. W. & Co., Inc., 1970), p. 180, quoting "A Century of Congress" by James A. Garfield, *Atlantic,* July 1877, p. 35.

19. Meldrim Thomson Jr., *One Hundred Famous Founders* (Oxford, NH, Mt. Cube Farm, 1994), p. 12.

New Hampshire — Josiah Bartlett

1. Cooke, *Our Nation's Great Heritage,* p. 38.

2. Dumas Malone, The *Story of the Declaration of Independence,* (New York: Oxford University Press, 1954), p. 98.

3. Dorothy Horton McGee, *Famous Signers of the Declaration* (New York: Dodd, Mead & Company, 1955), p. 38.

4. McGee, *Famous Signers,* p. 34.

5. David C. Whitney, *Founders of Freedom in America: Lives of the Men Who Signed the Declaration of Independence and so Helped to Establish the United States of America* (Chicago, IL: J.G Ferguson Publishing Company, 1964), p. 52.

6. McGee, *Famous Signers,* p. 25.

7. Ibid., p. 27.

8. Ibid., p. 27–28.

9. Ibid., p. 28–29.

10. Ibid., p. 30.

11. Ibid., p. 31.

12. Whitney, *Founders of Freedom in America,* p. 33.

13. John Sanderson, *Biography of the Signers to the Declaration of Independence* (Philadelphia, PA: R.W. Pomeroy, 1823), Vol. III, p. 147.

14. Ibid., p. 14.

15. Ibid., p. 149.

New Hampshire — Matthew Thornton

1. Goodrich, *Lives of the Signers,* p. 148.

2. Sanderson, *Biography of the Signers,* Vol. V, p. 49.

3. David C. Whitney, *Founders of Freedom in America: Lives of the Men Who Signed the Declaration of Independence and so Helped to Establish the United States of America* (Chicago, IL: J.G Ferguson Publishing Company, 1964), p. 219.

4. B.J. Lossing, *Biographical Sketches of the Signers of the Declaration of Independence; the Declaration Historically Considered; and a Sketch of the Leading Events Connected with the Adoption of the Articles of Confederation, and of the Federal Constitution* (New York: Derby & Jackson, 1856), p. 21.

5. Sanderson, *Biography of the Signers,* Vol. V, p. 61.

6. Ibid., p. 67.

7. Goodrich, *Lives of the Signers,* p. 144–145.

8. Ibid., p. 145–146.

9. Dennis Brindell Fradin, *The Signers: The 56 Stories Behind the Declaration of Independence* (New York: Walker & Company, 2002), p. 99.

10. Goodrich, *Lives of the Signers,* p. 148.

11. Sanderson, *Biography of the Signers,* Vol. V, p. 67.

12. Ibid., p. 64.

13. Ibid., p. 62–63.

New Hampshire — William Whipple

1. George E. Ross, *Know Your Declaration of Independence and the 56 Signers* (Chicago, IL: Rand McNally and Company, 1963), p. 25.

2. Fradin, *The Signers*, p. 96.

3. Lossing, *Biographical Sketches of the Signers*, p. 19.

4. McGee, *Famous Signers*, p. 30.

5. Goodrich, *Lives of the Signers*, p. 141.

6. Sanderson, *Biography of the Signers*, Vol. V, p. 84–87.

7. Whitney, *Founders of Freedom in America*, p. 223.

8. Ibid., p. 223.

9. Ibid., p. 223.

10. Sanderson, *Biography of the Signers*, Vol. V, p. 97–98.

Massachusetts — John Adams

1. Fradin, *The Signers*, p. 8.

2. Sanderson, *Biography of the Signers*, Vol. VIII, p. 334.

3. Whitney, *Founders of Freedom in America*, p. 34.

4. Ibid.

5. Ibid., p. 35.

6. Goodrich, *Lives of the Signers*, p. 97–98.

7. Ibid., p. 98.

8. Ibid., p. 37.

9. Ibid., p. 100–101.

10. John Adams, *Letters of John Adams, Addressed to His Wife*, Vol. I, p. 128. Charles Francis Adams, editor (Boston, MA: Charles C. Little & James Brown, 1841).

11. Goodrich, *Lives of the Signers*, p. 102.

12. Whitney, *Founders of Freedom in America*, p. 40.

13. Ibid..

14. Ibid., p. 41.

15. Ibid., p. 42.

16. Ibid.

17. Ibid.

18. Ibid., p. 43.

19. Ibid.

20. Ibid., p. 44.

21. Ibid.

22. Goodrich, *Lives of the Signers*, p. 111.

23. Fradin, *The Signers*, p. 10.

24. David Barton, *America's Godly Heritage* (Aledo, TX: Wallbuilders, 1992), p. 5.

25. David Barton, *Foundations of American Government* (Aledo, TX: Wallbuilders, 1994), quoting *The Works of John Adams, Second President of the United States*, Charles Francis Adams, editor (Boston, MA: Little and Brown, & Co., 1854), p. 7.

26. Barton, *Spirit of the American Revolution*, p. 7, quoting John Adams, *Letters*, Vol. II, p. 19, to Abigail Adams on December 15, 1777.

27. Fradin, *The Signers*, p. 9.

28. Whitney, *Founders of Freedom in America*, p. 37.

29. John Adams, *Letters*, Vol. I. p. 46, *to Abigail Adams on June 17, 1775*.

Massachusetts — Samuel Adams

1. Whitney, *Founders of Freedom in America*, p. 47.

2. Ross, *Know Your Declaration of Independence*, p. 26.

3. Ibid., p. 27.

4. Whitney, *Founders of Freedom in America*, p. 51.

5. Fradin, *The Signers*, p. 2.

6. Cooke, *Our Nation's Great Heritage*, p. 28.

7. Goodrich, *Lives of the Signers*, p. 41.

8. Sanderson, *Biography of the Signers*, Vol. IX, p. 326.

9. Ibid., p. 327.

10. Samuel Adams, *The Life and Public Service of Samuel Adams*, (Boston, MA: Little, Brown and Co., 1865, Vol. I, p.22 quoting a political essay by Sam Adams published in *The Public Advertiser*, 1749).

11. Adams, *The Life and Public Services of Samuel Adams* (taken from letters written by Sam Adams to John Adams), p. 412.

12. Adams, *The Life and Public Services of Samuel Adams*, p. 122–23.

13. Ibid., p. 124.

14. Lossing, *Biographical Sketches of the Signers*, p. 33.

15. Whitney, *Founders of Freedom in America*, p. 46.

16. Lossing, *Biographical Sketches of the Signers*, p. 34.

17. Ibid., p. 82.

18. Lossing, *Biographical Sketches of the Signers*, p. 83.

19. Goodrich, *Lives of the Signers*, p. 83.

20. Ibid., p. 84.

21. Ibid., p. 84–85.

22. Whitney, *Founders of Freedom in America*, p. 48.

23. Goodrich, *Lives of the Signers*, p. 86.

24. Whitney, *Founders of Freedom in America*, p. 48.

25. Goodrich, *Lives of the Signers* p. 86.

26. Ibid., p. 86–87.

27. Ibid., p. 87.

28. Ibid., p. 88.

29. Whitney, *Founders of Freedom in America*, p. 49.

30. Sanderson, *Biography of the Signers*, Vol. IX, p. 312.

31. Whitney, *Founders of Freedom in America*, p. 57.

32. Goodrich, *Lives of the Signers*, p. 89.

33. Ibid.

34. David Barton, *Original Intent: The Courts, the Constitution, and Religion* (Aledo, TX: Wallbuilder Press, 2000) p. 40, quoting *A Constitution or Frame of Government Agreed Upon by the Delegates of the People of the State of Massachusetts-Bay* (Boston, MA: Benjamin Edes & Sons, 1780).

35. Fradin, *The Signers*, p. 4.

36. Goodrich, *Lives of the Signers*, p. 90–91.

37. Samuel Adams, *The Last Will and Testament of Samuel Adams, attested December 29, 1790.*

Massachusetts — Elbridge Gerry

1. Fradin, *The Signer*, p. 13.

2. Sanderson, *Biography of the Signers*, Vol. VIII, p. 28–29.

3. Fradin, *The Signers*, p. 13.

4. Sanderson, *Biography of the Signers*, Vol. VIII, p. 38

5. Fradin, *The Signers*, p. 14.

6. Whitney, *Founders of Freedom in America*, p. 90.

7. Sanderson, *Biography of the Signers*, Vol. VIII, p. 10.

8. Ibid., p. 26.

9. Fradin, *The Signers*, p. 13.

10. Goodrich, *Lives of the Signers*, p. 122.

11. Ibid., p. 123.

12. Ibid., p. 125.

13. Sanderson, *Biography of the Signers*, Vol. VIII, p. 25

14. Whitney, *Founders of Freedom*, p. 92.

15. Goodrich, *Lives of the Signers*, p. 12.

16. Whitney, *Founders of Freedom*, p. 93.

17. Ross, *Know Your Declaration of Independence*, p. 29.

18. Sanderson, *Biography of the Signers*, Vol. VIII, p. 75–76.

19. Whitney, *Founders of Freedom*, p. 91.

Massachusetts — John Hancock

1. Sanderson, *Biography of the Signers*, Vol. I, p. 33–34.

2. Ibid., p. 34.

3. Ibid., p. 36.

4. Ibid., p. 35.

5. Ibid., p. 35–36.

6. Goodrich, *Lives of the Signers*, p. 80.

7. Whitney, *Founders of Freedom in America*, p. 98.

8. Fradin, *The Signers*, p. 5.

9. Whitney, *Founders of Freedom in America*, p. 100.

10. Ibid.

11. Fradin, *The Signers*, p. 6.

12. Sanderson, *Biography of the Signers*, p. 36–38.

13. Fradin, *The Signers*, p. 8.

14. Whitney, *Founders of Freedom in America*, p. 101.

15. Fradin, *The Signers*, p. 8.

16. Ibid., p. 5.

17. Whitney, *Founders of Freedom in America*, p. 105.

Massachusetts — Robert Treat Paine

1. Goodrich, *Lives of the Signers*, p. 113.

2. Ibid., p.113.

3. Fradin, *The Signers*, p. 112.

4. Goodrich, *Lives of the Signers*, p.115.

5. Ibid., p.115–116.

6. Ibid., p.117.

7. Ibid., p.119.

8. Ibid.

9. Barton, *The Role of Pastors & Christians*, p. 27, from "The Last Will & Testament of Robert Treat Paine, attested May 20, 1780."

Rhode Island — William Ellery

1. Merle Sinclair and Annabel Douglas MacArthur, *They Signed for Us* (New York: Duell, Sloan & Pearce, 1957), p. 30.

2. Sanderson, *Biography of the Signers*, Vol. IX, p. 179.

3. Ibid., p.279–280.

4. Lossing, *Biographical Sketches of the Signers*, p. 49.

5. Fradin, *The Signers*, p. 78.

Rhode Island — Stephen Hopkins

1. Malone, *The Story of the Declaration of Independence*, p. 122.

2. Sinclair and MacArthur, *They Signed for Us*, p. 57.

3. Ross, *Know Your Declaration of Independence*, p. 30.

4. Whitney, *Founders of Freedom in America*, p. 119.

5. Ibid.

6. Lossing, *Biographical Sketches of the Signers*, p. 46.

7. Sanderson, *Biography of the Signers*, Vol. VI, p. 254.

8. Ibid., p. 252.

9. Fradin, *The Signers*, p. 80–81.

10. Ibid., p. 81.

11. Cooke, *Our Nation's Great Heritage*, p. 43.

12. Sanderson, *Biography of the Signers*, Vol. VI, p. 257.

13. Ibid., p. 260.

Connecticut — Samuel Huntington

1. Fradin, *The Signers*, p. 86.

2. Ibid.

3. Cooke, *Our Nation's Great Heritage*, p. 34.

4. Malone, *The Story of the Declaration of Independence*, p. 133.

5. Lossing, *Biographical Sketches of the Signers*, p. 55.

6. Sanderson, *Biography of the Signers*, Vol. IV, p. 78.

7. Ibid.

8. Ibid., p. 77.

9. Ibid., p. 78.

10. Robert G. Ferris and Richard E. Morris, *The Signers of the Declaration of Independence* (Arlington, VA: Interpretive Publications, Inc., 1982), p. 89.

11. Sanderson, *Biography of the Signers*, Vol. IV, p. 78–79.

Connecticut — Roger Sherman

1. Sanderson, *Biography of the Signers*, Vol. III, p. 2.

2. Ibid.

3. Ibid., p. 5.

4. Ibid., p. 35–36.

5. Whitney, *Founders of Freedom in America*, p. 203.

6. Ross, *Know Your Declaration of Independence*, p. 32.

7. Cooke, *Our Nation's Great Heritage*, p. 31–32.

8. Lossing, *Biographical Sketches of the Signers*, p. 51.

9. Whitney, *Founders of Freedom in America*, p. 205.

10. Fradin, *The Signers*, p. 9.1

11. Whitney, *Founders of Freedom in America*, p. 208.

12. Sanderson, *Biography of the Signers*, Vol. III, p. 45.

13. Ibid., p. 56.

14. Ibid., p. 66.

15. Ibid., p. 606.

16. Ibid., p. 56.

17. Ibid.

18. Barton, *The Role of Pastors and Christians in Civil Government*, from *The Life of Roger Sherman* (Chicago, IL: A.C. McClung and Co., 1896,) p. 272–273.

Connecticut — William Williams

1. Fradin, *The Signers*, p. 88.

2. Sanderson, *Biography of the Signers*, Vol. IV, p. 86.

3. Lossing, *Biographical Sketches*, p.57.

4. Sanderson, *Biography of the Signers*, Vol. IV, p. 83.

5. Ibid., p. 85.

6. Ibid., p. 66–68.

7. Ibid., p. 90.

8. Ibid., p. 91.

9. Ibid., p. 92–93.

Connecticut — Oliver Wolcott

1. Whitney, *Founders of Freedom in America*, p. 233.

2. Sanderson, *Biography of the Signers*, Vol. III, p. 103.

3. Sinclair and MacArthur, *They Signed for Us*, p. 30.

4. Fradin, *The Signers*, p. 84.

5. Ibid., p. 84–85.

6. Lossing, *Biographical Sketches*, p. 62.

7. Sanderson, *Biography of the Signers*, Vol. III, p. 104–105.

New York —William Floyd

1. McGee, *Famous Signers of the Declaration*, p. 117.

2. Sanderson, *Biography of the Signers*, p. 119.

3. Goodrich, *Lives of the Signers*, p. 186.

4. T.R. Fehrenbach, *Greatness to Spare: The Heroic Sacrifices of the Men Who sSgned the Declaration of Independence* (Princeton, NJ: D. Van Nostrand Co., Inc., 1968), p. 49.

5. Sanderson, *Biography of the Signers*, Vol. IV, p. 111.

6. Ibid., p. 111–112.

7. Paul J. Scudiere, *New York's Signers of the Declaration of Independence* (Albany, NY: New York State American Revolution Bicentennial Commission, 1975), p. 22.

8. Fehrenbech, *Greatness to Spare*, p. 52–53.

9. Lossing, *Biographical Sketches*, p. 64.

10. Fehrenbach, *Greatness to Spare*, p. 51.

11. Ibid., p. 55.

12. Sanderson, *Biography of the Signers*, Vol. IV, p. 120.

13. Scudiere, *New York's Signers*, p. 23.

14. Sanderson, *Biography of the Signers*, Vol. IV, p. 120.

New York — Francis Lewis

1. Ibid., p. 195.

2. Ibid.

3. Ibid., p. 153.

4. Ferris and Morris, *The Signers of the Declaration of Independence*, p. 28.

5. Fehrenbach, *Greatness to Spare*, p. 51.

6. Sanderson, *Biography of the Signers*, Vol. VI, p. 153.

7. Whitney, *Founders of Freedom in America*, p. 149.

8. Sanderson, *Biography of the Signers*, Vol. VI, p. 159.

New York — Phillip Livingston

1. Fehrenbach, *Greatness to Spare*, p. 27.

2. Whitney, *Founders of Freedom in America*, p. 150.

3. Goodrich, *Lives of the Signers*, p. 190.

4. Sanderson, *Biography of the Signers*, Vol. III, p. 127–128.

5. Sanderson, *Biography of the Signers*, Vol. III, p. 129.

6. Sanderson, *Biography of the Signers*, Vol. III, p. 139.

7. Goodrich, *Lives of the Signers*, p. 192.

New York — Lewis Morris

1. Scudiere, *New York's Signers*, p. 17.

2. Cooke, *Our Nation's Great Heritage*, p. 49.

3. Sinclair and MacArthur, *They Signed for Us*, p. 40–41.

4. Sanderson, *Biography of the Signer*, Vol. IX, p. 151.

5. Ibid.

6. Ibid., p. 163.

7. Ibid.

8. Ibid., p. 164.

9. Ibid., p. 165.

10. Ibid.

11. Ibid., p.166–167.

12. Ibid., p. 172.

13. Ibid., p. 176.

14. McGee, *Famous Signers*, p. 108.

15. Scudiere, *New York's Signers*, p. 11.

16. McGee, *Famous Signers*, p. 108–109.

17. Sanderson, *Biography of the Signers*, Vol. IX, p. 177.

18. Goodrich, *Lives of the Signers*, p. 202.

19. Sanderson, *Biography of the Signers*, Vol. IX, p. 178–179.

20. Ibid., p. 177.

New Jersey — Abraham Clark

1. Sanderson, *Biography of the Signers*, Vol. VI, p. 301.
2. Goodrich, *Lives of the Signers*, p. 232.
3. Ibid., p. 33.
4. Sanderson, *Biography of the Signers*, Vol. VI, p. 300.
5. Ibid., p. 301.
6. Lossing, *Biographical Sketches of the Signers*, p. 23.
7. John and Katherine Bakeless, *Signers of the Declaration* (Boston, MA: Houghton Mifflin Co., 1969), p. 176.
8. Sinclair and MacArthur, *They Signed for Us*, p. 42.
9. Ibid.
10. Fehrenbach, *Greatness to Spare*, p. 85.
11. Ibid., p. 86.
12. Sanderson, *Biography of the Signers*, Vol. VI, p. 307.

New Jersey — John Hart

1. Ibid., Vol. IX, p. 296.
2. Cooke, *Our Nation's Great Heritage*, p. 52.
3. Bakeless, *Signers of the Declaration*, p. 174.
4. Sanderson, *Biography of the Signers*, Vol. IX, p. 286.
5. Bakeless, *Signers of the Declaration*, p. 174.
6. Sanderson, *Biography of the Signers*, Vol. IX, p. 283–284.
7. Ibid., p. 284.
8. Ibid., p. 285–287.
9. Ibid., p. 289.
10. Ibid., p. 298.
11. Ibid., p. 190.
12. Ibid., p. 288.
13. Ibid., p. 291–292.
14. Ibid., p. 292.
15. Ibid., p. 293–295.
16. Ibid., p. 297.
17. Goodrich, *Lives of the Signers*, p. 20.

New Jersey — Francis Hopkinson

1. Sanderson, *Biography of the Signers*, Vol. II, p.279.
2. Ibid., p. 277.
3. David C. Whitney, *Founders of Freedom in America*, p. 121.
4. Fradin, *The Signers*, p. 61.
5. Sanderson, *Biography of the Signers*, Vol. II, p. 264.
6. Goodrich, *Lives of the Signers*, p. 222.
7. Bakeless, *Signers of the Declaration*, p. 170.
8. Ibid.
9. Sanderson, *Biography of the Signers*, Vol. II, p.265.
10. Ibid, Vol. II, p. 268.
11. McGee, *Famous Signers*, p. 141.
12. Fehrenbach, *Greatness to Spare*, p. 75–77.
13. McGee, *Famous Signers*, p. 142.

14. McGee, *Famous Signers*, p. 145.
15. Barton, *The Role of Pastors & Christians in Civil Government*, p. 26.
16. Sanderson, *Biography of the Signers*, Vol. II, p. 268.
17. Ibid., p. 269.
18. Ibid.
19. Bakeless, *Signers of the Declaration*, p. 171.
20. Sanderson, *Biography of the Signers*, Vol. II, p. 271.

New Jersey — Richard Stockton

1. Ibid., Vol. III, p. 200.
2. McGee, *Famous Signers*, p. 128.
3. Ibid., p. 127
4. Ibid., p. 122–128
5. Bakeless, *Signers of the Declaration*, p. 165
6. Ibid., p. 167.
7. Sanderson, *Biography of the Signers*, p. 207.
8. McGee, *Famous Signers*, p. 125.
9. Bakeless, *Signers of the Declaration*, p. 168.
10. Scudiere, *New York's Signers*, p. 207.
11. McGee, *Famous Signers*, p. 126–127.
12. Sanderson, *Biography of the Signers*, Vol. III, p. 200–201.
13. Goodrich, *Lives of the Signers*, p.208–210.
14. Barton, *The Role of Pastors & Christians in Civil Government*; quoting *The Last Will and Testament of Richard Stockton, attested May 20, 1780*.

New Jersey — John Witherspoon

1. Goodrich, *Lives of the Signers*, p. 84.
2. Sanderson, *Biography of the Signers*, Vol. III, p. 265–256.
3. Ibid., p. 217.
4. Fradin, *The Signers*, p. 62.
5. McGee, *Famous Signers*, p. 136.
6. Ibid.
7. Bakeless, *Signers of the Declaration*, p. 161.
8. Barton, *The Role of Pastors & Christians in Civil Government*, p. 25.
9. Bakeless, *Signers of the Declaration*, p. 161.
10. McGee, *Famous Signers*, p. 130.
11. Ibid., p. 131.
12. Sanderson, *Biography of the Signers*, Vol. III, p. 109.
13. McGee, *Famous Signers*, p. 132.
14. Ibid.
15. Ibid., p. 132–133.
16. Ibid., p. 134.
17. Ibid.
18. Sanderson, *Biography of the Signers*, Vol. III, p. 232.
19. Barton, *The Role of Pastors & Christians in Civil Government*, from Witherspoon Works (1815), Vol. V, p. 276–278, *The Absolute Necessity of Salvation Through Jesus Christ*, Jan 2, 1758.

❧ Endnotes ❧

Pennsylvania — George Clymer

1. Sanderson, *Biography of the Signers*, Vol. IV, p. 226.
2. Ibid., p. 223–224.
3. Fradin, *The Signers*, p. 44.
4. Bakeless, *Signers of the Declaration*, p. 145.
5. Sanderson, *Biography of the Signers*, Vol. IV, p. 227–229.
6. Ibid., p. 180.
7. Goodrich, *Lives of the Signers*, p. 285.
8. Sanderson, *Biography of the Signers*, Vol. IV, p. 188.
9. David C. Whitney, *Founders of Freedom in America: Lives of the Men Who Signed the Declaration of Independence and so Helped to Establish the United States of America* (Chicago: J.G Ferguson Publishing Company, 1964), p. 71.
10. Sanderson, *Biography of the Signers*, Vol. IV, p. 193.
11. Ibid., p. 197.
12. Whitney, *Founders of Freedom in America*, p. 72–73.
13. Sanderson, *Biography of the Signers*, Vol. IV, p. 207–208.
14. Ibid., p. 220–221.
15. Goodrich, *Lives of the Signers*, p. 291.
16. Bakeless, *Signers of the Declaration*, p. 119.

Pennsylvania — Benjamin Franklin

1. Whitney, *Founders of Freedom in America*, p. 80.
2. Bakeless, *Signers of the Declaration*, p. 109–110.
3. Ibid., p. 110.
4. McGee, *Famous Signers*, p. 179.
5. Ibid.
6. Barton, *The Role of Pastors & Christians in Civil* Government, p. 23–24.
7. McGee, *Famous Signers*, p. 172.
8. Ibid., p. 180.
9. Ibid., p. 185.
10. Fradin, *The Signers*, p. 78.
11. David Barton, *Four Centuries of American Education*, (Aledo, TX: Wallbuilder Press, 2004), p. 36.
12. McGee, *Famous Signers*, p. 175.
13. Bakeless, *Signers of the Declaration*, p. 112.
14. Ibid., p. 108.
15. Whitney, *Founders of Freedom in America*, p. 80.
16. Bakeless, *Signers of the Declaration*, p. 110.
17. Whitney, *Founders of Freedom in America*,, p. 80.
18. Bakeless, *Signers of the Declaration*, p. 113.
19. Lossing, *Biographical Sketches*, p. 106.
20. Bakeless, *Signers of the Declaration*, p. 115.
21. Ibid., p. 118.
22. Fradin, *The Signers*, p. 36–37.
23. Whitney, *Founders of Freedom in America*, p. 83.
24. Bakeless, *Signers of the Declaration*, p. 118.

25. Whitney, *Founders of Freedom in America*, p. 86.
26. Whitney, *Founders of Freedom in America*, p. 86.
27. Bakeless, *Signers of the Declaration*, p. 123.
28. Ibid., p. 123–124.
29. Whitney, *Founders of Freedom in America*, p. 87.
30. Lossing, *Biographical Sketches of the Signers*, p. 110.
31. Whitney, *Founders of Freedom in America*, p. 87.
32. Ibid.
33. Bakeless, *Signers of the Declaration*, p. 124–125.
34. Whitney, *Founders of Freedom in America*, p. 87.
35. Ibid., p. 89.
36. Bakeless, *Signers of the Declaration*, p. 126.
37. Benjamin Franklin, *A Biography in His Own Words*, Vol. 2 (New York: Thomas Fleming, 1972), p. 393.
38. McGee, *Famous Signers*, p. 187–188.
39. Whitney, *Founders of Freedom in America*, p. 89.
40. Goodrich, *Lives of the Signers*, p. 282.
41. Ibid.

Pennsylvania — Robert Morris

1. Fradin, *The Signers*, p. 39.
2. Bakeless, *Signers of the Declaration*, p. 127.
3. Ibid., p. 128.
4. Ibid., p. 127.
5. Ibid., p. 130.
6. Ibid., p. 131.
7. Ibid.
8. Sanderson, *Biography of the Signers*, Vol. V, p. 227–228.
9. Ibid., p. 201.
10. Bakeless, *Signers of the Declaration*, p. 132.
11. Ibid.
12. McGee, *Famous Signers*, p. 158.
13. Sanderson, *Biography of the Signers*, Vol. V, p. 200–201.
14. Bakeless, *Signers of the Declaration*, p. 132–133.
15. Barton, *Four Centuries of American Education*, p. 25.
16. Goodrich, *Lives of the Signers*, p. 242.
17. Sanderson, *Biography of the Signers*, Vol. V, p. 204–205.
18. Whitney, *Founders of Freedom in America*, p. 168.
19. Sanderson, *Biography of the Signers*, Vol. V, p. 294.
20. Bakeless, *Signers of the Declaration*, p. 135.
21. Sanderson, *Biography of the Signers*, Vol. V, p. 318.
22. Ibid., p. 223–224.
23. Ibid., p. 247–248.
24. Ibid., p. 297.
25. Whitney, *Founders of Freedom in America*, p. 165.
26. Sanderson, *Biography of the Signers*, Vol. V, p.207.
27. Whitney, *Founders of Freedom in America*, p. 170.
28. Sanderson, *Biography of the Signers*, Vol. V, p. 237.

29. Ibid., p. 349.

30. Sanderson, *Biography of the Signers*, Vol. V, p. 232.

31. Ibid., p. 354–355.

32. Ibid., p. 358.

33. McGee, *Famous Signers*, p. 163.

34. Ibid., p. 155.

35. Bakeless, *Signers of the Declaration*, p. 136.

36. Ibid.

37. Sanderson, *Biography of the Signers*, Vol. V, p. 358–359.

38. Botta's War of Independence, Vol. III, p. 345, translated from Sanderson, *Biography of the Signers*, p. 357.

Pennsylvania — John Morton

1. Sanderson, *Biography of the Signers*, Vol. VI, p. 222.

2. Ibid., p. 213.

3. Ibid., p. 217.

4. Bakeless, *Signers of the Declaration*, p. 142.

5. Sanderson, *Biography of the Signers*, Vol. VI, p. 219–220.

6. Ibid., p. 220–221.

7. Goodrich, *Lives of the Signers*, p. 284.

Pennsylvania — George Ross

1. Ross, *Know Your Declaration of Independence*, p. 49.

2. Goodrich, *Lives of the Signers*, p. 312.

3. Bakeless, *Signers of the Declaration*, p. 156.

4. Whitney, *Founders of Freedom in America*, p. 193.

5. Sanderson, *Biography of the Signers*, Vol. VIII, p. 199.

Pennsylvania — Benjamin Rush

1. David Barton, *Benjamin Rush* (Aledo: Wallbuilder Press, 1999); quoting "Eulogium on the Late Dr. Rush," by Dr. David Hosack, *The Analetic Magazine,* Vol. III (1814): p. 46.

2. Barton, *Benjamin Rush*, p. 10.

3. Barton, *Benjamin Rush*, p. 10–11, from *Letters of Benjamin Rush* by Benjamin Rush, edited by L. H. Butterfield, editor of Princeton University Press, 1934, p.12.

4. Barton, *Benjamin Rush*, p, 14, from Ramsay, *Eulogium upon Benjamin Rush, M.D.* (Philadelphia, PA: Bradford and Inskeep, 1813), p. 129–130.

5. Barton, *Benjamin Rush* (written by one of Rush's students), p,14, from Hosack, *Eulogium,* p. 46.

6. Barton, *Benjamin Rush*, p. 29–30.

7. Barton, *Benjamin Rush* p.31, from Benjamin Rush, George W. Corner, editor*, The Autobiography of Benjamin Rush* (Princeton, NJ: Princeton University Press for the American Philosophical Society, 1948), p. 108.

8. Barton, *Benjamin Rush* p.32–33, from Rush, *Autobiography,* p. 162–166.

9. Barton, *Benjamin Rush*, p. 34, from Nathan G. Goodman, *Benjamin Rush* (Philadelphia, PA: University of Pennsylvania Press, 1934), p. 348.

10. Barton, *Benjamin Rush* p, 35, from Rush, *Letters ,* Vol. I, p. 1xxiii.

11. Barton, *Benjamin Rush*, p. 40, from Rush, *The Autobiography of Benjamin Rush,* p. 31–32.

12. Barton, *Benjamin Rush* p. 42, from Rush, *Consecration of the German College at Lancaster,* p. 30.

13. Barton, *Benjamin Rush*, p. 46.

14. Ibid., p. 50.

15. Barton, *Benjamin Rush,* p. 50, from Rush, *Essays,* p. 82.

16. Barton, *Benjamin Rush*, p. 51, from Rush, *Letters,* Vol. II, p. 521, to Jeremy Belnap on July 13, 1789.

17. Barton, *Benjamin Rush*, p. 106–107.

18. Ibid., p. 107.

19. Ibid., p.184.

20. Barton, *Benjamin Rush*, p. 207, from Rush, *Letters,* Vol. I, p. 455–456 to John Montgomery on April 9, 1788.

21. Barton, *Benjamin Rush* p. 208–209, from Rush, *Letters,* Vol. II, p. 132 to Julia Rush on Jan. 31, 1777.

22. Barton, *Benjamin Rush*, p. 210–211, from Rush, *Letters,* Vol. II, p. 776 to John Rush on May 18, 1796.

23. Barton, *Benjamin Rush*, p. 213, from Rush, *Letters,* Vol. I, p. 1xxii.

24. Barton, *Foundations of American Government*, p. 6.

25. Barton, *The Role of Pastors & Christians in Civil Government*, p. 25–26.

26. Goodrich, *Lives of the Signers*, p. 252.

27. Ibid., p. 253.

28. Ibid., p. 257.

29. Ibid.

30. Ibid., p. 259.

31. Ibid., p. 259–260.

32. Ibid., p. 260.

33. Lossing, *Biographical Sketches of the Signers*, p. 101.

34. Barton, *Spirit of the American Revolution*, p. 15.

35. Goodrich, *Lives of the Signers*, p. 244.

36. Whitney, *Founders of Freedom in America*, p. 196.

37. Fradin, *The Signers*, p. 42.

38. Ibid., p. 42.

39. Whitney, *Founders of Freedom in America*, p. 198.

40. Goodrich, *Lives of the Signers*, p. 246–247.

41. Ibid., p. 248.

42. Sanderson, *Biography of the Signers*, Vol. IV, p. 261.

43. Whitney, *Founders of Freedom in America*, p. 198.

44. Ibid., p. 198.

45. Barton, *The Role of Pastors and Christians in Civil Government*, from Rush, *The Autobiography of Benjamin Rush*, p. 166.

Pennsylvania — James Smith

1. Goodrich, *Lives of the Signers*, p. 296.

2. Ibid., p. 296.

3. Sanderson, *Biography of the Signers*, Vol. VII, p. 182.

4. Bakeless, *Signers of the Declaration*, p. 146.

5. Whitney, *Founders of Freedom in America*, p. 210.

6. Sanderson, *Biography of the Signers*, Vol. VII, p. 225–228.

Pennsylvania — James Wilson

1. Lossing, *Biographical Sketches of the Signers*, p. 129.

2. Sanderson, *Biography of the Signers*, Vol. VI, p. 154.

3. Fradin, *The Signers*, p. 48.

4. Sanderson, *Biography of the Signers,* Vol. VI, p. 175.

5. Goodrich, *Lives of the Signers*, p. 301.

6. Sanderson, *Biography of the Signers*, Vol. VI, p. 113.

7. Ibid., p. 167.

8. Bakeless, *Signers of the Declaration*, p. 151.

9. Ibid., p. 154.

10. Ibid.

11. Whitney, *Founders of Freedom in America*, p. 228.

12. McGee, *Famous Signers of the Declaration*, p. 146.

13. Ibid., p. 151.

14. Whitney, *Founders of Freedom in America*, p. 229.

15. Sanderson, *Biography of the Signers*, Vol. VI, p. 173–174.

Delaware — George Read

1. Bakeless, *Signers of the Declaration*, p.186.

2. Whitney, *Founders of Freedom in America*, p. 186–187. (Description of George Read by John Meredith Read Jr., one of his great-grandsons.)

3. Goodrich, *Lives of the Signers*, p. 321.

4. Whitney, *Founders of Freedom in America*, p. 187.

5. Fradin, *The Signers*, p.74.

6. David Barton, *Keys to Good Government* (Aledo, TX: Wallbuilders Press, 1994), p. 5, quoting *The Constitutions of the Several Independent States of America*, Published by Order of Congress (Boston, MA: Norman and Bowen, 1785), p. 99–100.

7. Goodrich, *Lives of the Signers*, p. 323.

8. Sanderson, *Biography of the Signers*, Vol. IV, p.74–75.

9. Ibid., p. 81.

10. Ibid., p. 82.

Delaware — Caesar Rodney

1. Whitney, *Founders of Freedom in America*, p. 190

2. Goodrich, *Lives of the Signers*, p. 319.

3. Sanderson, *Biography of the Signers*, Vol. VIII, p. 119–120.

4. Ibid., p. 122.

5. Goodrich, *Lives of the Signers*, p. 315.

6. Ibid., p. 316–317.

7. McGee, *Famous Signers*, p. 191–192.

8. Sinclair and MacArthur, *They Signed for Us*, p. 10.

9. McGee, *Famous Signers*, p.194.

10. Cooke, *Our Nation's Great Heritage*, p. 58.

11. Sanderson, *Biography of the Signers*, Vol. VIII, p. 105.

12. McGee, *Famous Signers*, p. 196.

Delaware — Thomas McKean

1. Sanderson, *Biography of the Signers*, Vol. VI, p. 337.

2. Ibid., p. 321–322.

3. Ferris and Morris, *The Signers of the Declaration of Independence*, p. 100.

4. Dorothy Horton McGee, *Famous Signers of the Declaration* (New York: Dodd, Mead & Company, 1955), p. 200.

5. Ferris & Morris, *The Signers of the Declaration of Independence,* p. 101.

6. McGee, *Famous Signers,* p. 193.

7. Ibid., p. 193–194.

8. Ibid., p. 287–289.

9. Whitney, *Founders of Freedom in America*, p. 156–157.

10. Barton, *The Role of Pastors and Christians in Civil Government*, p. 26, taken from William B. Reed, *Life and Correspondence of Joseph Reed* (Philadelphia, PA: Lindsay and Blakiston, 1847).

11. Whitney, *Founders of Freedom in America*, p. 157.

12. Ibid., p. 159.

13. Ibid.

14. Ibid.

15. Ibid.

16. Ibid.

17. Ibid.

Maryland — Charles Carroll

1. Lossing, *Biographical Sketches of the Signers*, p. 161.

2. Sanderson, *Biography of the Signers*, Vol. VII, p. 260–261.

3. Cooke, *Our Nation's Great Heritage*, p. 51.

4. Barton, *The Role of Pastors & Christians in Civil Government*, p. 5.

5. Fradin, *The Signers*, p. 108.

6. Sanderson, *Biography of the Signers*, Vol. VII, p. 245–246.

7. Whitney, *Founders of Freedom in America*, p. 59.

8. Ibid., p. 59–60.

9. Ibid., p. 61.

10. Sanderson, *Biography of the Signers*, Vol. VII, p. 253–254.

11. Lossing, *Biographical Sketches of the Signers,* p. 160.

12. Goodrich, *Lives of the Signers*, p. 302.

13. Sanderson, *Biography of the Signers*, Vol. VII, p. 260.

14. Ibid., p. 232–233.

15. Barton, *The Role of Pastors and Christians in Civil Government*, from a letter he has in his possession written by Charles Carroll to Charles W. Wharton, Esq., on September 27, 1825, from Doughorgen, Maryland.

Maryland — Samuel Chase

1. Whitney, *Founders of Freedom in America*, p. 67,

2. Ross, *Know Your Declaration of Independence*, p. 53,

3. Ibid., p. 49.

4. Goodrich, *Lives of the Signers*, p. 345.

5. Whitney, *Founders of Freedom in America*, p. 64.

6. Ibid.

7. Ibid., p. 65.

8. Ibid., p. 66.

9. Lossing, *Biographical Sketches of the Signers*, p. 150.

Maryland — William Paca

1. Lossing, *Biographical Sketches of the Signers*, p. 156.

2. Fradin, *The Signers*, p. 104.

3. Ibid.

4. Goodrich, *Lives of the Signers*, p. 357.

5. Ibid., p. 350.

6. Ibid.

7. Whitney, *Founders of Freedom in America*, p. 181.

Maryland — Thomas Stone

1. Sanderson, *Biography of the Signers*, Vol. IX, p. 357.

2. Whitney, *Founders of Freedom in America* (a member of the Maryland state senate, describing Thomas Stone), p. 214–215).

3. Sanderson, *Biography of the Signers*, Vol. IX, p. 165, letter addressed to Congress by Representative Stone to accept Articles of Confederation.

4. Goodrich, *Lives of the Signers*, p. 352–353.

Virginia — Carter Braxton

1. Whitney, *Founders of Freedom in America*, p. 55.

2. Sanderson, *Biography of the Signers*, Vol. VI, p. 107.

3. Cooke, *Our Nation's Great Heritage*, p. 55.

4. Whitney, *Founders of Freedom in America*, p. 55.

5. Lossing, *Biographical Sketches of the Signers*, p. 199.

6. Fradin, *The Signers*, p. 29–30.

7. Ibid., p. 30.

8. Lossing, *Biographical Sketches of the Signers*, p. 420.

9. Whitney, *Founders of Freedom in America*, p. 57.

10. Fradin, *The Signers*, p. 30.

Virginia — Benjamin Harrison

1. Ibid., p. 33.

2. Goodrich, *Lives of the Signers*, p. 407.

3. Fradin, *The Signers*, p. 32.

4. Ibid., p. 32.

5. Ibid., p. 107.

6. Ibid., p. 32.

7. Ibid., p. 33.

8. Whitney, *Founders of Freedom in America*, p. 108.

9. Sanderson, *Biography of the Signers*, Vol. VIII, p. 36.

Virginia — Thomas Jefferson

1. Whitney, *Founders of Freedom in America*, p. 126.

2. Ibid., p. 137.

3. Lossing, *Biographical Sketches of the Signers*, p. 180.

4. Fradin, *The Signers*, p. 25.

5. Goodrich, *Lives of the Signers*, p. 384.

6. Ibid., p. 384–386.

7. Barton, *The Role of Pastors and Christians in Civil Government*, p. 24.

8. Whitney, *Founders of Freedom in America*, p. 127.

9. Goodrich, *Lives of the Signers*, p. 383.

10. Whitney, *Founders of Freedom in America*, p. 129.

11. Ibid.

12. Ibid.

13. Ibid., p.130–131.

14. Ibid., p. 133.

15. Goodrich, *Lives of the Signers*, p. 390–391.

16. Whitney, *Founders of Freedom in America*, p. 133.

17. Ibid., p. 134.

18. Ibid., p. 132.

19. Ibid., p. 137.

20. Goodrich, *Lives of the Signers*, p. 399.

21. Ibid., p. 402.

22. Whitney, *Founders of Freedom in America*, p. 137.

23. Lossing, *Biographical Sketches of the Signers*, p. 181–182.

24. Ibid., p. 182.

25. Ferris and Morris, *The Signers of the Declaration of Independence*, p. 58–59.

26. Sanderson, *Biography of the Signers*, Vol. VII, p.139–141.

27. Ibid., p. 142.

Virginia — Francis Lightfoot Lee

1. Lossing, *Biographical Sketches of the Signers*, p. 96.

2. Ferris and Morris, *The Signers of the Declaration of Independence*, p. 91.

3. Lossing, *Biographical Sketches*, p. 195.

4. Sanderson, *Biography of the Signers*, Vol. IX, p. 84.

5. Ibid., p. 85–86.

6. Sanderson, *Biography of the Signers*, Vol. IX, p. 78.

7. Whitney, *Founders of Freedom in America*, p.41.

8. Goodrich, *Lives of the Signers*, p.418.

9. Sanderson, *Biography of the Signers*, Vol. IX, p. 86.

Virginia — Richard Henry Lee

1. Whitney, *Founders of Freedom in America*, p. 142.

2. Lossing, *Biographical Sketches of the Signers*, p. 171.

3. Ibid., p. 173.

4. Sanderson, *Biography of the Signers*, Vol. IX, p. 64.

5. Ibid., p. 41.

6. Lossing, *Biographical Sketches of the Signers*, p. 171.

7. Whitney, *Founders of Freedom in America*, p. 142.

8. Lossing, *Biographical Sketches of the Signers*, p. 167.

9. Ibid.

10. Whitney, *Founders of Freedom in America*, p. 142–143.

11. Sanderson, *Biography of the Signers*, Vol. IX, p. 30–31.

12. Whitney, *Founders of Freedom in America*, p. 144.

13. Ibid.

14. Ibid.

15. Ibid.

16. Ibid., p. 145.

17. Sanderson, *Biography of the Signers*, Vol. IX, p. 48-49.

18. Lossing, *Biographical Sketches of the Signers*, p. 169–170.

19. Sanderson, *Biography of the Signers*, Vol. IX, p. 55–56.

20. Whitney, *Founders of Freedom in America*, p. 147.

21. Sanderson, *Biography of the Signers*, Vol. IX, p. 58.

22. Ibid.

23. Goodrich, *Lives of the Signers*, p. 378.

24. Sanderson, *Biography of the Signers*, Vol. IX, p. 65.

25. Ibid., p. 62–63.

Virginia — Thomas Nelson Jr.

1. Whitney, *Founders of Freedom in America*, p. 175.

2. Sanderson, *Biography of the Signers*, Vol. VII, p. 290–292.

3. Ibid., p. 291.

4. Ibid., p. 267–268.

5. Fradin, *The Signers*, p. 27.

6. Sanderson, *Biography of the Signers*, Vol. VII, p. 270.

7. Ibid., p. 272.

8. Whitney, *Founders of Freedom in America*, p. 176.

9. Sanderson, *Biography of the Signers*, Vol. VII, p. 277.

10. Ibid., p. 278.

11. Lossing, *Biographical Sketches of the Signers*, p. 191.

12. Whitney, *Founders of Freedom in America*, p. 176.

13. Ibid.

14. Sanderson, *Biography of the Signers*, Vol. VII, p. 288–289.

15. Whitney, *Founders of Freedom in America*, p. 177.

16. Lossing, *Biographical Sketches of the Signers*, p. 192.

17. Sanderson, *Biography of the Signers*, Vol. VII, p. 288.

18. Ibid., p. 284.

19. Whitney, *Founders of Freedom in America*, p.179.

20. Lossing, *Biographical Sketches of the Signers*, p. 192-193.

21. Sanderson, *Biography of the Signers*, Vol. VII, p. 295.

22. Ibid., p. 297–298.

23. Ibid., p. 298.

24. Ibid., p. 500–501.

25. Ibid., p. 304.

26. Ibid.

Virginia — George Wythe

1. Whitney, *Founders of Freedom in America*, p. 235–236.

2. Lossing, *Biographical Sketches of the Signers*, p. 165.

3. Fradin, *The Signers*, p. 22.

4. Sinclair and MacArthur, *They Signed for Us*, p. 21.

5. Ross, *Know Your Declaration of Independence*, p. 56.

6. Goodrich, *Lives of the Signers*, p. 371.

7. Ferris and Morris, *The Signers of the Declaration of Independence*, p. 154–155.

8. Ibid.

9. Whitney, *Founders of Freedom in America*, p. 236.

10. Goodrich, *Lives of the Signers*, p. 369.

11. Whitney, *Founders of Freedom in America*, p. 237.

12. Lossing, *Biographical Sketches of the Signers*, p. 165.

13. Fradin, *The Signers*, p. 23.

14. Goodrich, *Lives of the Signers*, p. 370.

15. Lossing, *Biographical Sketches of the Signers*, p. 165.

North Carolina — Joseph Hewes

1. Whitney, *Founders of Freedom in America*, p. 111.

2. Sanderson, *Biography of the Signers*, Vol. VII, p. 433.

3. Lossing, *Biographical Sketches of the Signers*, p. 206.

4. Cooke, *Our Nation's Great Heritage*, p. 60.

5. Fradin, *The Signers*, p. 116.

6. Ross, *Know Your Declaration of Independence*, p. 63.

7. Fradin, *The Signers*, p. 117.

North Carolina — William Hooper

1. Sanderson, *Biography of the Signers*, Vol. VII, p. 426.

2. Fradin, *The Signers*, p. 78.

3. Goodrich, *Lives of the Signers*, p.426.

4. Malone, *The Story of the Declaration of Independence*, p. 226.

5. Lossing, *Biographical Sketches of the Signers*, p. 204.

6. Fradin, *The Signers*, p. 112.

7. Sanderson, *Biography of the Signers*, Vol. VII, p. 175.

8. Whitney, *Founders of Freedom in America*, p. 115–116.

North Carolina — John Penn

1. Fradin, *The Signers*, p. 114.

2. Ibid., p. 117.

3. Whitney, *Founders of Freedom in America*, p. 284.

South Carolina — Thomas Heyward

1. Malone, *The Story of the Declaration of Independence*, p. 233.

2. Ibid.

3. Sanderson, *Biography of the Signers*, Vol. IV, p. 199.

4. Lossing, *Biographical Sketches of the Signers*, p. 217.

South Carolina — Thomas Lynch

1. Sanderson, *Biography of the Signers*, Vol. V, p. 217.

2. Ibid., p. 276.

3. Ibid., p. 217.

4. Cooke, *Our Nation's Great Heritage*, p. 63.

5. Sanderson, *Biography of the Signers*, Vol. V, p. 214.

South Carolina — Arthur Middleton

1. Ibid., p. 229.

2. Ibid., Vol. VI, p. 234.

3. Lossing, *Biographical Sketches of the Signers*, p. 10.

4. Ibid., p. 228.

5. Sanderson, *Biography of the Signers*, Vol. VI, p. 240.

6. Ibid., p. 241–242.

7. Ibid., p. 248.

South Carolina — Edward Rutledge

1. Fradin, *The Signers*, p. 120.

2. Lossing, *Biographical Sketches of the Signers*, p. 213.

3. Sanderson, *Biography of the Signers*, Vol. III, p. 182.

4. Ibid., p. 178.

5. Whitney, *Founders of Freedom in America*, p. 201.

6. Ibid., p. 262.

7. Lossing, *Biographical Sketches of the Signers*, p. 214.

8. Sanderson, *Biography of the Signers*, Vol. III, p. 175.

9. Ibid., p. 179.

Georgia — Button Gwinnett

1. Sanderson, *Biography of the Signers*, Vol. III, p. 260–261.

2. Whitney, *Founders of Freedom in America*, p. 94.

3. Ibid., p. 63.

Georgia — Lyman Hall

1. Whitney, *Founders of Freedom in America*, p. 96.

2. Sanderson, *Biography of the Signers*, Vol. III, p. 269–270.

Georgia — George Walton

1. Ibid., Vol. IV, p. 280.

2. Ross, *Know Your Declaration of Independence*, p. 70.

3. Sanderson, *Biography of the Signers*, Vol. IV, p. 252.

4. Ibid., p. 237.

Epilogue

1. Stoker and Clegg, *Our Heritage of Freedom*, p. 43.

2. Barton, *The Role of Pastors and Christians in Civil Government*, p. 36, quoting Charles Finney, *Lectures on Revivals of Religion* (New York: Fleming H. Revell Co., 1868, first published in 1835), Lecture XV, p. 281–282.)

3. Barton, *The Role of Pastors and Christians*, p. 37, quoting Matthias Burnett, *An Election Sermon, Preached at Hartford on the Day of the Anniversary Election,* May 12, 1803 (Harford, CT: Hudson & Goodwin, 1803), p. 26–27.)

Appendix B

1. Stoker and Clegg, *Our Heritage of Freedom*, p. 39, taken from *The Boston Journal.*

Appendix C

1. Barton, *Keys to Good Government,* , p. 4.

2. Robert T. Taylor, editor, *Papers of John Adams* (Cambridge, MA: Belknap Press of Harvard University Press, 1977), Vol. I, p. 81.

3. David Barton, *Original Intent: The Courts, the Constitution, and Religion* (Aledo, TX: Wallbuilder Press, 2000), p. 40, quoting *The Constitution of the Several Independent States of America, Published by the Order of Congress* (Boston, MA: Norman & Bowen, 1785), p. 99–100.)

4. Barton, *Keys to Good Government*, p. 4.

5. Barton, *Keys to Good Government*, from the Constitutions (1785, p. 138, North Carolina, 1776, Article 32), p. 12.

6. Barton, *Original Intent*, quoting *A Constitution or Frame of Government Agreed Upon by the Delegates of the People of the State of Massachusetts Bay* (Boston, MA: Benjamin Edes & Sons, 1780), p. 44, Chapter VI, Article I, p. 40.

Appendix D

1. Barton, *Original Intent*, p. 81, quoting Benjamin Pierce, *A History of Harvard University* (Cambridge, MA: Brown, Shattuck & Co, 1833), Appendix p. 5.

2. Barton, *Original Intent*, p. 8, quoting *The Laws of Harvard College* (Boston, MA: Samuel Hall, 1790), p. 7–8).

3. Barton, *Original Intent*, p. 82, quoting *Documentary History of Yale University, Franklin* B. Dexter, editor (New Haven, CT: Yale University Press, 1916), Nov. 11, 1701, *Proceedings of the Trustees*, p. 27.

4. Barton, *Original Intent*, p. 82, quoting *Documentary History of Yale University*, p. 32.

5. Barton, *Original Intent*, p. 82, quoting *The Catalogue of the Library of Yale College in New Haven* (New London: T. Green, 1743).

6. David Barton, *Four Centuries of American Education* (Aledo, TX: Wallbuilder Press, 2004), p. 11, quoting *The Laws of Yale College in New Haven Connecticut* (New Haven, CT: Josiah Meigs, 1787), p. 5–6.

7. Barton, *Original Intent*, quoting *The Laws of Yale College in New Haven Connecticut*, p. 5-6.

8. Barton, *Original Intent* (quoting *The Laws of The College of New Jersey* (Trenton, NJ: Isaac Collins, 1794), p. 28–29.

9. Barton, *Four Centuries of American Education*, p. 12, quoting *The Works of the Rev. John Witherspoon*, Vol. III, from *The Dominion of Providence Over the Passions of Men,* delivered at Princeton on May 17, 1776 (Philadelphia, PA: William W. Woodard, 1802), p. 42).

10. Barton, *Four Centuries of American Education*, p. 12, from Thomas Jefferson Westinbaker, *Princeton: 1746–1896* (Princeton, NJ: Princeton University Press, 1946), p. 99; Lawrence A. Cremin, *American Education: The Colonial Experience, 1607–1783* (New York: Evanston, and London: Harpers Row, 1970,) p. 301.

11. Barton, *Original Intent*, p. 82, quoting *The Charter and Statutes of The College of William and Mary in Virginia* (Williamsburg, VA: William Parks, 1736), p. 3).

12. Barton, *Original Intent*, p. 82, quoting *William and Mary Rules* (Richmond, VA: Augustine Davis, 1792), p. 6).

13. Barton, *Four Centuries of American Education*, p. 23, from Warren A. Nord, *Religion and American Education* (Chapel Hill, NC: The University of North Carolina Press, 1995), p. 84, quoting James Trunstead Burtchaell, *The Decline and Fall of the Christian College I, First Things* (May 1991), p. 24, and George Marsden, *The Soul of the American University* (New York: Oxford University Press, 1992), p. 11.

14. Barton, *Four Centuries of American Education*, p. 23 (quoting Nord, *Religion and American Education*, p. 84, and Marsden, *The Soul of the American University*, p. 11.

Bibliography

Barton, David. *Benjamin Rush: Signer of the Declaration of Independence*. Aledo, TX: Wallbuilder Press, 1999.

———. *The Role of Pastors & Christians in Civil Government*. Aledo, TX: Wallbuilder Press, 2003.

Bakeless, John and Katherine. *Signers of the Declaration*. Boston, MA: Houghton Mifflin Co., 1969.

Cooke, Donald E. *Our Nation's Great Heritage: The Story of the Declaration of Independence and the Constitution*. Maplewood, NJ: Hammond Incorporated, 1972.

Fehrenbach, T.R. *Greatness to Spare: The Heroic Sacrifices of the Men who Signed the Declaration of Independence*. Princeton: D. Van Nostrand Co., Inc., 1968.

Ferris, Robert G., and Richard E. Morris. *The Signers of the Declaration of Independence*. Arlington, VA: Interpretive Publications, Inc., 1982.

Fradin, Dennis Brindell. *The Signers: The 56 Stories Behind the Declaration of Independence*. New York: Walker & Company, 2002.

Goodrich, Charles A. *Lives of the Signers to the Declaration of Independence*. New York: Thomas Mather, 1832.

Lossing, B.J. *Biographical Sketches of the Signers of the Declaration of Independence; the Declaration Historically Considered; and a Sketch of the Leading Events Connected with the Adoption of the Articles of Confederation, and of the Federal Constitution*. New York: Derby & Jackson, 1856.

Malone, Dumas. *The Story of the Declaration of Independence*. New York: Oxford University Press, 1954.

McGee, Dorothy Horton. *Famous Signers of the Declaration*. New York: Dodd, Mead & Company, 1955.

Ross, George E. *Know Your Declaration of Independence and the 56 Signers*. Chicago, IL: Rand McNally & Company, 1963.

Sanderson, John. *Biography of the Signers to the Declaration of Independence*, Volumes I–IX. Philadelphia, PA: R.W. Pomeroy, 1823.

Scudiere, Paul J. *New York's Signers of the Declaration of Independence*. Albany, NY: New York State American Revolution Bicentennial Commission, 1975.

Sinclair, Merle, and Annabel Douglas MacArthur. *They Signed for Us*. New York: Duell, Sloan & Pearce, 1957.

Stoker, Darlene P., and B. Elaine Clegg. *Our Heritage of Freedom*. SC Enterprises, 1998.

Whitney, David C. *Founders of Freedom in America: Lives of the Men Who Signed the Declaration of Independence and so Helped to Establish the United States of America*. Chicago, IL: J.G. Ferguson Publishing Company, 1964.

 Suggested Reading

The following books I found helpful in my study of the signers. You may want to read some of them also.

Barton, David. *Original Intent*. CD ROM. Aledo: Wallbuilder Press, 2000.

———— *Life and Correspondence of Charles Carroll, Signer of the Declaration*. CD ROM. Aledo: Wallbuilder Press, 2004.

———— *America's Godly Heritage*. Aledo, TX: Wallbuilder Press, 1993.

———— *The Foundations of American Government*. Aledo, TX: Wallbuilder Press, 2000.

———— *The Spirit of the American Revolution*. Aledo, TX: Wallbuilder Press, 2000.

Burnett, Edmund C. *Letters of the Members of the Continental Congress*. Washington, DC: Carnegie Institution of Washington, 1923.

Butterfield, L.H., Marc Friedlaender, and Mary-Jo Kline, editors. *The Book of Abigail and John: Selected Letters of the Adams Family*. Cambridge: Harvard University Press, 1975.

Collins, Gene. *The Signing of the Declaration of Independence*. Woodbury, MN: Resurrection Resources LLC, 2000.

Commager, Henry Steele, and Richard B. Morris, editors. *The Spirit of 'Seventy-Six*. New York: Harper and Row, Publishers, 1958.

DeMar, Gary. *America's Christian History: The Untold Story*. Atlanta, GA: American Vision, Inc., 1993.

Ford, Worthington Chauncey, editor. *Journals of the Continental Congress*. Washington, DC: Government Printing Office, 1907.

Hamburger, Kenneth E., Ph.D., Joseph R. Fischer, Ph.D., and Lt. Col. Steven C. Gravlin. *Why America Is Free: A History of the Founding of the American Republic, 1750–1800*. Washington, DC: The Society of the Cincinnati, 1998.

McCullough, David. *1776*. New York: Simon and Schuster Paperbacks, 2005.

———— *John Adams*. New York: Simon and Schuster, 2001.

Meltzer, Milton. *The American Revolution: A History in Their Own Words*. New York: Thomas Crowell Junior Books, 1987.

Parry, Jay A. *Soldiers, Statesmen, & Heroes*. Washington, D.C.: National Center for Constitutional Studies, 1990.

Plumb, Dr. J.H., and Bruce Lancaster. *The American Heritage Book of the Revolution*. New York: American Heritage Publishing Co., Inc., 1958.

Scheer, George F., and Hugh F. Rankin. *Rebels and Redcoats*. New York: World Publishing Company, 1957.

Stedman, W. David. *Rediscovering the Ideas of Liberty*. Asheboro, NC: W. David Stedman Associates, 1994.

The Signers of the Declaration of Independence. *Signers of the Declaration of Independence Letters and Documents*. New York: Parke-Bernet Galleries, Inc., 1967.

Willard, Margaret Wheeler, editor. *Letters of the American Revolution, 1774–1776*. Boston and New York: Houghton Mifflin Company, 1925.